Discarded
SSCC

Acting in Musical Theatre

Acting in Musical Theatre is the only complete course in approaching a role in a musical. The musical theatre performer must be a master of many styles of acting, singing and dancing, and this is the first book to combine these disciplines into a comprehensive guide.

Just starting out? This book will guide you from the beginning of your training through years of professional work. If you are an acting instructor, it will lead your students through a complete training programme. If you're an experienced actor, this book will help you achieve real performing power.

Drawing on decades of experience both on-stage and in the classroom, the authors provide crucial advice on all elements of the craft, including:

- Fundamentals of acting applied to musical theatre
- Script, score and character analysis
- Personalizing your performance
- Turning rehearsal into performance
- Acting styles in the musical theatre
- Practical steps to a career

Acting in Musical Theatre's chapters divide into easy-to-reference step-by-step units, each containing related group and solo exercises, making it the definitive textbook for students, teachers and professionals alike.

Joe Deer has been a musical theatre educator, director/choreographer and performer in Broadway, National Tour, regional theatre, and university productions for the last twenty-five years. Founding President of the Musical Theatre Educators' Alliance International, he is head of Musical Theatre at Wright State University.

Rocco Dal Vera is a Professor at the University of Cincinnati's College-Conservatory of Music, whose graduates populate virtually every Broadway and National touring stage. He is co-author of the book *Voice: Onstage and Off*, and has coached hundreds of musicals and plays at America's best regional theatres.

"This is the book we have all been waiting for! Every actor needs a guide to help solve the complex array of puzzles that emerge when we begin to dissect a lyric, a song, or a complete role in a musical. And here it is. Written in an engaging generous style, and full of examples and exercises, this book makes the textured work involved in the technique of acting in a musical more of a game and exploration than a chore. Whether for the beginner or the experienced professional, the student or the teacher, the fan or the critic, this text is a must-have and a must-read."

Victoria Clark, Tony Award-winning actress, *The Light In The Piazza*

"Though I attended a highly respected drama department for six years (two degrees), there was never a single course offered having anything to do with musical theatre. Therefore, I am all the more impressed by *Acting in Musical Theatre*, which gives a comprehensive and thought-provoking guideline to the study of performing on the musical stage. I found it fascinating and functional, and I am sure you will, as well."

Tom Jones, Tony Award-winning author/lyricist of *The Fantasticks, 110 In The Shade* and *I Do, I Do!*

"The method for acting in a musical has finally arrived! Deer and Dal Vera have de-mystified with articulate clarity a fully internalized, assimilated, and yet somehow flexible approach to the actual method of rehearsing, performing, and auditioning for the musical theatre."

Lara Teeter, Tony Award Nominee, *On Your Toes*, and Head of Musical Theatre, Webster University

"At last a book that assists us in guiding our students to inhabit characters in musicals organically! A major milestone in musical theatre pedagogy."

Robert Barton, author of *Acting: Onstage and Off*

"*Acting in Musical Theatre* covers it all – acting, musical terminology, style and auditions. It is a must-have resource for all teachers and students of performing in musical theatre."

Mary Jo Lodge, Lafayette College, USA

"Whether you are a fledgling musical theatre artist or a seasoned professional, this book offers an array of insights, suggestions, guideposts and exercises which you will find invaluable."

Michael Ellison, Bowling Green State University, USA

"A lively, engaging read that, as a comprehensive guide to acting in musicals, in many ways fills a heretofore empty niche. The authors do not patronize, but help the student focus on those aspects of the profession under his or her control."

Judith A. Sebesta, University of Missouri-Columbia, USA

"A great handbook for the serious student, giving relevant information for all stages of development."

Kathleen Savage, Performer's College, Essex, UK

Acting in Musical Theatre

A Comprehensive Course

Joe Deer and Rocco Dal Vera

Routledge
Taylor & Francis Group

LONDON AND NEW YORK

First published 2008
by Routledge
2 Park Square, Milton Park, Abingdon, Oxon OX14 4RN

Simultaneously published in the USA and Canada
by Routledge
270 Madison Avenue, New York, NY 10016

Transferred to Digital Printing 2008

*Routledge is an imprint of the Taylor & Francis Group,
an informa business*

Typeset in Univers by
Keystroke, 28 High Street, Tettenhall, Wolverhampton, UK

Printed and bound in the Great Britain by TJI Digital, Padstow, Cornwall

British Library Cataloguing in Publication Data
A catalogue record for this book is available from the British Library

Library of Congress Cataloging in Publication Data
Deer, Joe.
Acting in musical theatre : a comprehensive course / Joe Deer,
Rocco Dal Vera.
p. cm.
Includes index.
1. Acting in musical theater. 2. Musical theater—Instruction and study.
I. Dal Vera, Rocco. II. Title.
MT956.D44 2008
792.602'8—dc22   2007034017

ISBN13: 978–0–415–77318–8 (hbk)
ISBN13: 978–0–415–77319–5 (pbk)
ISBN13: 978–0–203–93107–3 (ebk)

ISBN10: 0–415–77318–0 (hbk)
ISBN10: 0–415–77319–8 (pbk)
ISBN10: 0–203–93107–6 (ebk)

Contents

CHAPTER 5 Working with Words – The Language of the Lyric and Libretto **75**

We dedicate this book to

Our Producers
Harriet Deer and Irving Deer
Polly Keys and Roger Dal Vera

Our Leading Ladies
Caitlin Larsen Deer
Denise Dal Vera

and

Our Rising Stars
Leo Deer
Kendall Dal Vera

Foreword

The first musical I ever saw as a child was not on a stage but in the movies – the film version of *West Side Story*. My memory of it is this: for the first half hour, I was utterly baffled – why were all those boys dancing down the street, snapping their fingers and singing at the top of their lungs? For the rest of the time, I was enraptured.

That seminal experience sums up, what is for me, the essence and the contradiction of musicals: in real life, people don't dance down streets, snapping their fingers and singing at the top of their lungs. And yet, it's become my job, as a writer of musicals, to make an audience accept and believe that this is exactly how real life is – a place where we burst into song and dance when we can't contain our emotions any longer, and where music wells up even when we speak.

Making such a fantastical world ring true is the job of the writer, but also the job of the actor, and it requires prodigious skill. Not only do performers need to master the extremely difficult discipline of acting itself, but they must learn to act within the strictures of rhythm and rhyme and melody. They must speak on the beat, sing their feelings, and somehow make it feel honest. I stand in awe of those who can do it.

Coincidentally, as I write this, I'm about to start previews for a new musical at Lincoln Center Theatre – it's the story of "The Glorious Ones," a fictionalized troupe of *commedia dell'arte* players in sixteenth- century Italy. It's all about actors.

Our cast of seven is perfect. Every day in the rehearsal room these past weeks, I've marveled at their unselfconsciousness, their wit, their constant exploration of their own hearts, and the hearts of their characters. These are serious actors, one and all. And yet, I've seen them hurl themselves into pratfalls, gallop like horses around the stage, dash up and down staircases – all the while, singing. How do they do it, I marvel? Is being a musical actor something genetic, instinctive, or can it be taught? I suppose the answer is "yes."

Interestingly, some of our "Glorious" cast members are seasoned performers in musical theater, with voices that could easily reach to the last row of the Minskoff, while others have smaller "actor voices," and have performed more often in plays. This particular musical is a character-driven piece. What mattered most to us in casting each role was how well the actor could act, how well he or she embodied the role and whether or not the actor understood the specific world we were trying to create. Thus, it isn't always a great voice that wins a role. It can be the actor's understanding of the role that matters more – the emotional weight, intelligence, training and background he or she brings to bear. With luck, some are born with beautiful voices in their bodies and dancin' shoes on their feet. But even those who are not can develop and train the instruments they've been given; even without a great voice, they can learn to act songs.

Music, of course, is what creates the rhythm, pace and tone of a show. It also provides the inherent emotionality. How lyrics are set on top of that music indicates the way lines should, and must, be "read." I try to make sure that my lyrics are conversational and sit naturally on the music – that words and phrases are not mis-accented, that rhymes do not call attention to themselves – because my goal is always to make the singing sound as easy and natural as speech. I want the character who's singing to sound like the same character who was speaking just a moment before. The song is simply a heightened extension of the dialogue, and if we – actors and writers – make that transition appear seamless and natural, it helps to convince the audience that what they're seeing is real life.

Most musicals are gnarly beasts, requiring constant wrestling and revision before they're tamed. Throughout the writing process, and usually well into previews, the writers, director and music staff work tirelessly to weave the spoken word, movement and song into a seamless dramatic structure. We have to make hundreds of tiny decisions per square inch: Should her final note cut off on beat 2 or beat 3? When should she pause in the phrase to catch her breath? Can she fit her dialogue over two bars or do we need more music? Is the orchestration overpowering the emotion of the moment? Can we lower the key a half step to take advantage of her "money note?" With that big hat on, the song isn't funny! With those lights so bright, the song isn't dramatic! The actor is doing a great job on the song, but is the song the right one? Maybe we should cut it!

To some actors, this might all seem limiting, daunting, even hellish. ("You mean I have to say my lines, sing the last three words and get off the stage by the downbeat of measure 4?") To others, the demands of musical theater are a challenge and a joy. These are the actors we look for. No, these are the actors we pray for!

We strive to make our actors look good and sound good. In return, we expect that they will do their best to honor our intentions. In the end, the most important thing is not any single ego, but the artistic aims of the show itself – we are all collaborators toward that goal.

I'm sure this book will be a valuable resource in nurturing the development of many actors – I hope I'll meet them dancing down the street, snapping their fingers and singing at the top of their lungs, on their way to some universal, human truth. Such actors enthralled and inspired me as a child, and continue to do so every day.

Lynn Ahrens

Lynn Ahrens won the Tony Award, Drama Desk and Outer Critics Circle Awards for the score of the Broadway musical Ragtime. *For her extensive work in theater, film and television, other honors include the Emmy Award, London Olivier Award, three Grammy nominations and two Academy Award nominations. She has collaborated with composer Stephen Flaherty since 1983.*

Special Thanks and Acknowledgments

Talia Rodgers for adopting our proposal. Minh Ha Duong at Routledge for her gentle guidance and support in this process.

The students and our colleagues at Wright State University, especially W. Stuart McDowell, Joseph Bates, Richard Church, Jamie Cordes, Sandra Crews, Bruce Cromer, Mary Donahoe, David Hapner, Greg Hellems, Teressa Wylie McWilliams, Lee Merrill, Victoria Oleen, D'Arcy Smith and Sherri Sutter. WSU's College of Liberal Arts and Office of Research and Sponsored Programs for support in preparing this book.

The students and our colleagues at the University of Cincinnati's College-Conservatory of Music, especially David Adams, Thomas Baresel, Aubrey Berg, Michael Burnham, R. Terrell Finney, Jr., Roger Grodsky, Julia Guichard, Thomas Haines, Kelly Hale, Patti Hall, Richard Hess, Barbara Honn, K. Jenny Jones, Diane Kvapil, Diane Lala, Wendy LeBorgne, Patricia Linhart, Terry Lusk, Karen Lykes, Nick Mangano, William McGraw, Nicholas Muni, Barbara Paver, Bob Pavlovich, Sylvia Plyler, Anne Schilling, Kenneth Shaw and Mary Henderson Stucky.

We gratefully acknowledge the influence and insight of many fine teachers, scholars and artists who have inspired us: Ron Arden, Wesley Balk, Robert Barton, Steven Beckler, Judith Blazer, Susana Bloch, Marina Caldarone and Maggie Lloyd-Williams, Christopher Chadman, Bill and Irene Chapman, Victoria Clark, Dave Clemmons, David Craig, Robert Cohen, Marcia Milgrom-Dodge, John Harrop and Sabin R. Epstein, Gerald Freedman, Michael Garber, James Jamison, Tom Jones, Finis Jhung, Robert and Sandy Karl, Mladen Kiselov, Gregory Lehane, Henry LeTang, Gary Logan, Kathy Maes, DeVera Marcus, Pat McCorkle, Roxane

Rix, Mars and Arthur M. Sanderson, Ron Scherer, Michael Shurtleff, Michael Smuin, John Stefano, Dennis Turner, Jack Tygett, Ira Weitzman and Jerry Zaks.

The helpful observations of Michael Ellison (Bowling Green State University), Judith Sabesta (University of Arizona) and Mary Jo Lodge (Lafayette College), whose careful reviews of the manuscript provided many useful suggestions.

Don Corathers and *Dramatics Magazine* for their eager interest in our work and for helping bring it to another generation of musical theatre performer.

Our colleagues across the country and around the globe who have offered us opportunities to develop this material: Thomas Albert, Margaret (Meg) Bussert, Rena Cook, Charles Gilbert, Cary Libkin, Kim Moke, Kip Niven, Lara Teeter and Neil Vanderpool. Also to the members of the Musical Theatre Educators Alliance-International, the Association for Theatre in Higher Education Music Theatre and Dance focus group, and the Voice and Speech Trainers Association.

For opportunities to explore this work and support in developing a perspective on applying it: Lee Theodore and the members of the American Dancemachine, Ed Stern, Michael Haney, Bert Goldstein and the Cincinnati Playhouse in the Park, D. Lynn Meyers and the Ensemble Theatre of Cincinnati, Brian Isaac Phillips, Jasson Minadakis and the Cincinnati Shakespeare Company, Kevin Moore, Marsha Hanna and the Human Race Theatre Company, Teresa Stoughton-Marafino, Scott "Biff" Baron, Audrey Tischler and the Mountain Playhouse, Charles Tranter and Struthers Library Theatre, and all the professional and student actors who have allowed us to develop this work in the classroom and rehearsal studio.

Lyric permissions

Introduction

We all agree that good acting is about truth. Okay. Can you find the truth in a character who:

. . . sings when she's sad?
. . . dances to get the girl to go out with him?
. . . is a cat?

Welcome to musical theatre, where truth and the logic of everyday reality are often completely separate, which can make this the most difficult kind of acting. Yet, we willingly and eagerly suspend our doubts and disbelief in order to relish the passion, joy, humor and pain of these musical stories because logic has very little to do with why we are drawn to act in or attend musicals. Whether we call it catharsis, escape or just a desire for entertainment and emotional engagement, the musical theatre can take an audience to places that few other experiences can claim.

Training for the musical theatre

The musical actor must also be able to handle a wide range of performance conventions, training requirements and styles that are unique to the musical theatre.

Training for this exciting and challenging field has traditionally been piecemeal, leading students to study singing, dance and acting independently with the hope they will somehow figure out how to put them all together when the time comes. Even those training programs that do attempt to pull the various strands together rarely do so with a technique students can reliably access on their own.

Until now there has been no guiding text or established methodology for integrating all the elements of musical theatre acting, often requiring teachers to direct their students into an integrated performance by using the teacher's personal experience and instinct to select useful choices *for* the actor. The teacher's hope is that this experience will ultimately accumulate and add up to a technique the student actor can take into a career. This approach is unsatisfactory for a number of reasons. First, it is difficult for the student to ever exceed the instructor's skill level. Second, without a clearly articulated method for approaching musical theatre acting, the performer won't ever be able to approach her work with a sense of confidence in her craft and technique. Also, without a clear technique for approaching her craft, the actor becomes dependent on someone else to hand her strong direction and will never be a full partner in the creative process. In short, without a clear system for approaching musical theatre acting, the student is at a great disadvantage.

Acting in Musical Theatre – the book

If you are an actor just starting out, this book will put you on the right path and give you a set of tools to take you from the beginning of your training through years of professional work. The approach of *Acting in Musical Theatre* can form the cornerstone of your musical theatre technique. If you are an acting instructor, this book will provide you with a series of potent experiences to lead your students to a solid, reliable acting technique. If you are an experienced actor, this book will help you put a frame around many of the techniques you have been using, but perhaps not mastering with the clarity and detail that is the source of real performing power.

There are several elements of this text that make it particularly useful:

1. *Acting in Musical Theatre* **is easy to understand**. Acting in a musical doesn't need to be a confusing process. One of our goals is to demystify and clarify the subject without sacrificing a rigorous approach.
2. *Acting in Musical Theatre* **is a step-by-step process**. Good technique is built in stages. We take the actor through a gradual process of skill building designed to ground him in a reliable, fully internalized and assimilated way of working.

3. *Acting in Musical Theatre* **is comprehensive**. We explore the process of acting in the full range of musical theatre circumstances from the simple to the complex, from the beginning of study right through to starting a full professional career.

4. *Acting in Musical Theatre* **capitalizes on established approaches**. We incorporate traditional, classical acting methods and expand upon them as required for the specialized techniques of musical theatre. If you have studied traditional acting, you will be familiar with many of the terms we use. If you are new to acting, this will ground you in techniques and terminology that will dovetail with later non-musical acting classes.

5. *Acting in Musical Theatre* **is flexible**. This approach can be tailored to suit individual study, group classes, and courses lasting from one semester to several years. This book can be the primary text used in an intensive professional training program, or selectively employed in a shorter course. The text provides solo activities for the individual or unenrolled reader and group projects on which class members can collaborate.

6. *Acting in Musical Theatre* **encourages fun**. It takes a lighthearted approach to a serious study.

Structure

We have broken the many components of the musical theatre actor's tool belt into six major areas and offer step-by-step instruction and exercises to help students master each of these in a logical, progressive order.

Section I: Fundamentals of Acting in Musical Theatre addresses how to approach the imaginary circumstances of musical acting by working with objectives, obstacles, tactics, relationships, beats and personalization.

Section II: Score and Libretto Analysis and Structure explores the music, lyrics and libretto of a musical and teaches the reader to look at (and listen to) these components of a musical for clues to character development.

Section III: The Journey of the Song provides a process for revealing the dramatic shape of a song, for intensifying the character's needs, for establishing and building character relationships and for making the song, the most essential element of a musical, come to life.

Section IV: Making It a Performance takes the musical actor from the classroom or rehearsal hall to the stage, building a performance step-by-step from staging and use of gesture, through exploring musical phrasing and into the full rehearsal process.

Section V: Style in Musical Theatre provides the actor with a specific method to assess the various styles and genres of musical theatre and how to act in each.

Section VI: The Profession answers the many questions about how to become a professional musical theatre actor. From agents to creating zed cards, this chapter covers it all.

How to use this book

Each section of the book is made up of a series of chapters with individual study units covering a specific skill or concept. Each unit builds on the last and leads to the next so you will have a clear sense of how to apply these important concepts by the end of every chapter. We've supplied numerous exercises that guide you to a hands-on mastery of those concepts. You may want to select exercises from each group, or delve into the concept in greater detail by exploring all of them.

For teachers who are using this textbook as a basis for a one-term course, you may find that covering two chapters each week will carry you through a clear curriculum. Assigning readings from *Section VI: The Profession* concurrent with other in-class acting exercises will allow students to concentrate on professional preparation while they build a solid acting technique.

Teachers who have more time can explore the material in greater detail. The ideal teaching method for this book includes focusing on a chapter for long enough to allow each student in the group to fully develop individual concepts in class and to apply instructor notes and feedback. Even in these more detailed courses, teachers may also wish to have students begin reading and exploring units from *The Profession* early on, with class time devoted to those ideas. Offering days for practice auditions throughout the course helps focus student energies and varies the structure of the course to keep students engaged.

Actors using this book on their own will find they can apply it to work they do with their singing teacher or coach. You may choose to find a workout buddy (as recommended in the last section of this book) who will want to engage in a short course with you. Arranging a regular group to get together one night a week to work on these ideas is another useful way of staying fresh.

With the amount of good musical theatre performance available on video it is possible for students to see landmark performances of classic and contemporary musicals. *Section V: Style in Musical Theatre* includes a list of representative performances that are commercially available. Setting up regular viewings of these recordings and attending professional theatre is an irreplaceable part of what is sure to be a life-long study.

Welcome

If you feel things so deeply and passionately that you just need to sing about them; if you are so filled with emotion that your body just has to dance; if you love standing in someone else's shoes, reveling in that person's thoughts and feelings, then you are a musical theatre actor and you've just found a home here.

SECTION I: FUNDAMENTALS OF ACTING IN MUSICAL THEATRE

CHAPTER 1

Fundamentals of Acting in Musical Theatre

ACTING BASICS–THE FOUNDATION

You're sitting in a theatre as the houselights dim. The crowd hushes. The piano picks out a single note and a pinspot reveals a face. The singer begins . . . and the magic happens. We are touched, moved, changed.

Why? What happened? What is it that makes a performance more than a beautiful piece of music, or an insightful lyric, or some snappy choreography? What makes us disregard the artificial theatricality of the event and connect with the singer on a deep, personal level?

Acting.

For many, the term acting carries connotations of pretense, posturing and artful lying. To those who practice it as a profession, it is just the opposite. It is the expression of the artist's personal truth through the lens of a role. When we watch a performance filled with this personal truth we are drawn to it and are touched by a universal human experience. This is the magic of the theatre. It is why people pay huge sums for a ticket, sit transfixed for the evening, then argue about the show over coffee, and can't get the experience out of their heads for weeks afterward. They are transformed, not merely entertained, by the event.

What makes good acting?

Can acting be taught? Talent can't be taught, and there will always be those who possess an instinctive aptitude for an art form. Acting is an art, but it is also a craft that can be learned. Even the most talented individual needs to master the skills of her discipline. A piano prodigy only becomes a virtuoso after spending many long hours at the keyboard. Acting works the same way. If you have a gift for it, there are ways to develop the craft. Musical theatre as an art form requires many talents and skills. You need to sing and dance well, but those abilities alone aren't enough. Hitting a high C or doing a triple pirouette isn't going to move the audience unless it comes from a believable character expressing a rich inner truth. Acting is the connective tissue that holds the whole performance together.

How do you recognize good acting? We know it when we see it, or, even more likely, excellent acting is so transparent that we are unaware we are seeing it at all and simply become involved in the character's experience without thinking about the acting. When watching anything that is done excellently, one doesn't notice the technique. It looks so natural it is easy to believe anyone could do it. A winning golf swing is effortless poetry in motion (and looks simple until you try it), but it is poetry that can be learned. There are principles and techniques involved and those can be studied and incorporated into the seamless, graceful whole. This is also true for acting. And just as you can't become a championship athlete without dedicated concentration on the fundamental skills of the sport, you won't fulfill your potential as an artist without mastering the fundamental elements of your craft.

UNIT 1.2   **Preparing to work**

For the work we are about to do it will be helpful if you have some material to use to frame the exercises. If you are working in a group, you can choose a specific show to work on together or study a range of roles in a variety of shows. If you are working alone, you might enjoy exploring a single role you're interested in or use this to prepare a portfolio of material. To start with, you should have at least two contrasting songs and the accompanying script. It will also help you to have accompaniment recordings for these two songs or an accompanist to work with.

Come to class on time, vocally and physically warmed up, and ready to work. Wear clothing that is easy to move in and doesn't restrict your breathing. Or wear clothes that suit the character. It isn't necessary to have an actual costume, but if your character would wear dress shoes, a hat, or a coat and tie, or a long dress and heels, give yourself the advantage of working in those accoutrements from the start. If you have long hair, keep it back out of your face. Don't wear any unnecessary accessories, piercings or jewelry.

Giving and taking feedback

The work that actors do is deeply subjective. The raw material of our art is our own psyche, emotions and internal processes. As you gain experience, you'll also gain deeper insight and self-knowledge, but many of us are inexperienced at understanding and articulating our feelings, thoughts and impulses. It is not uncommon for beginning actors to believe they are doing one thing, while the rest of the world sees something quite different. Probably the most important single issue at this stage of the actor's journey is learning to reconcile the disparity between what something feels like inside and what others receive outside. To help us reconcile this difference, we need to get quality feedback from our colleagues as well as from our directors and teachers. Then we need to learn how to use those responses effectively.

Taking feedback

The audience is never wrong. When receiving responses to your work, remember that what the audience discerns is all that matters. It doesn't make any difference what you *meant* to communicate; communication is what the other person understood or felt. What they got was what you did. If you don't like the response, try doing something else until you get the reaction you want.

Take the note and be grateful for it and gracious about it. One of the most vulnerable times in your training process is when you stand before a teacher and classmates to receive feedback on a song or a scene. You may not always like what you hear, or you may have thought your work was just perfect. But, remember why you're there – to learn so you can achieve your dream of becoming a working actor. Most teaching is done through oral feedback. So, if you can think of every bit of constructive criticism as a gift from your teacher or classmate that helps you get closer to your dream, you will look forward to the notes, not dread them. Few teachers get satisfaction out of tearing a student apart. They only enjoy helping you. So, the note is probably offered in the spirit of support.

Yes! And? Once you've learned to release yourself from the insecurity of getting notes in public, you can begin to adopt the hungry attitude of a real professional, where each note is greeted with the response "Yes, And?" Not only does this signal that you are really interested in what is being offered, but it also helps establish and maintain an atmosphere of openness for every class or rehearsal.

Don't defend or explain your performance. The only communication that matters is what happens in your performance, even though you will have a strong personal need to explain what you are doing (especially when it seems you haven't been accurately received). Put your attention back into the work and communicate through your acting. The audience won't have the benefit of your annotated study guide, so telling your classmates or your director what you meant to do won't help you. This may require a lot of self-restraint.

Your audience is your mirror – don't cloud it. You risk something else important if you tell your observers too much. If you explain what you are doing or are about to do, you may reduce your director and classmates' ability to see your work objectively and to reflect back to you what they actually saw. Objectivity is a fragile thing and if you rob yourself of an unbiased audience, you won't be able to get it back.

UNIT 1.3.2   *Giving feedback*

Say what you saw and felt, not what you wished or expected to see and feel. When giving feedback to a fellow actor, learn to make a distinction between what you *wanted* to see, and what you *actually* saw. Actors need to hear how they're coming across. Be a good mirror.

Clear notes that reflect what you experienced are most useful. Try phrasing it like, "When you did that I felt . . .," "I understood . . ." or "I saw . . ." These sorts of comments are most likely to help the actor who needs an accurate reflection of his work. Avoid statements that start with, "How about . . ." or "Try it like . . ." or "I would have . . ." These put you in the situation of acting the role for him. That's not your job as a responder.

Restrain your ego. Without realizing it, you may be subtly knocking down your peers in order to gain stature for yourself. Giving notes to classmates that are really about proving how smart you are, or that reinforce someone else's insecurities, has nothing to do with being a member of an ensemble. Instead, try reaching out to help every member of your company to be as good as he can be. The reflection of their success will shine on you and your entire production.

In rehearsal, you are a character in the play, not the director. Questions of interpretation are best left to the teacher or director and the actor who is working. Fellow actors need to be careful not to intrude on that relationship. There are many interpretations for every role and an infinite range of possibilities for playing any moment. Comments on interpretation from too many sources can confuse an actor, and may send the role off in a direction that is contrary to what the director wants. Further, if you are focusing on a colleague's work in that way, you may not be living subjectively in your own role. Respond intuitively as a character to what you see going on around you, not as a person whose job is to objectively see the whole play. That's the job of a director. Do your job.

Don't give other actors notes in rehearsal. In rehearsal, it is a customary courtesy to avoid giving another actor any kind of note at all. In classes, discussion and response to the work of your fellow students is a frequent and useful component of training. Don't confuse the different environments.

Asking for feedback

Don't be general. Ask specific questions. "So, what did you think?" will get you vague responses like, "nice job, man." Or "I liked/didn't like it." These may be affirming or hurtful, but they're never helpful. You're looking for feedback that helps you pinpoint effective moments and to eliminate vague ones. Try asking questions like: "Tell me who you thought I was?" "What do you think my objective was?" "What was standing in my way?" "Who I was speaking to?" and "What was our relationship?" etc. The most general questions you should ever ask are: "What moments stand out for you? Why?" With specific questions, you're more likely to elicit responses you can use.

Learning to give and receive feedback is an important element of your training. Develop your observational skills as well as your ability to articulate your thoughts and feelings so you can tune your instrument to internalize and respond to feedback from others.

EXERCISE 1A CREATING A WORKBOOK

It's important to listen attentively while getting notes. But, it's also important to write them down quickly so that you can digest the notes later, when you are able to separate yourself from the conversation. Create a workbook to hold notes and the various kinds of homework you'll do for every role. This can be a three-ring binder, a composition book or a special book that you purchase for the purpose. It doesn't matter as long as you use it. Some actors create a separate journal/workbook for every project and production or class. Feel free to journal in your workbook if that's part of your process. But we suggest that you use the book for at least these tasks:

- Write your character analysis (which we'll cover throughout this book).
- Take notes from rehearsals and class.
- Collect important research for your development of a character and understanding of the world of the musical.

UNIT 1.3.4   *Safe space*

You'll put yourself on the line every time you perform in class, in an audition or onstage. Few things in life are more personally exposing than acting. Training as an actor, especially in the musical theatre, requires you to wake up your impulses and enter the role without barriers or emotional protection. You won't be able to do that if you don't feel emotionally and physically safe in the studio. Behavior is everything. Even small practical courtesies can make a big difference. What you do will set the tone for everyone.

Working safe and working smart

Twenty practical ways to turn your work space into a safe space

1. Show up on time, warmed up and ready to work.
2. Know your music, lines and choreography before being asked.
3. Do your homework and research on the role and bring in ideas.
4. Remove outside distractions. Turn off cell phones.
5. Leave personal problems at home. If you have an argument or even if you fall in love with someone, keep it outside the studio.
6. Respect the physical space. Don't throw chairs to indicate your passion, or to rev up your energy.
7. Be sober.
8. Be hygienic. Don't kiss your partner when you have a cold sore. Check your breath.
9. Stay clean. Theatre requires intimacies and musical theatre requires lots of physical exertion. That isn't always a delightful combination. Avoid perfumes or scented products since some people have allergies to them.
10. Be respectful about touch. Characters will do private things onstage and while it can help to be uninhibited, it is fine to have personal boundaries. Communicate well with your partners and honor their limits.
11. Theatres are often physically dangerous spaces. In a blackout or stage fog, you can fall off a platform, trip into the pit, get scenery lowered onto your

head or be bitten by a tiger. There are gunshots, strobe lights, turntables, high heels and bayonets. Stay focused.

12. Respect all the many collaborators. A production requires of number of exceptional artists. Performers depend on a small backstage army never seen by the audience. When you receive applause at the end of a show, take that praise with the awareness that you didn't do this by yourself. Spend some time working backstage. Learn that side of theatre so you can interact effectively and gratefully with these professionals.

13. Don't play with props, and be responsible about checking your own props.

14. Don't smoke or eat in costume.

15. Listen and be open to new ideas. Remain fully present and receptive to direction and to the multiple layers of information coming from the other characters onstage.

16. Pay attention and don't ever get the same note twice. Write it down to make it stick.

17. Be worthy of trust. Don't gossip. Make the rehearsal and classroom environment into an ideal society of collaborative artists. Gossiping and complaining can only flourish if someone else feeds them.

18. Be childlike but never childish. Act with creative impulse but never with thoughtlessness.

19. Set high standards for yourself and compete only with yourself.

20. Inspire others by your example.

Once you start making these behaviors part of your daily work practice you'll discover that creating a safe space also requires you, your colleagues and leaders to treat those spaces as special, where the painful behaviors of subtle attack and counterattack aren't permitted. Many people are attracted to the theatre because it is an embracing, supportive and emotionally open society. It all adds up to a word theatre folk hold sacred: ensemble. It is that troupe of special people who seem to function in an effortless harmony. That doesn't happen by accident. It needs to be cultivated.

Being an actor

The career you're embarking on can be desperately challenging, and endlessly rewarding. It takes a special set of attitudes and aptitudes to do it well. We want to outline a few of those as you begin this work.

UNIT 1.4.1   *The Magic "IF"*

The great acting teacher and director Konstantin Stanislavski coined a term that actors have used since he first came up with it a century ago called the *Magic "IF."* He simply asked us to consider one question: How would I act *if* I were in this situation? It is on that little idea that most contemporary acting theory is based, because it begs us to pretend that we are someone else with specificity, sensitivity and commitment. The test of your choices as an actor will often reside in that question. If what you've chosen to do doesn't help you respond truthfully to the imaginary circumstances of the character, then it is probably not a good choice.

UNIT 1.4.2   *Believability and truth*

All theatre is inherently artificial because the very essence of acting is that we are pretending to be someone we are not. So, when we observe the work of our peers in production or in class, the term real is less useful to us than the terms believable under the circumstances or truthful.

In the theatre, believability has to do with our innate feeling that the actions and behaviors of the person inhabiting a role are in line with the reality the writers have created. When those actions and behaviors all line up with the specifics of the character, the relationships and the story, then we call the acting believable. And when they fall out of sync with that theatrical reality we instinctively recognize the disconnect.

Part of believability has to do with our sense of the actor's truthfulness in any given moment. Truth in acting is the alignment of the character's reality and the actor's reality. The thoughts, needs and feelings of the character are expressed in a way that is particular to that actor under the circumstances of the character. Although there is a great deal about theatre that is artificial, a truthful performance seems to be without artifice.

As actors, we seek to inhabit the role completely, reacting to all of the many stimuli we receive from the actors onstage with us, the imaginary world of the writers, the historical context of the piece and our own imagination. Believability and truth are central to achieving this goal.

We encourage you to focus on believability and truth because they express two fundamental aspects of acting in a specific way that avoids judgment or vagueness. A working vocabulary that allows us to say what we mean is one of the essential tools of your trade.

First time

A natural extension of Stanislavski's *Magic "IF"* is the idea that what we are pretending to live through is happening for the first time. That means you will experience every part of the carefully planned performance as if it never happened before. Discoveries must feel fresh, defeats be suffered and victories relished in the immediacy of the moment. And the words you speak, steps you dance and songs you sing must spring from you as if newly minted. This is all part of living truthfully in an imaginary world before an audience.

Public solitude and relishing exposure

Actors experience their most private and revealing moments in public. Think of this as *public solitude*. All actors need to learn that this is a fundamental part of their art. It takes some getting used to, this exposing our innermost feelings before a teacher or director, a classroom or cast, or a paying audience. That public sharing of private moments is why audiences are drawn to live performance. They want to be allowed to watch someone else live through experiences they might not get to, or would be afraid to have. Actors are brave emotional warriors. Your willingness to relish this kind of personal exposure is central to becoming a great actor in any medium.

Acting is believing – the difference between acting and performing

For many of us, the reason we first got into theatre is because we love being onstage in front of an audience. The energy we get from that kind of attention, and the chance to share our deepest feelings of joy or sadness in such a public way can be intoxicating. As heady as that experience can be, there is a difference between performing to satisfy yourself, and stepping into the shoes of a character and serving the writer's purpose. As you develop in your training you'll probably discover the old thrill of pure performance is replaced, or augmented, by another kind of excitement: engaging a musical text so fully you really do imagine yourself in that world and find great freedom in doing so. You will still get the thrill of performance as you live truthfully in the imaginary circumstances of your role. But, that is no longer the goal. It has become a side effect. This transition from one who needs the attention of the audience to one who seeks to serve the dramatic moment is a hallmark of great actors. And this is the difference between being a performer and being an actor.

Many of the best cabaret and concert artists make this same transfer by treating each song as a one-act play. The immersion into the given circumstances of the characters they create song-by-song is no less dramatic than when working on an evening-length role.

For sheer personal satisfaction and a love-fest between you and the audience, you always get a curtain call at the end of the evening, where it is your right and privilege to bask in their adoration.

UNIT 1.4.6   *Playful work, disciplined play*

It can be fun to be in a musical, whether in a high school production, a community theatre or on Broadway. But it is also a lot of hard work. And there are times when it is more work than fun to get the job done. This is where your commitment to building and sustaining excellence must take over. Artists are willing to toil over a single moment until it serves the production. Amateurs settle for the first, easiest choice.

There is a discipline to working as a theatre artist that extends to your willingness to meet the emotional demands of the scene or song exactly when you're called on to do so. As harsh as this may sound, you're simply not allowed to "not feel it" when the text tells you that you must. Of course, you will develop technique that allows you to call upon your personal and physical resources to get you to the place you need to go, even under difficult circumstances. But a professional actor not only hits his physical marks every time, he also hits the emotional marks.

UNIT 1.4.7   *Theatricality*

When we see the work of a great actor, we are compelled by his power onstage, the specificity of his choices in expressing the character, the technical mastery that he possesses, and the sheer interesting-ness of the performance. By expanding his vocal and physical expression, he conveys the truth of the character in a way that reaches us in the back of the balcony. This is called theatricality. It is *life* plus *magnitude*. All theatrical performance involves some degree of theatricality. The appropriate degree of magnitude has a great deal to do with where your audience is, how large it is and the imaginary world of the musical.

Musical theatre can be a difficult art form for the serious actor because it comes with some built-in challenges. Most of these stem from this overt theatricality.

If asked, most people would say that good acting should look just like life itself; it should be natural, truthful, believable, artless and unaffected. But when was the last time your real life required you to all at once perform a complicated dance step, sing in witty rhyming couplets, and fill a five thousand seat theatre with the intimate discovery that you're in love for the first time? This is part of the joy of doing musicals, and is also a job requirement.

You may periodically feel a conflict between your desire to express a moment truthfully and your requirement to share that moment with the audience. There is no need to choose one or the other. In fact, you can't successfully meet the demands of any good theatrical text unless you can do both simultaneously. In many cases, the energy required to express your truth to the audience will amplify that truth in ways that make the moment more powerful for you and them. Remember, in theatrical terms, if we can't see it and hear it, it didn't happen.

Inside out/outside in

UNIT 1.4.8

As you work the exercises in this book you'll see we spend time approaching this work from at least two different perspectives. The first has you find the character through emotional and psychological means that eventually result in physical and vocal choices that are stageworthy. This is a valid approach and probably falls in line with many of the acting classes you have already taken. We call it *inside out* because it asks you to start internally and then manifest your experience in behavior.

But we also offer a good number of exercises that ask you to start with external physical and vocal choices that we want you to work inward from. So, you may adopt a physical shape and then be asked to let that shape affect you emotionally. We call this *outside in*. This is also a valid approach to training that artists in every branch of acting, movement and singing have used for years.

Regardless of where you start your process, you are ultimately working toward the same goal of creating a performance that is internally rich and externally expressive. The interplay between these two aspects of your artistic self is constant and seamless. You'll need to allow the outside in and be affected by it, and you'll need to let your inside out and express it with clarity and power. It doesn't matter where you start this loop, as long as it circulates.

Don't reject any approach to training outright unless it is physically or emotionally destructive, or unless it results in untruthful or uninteresting performances. Training as an actor is a life-long process. You create and refine your technique by accumulating useful practices from every realm of your life. Recognize that what works for one person may not work for another. There is no one-size-fits-all approach to artistic training. It is a process of lots of trial and almost as much error. If you can approach your work with an open mind, who knows where you'll find your next learning opportunity?

Let's now start exploring the fundamental acting elements in more depth.

SECTION I: FUNDAMENTALS OF ACTING IN MUSICAL THEATRE

CHAPTER 2

Acting fundamentals

It is helpful to have a clear way to speak about the acting process. So we'll lay out some common terms and examine them in detail.

These are the fundamental elements of the acting process:

Given circumstances – the context your character lives in; all the facts of her life, personal history, relationships, social and physical environment

Relationship – who you are in association to everyone and everything around you

Objective – what your character wants

Beat – a unit within a scene where what you want changes, because you either achieved, discarded or replaced your former objective

Obstacle – anything that gets in the way of what you want

Strategy – either an instinctive or an intentional plan to get what you want

Tactics – the moment-to-moment actions taken to implement your strategy

Evaluation – a moment when an impulse is restrained and multiple possibilities for action are considered, rejected or accepted

Text – all the tangible elements established by the author, composer, choreographer, director and designers, particularly the script and the lyrics

Subtext – all the intangible things implied by the actor but not expressly stated in the text; what you mean as opposed to what you say, for example

Inner monologue – the constant stream of interior thoughts, feelings, sensations and impulses that are experienced but not necessarily expressed.

As with any skill, success rests on mastering the fundamentals. Experienced actors use the rehearsal process to consciously, then instinctively, address all these elements for every moment of every role.

UNIT 2.2   ## Given circumstances

Welcome to the land of *IF*.

IF is a terrific place to visit. If it is 1962 and the most important thing in my life is getting my hair to flip up perfectly, or if the year is 1957 and a Puerto Rican gang named the Sharks is threatening to take over my territory, or if it's 1907 and Oklahoma is the territory and I punch cattle for a living . . . but . . . wait, it's actually now and I've been hired to live in all those places this season. I'm still just little old me and I have to transform into people from places I've never been, with concerns I've never had. How?

UNIT 2.2.1   ## *Facts of the world of your script*

First, understand. Learn everything you can from the script. The circumstances your character lives in spring from the world of the play. This is a fabricated world. Even in a musical that has a historical and factual basis like *1776*, the viewpoint of the story and the lives of the characters are inventions. In order to enter that world, you'll need to understand it.

Initially, read the play looking for facts. Search out things that help you understand the plot, the characters, and the social and physical environment. Different specific facts will be relevant for each show. Ask questions like:

1.   What is the story?
2.   Who are the characters? (Define their age, social level, physical description, education, occupation and community.)
3.   What are their relationships?
4.   Where does this story take place? (Answer this for each scene and do some research to learn about these places.)
5.   When does the story take place? (Look at the year, the season, time of day, weather, etc. for each scene.)

At this stage, restrict yourself to just the facts that are established in the script and from your research. Get the facts straight before drawing inferences from them.

EXERCISE 2A   BRINGING IN YOUR RESEARCH

For this exercise you'll need to select a musical that you can get a full script and complete recording of. If you can get a score, so much the better. If you're in a class, it's useful to pick the same musical for everyone to explore together. Make a list of all the areas that you can examine as you investigate the world of your show. List everything that comes to mind (this is a good time to start using your workbook). Once you've made a comprehensive list, select the most important items. Divide into groups, solos or pairs (if you're part of a larger group). Assign the tasks and start to research that part of your dramatic world.

You're going to research one component and make a presentation to the cast. Be creative in how you present the information. Bring in pictures, video, food and music. Decorate the room with images from that world. Create a mock newscast. Stage a community gathering, a political debate or a place in the world of your musical. Select a day when everyone presents their findings.

Inferring given circumstances

Once you understand the objective facts of the given circumstances, you will begin to deduce information that isn't explicitly stated. But don't leap to this step until you understand the factual world of the play or you run the risk of making the wrong inferences.

Inferring is the beginning of entering the land of *IF*. Place yourself personally in the worldview of the character: if I was [——] and you were [——] then we would [——]! And you're off and running. Now you're at the place where you can begin projecting yourself into the given circumstances. The primary rule about inference is that it can never negate the facts. Inference must always be consistent with the circumstances of the characters as given by the writers.

UNIT 2.2.3 *Worldview*

Characters are shaped and limited by their perceptions of the world – what we call a worldview. It affects their sense of what is real as well as what is possible. Certain things will be unthinkable for your character. Though many times a character is on the cusp of an insight that is revolutionary (Tony and Maria thinking they could be together in *West Side Story*), every worldview contains limitations. In *1776*, Abigail and Jon Adams can't even think the thought that she might become president of the emerging nation. The gender roles of the time simply couldn't allow the question to be raised in their own minds.

A worldview is pervasive. We could all be cats cavorting around a junkyard or villagers in a shtetl in danger of a pogrom, or gangsters who love to shoot craps. Each of these worlds is unique and complete. And none of them is like yours. Understand the world of the musical for what it is rather than interpreting it through the world we're living in now.

It is always difficult to suspend our own worldview (because we don't tend to admit that we have one) and enter that of the musical, but that's half the fun of being an actor. Large sections of this book are dedicated to help you with this process.

EXERCISE 2B   WHAT IS MY WORLDVIEW?

Use your earlier research to compare your worldview with that of the characters in the musical. Answer these questions for yourself and your character?

1. Where do I live? (urban, rural, east/west coast, desert, mountain, apartment, tenement, tent, palace . . .)
2. How do I speak? (formal, slang, hip, scholarly)
3. What is beautiful?
4. What is sexy? (turn-ons and turn-offs)
5. What are the gender roles? (what are you allowed/not allowed to do, stereotypes)
6. What is good etiquette and what is taboo?
7. What do you do for fun?
8. What are your religious beliefs and sense of an afterlife? What is a sin?

9. Who is in charge? (social justice, politics) What is your relationship to authority?
10. What is your education?
11. What is your profession?
12. What are the recent advances in science, exploration and technology?

Use this information to create a list of worldviews that you share with your character, and another list of areas where you are divergent. Write this in your workbook and present them to the class. Address how your daily experience would change if you had the same worldview as your character.

Relationships

UNIT 2.3

You are in a relationship with everyone and everything in the musical. From the central characters, to the smallest prop, to the memory of your character's grandmother, you have a personal relationship with all of it. It or they mean something to you.

EXERCISE 2C LIST THE RELATIONSHIPS

1. List the five most important people in your life. They don't have to be family, though they might be. And they don't have to be the people you're told you "should" care about, though they might be that, as well. These just need to be the five most important people in your life. Next to each name, write why they matter to you in one sentence.
2. Now, list the three most important items in your life. Not most valuable in terms of replacement cost, but most important to you, for any reason. Next to those items, write a single sentence that describes why it is important.
3. You've just articulated relationships! Repeat this exercise asking those same questions of your character.

UNIT 2.3.1   *My world and welcome to it*

Do you take things personally? If you're being honest, you should answer, "Yes," because there is really no other way to take them. Every person believes she is the center of the universe. This isn't a flaw. There is simply no other way to be. Everything in the world exists as something that is *mine*: this is my house, my school, my dog, my bank, etc. Even things we reject are conceptualized in terms of ourselves: my ex-boyfriend, my rival school attended by all those kids who are richer than I am, that church where they profess odd things I don't believe, etc. Personalization is the key here. Admit that everything is "mine."

EXERCISE 2D   EVERYTHING IS MINE

Go back to the list that you created in the last exercise and rephrase everyone and everything on it as "mine." Were you already doing this? You wouldn't be alone if you were. Do this for yourself and for your character.

UNIT 2.3.2   *Endowment*

Implicit in owning everything is that it is all framed and conceived through the lens of our needs, judgments, values and beliefs: how I feel about them. That's not just my dog; it is my dog I see as cute, scary, a cesspool of allergic stimulant, my protector, etc. Since the same dog can be feared by one person and adored by another, the objective truth about the dog is immaterial. Your character's truth is the only one you can play. This process of assigning qualities to other people or things is called *endowing*. When you say that the dog is "my little cutie-pootie," or a "monster that will bite me," you are endowing the dog with qualities and defining your relationship with it.

We can also endow inanimate objects with special relationships. When Pseudolus goes off in search of mare's sweat in order to create a sleeping potion in *A Funny Thing Happened on the Way to the Forum*, that vile vial is "a stink bomb" to the people he encounters, but to him it is "my holy grail" because it will lead directly to his freedom. In each case you are setting up a complex and layered relationship that has memories, expectations, blind spots and all the richness of real human interaction. So be judgmental. Endow.

EXERCISE 2E ENDOWING

Use the earlier list of personal and character relationships. Add a column describing or characterizing the other person or thing. Phrase it as "my (adjective phrase) (noun)" as in "my devoted fantasy-cheerleader girl-friend," or "my evil, drunken, trailer-trash brother-in-law."

Compare your descriptions of your character relationships with others in your group and celebrate the differences.

EXERCISE 2F THE LIARS' CLUB

Bring in three random items that mean nothing much to you. If you can, bring items in and then trade with a friend. Or perhaps you have access to a property storage area in a theatre. Go there to find items.

For each item, create a story about what the object is, where it came from and why it matters to you. It's important that you make this up and that it is not the real story of the object. Perhaps you have a pocketknife that you are pretending belonged to your grandfather. Pretend he gave it you when you went camping. Create some special event around the object (that doesn't even belong to you!).

Use all your senses to engage this endowment and the memories associated with it. Smell the campfire, taste the roasted marshmallows, and hear your grandfather's voice as you feel him hand you the gift.

Once you've established this imaginary reality, try singing a song from your repertoire and use one object in the song. You can probably find a song that you know where you can employ a prop easily.

Did you find that you were affected by the use of this borrowed object with a made-up history?

Metaphoric relationships

UNIT 2.3.3

The way we conceptualize relationships may be irrational, metaphoric, out of date or otherwise idiosyncratic. A girl can baby her boyfriend. Parents can think of their adult children as irresponsible, pimply teenagers forever. A mom might be a best friend to her daughter. You can make someone else the bad guy, the hot guy or the nerd just by thinking it, and it will be true for you. Your best friend might see you as his confessor, his smarter half, his dupe, his brother, his counselor, etc. Endow every relationship with a strong metaphoric side by giving it a relationship title. If you chose bland descriptors like buddy, wife or cousin you will miss the potential of this. Don't be afraid of strong characterizations such as you are my nemesis, my delicate flower, my obligation, my solace, etc., and look beyond the literal to the deeper nature of your relationship.

Here is a short listing of some metaphoric relationships:

my savior	my slave	my captor	my healer
my mentor	my protégé	my seducer	my attacker
my henchman	my accomplice	my co-conspirator	my playmate
my captive	my side-kick	my oppressor	my nag
my nemesis	my inspiration	my mill-stone	my suck-up
my love-slave	my addiction	my crutch	my master
my cellmate	my tiger	my lieutenant	my captain
my competitor	my cutie-pie	my patron saint	my angel

You can add hundreds of richly stimulating metaphoric relationships to this list. Dig through a thesaurus and keep looking until you find the metaphoric characterization that engages the essential nature of your relationship.

You are characterizing the other person when you endow a relationship. This characterization may or may not be objectively true. It only matters that it is true for you. In *110 in the Shade*, Starbuck is Lizzie's savior, but he is her brother Noah's enemy. He is, in addition, the romantic rival to File, the town's sheriff. Those opinions don't tell us much about who Starbuck really is, but they do tell us about the people who hold them. What's interesting is that in the process of characterizing all the people and things around you, you'll solve another important acting issue – you'll establish your own character.

EXERCISE 2G   PLAYING THE RELATIONSHIPS

1.   Choose a song as a neutral text, work with a partner.
2.   Put a range of metaphoric relationships on paper and cut them up into individual slips. Place them in a hat or cup, then draw a relationship,

> but don't tell your partner, and play that relationship using the song as your text.
>
> 3.   Do it again and have you and your partner each choose a relationship slip at random. Don't tell each other what the relationships are.
>
> 4.   After you're done, ask each other and your classmates what they thought the relationships were. Then you can reveal what they really were.
>
> 5.   Try this again, but, doing it in the open, select a relationship that you think would be ideal for your song. Allow your partner to pick a complementary relationship (either sympathetic to your need or in conflict with your need). After you're done, discuss what it did for you in the song.
>
> 6.   Try it a last time, but this time, be sure that your partner has picked a relationship that is contrary to the one you want. If you are calling her your savior, she cannot make you her apostle. Let her make you her competitor. Now see what happens.

Relationships change

UNIT 2.3.4

Relationships are multi-faceted. A wife can shift from being my playmate, to my nag, to my comfort in a single encounter. The changing qualities of a relationship can also mark your character's journey or arc through a play as your enemy might evolve into your ally, then your lover. At the beginning of *110 in the Shade*, Lizzie views Starbuck as her charlatan, and proceeds to treat him that way until she begins to view him as her romantic savior. Finally she sees him as her charming dreamer. The relationship shifted radically as her experiences with him redefined it.

EXERCISE 2H   METAPHORIC RELATIONSHIPS

1.   Go back to your list of personal and character relationships and intensify them by reinforcing the metaphoric aspect. So "my devoted fantasy-cheerleader girlfriend" might now be "my devoted fantasy-cheerleader love-slave," or "my evil, drunken, trailer-trash brother-in-law" might now be "my evil, drunken, trailer-trash nemesis".

2. For your character relationships, see if they change over the course of the show. For example, your brother-in-law might start as "my best-buddy drinking-partner" before turning into "my prissy, judgmental, puritan nun."
3. As in the earlier exercise, play this relationship in two ways with the same person, using your neutral text song.

UNIT 2.3.5   *Who am I, anyway?*

Actors tend to turn inward at the first mention of characterization. They can get caught up in worrying how they will behave or how they will be seen or under-stood by the audience. That way of looking at the issue has a built-in problem: if you set out to show something it will look shallow and artificial. You'll also be focusing on yourself and not as available to listen and respond to the other characters onstage. Instead, a focus on relationships will get you out of a con-centration on yourself and make you interactively present onstage. Get out of yourself and into the other person. You can't focus on yourself when you're intent on changing someone else.

Imagine you are playing a character described as greedy. How do you show that? Try it and you'll start to feel frustrated. The problem is you're asking the wrong question. The right question is: how do you endow the other characters and what will that tell us about you? Look at a character like Fagin in *Oliver!* He's a cunning person, motivated by greed and a ruthless survival instinct, with a willingness to lie and use others, especially helpless orphan children. If you endow the other characters with relationships that are experienced through the lens of his greed you may start to see them as: my tool, my fool, my opportunity, my conspirator, my dupe, my weak spot, my loose cannon, etc. Notice the absence of: my love, my friend, my comfort, etc. You might see Oliver as my opportunity whereas Nancy will see him as my child. Oliver is just himself, but the way characters define him reveals who *they* are. Relationships define who you are by the way you see your world.

In addition, the way you have defined the relationship triggers the other person to have feelings and impulses and strong reactions to you. Because you have a clear sense of who she is to you and how you feel about her, she will naturally have a strong response to that identification. In *A Funny Thing Happened on the Way to the Forum*, Miles Gloriosus characterizes every one else as his cadets.

As a result, people either accept this characterization and obey him, or they mightily resist it and encounter opposition from a formidable foe. This is one of the most effective ways to begin the interactive dance of characters. As soon as you start getting a sense of the character's given circumstances, turn your focus to the process of endowing relationships. You'll solve the problem of character-ization and put yourself interactively into the play.

Your character can be defined in interesting ways by how you endow the *things* in your world, as well. In *You're a Good Man, Charlie Brown*, Linus endows his blanket as his best friend, his talisman, his life raft, and many other positive things. That process defines him as being unlike any other little boy in the show. It also gives the actor in that role so many interesting things to do. Linus' world is defined by his relationship with his blanket. In fact, every character in that show endows the blanket with a specific relationship.

Relationships with people and things have stakes. There is risk, a need and a potential for success and failure attached to everything in your character's world. What would happen if that person rejected you, or embraced you? What would happen if that person stopped trusting you or that blanket ripped? What would happen if that person suddenly died, or the blanket was stolen?

Objectives

UNIT 2.4

Characters aren't static. They move through a musical by doing things. *What* does my character do? This addresses the question of your character's actions in the story. When a character does something, we call that an *action*. Things like confronting an enemy, calming someone down, confessing a secret or avoiding an awkward subject are all actions because they're things that you do.

Why versus what for

UNIT 2.4.1

Why does he do the things he does? This question addresses the character's *motivation*. It is necessary to understand your character's motivation because it gives you a context and a history, and can help you comprehend the psychological and emotional reasons for a character's behavior – all important things to know when going into a role. But that information will usually precede the action of the scene. It's really part of the character's past. Answering a why question won't help you act. It will provide you with a dry, reasonable rationale containing *because*. For example: why did Valjean steal that loaf of bread? He stole because he was hungry and impoverished and he saw no other solution. All true – but not active.

Acting needs to be active. Characters need to do. Ask, "*What* does my character *do*?" Then, instead of asking, "*Why* does my character do that?" try asking, "What is my character acting *for*?" "What does he want to make happen?" Now you're addressing the character's *objective*. That is not only actable, it will force you to act. An objective is the rocket fuel that drives the character's behavior. The distinction between motivation and objective may seem subtle at first, but notice the difference between how you feel when you say, "I steal the bread because I'm hungry," and "I'm stealing the bread to save my life." The first is the rational *why*; the second is the passionate and desperate *what for*. The trigger word to watch for is *because*. It will make you focus on rational explanations and keep you in your head. In contrast, "I'm stealing bread *in order to* save my life" will focus you on your objective and put you into action.

As you analyze your role you'll need to note your character's actions, motivations and objectives. They are related but they aren't the same thing. Ask yourself these questions:

- *What does my character do?* This will describe your action. Look for answers that have strong verbs in them: I fight, I seduce, I tease, I savor, I kill . . .
- *Why does my character do this?* This will give you your motivation. Look for answers that have *because* in them: because I'm lonely, because I'm sad, because I'm hurt, because you begged me . . .
- *What am I fighting for?* This will tell you your objective. Look for answers that start with "I want" and have "to" in them: to possess, to live, to change, to revenge, to have, to know . . .

EXERCISE 21 WHY VERSUS WHAT FOR

1. Using your workbook, make a list of some of the things your character does.
2. Now create a chart like the one opposite. Label the columns and place the list of actions in the first. Then proceed to answer each of the following questions about that action.

Table 2-1

Action	Motivation	Objective
What do I do?	Why do I do that?	What am I doing that for?

Be sure to make a clear distinction between your reasons for doing something and what you actually want. Reasons aren't playable. A focus on reasons will tend to make you stand outside the musical, whereas fighting for something you want puts you directly into the character's experience. Another way of saying this is *why* is about the past; *what for* is about the future.

Superobjective

UNIT 2.4.2

Seen from the perspective of the whole story, characters usually want one important overarching thing. We call this the superobjective. The character proceeds in the direction of the superobjective through a series of smaller objectives. Every act, scene and song – right down to the smallest action – has its own objective, but they all point congruently toward the big important thing your character wants. This is called an *objective hierarchy*.

Sometimes a character isn't quite aware of what is driving his actions. Many characters fiercely deny what they are actually after. Gaining insight into his own behavior is often the journey that character makes through the musical, and enlightenment, realization and comprehension of the nature of his actions comes only at the climax of the show. In *Pippin*, for example, Pippin would never have said that being a father, husband and simple farmer were what he had in mind when he sang 'Corner of the Sky'. In fact, his conscious desire could be phrased as "to live an extraordinary life." It's only after he has tried and rejected all the obvious roads to self-fulfillment that he embraces this decidedly humble path. The actor needs to understand the character's superobjective even when the character himself doesn't. In Pippin's case, he states his superobjective as "be[ing] where my spirit can run free . . . find[ing] my corner of the sky." He discovers that his earlier picture of what that means was naive, but his journey toward his superobjective is consistent.

A superobjective can be consciously chosen, but, more typically, it seems to choose the character. It might be a basic need like, "I must protect my nation" (King in The King and I). It can be a compulsion as in, "I must win at all costs" (Mama Rose in Gypsy). It can also be something the character is forced to assume by circumstance such as, "I must avenge my father's death" (Simba in The Lion King).

It can take some careful analysis to establish a character's superobjective. An actor needs to be able to both zoom in on a single small moment and also zoom out to see the character's behaviors from the perspective of the whole show. From the larger perspective, small, seemingly contradictory actions take on coherence.

One of the most important uses of the rehearsal process is to test and refine your character's superobjective. You're looking for the single driving force that contains and organizes all the character's behaviors into a throughline of action.

The concept of a throughline of action rests on the awareness that everything your character does points toward one primary thing he wants. If you can find the right superobjective, that want will bring a focus and structure to all the character's actions.

A superobjective is the most powerful force in your character's life. It has no means of escape. It reaches backwards from the end of the story, grabs your character by the throat and yanks you through the musical. If you are working on Anita in West Side Story, for example, you might consider these for her: "I must fight for my place in America," or "I must protect Maria from the dangers of this new country," or "I must control Bernardo and make him desire me." Those are all things she wants and fights for. The superobjective will be the most significant of those wants.

In many cases a character will have conflicting desires and will be forced to choose between them. That choice is telling, because the one he selects is his true superobjective. In Anita's case, she wants her people to be respected, wants Bernardo's love, wants to avenge his death, and, in direct contradiction to all that, agrees for Maria's sake to warn Bernardo's killer that he is in danger. If, in the midst of all those extreme emotional demands, Anita chooses to act in Maria's interest, it is a major clue to what is the most important thing for her. Her superobjective might be "to protect and support Maria."

Once you have established a clear superobjective, all the other contrary impulses become conflicts that the character must confront and reconcile or overcome. Anita can't maintain her loyalty to her people or avenge Bernardo and still protect and support Maria. Those are intense dramatic obstacles for her character. We'll discuss more about the usefulness of obstacles in a moment.

Many of the things we want in our deepest hearts are irrational and unobtainable – yet these unconscious imperatives are the forces driving our lives. Pippin wants complete and utter fulfillment at all times or else he feels trapped in a mundane existence. How possible is it for anyone to achieve that goal? But winning isn't the issue. It is the pursuit of the superobjective that keeps you active and keeps the musical going. An objective may be unachievable and can have an element of insane compulsion even in otherwise rational characters: "I must enact my revenge by killing God," for example.

In developing your character's hierarchy of objectives, start by outlining the main units where your character appears and find the objective for each.

EXERCISE 2J   OBJECTIVE HIERARCHY

Using an outline form, divide the show up into its component pieces. Work from the large scale to the small, noting what your character wants for each.

   Superobjective for the whole show

      Act objective

         Scene objective

            Unit or song objective

Remember that discovering clear objectives is one of the primary goals of the rehearsal process. That means you'll need to try on a few in order to find the ones that fit best. You should do this consciously and intentionally and revise it regularly as your understanding of the role deepens.

UNIT 2.4.3   *Testing the objective*

Objectives need to be tested in rehearsal to see if they inspire you to a passionate connection with the role. Every objective comes with an expected outcome. The questions to ask are:

> If I got exactly what I wanted, what would happen?
> How would I know I got what I wanted?
> What does winning my objective look like?

We can test these questions with '*I Have a Love/A Boy Like That*', a duet between Maria and Anita from *West Side Story*. Bernardo has just been killed. Anita, his love, confronts Maria, his sister, about Tony, Maria's love and the boy who killed Bernardo in a gang fight (see Table 2-2).

In almost every case, you would know you got what you wanted because someone else would do something. So achievement of your objective usually depends on the other person. In this case, Anita does what Maria wants, and Maria knows she's won her fight for support and endorsement because of Anita's response. The advantage of seeing an objective in terms of your acting partner is that it puts you into relationship with the other person. Your need is focused into your partner and in working to change her or demanding that she act you are raising the stakes for the other character as well as yourself. Maria did change Anita from a condemner to a supporter. She only knows this has happened because of what Anita does.

Table 2-2

Maria's objective is to gain Anita's support for her love of Tony.	**Anita's objective is** to convince Maria of Tony's deceit and end their relationship.
Maria would know she got what she wanted because Anita would stop her condemnation and offer support to Maria and Tony.	**Anita would know she got what she wanted because** Maria would renounce Tony.
For Maria, winning looks like her dear friend and counselor, Anita, embracing her and shaking her head "yes" to Maria's request for support.	**For Anita, winning looks like** Maria weeping and praying for forgiveness for her betrayal of her family.

Specific ideal outcome

Require your partner to respond to you in specific ways. For example, "I want to be saved" risks being a generalized need as opposed to knowing that you must be rescued from destitution on the streets of Berlin in a specific way. This is exactly what Sally Bowles wants from Cliff Bradshaw in *Cabaret*. She will know she's been rescued when Cliff puts her suitcase on the bed. Another way she'd know is if he grabbed her, tossed her on the bed and kissed her. Or he could simply drop his head in weary surrender to the inevitable. Every character has a specific idea of what winning looks like. The more precise the intended outcome is, the easier and more exciting it is to play it. Once you know what your objective is, you'll no longer think of it in general terms like, "I want you to suffer for what you did." Rather, you'll pursue the *specific ideal outcome* like, "I demand that you burst into flames and disappear screaming into a cloud of black smoke. I will settle for nothing less." Then you can keep your mind focused directly on getting Cliff to toss you into bed, Anita to embrace you, or your enemy to burst into flames.

EXERCISE 2K   SPECIFIC IDEAL OUTCOME

Work from the Objective Hierarchy list you have been evolving. For every objective, ask the question, "If I got what I wanted, what specific things would happen, and what exactly would that look like?"

Take that list back into rehearsal and instead of abstractly focusing on what you want, fight to make the specific ideal outcome happen. See if that isn't easier and clearer.

Use this as a way to test whether your objectives need to be adjusted.

Notice that all the work we're doing overlaps. Understand the character's given circumstances. Act from clear, specific relationships. Characterize and endow all the people and things you relate to. Pursue specific objectives that are focused on other characters and have clear expected outcomes. All these will place you inside the character and keep you passionately moving forward through the musical.

UNIT 2.5 **Beats**

Sometimes during a scene you win your objective. Or it is replaced by something more pressing. Or something happens that changes the game and alters what you want. Winning, or changing your objective, signals the shift to another small unit within a scene or a song. The traditional actor terminology for this small section is a *beat*.

If you neglect to identify the beats and when they change, you will miss the author's intention and fail to lead us through the character's experience in truthful detail. Like so many issues in acting, this requires attentive script analysis and the ability to project yourself imaginatively into the character's experience. It is at the smaller units of a performance that the audience finds a connection to the performer and a belief in the reality being established.

UNIT 2.5.1 *Identifying beats*

Start by asking what you want, and when that seems to change.

For example, let's look at Anita again. When we first meet her, she and Maria are working in the bridal shop. Anita is converting a white communion dress into a party outfit for Maria. Maria is begging Anita to make the dress sexier. Anita's objective in this section is clear: she needs to try to contain Maria's guileless nubile enthusiasm. Anita, being older and more experienced, knows what happens when a girl flaunts herself, and in her superobjective of protecting Maria needs to keep her from provoking more than she can handle. Maria tries a variety of tactics to persuade Anita, who remains firm. The beat ends when they arrive at a compromise – the neckline will go a little lower, but just a little, and the dress will be white, not red. When that beat is ended, Bernardo and Chino enter and we're into the next unit.

West Side Story is a tightly composed, episodic script. In this musical the beats and the units of action are sometimes the same. At other times, beats are small units within larger scenes or song sections. The distinction is that a *unit of action* contains one important *story event*. A beat contains one small *objective* for your character. The unit of action is about the story. The objective is about what your character wants. Sometimes they coincide, but frequently the beats are much smaller units. It is important to identify the story element of the unit of action so you can keep a clear sense of what is going on. But story elements aren't playable; objectives and the behaviors they lead to are.

Later, Anita, Bernardo, the Sharks and their girls have gathered after the dance. In this section, Anita's scene objective is to control, dominate and fascinate Bernardo, and to do it in a way that establishes her prerogative to act as a strong, independent American woman, free of the confining roles forced on women in traditional Puerto Rican society. When they enter, Bernardo (Maria's brother) is preoccupied with wondering if Maria is safely at home. Anita's first beat objective is to get Bernardo's attention focused back onto her. She wins this objective six lines in. She knows she's won because Bernardo starts cooing her name. With that success, Anita's objective shifts and we're into her next beat.

EXERCISE 2L FINDING THE BEAT

1. Choose a scene to work on that includes a song.
2. Ask yourself, "What happens in this scene?" Don't look at your script; just tell the story of the scene. If you're working with a group, sit in a circle and take turns telling one simple story element each and handing it on to the next person by saying, "and then . . . " You'll instinctively break the scene up into units of action – the important story elements.
3. Identify your character's scene objective, then your objective for every unit of action.
4. Then look even more closely to see the smaller things your character wants and most importantly where those small specific wants are either fulfilled, stymied or renegotiated and then are replaced by a new objective. Those changes mark the end of one beat and the start of another.
5. Score your script with bold markings that show these beats. Choose a clear objective and an ideal intended outcome for each.
6. Rehearse the scene, working to make each of those outcomes come true and notice how you and your partner respond to this way of working.

Fight only for what you want right now

UNIT 2.5.2

Even though characters may want many things in a scene (and may often want contradictory things) it is usually wise to pursue one clear beat objective at a time. Don't worry about whether the objective is reasonable or achievable. Don't worry about whether it is the exact opposite of what you were after a moment before. Fight for what you want, now, in this moment. Much of human behavior is irrational and a truthful embodiment of a character will include all the rich ridiculousness of our fallible psyches. As Stephen Sondheim wrote in *Follies*, "God-why-don't-you-love-me-oh-you-do-I'll-see-you-later."

Apt. Witty. And did you notice that it has at least three distinct beats with contradictory objectives in one rapidly sung line?

> God, why don't you love me? (Fall to your knees and worship me!)
> Oh, you do! (Wait! Stop!)
> I'll see you later . . . (Get me out of here!)

One of the challenges of musical theatre is it can go from this kind of compression of thought and objective (three beats in two seconds) to soaring extended moments where time seems to stop. An understanding of the character's beat objective is critical to making these moments truthful.

UNIT 2.6 ## Obstacles

If you have something to fight *for*, you'll need something to fight *against*. Drama is about conflict. Obstacles, those things we fight against, create that conflict. Just as an airplane takes off more quickly when facing into the wind, a challenging obstacle will provide the resistance to make the beat take off.

In our offstage lives a psychologically healthy person will try to defuse conflict and resolve differences amicably. In all forms of drama, characters pursue their objectives regardless of the obstacles they face. The obstacles make them fight harder, more cleverly, and discover tactical resources they never knew they had. The dynamic interplay between fighting to pursue what you want and meeting defiant opposition will also provoke strong emotional responses in both the actor and the audience, not to mention the person you're fighting against.

UNIT 2.6.1 ### *External and internal obstacles*

Obstacles come from sources that are both external (physical hurdles, other characters' conflicting wants) and internal (emotional conflicts, psychological struggles, moral compunctions, contradictory impulses).

External obstacles are usually obvious. Maria is on the fire escape and Tony is on the ground. It's a metaphor for all that separates them, and it is also usefully physical. They have a literal gap to cross in order to be together. When they are with each other, the risk they take is also literal: Bernardo would kill Tony if he found them together. Characters are frequently faced with external physical obstacles.

Internal obstacles are even more frequent. Remember that characters often want contradictory things. There will be a primary objective, but usually a number of strong impulses running in opposition to that desire. After the dance at the gym, Maria wants to embrace Tony when he comes to her window, and she has the external obstacles that her father may come out onto the fire escape to get her or, worse, that her brother will discover the liaison. Internally, she has other conflicts. She has been taught to be an obedient daughter, a loyal sister and a chaste Catholic girl. Meeting secretly with an American boy is contrary to all of that. She fears Bernardo and his friends are right about American boys only wanting one thing from girls, but she is feeling things she's never felt before and is in the grip of powerful new longings. All of these thoughts might rush through her mind as she meets with Tony, causing her to struggle between her desires and her reservations.

EXERCISE 2M IDENTIFYING OBSTACLES

Choose a unit in your script that contains at least three beats. Define your objectives and ideal outcomes. Then, for each beat say, "If my objective is [——], then my obstacles might be [——]."

Identify at least two external obstacles and five internal obstacles to each objective. Now play this section and use the obstacles. Which obstacles worked most effectively to force you to work harder, or differently on the objective?

Physicalizing the struggle

UNIT 2.6.2

Though internal, your personal obstacles will seem to literally pull your character in different directions. And that is the secret to acting them: make them physical. It is an axiom of human behavior that anything that lives in the heart or in the head also lives in the body. If you have a thought or a feeling, your body will respond. Your breath will shift; certain muscles will tighten or relax; your posture and balance will adjust. There is really no such thing as a purely internal thought or feeling, even though the physicalization can be subtle. One of the jobs of an actor in training is to wake up and sensitize your voice and body so that you are ready, willing and able to respond with all parts of your instrument when an impulse strikes.

Although the physical experience of a feeling or thought can be delicate, the theatre, and musicals in particular, require expressive acting. To help find a large, truthfully physical character experience, let's make the obstacles your character is facing literal.

EXERCISE 2N OBSTACLES: WHAT'S IN YOUR WAY?

1. Use the same beats and list of internal and external obstacles as in the last exercise.
2. Place your partner across the room. Imagine that in order to achieve your ideal outcome you need to get to your partner.
3. Use other members of your group to physically hold you back from crossing the room, so you have powerful literal obstacles to work against. If you're one of the obstacles, work safely, but make the actors fight hard. Let them win when the script establishes that. If you're the actor, don't just struggle, use all the tactics you can find to win: charm, seduce, threaten, intimidate, tease, please, etc.
4. Explore this with creative obstacles. Put furniture pieces in the way. Make the goal retreat or dodge. Have fun.

UNIT 2.6.3   *Emotions are obstacles (but in a good way)*

Notice how that last exercise made you feel. It can be frustrating to be stymied and thrilling to win. Did you get angry and have to deal with that? Without trying at all, you probably felt some strong emotions. Excellent.

It isn't unusual for actors to feel a certain pressure to generate emotions. Roles can come with specific emotional obligations. At one point in *Guys and Dolls*, Sarah Brown, speaking to Adelaide, is clearly distraught. "In the Bible, it tells us in Isaiah . . . Isaiah . . . (The thought is too much for her.) . . . Isaiah . . ." Adelaide says, "Nobody cries like that over an old guy. Whoever it is, you got it bad."

There is no getting out of this. Sarah has to be in the emotional state demanded by the script. She has to have it bad.

Even an experienced actor might feel intimidated by that requirement. You know you have to get there, but how? Conversely, we have all seen actors whose performances were a riot of generalized emoting sprayed all over the stage. Both are problems. As with many acting problems, these are difficulties born of looking at the issue from the wrong direction.

In real life, emotion is almost never the goal. We don't spend our days trying to feel something. If we are living inside a character we also shouldn't be pre-occupied with trying to feel. Quite the opposite of emotions being a goal, they are usually one of the main obstacles preventing us from getting what we want. Sarah doesn't want to cry. She doesn't want to feel the way she does at all. Emotional states are a byproduct of fighting to achieve what you want in the face of resistance. It is the product of being present with your partner and being available to be affected by what she does. It is the product of being filled with conflicting irreconcilable desires that make you need opposing things. In short, emotions will show up of their own accord if you focus on the basics of objective and obstacle. Then when they come they will be truthful and will fit the moment. Even better, emotions will drive your character forward and conflict with your character in useful ways. If your feeling doesn't seem strong enough, then increase the importance of what you want and plant larger obstacles to fight against. Don't look for larger feelings, look for larger needs and bigger problems. Onstage, unlike in real life, big desires and big problems are an actor's best friend.

If your character has a clear emotional obligation presented by the text (like "I can't keep from crying"), then back out of that moment and plant an accelerating series of overwhelming conflicting needs that bring you to that point. Start the progression to that place much earlier.

Occasionally a character has to enter or begin a scene in a strong emotional place. That only means you have to do your imaginary work offstage. In *Cabaret*, when Sally Bowles has to enter and break the news to Cliff that she's had an abortion, she has to walk through the door bringing that whole experience with her. She is a mess of conflicting desires, regrets, needs, and is in actual physical pain. Rehearse each objective and obstacle of that complex knot of feeling one at a time to get them clear. Then develop an offstage preparation that layers each of those into the moment.

EXERCISE 20   PUSH-ME-PULL-YOU

1. Use the same beats and list of internal and external obstacles as in the last exercise.
2. As before, place your scene partner across the room, and make reaching him your physical goal. Reaching him represents your scene objective.
3. Find a strong, wide belt to wear loosely around your waist. Pick two classmates to help, one in front and one behind. It helps if they are familiar with the scene section or song you'll be using for your text. They will use your belt to push and pull you.
4. Resist these helpers on your journey across the space. The one in front pulls you forward (representing your primary objective drawing you on) but you have fears or conflicting desires. True to human nature, when something pulls you forward, have compunctions that pull you back. When you are separated from the main thing you want, you'll recover your need for it and fight your way forward again. Don't let this become a wrestling match. Let each contrary desire have its little victory in a neurotic dance of internal conflict made physical. The helpers need to exercise sensitivity and read the actor's cues in order to create useful opposition. This can become quite forceful, but no one should lose control. Play safely.

Playing emotion as an end in itself will feel unspecific and indulgent, and will push the audience away, rather than draw them in. Don't play the emotion, play the intention, overcome the obstacle and let your emotions show up.

UNIT 2.7   **Strategy and tactics**

You'll notice in the last exercises that you instinctively searched for ways around your obstacles. If someone moved left, you countered right. They pushed and you pushed back, or ran, or dodged. Since you had a clear sense of what you were fighting *for* (objective), and what you were fighting *against* (obstacle), you were spontaneously developing *how* (tactics) to pursue those goals and overcome those obstacles. Strategy is the big how. Tactics are the little hows. Strategy is the big plan and tactics are the moment-to-moment lunges, feints, jabs, retreats and counterattacks that respond to what is happening, now. Your objective might be to get the girl. Your strategy might be to drive a wedge between that beautiful girl and her boyfriend. Your tactics might be to plant suspicion about her loyalty in his mind, to make him think she isn't good enough for him, or that there is a better girl out there. Strategy is the way you plan to win large unit objectives, and tactics are the ways you pursue beat objectives. Tactics are the moment-to-moment thrusts and parries that really make up the details of an encounter. It is here that the richness of a performance will live.

Let's apply all the concepts we've been exploring by using the character Ursula and the song 'Poor Unfortunate Souls' from the stage musical The Little Mermaid.

Superobjective: Get revenge on King Triton for banishing me from his undersea kingdom.

Strategy: Trap his favorite daughter, Ariel, for eternity by stealing her soul.

Song objective: Get Ariel to sign the pact and give up her voice for three days in exchange for being able to walk on land to win the heart of a prince.

Tactics: Ursula's moment-to-moment tactics for tricking Ariel have to do with winning her trust, weakening Ariel's confidence, dismissing her hesitations, inflating the impact of being able to walk, diminishing the importance of talking.

Obstacles: Ursula has so many obstacles that she has to go on for several verses before Ariel willingly signs the pact. The obstacles to Ursula are primarily Ariel's internal obstacles: her fear of breaking her father's rules, her hesitation about whether this is the best course of action, her uncertainty about her own beauty, her reluctance to give up her voice while wooing her new love, her fear that he might not like her enough to kiss her before three days are up, her fear that three days won't be enough time, and so forth. However, Ariel may present physical obstacles like turning away, starting to leave, speaking too loudly. Other external obstacles include the presence of Ariel's friends, who might overhear the conversation and spoil the deal.

Objective test: Ursula will know she has achieved her immediate objective when Ariel signs the pact and releases her voice to Ursula's magical jar.

Every aspect of the dramatic situation stems from the superobjective and leads back to it through a chain of smaller objectives, strategies and tactics.

Pick one song from the show you have chosen to work on. Identifying the character that sings it, apply the concepts we described above to several objectives in the song.

UNIT 2.8   ## Evaluation, discovery and adjustment

Mostly, tactics need to be explored rather than planned, because they depend so much on being in a living relationship with your partner and on your responses to what that partner is doing at any given moment. When you are responding tactically, you'll be constantly on the alert to what is and isn't working for you (unless your character has a blind spot and is socially tone deaf – something that does happen a lot in musicals). Part of the moment-to-moment interplay between characters consists of ongoing *evaluations* of the situation, *discovery* of what is happening and *adjustments* to your tactics. These tiny moments usually spring from being deeply invested in and observant of your partners, and from listening attentively to assess and respond to the new information they are bringing and the tactics they are pursuing. If you are in a duel of competing objectives, your character will be preparing a range of tactical options and will be investigating the other character's behavior for chinks in his armor. You'll consider all the things you might do or say before you act. But you can only do this in the instant before you respond because you can't really know what they're going to do until they do it! These rapid evaluations and adjustments take place, not so much in lengthy pauses, but more often, during the other character's line.

Evaluation, discovery and adjustment are all about "the other guy." This is why we so often find ourselves struggling to invent reactions when we do solo exercises with an imaginary partner, but find ourselves so free to respond when we have an actual partner. Their reactions fuel our reactions. The cycle continues with vitality and excitement as two or more people play good acting tennis with each other. It is as much your job to respond with full investment in the actions of your partners as it is theirs to work intently off of you.

The creative mood and preparation

We do offer a word of caution about depending on your partner to stimulate your performance, though. As freeing as working with a partner is, you still must each come into every rehearsal or performance with a powerful set of needs and a sense of what's happening in the text at every given moment. Otherwise, all of your acting becomes a game of pure chance. Some actors, especially young ones, feel that it's artificial to plan too much and that it inhibits their creativity and ability to respond freely. They fear that if they make clear moment-to-moment choices the spontaneity will be removed from the experience. So, their instinct is to avoid making any choices.

This is an understandable fallacy to fall victim to. After having watched thousands of good student and professional actors rehearse with such clarity and specificity that the performances seem completely spontaneous, we will assure you that preparation doesn't have to kill spontaneity. This artistic death only occurs when you allow the homework to be all you work with rather than a springboard. If the homework becomes a foundation you build each living moment upon, you will be empowered by it.

One of the dangers of refusing to make choices is that everything in your performance will flatten out and you'll lose the highs and lows that make it exciting. A resistance to making choices also frequently denies your ability to embrace given circumstances of the character that are different from your own. It's a slippery slope that almost always leads to bland acting.

Making choices about objectives, tactics and strategies is really no more restrictive than learning notes, lyrics and dialogue, or rehearsing choreography until you're confident with it. Can you imagine telling a musical director that you're afraid to sing the notes accurately or you'll lose the spontaneity of the song?

Just as you rehearse notes and steps so you don't have to think about them anymore, you do the same thing with other kinds of actor homework. Only when you no longer have to consciously think about your analysis can you work freely onstage in the imaginary circumstances of the character. Until then, you're either fighting to keep up or ignoring the text.

What we really crave, both as actors and as audience members, is a combination of improvisational spontaneity with the clarity of having accumulated a series of good choices in rehearsal. You can live freely in the moment, but have the security of a solid framework to support it. The goal of rehearsal is to wake moments up by exploring the imaginary world that the author, composer and lyricist have provided, not to deny it.

UNIT 2.9   **Text, subtext and inner monologue**

In plays, the text is the script. In musicals, it is useful to think of your text as what you speak, sing and dance. If you consider text to be the material you're handed by the author, lyricist, composer and choreographer, then your subtext is all the meaning and feeling you infuse into your lines, songs and movement.

Some communication theorists have estimated that in a typical interaction, only 7 percent of the full communication comes from the meaning of the words spoken. That would mean 93 percent of the message resides in the subtext!

This is why some people find reading scripts a difficult chore. Scripts aren't written like novels. They need actors to bring them to life. In the first reading the characters may not be distinct and the important meanings that lie under the lines may not be immediately apparent. But watch the show, hear the lines spoken, see the character's behavior and we understand everything easily.

You can look at the journey from page to stage as a journey from text to subtext. As you develop a sense of the given circumstances, establish relationships, get a clear sense of the character's objectives and begin acting tactically on the other characters, you'll reveal the meaning inside the lines, lyrics and movement.

You'll also start living inside the character's thinking. You'll engage the internal cinema of the mind, the *inner monologue* – a conversation we are constantly having with ourselves inside our heads. This stream-of-consciousness is made up of images, memories, fantasies, projections, the character's commentary and obsessions, and all the rational and irrational, linear and non-linear elements of our complex psychology. This inner monologue is probably the most authentic set of ideas a character can have. Here is where the character's ideations are uncensored, filled with taboos and thoughts of the unthinkable.

Even in songs where the character is alone onstage, singing something like Billy's 'Soliloquy' from *Carousel*, where he doesn't need to present a modified version of his feelings to someone else, the character still has an inner monologue because he will invariably reflect on the things he says. His fantasies about what his boy will become all give cause for reflection, opinions, memories and reactions. Characters can still lie to themselves, exaggerate, avoid the truth, try to convince themselves to accept a distasteful choice or have any number of other contrary reactions to what they say, even when they are alone.

When you find yourself thinking the character's thoughts, you've arrived at the place where you can freely improvise via the character and trust that your impulses have become merged with the character's. The journey inside a character will result from engaging the steps we've outlined: a process of consciously evoking the unconscious.

EXERCISE 2Q   SUBTEXT AND INNER MONOLOGUE

1. Choose a partner to work with. She will be your inner voice as you sing one of your songs. As you sing, she will speak the character's inner thoughts and feelings. See how you can respond to what your "inner self" is saying.
2. In the next phase, you'll play both roles yourself. For this exercise you'll sing without accompaniment. Don't worry if you change key or mess up rhythms. That's not the point of this exercise. You will sing each idea or image in your song, stopping after it to speak your inner monologue. Simply respond to the image or idea immediately and without planning your reactions. Then move on to the next idea. This is a great way of responding truthfully in the shoes of the character. You will also be able to give full attention to both the subtext and the sung text.
3. Sing the song again, with accompaniment this time, and allow yourself to respond to the inner monologue you just rehearsed.

SECTION I: FUNDAMENTALS OF ACTING IN MUSICAL THEATRE

CHAPTER 3

MAKING IT MATTER

If you've been going over this material with a class or if you've been applying it in rehearsal, you may have had the opportunity to receive feedback from teachers, directors and classmates. Sometimes a surprising thing can happen. You might pick an objective, like "I want to kill you." Specific. Clear. Direct. No problem. You play the moment and your director suggests, "Why don't you try to kill him?" as if that was a new idea, and you feel like killing yourself. Nearly every actor has something like this happen, at some point, and it can be quite upsetting since it suggests that nothing you were thinking was being communicated. Frustrating.

The problem may go back to the difference between the kind of behaviors that have worked to make you successful in life and the kind of actions necessary to communicate effectively on stage. You might think that there should be no difference, because, after all, truthful behavior should really be the same, regardless. But that isn't necessarily correct.

Success in society, after the age of two, depends on controlling our impulses and not saying everything that comes into our heads, or throwing a fit because we're unhappy, or taking something from a store just because it catches our eye. From the time we start having to pay attention to others' feelings we begin learning to mask our own. We can't just blurt, "Yuck, who cuts your hair?!" even though our inner monologue is saying exactly that. We can't even show it on our faces for fear of hurting someone's feelings or incurring her wrath. Usually during puberty the external forces that control our behavior switch from being teachers and parents to being our peers. The social games take on more elaborate and obscure rules. In this environment it is safer to be cautious, so we become even more guarded. Our inner monologues are as loud as ever, though. The difference between our inner voice (loud) and our outer expression (noncommittal) often goes unconsidered. We just don't realize how unexpressive we have become.

This situation works fine for most people. Just not for actors. Our job is to provide a window into the psyche. Our inner monologue needs to live a lot closer to the surface. Our truth needs to be an expressive, uncensored truth – especially in musical theatre.

EXERCISE 3A   TELL THE TRUTH. NOW, LIVE IT LARGE

1. Choose a small section of dialogue (no longer than two minutes). Work in a large studio space, a theatre or outside (try the football stadium). You will play the scene as a loop. When you reach the end, go straight back to the beginning and start over. Have a third person act as a referee.

2. Start in the middle of the space. Act the scene as intimately as possible, looking for a personal truth that isn't shared with anyone other than your partner. Deliberately make this audible only to your partner. Speak not only to the ears of your partner, but also to her eyes. Get her to see what you see. Sing to her skin. Get her to feel you. Make the connection.

3. Don't wait for the scene to finish. As soon as the referee senses that you are connecting with each other, he will give a signal (like a hand clap) that will cue each actor to take two large steps away from each other. Continue working with the intention only to reach your partner. This never becomes about projection, only about connection. Reach your partner.

4. Continue progressively widening the gap until you are working as far away from each other as you can. If you ever feel you're losing the honesty, reset closer until you reconnect.

5. When you've expanded your playing size to fill the whole space, rapidly come together so you are as close as when you started.

6. Do one more run of the scene, close together, but at the same playing size as when you were far apart. See if you can maintain the intimate truthfulness even when filing a large space. What does this teach you about issues of truth and theatrical size?

Raising the stakes

Have you ever witnessed someone become irrationally angry over a seemingly insignificant incident? Here's a scenario. A fellow goes into a drycleaner to pick up a suit. It isn't ready. He unleashes a torrent of abuse on the clerk even though it clearly is not her fault. What could be happening? Here is what his inner monologue could be saying:

> I need this suit for an important date tonight.
> If I don't wear this suit I won't look good enough.
> If I don't look good enough, I won't impress this girl.
> If I don't impress this girl, I'll miss out on my one chance for happiness.
> If I miss this one chance, I'll die lonely and alone.
> If that's what I have to look forward to I might as well die right now.
> So, by failing to give me that suit, you're killing me right now. No suit = death.

You can see why a character could say, "If I don't get these new shoes, I'll die!" It is irrational, but congruent to the inner reasoning. It is an example of how a normal situation gets dramatically intensified. It's never about the suit. It's about what the suit means. In *She Loves Me*, when Amalia sings about '*Vanilla Ice Cream*', it isn't because she cares about the flavor. It's about being loved by Georg. He brought her ice cream, and that act transforms him in her eyes and transports her. Ice cream = happy ever after.

Musicals operate on a heightened dramatic scale. Even when they are about commonplace things, successes tend to be incredible and failures will be tragic. These wins and losses affect your character so strongly that you're driven to dance and sing about it. The need to speak, sing or dance arises from the character's overwhelming feelings – emotions that are too large to be contained and so must have their expression. Those feelings will be large enough when it feels like life or death for your character.

Meeting the emotional demands of the music

A good rule of thumb is that you must match the emotional impact of the music. Amalia's celebration of her new feelings for Georg reaches exuberant heights musically. If you don't meet those musical demands, you'll know that you've fallen short. If you think of the musical shape as a balloon, you will see that it takes a certain degree of emotional helium to fill it properly. Too much and you'll burst the balloon. Too little and it will sag and droop. Big doesn't mean phony. Only phony means phony.

> **EXERCISE 3B OR ELSE I'LL DIE**
>
> Pick an objective and play a scene beat or sing a section of a song. Think about what you could lose (I'll die) or think about what you could win (your heart's desire). Play the section again with these stakes in mind.

UNIT 3.3 **Citizenship in the Land of *IF* – the creative state**

Art and creativity flow from the unconscious. Craft is the product of conscious processes. The craft of acting uses a conscious means of engaging the unconscious. The development of a role requires an actor to move in and out of unconscious and conscious behavior fluidly and easily. Become comfortable with this cycle, because it is easy to lose faith in the instinctive and the creative when you're operating consciously.

We've outlined what may seem like a series of steps you can take to engage the acting process. It isn't that linear, however. There is a kind of progression, but sometimes one acting element will prove to be a key for a certain role. At other times your inspiration will come from a completely different element. Still, you'll want to make sure that you don't ignore any of the ingredients we've listed because they are all essential for a complete, truthful and detailed performance. Get good at all of them.

You may have started this chapter as a tourist visiting the Land of *IF*. You may also remember that you used to live here as a child. Welcome back. Welcome home. We hope you've come back to stay.

SECTION II: SCORE AND LIBRETTO ANALYSIS AND STRUCTURE

CHAPTER 4

Score and Libretto Analysis and Structure

The best musical actors have a full and considered grasp of their texts and have made strong, appropriate and exciting choices based on that analysis. The three chapters that follow will give you a methodology for exploring the music, lyrics and script, and ways to apply them to a role.

The key element that distinguishes musicals from other theatrical forms is the song, where we experience the emotional high points in the characters' lives. In the wide range of styles from Verdi's *Aida* to Elton John's, what makes each event a musical theatre piece is the presence of songs as an integral part of the theatrical text.

MUSICAL ANALYSIS – LISTENING FOR CLUES   CHAPTER 4

Introduction   UNIT 4.1

Perhaps the only factor that unifies all types of song in musicals is that each is a heightened expression of a character's experience – a slice of life we go through via the combination of sung words and music. Unlike popular music we listen to on the radio, songs in musicals depend on the story and characters that surround them for specific meaning. Songs in the theatre are written with the knowledge that the audience member will hear the song in the context the authors intended and with all the necessary background information in place.

As we listen to the music a character sings with and speaks over, we're given a lot of information about that character, her mood and the emotional changes she goes through. Even though it is not the linguistic information you find in the libretto and lyrics, it is still specific to the character and provides you with character building information. It is this musical information we'll be exploring next.

UNIT 4.1.1   *Learn to listen*

Most of us listen to music uncritically. It affects us below our awareness. Take a look at film scores to understand how this works. So, we need to develop the skills to consciously notice and use musical information that the audience will take in unconsciously. You don't need to be a musicologist or even be able to read music to find this information. Probably the most valuable skill you'll need to acquire for the musical analysis of your songs is the ability to listen to different aspects of the music and to identify how they express the emotional experience of your character over the course of a song.

UNIT 4.1.2   *The music never lies*

Let's start with a basic premise that the accompaniment and underscoring for a song or musical scene are always telling the truth about a character's feelings. This is an important assumption because in the verbal text of a scene, speech or song your character may lie about how she feels, or she may hide the true extent of her feelings to the people with whom she's talking or even to herself. This is not unusual in drama. In non-musical theatre we often have to guess at the true emotional content of a scene or look for indirect signals to it. This allows for a great deal of flexibility in interpretation. But, in the musical theatre we have the added textual layer of music to tell us what is going on under the surface of the scene. Subtext is often explicitly delivered through music. The audience can have the simultaneous experience of the characters saying or singing one thing while the music tells us something else. The music can also agree with what the characters are saying and support it with new, different or varied information. Even when the words are repeated exactly, the music can amplify, diminish or change their emotional impact and meaning. This chapter will outline some of the many ways music can illuminate a character's experience.

Kinds of musical information

As we begin to hunt for character information in the score we'll see it's made up of the following layers:

Melody: The tune. More formally, it is the arrangement of pitches in musical time, upon which the lyrics are sung.

Accompaniment: What the piano or orchestra plays while you sing the *melody*.

Underscoring: Music that has been composed or arranged to be played during the dialogue portions of a musical scene. This music is intended to reveal emotional mood and the character's inner experience.

Because music is in many ways another language, a specialized vocabulary has evolved over many centuries to refer to its various components. The following are a few central terms that will help you discuss music with coaches and music directors:

Tempo: How fast a piece of music is played or sung.

Rhythm: The arrangement of short and long notes in relationship to each other.

Key: The arrangement of pitches in a song around an organizing pitch, also known as the *tonic*. The organizing pitch can be shifted higher or lower, changing all of the other pitches in a song in the same relationship. This is called *changing the key*.

Time signature or *meter*: A set of numbers, one over the other, which indicates the number of pulses in each measure of music, as in 2/4 (two beats per measure), 4/4 (four beats per measure) or 3/4 (three beats per measure), etc.

Bar or *measure*: A unit of music containing the number of pulses indicated by the upper number in the *time signature*. *Bars* are separated by a vertical line drawn through all five lines of the musical staff.

This is just a handful of terms. If you expect to build a career in musical theatre, it is essential that you eventually get some musical training and develop basic sight-singing skills. But for now, we're going to listen.

EXERCISE 4A WAYS OF LISTENING

Pick two songs from musicals to listen to and work on: one slower song (a ballad) and an up-tempo song. At least one should be from a traditional musical theatre piece; the other will be from something written since 1980. Get copies of the sheet music that you can write on. Have recordings of your songs available in these ways:

1.   The song with piano accompaniment *and* melody (but, no words).
2.   Just the piano accompaniment, *without* melody or words.
3.   Just the melody, without accompaniment or words. Be sure that it is played with accurate note value and in consistent tempo.
4.   Finally, try to find a recording of the song with full orchestral accompaniment. If you can do this with no singing on that recording, so much the better. But a recording with voice and orchestral accompaniment that matches your piano accompaniment will work, too. Many scores have been recorded for music-minus-one or karaoke singing.

These different ways of listening to your songs are useful because all of the musical information we'll discuss in this section is either part of the underscoring for the surrounding scene, the accompaniment or the melody for the song.

EXERCISE 4B EASY LISTENING

Before we begin any formal analysis or get too involved in what to listen for, listen to each song in the ways that we asked you to record it. Go somewhere quiet and close your eyes as you listen. Don't sing along or read the lyrics or music as you listen. Just listen. You may want to do this several times with each song. It's important that you can separate the melody from the lyrics for a while as you do these exercises. It can take some focus to resist filling in the words as you listen. But, persevere until you're able to hear only melody and accompaniment. Take note of the impressions you have of the song.

•   Did you hear anything new or different from one recording to the next?
•   Did the accompaniment suggest anything to you without the melody?
•   Did the melody reveal anything new to you without the accompaniment?

Now that you're familiar with the different layers of your song, let's look at some types of information you might find. This information can have a powerful impact on your acting choices.

Composer's markings

UNIT 4.2.1

In almost every case, the composer has given you very specific notations about tempo, vocal qualities and when these dynamics change, which you would be wise to consider seriously. If you choose to interpret the song differently, it should be a specific choice for a good reason, rather than a mistake or a whim. Here is a list of some of the most common terms that you will find in musical scores.

Accelerando: Gradually quicken tempo.

Adagio: A tempo with slow movement; restful at ease.

Adagissimo: Very slow.

Ad libitum (also *ad lib*): At liberty; the speed is left to the performer.

Affettuoso: Tenderly.

Afrettando: Hurrying, pressing onwards.

Agile: Swiftly.

Agitato: Agitated.

Allargando: Broadening, becoming a little slower.

Allegretto: A little lively, moderately fast.

Allegro: Lively and fast.

Andante: At a walking pace; moderate tempo.

Appassionato: Passionately.

A tempo: In time; return to the main tempo of the song.

Brillante: Brilliantly, with sparkle.

Common time: In 4/4 time.

Crescendo: Becoming louder.

Cut time: In 2/2 time.

Da capo: Repeat the beginning of the piece before stopping on the final chord.
      Sometimes also used to mean "Take it from the top."

Diminuendo or *decrescendo*: Getting softer.

Doloroso: Sorrowfully.

Energico: Energetically.

Espressivo: Expressively.

Forte: Loud (denoted as *f*, with *ff* and *fff* as signals to louder volumes).

Grazioso: Gracefully.

In modo di: In the style of.

Largo: Broadly.

Legato: Smoothly.

Lento: Slowly.

Mezzo: Medium speed.

Parlando: Speechlike.

Piano: Softly (denoted as *p*, with *pp* and *ppp* as signals to softer volumes).

Piu moso: More rapidly.

Poco piu moso: a little more rapidly.

Poco a poco: bit by bit, a little bit at a time.

Presto: Quickly.

Rallentando: Slowing down.

Ritardando: Gradually slowing down.

Rubato: An indication that the strict tempo is temporarily abandoned to accommodate feeling.

Segue: Continue to the next section or song without stopping.

Sotto voce: Softly, as if whispering, under the breath.

Staccato: Sharply and with attack.

Stop time: Accompanied by only crisp chords, usually played on the first beat of a bar.

Tacet: Sung without accompaniment.

Vivace: Brisk, lively and spirited.

There are many more terms, all of which are easily translated using a standard musical dictionary. If you don't understand a term look it up.

UNIT 4.2.2   *Emotional qualities*

Every piece of music you sing or listen to affects you and your audience emotionally. This is one of the aspects of music that is hardest to talk about because this type of response is on an intuitive, gut level, not on an intellectual one. But it's clearly present in all music. The emotional quality of the music is probably the most important and basic piece of information you can sensitize yourself to because it expresses the experience of the character that sings it. It is your barometer of his emotional experience. As the emotional quality of a song changes, so does the mood of the character. This aspect of a song is described best using adjectives like jubilant, joyous, brooding, agitated, somber, pensive, giddy and so forth. Those emotional qualities in the music can change from section to section within a song and from our initial encounter with the song to later reprises, where it might have a very contrasted meaning. Sensitize yourself to this information.

EXERCISE 4C   EMOTIONAL QUALITIES

As you listen to the song (melody and accompaniment), make a list of adjectives that describe how it makes you feel. Next, note these adjectives next to the musical passage that they apply to. Notice the changing emotional terrain of the song based solely on the musical information you're given. Try to resist imposing on the music your prior knowledge of the lyrics and the dramatic situation.

Melodic shape   UNIT 4.2.3

This refers to when and how extremely the melody changes from note to note throughout a song. The melody may progress to higher or lower pitches in very short leaps of only one or two steps up or down, or it may leap an interval of five to eight notes on a scale. The broadness or narrowness of these changes can have an emotional effect on the singer and the listener and may suggest something about how emotionally active or subdued a character is at that dramatic moment. You can certainly hear this when you listen to the melody played or sung. And even if you don't read music, you can still see how quickly and widely the melody of your song changes by looking at the musical notation as if it were a heartbeat monitor. Notice when the changes in pitch are very close to each other or when there are big leaps from low to high or vice versa. Melodic shape can be like gently rolling hills, jagged cliffs or mountain peaks. This musical texture can reveal the character's emotional nature. Recognize when a melodic shape is repeated and when the composer chooses to alter the established shape. Why do this? What does it make you feel? What does it suggest about the character's experience?

EXERCISE 4D   MELODIC SHAPE

Listen to just the melody of your song and note its melodic shape by using hand gestures. This will help you physicalize the shape of the song.

- Are there places where the melody changes in larger or smaller leaps?
- What kind of musical terrain would you say you're listening to?

- Does that change from section to section of the song?
- What does this suggest to you about the emotional state and journey of the character?
- Are there clear melodic phrases that repeat, change key or vary slightly from each other?
- Look at the sheet music to see how the notation corresponds to what you heard.

Again, resist imposing prior knowledge of the show and song on this exercise. Allow yourself to hear the song as if for the first time.

UNIT 4.2.4   *Tempo quality and changes*

All music is played or sung in tempo. And that tempo gives us more information about how a character feels. She may be excited, despondent, deliberate, confused, or any number of other feelings that are directly expressed through the speed of the music. As the emotional experience of a character changes, the tempo in which she expresses herself may change, as well. It is not unusual for a character to go through an enormous change of mind during a song and for the tempo to reflect that. The composer's dynamic markings will tell you what these changes were intended to be.

EXERCISE 4E   TEMPO CHANGES

As you listen to your song, notice any changes in tempo.

1. Look at the sheet music to see if the composer indicated any tempo changes
2. What do the changes in tempo or the steady tempo throughout suggest to you?
3. Try slowing the song down or speeding it up. What does that do to the emotional meaning of the song?

Rhythmic quality

This refers to how quickly the melody changes, how long a note is held compared to those notes around it, and how often a rhythmic pattern is repeated. A great example of a clear rhythmic pattern that informs us about character is in George Gershwin's 'Fascinatin' Rhythm'. Clap the rhythm of the chorus for this song and you'll see that Gershwin created a couple of very clear rhythmic shapes that he uses over and over again. Notice how the bridge of the song has a very different rhythmic quality than the other parts of the chorus. It is common for different parts of a song to have strongly different rhythmic qualities. Along with melodic variety, rhythmic variation can help convey different aspects of the changing experience (beat changes, new tactics, reactions to others, etc.). All this also happens in the context of structural form like a waltz, a foxtrot, a march, a cha-cha, a tango, etc. Each of these musical forms is written within a rhythmic convention.

EXERCISE 4F   RHYTHMIC STYLES

Assign each member of your group a different rhythmic song form. Have each person bring in a recording of that form to play for the class. Select from among these forms:

> Waltz – All of *A Little Night Music*, 'Out of My Dreams' from *Oklahoma!*
> Fox trot – '*I've Never Been in Love Before*' and '*If I Were a Bell*' from *Guys and Dolls*
> Tango – '*Whatever Lola Wants*' from *Damn Yankees*
> Charleston – '*Not for the Life of Me*' from *Thoroughly Modern Millie*
> Ragtime – '*Gettin' Ready Rag*' from *Ragtime*
> Swing – '*I Can Cook, Too*' from *On the Town*
> March – '*Seventy-Six Trombones*' from *The Music Man*
> Dirge – '*Poor Jud Is Daid*' from *Oklahoma!*

Can you identify others?

Research the songs that you're using for these exercises to find out what rhythmic form they are written in.

UNIT 4.2.6   *Musical key*

Songs are played in different keys for various reasons. If the original singer of a song had a difficult time with the higher or lower extremes of the melody, then the key may have been raised or lowered accordingly to flatter her voice. But composers choose different keys for other reasons, as well. The key that a song is written in can suggest emotional qualities and moods. If the song is in a major key, it may suggest emotional balance or strength, while minor keys can sometimes suggest tension, sadness or emotional struggle. Allow yourself to personalize this and absorb the qualities that the key suggests to you.

UNIT 4.2.7   *Modulations*

Sometimes a composer will change keys within a song. This is most often done to change the emotional mood of the moment. In pop music and theatre music that is influenced by that form it is common for the key to shift, or modulate, upwards several times before the song is finished. This is done to create a sense of growing excitement or enthusiasm on the part of the character that's singing. But these modulations can also move downward, indicating a very different emotional journey. Some composers use subtle changes of key to express nuances of emotional experience (as in Jerome Kern's '*All the Things You Are*'). These shifts of key can create bold or subtle tensions and releases throughout a song, implying a richly varied experience for the character.

> **EXERCISE 4G   CHANGING KEYS**
>
> As you listen to your song with melody and accompaniment, note any key changes within the song. What do these changes suggest to you? Look through the songs in your repertoire or those songs that the members of your group are using for this chapter to identify and compare the way different composers employ this tool.

UNIT 4.2.8   *Tensions and releases*

Listening just to the accompaniment of a song, you will find that there are sequences that seem to build in tension, where the music seems to press against something and then later release or resolve itself. This can happen through subtle changes in tempo or key, through musical builds, through a series of modulations and through the artful manipulation of every musical element we've discussed. These changes in tension and release are another barometer of your character's thoughts and feelings. It is common for the verse of a song to build in tension that is finally released as the chorus begins. The bridge of a song may do the same thing as it approaches a final phrase. We can also hear tensions and releases in the way that accompaniment and melody play against each other. Tension in a song builds a need for release or resolution.

Musical accents

In many songs for the theatre, the accompaniment is peppered with a range of musical high and low points that provide specific texture to the character's experience. These little bumps, twinkles and booms are most present in songs with brisk tempos, but may also be found in slower songs, as well. These accents usually occur when a character is not singing, but on the pauses or breaths between and within musical phrases. Dance music and musical interludes within songs (those passages where there is accompaniment, but not singing) are frequently full of this kind of specific musical emphasis. These accents often help to identify sudden shifts in attention or in the character's thought process. They may also indicate physical action that helps to punctuate part of the character's experience. As you begin staging your song, you'll see that these musical accents almost beg to be utilized. Try ignoring a sharp accent in your music and you'll quickly see how important it is.

EXERCISE 4H USING ACCENTS

Listening to the full orchestral accompaniment for your song, identify a passage that contains clear musical accents. You may discover that the final musical moment of your up-tempo song requires a "button," for example. Experiment with different ways of physicalizing that musical point. Use different kinds of natural behavior (sitting into one hip, crossing your arms, sharply placing your hands on your hips, sitting), and then explore overtly theatrical "dance-like" movement (various poses with arms in the air, grabbing a piece of the sky, arms straight out to the sides). You'll instinctively feel how these musical accents demand to be used and those shapes and movements that seem right for you.

UNIT 4.2.10   *Musical dynamics*

As a character experiences a range of feelings, thoughts and needs over the course of a single song, the music that accompanies that complex experience will change from moment to moment. We've talked about a range of possible changes already. But the musical dynamics of a song can often reflect those changes as well. Musical dynamics are contrasts in a song and its accompaniment between loud and soft, low and high, booming and whispering, fast and slow, crescendo and decrescendo, etc. The composer has often given you some of this information in the form of dynamic markings (which are often written in Italian above the appropriate passage of music). These are invaluable to you in understanding the composer's intentions and giving you a precise musical roadmap. In addition, you will begin to add your own musical dynamics as you interpret a song, making choices for yourself about what is more or less important. All of the ways we've just described are available for you to explore.

EXERCISE 4I   DYNAMIC CHANGES

Pick a phrase from your ballad that will allow you to explore some dynamic contrasts easily. It's most useful if you have some sustained notes. Using this phrase as an open text, apply each of the following dynamic contrasts to the phrase. See if you can use both extremes within the one phrase.

   loud/soft   crisp/smooth   angry/gentle   crescendo/decrescendo

Next, try to modulate from one to the next and back again. Now, reverse the order. Try mixing dynamic possibilities (loud and smooth, crisp and whispered, etc.).

UNIT 4.2.11   *Musical idiom*

Just as the words in the lyrics and libretto can be written with an "eye dialect" that prompts you toward a specific way of speaking (such as in '*Cain't Say No*' from *Oklahoma!*), songs are also written with musical qualities that can suggest a number of given circumstances. Location can be suggested or alluded to by incorporating regional musical styles as in *The King and I* when practically everyone except Anna sings in an "Asian" mode, in *West Side Story* when the

Puerto Rican girls sing '*America*' with a distinct Latin flavor, or in *Brigadoon* when Charlie Dalrymple or Meg Brockie sing in what feels like a Celtic folk song form. Composers carefully select these musical idioms to remind the audience of the world of the story and the given circumstances of the character. Does your song belong to any region or national identity based on its musical idiom? An important exception to this is when a composer may borrow a specific regional or ethnic form to comment on or make fun of a situation, character or relationship.

Musical character quality

UNIT 4.2.12

In the same way music can suggest nationality or region, it can also subtly suggest intelligence or character quality. Just listen to Curly's '*Surrey with the Fringe on Top*' compared to Will Parker's '*All 'Er Nuthin''* in *Oklahoma!* The music suggests the great differences in these two men who share many of the same given circumstances (age, occupation, regional identity, education, etc.). But the fundamental nature of their contrasting personalities is blatantly apparent in the musical qualities of their songs.

The relationship between melody and accompaniment

UNIT 4.2.13

So far, we've been listening to either the accompaniment or the melody independent of each other. But, accompaniment must accompany something else. In this case, it is the melody, or sung musical line. As you listen to your recording of the melody and accompaniment (without the words), see how all of that musical information that you gathered relates to the melody. When there are tensions and releases in the accompaniment, does the melody reflect them, as well? Or does it continue in a steady fashion? How do the musical dynamics affect the melody? How do the changes in tempo affect the course of the melody line? Does the accompaniment change rhythmically when the melody does?

The relationship between dialogue and underscoring

UNIT 4.2.14

When you're performing musical scenes you will often have sections of dialogue before, after and sometimes during the song that are underscored. Listen to the underscoring to hear melodic themes from the central song of the scene and from other moments in the show that may suggest emotional qualities and how they relate to (or are juxtaposed with) the dialogue being spoken. As the subject matter and relationships change, the orchestration of the musical themes will reflect this. Composers, or often the arrangers, invest time and care in designing music that is played under dialogue. As an actor in the underscored scene, you will find the author's and composer's intentions clearly expressed in this music. Your job is to create a performance that agrees with that musical information, and is still authentically your own. The underscore is your friend in this regard and it specifically tells you your subtext. With practice and awareness you can develop a nuanced performance that works in tandem with the underscoring to provide maximum impact.

EXERCISE 4J   REUNITED . . . AND IT SOUNDS SO GOOD

Now, place the lyric back over that accompaniment and melody to see how your understanding of the words is influenced by this new musical information. It can be quite a revelation. Sing the song as you listen closely to the accompaniment and allow it to inform your performance.

Although we've just outlined a long list of different musical aspects that can help to reflect the emotional experience of the character you're playing, the key relationship in every theatre song is the one between the music and the lyrics. It is this marriage of the emotional and the specific that makes a great performance.

UNIT 4.3   ## Architecture of the traditional theatre song

We've been talking about the kinds of information you can find by listening to the musical layers of your song. Now we'll look at the structure that lies underneath. You probably already understand the basic structural conventions of the popular song, even if you've never thought about them or taken a music theory class. There are consistent conventions, or agreed upon practices, that most song-writers observe to some degree. As even casual listeners to popular music, we are used to hearing songs that obey these conventional forms and can anticipate structural changes. In fact, if a song doesn't obey the traditions of popular song-writing we might perceive it as being "wrong." Composers like George Gershwin and Irving Berlin confirmed many of these conventions in early twentieth-century popular songs. We still see them used in songwriting today, including writing for the musical theatre, although there are many variations on the form. First among those conventions is the idea that a song will usually be made up of the following parts: introduction (or "intro"), verse, chorus and ride-out.

Introduction or "intro"

UNIT 4.3.1

The introduction is the music we hear before you start singing. It sets the mood of the song, establishes what key you'll be singing in and the tempo. This intro can be brief, as short as just a bell tone or a few bars, or lengthy as it sets the musical mood of the song elaborately or makes room for dialogue or physical action. There are no rules about its length. The introduction often uses melodic material from the chorus of the song and usually creates tension that is released when we begin the next part of the song – the verse. The version of the intro that you hear in vocal selections sold commercially may not be the same as we hear in the full score because songs often emerge out of underscored dialogue or a more complex musical texture that has built for some time. But publishers usually make some effort to establish the same mood for the published vocal selections. Whenever possible, work from the complete score.

Verse

UNIT 4.3.2

The verse of a song begins the sung portion and leads us to the main musical theme(s), which we hear in the chorus. The verse is musically different from the main theme(s). Melodically, it can be somewhat meandering or it might have very clear musical components that even repeat themselves, feeling melodically complete. Again, there are no rules about how long this part must be. It is not unusual for this portion to be as short as a dozen bars or as long as thirty or forty bars. The verse is not intended to stand on its own, but exists only to set up the main body of the song, both musically and lyrically. In terms of lyrics, the verse often serves the overall song by presenting us with exposition of the character's problem, which is ultimately worked out in the chorus. The verse usually clarifies the urgent need of the character in that dramatic moment. A well-written verse leads the listener musically and lyrically to the doorstep of the chorus, opens that door and finally allows us to step in as the chorus begins. It also creates antic-ipation for the chorus. Note that some composers skip the verse completely and start right with the chorus. This is more common in contemporary musical theatre than in older shows.

The word verse has many different uses and meanings, sometimes even in a musical context. You may be asked to sing the second verse of a song, but be expected to sing the second chorus. Get your terms straight with whomever you're working with.

UNIT 4.3.3   *Chorus or refrain*

This is the main body of the song. It is often musically and lyrically more sub-stantial and clearly structured than anything we've heard before. In many cases, this is the part of a song that we hum to help others identify that song. The chorus is usually able to stand on its own without the verse, though the performance of a well-written song almost always benefits from the inclusion of the verse. The chorus is made up of at least one, and usually two or three, melodic themes that alternate in some clear pattern. There may be slight variations on these themes through small melodic changes or even changes of key. But, the pitch relationship usually remains identifiably consistent within each theme.

In many songs there is a repeated alternation between verse and chorus. The lyrics in the verse usually change from one repetition to the next, while the chorus may or may not change.

UNIT 4.3.4   *Playoff or ride-out*

This is the last musical material that we hear in a song. It follows the final sung portion of the chorus, though it may happen at the same time, with singing and accompaniment finishing simultaneously. This portion of the song is usually a repetition or variation on some piece of the musical material in the chorus. Part of its dramatic function in a song is to bring closure to the character's experience and leave us with a sense of her emotional state at the end of the song: resolved, agitated, uneasy, peaceful, etc. Even though you're not singing, you're still acting. Carry the experience through to the end of the last note of the ride-out.

EXERCISE 4K   NAMING OF PARTS

With a spare copy of your song, use a pencil to mark the beginnings and endings of the intro, verse, chorus and playoff for each. Listen to your recording of the song's melody and accompaniment as you do this. You'll hear that these large sections are clearly and obviously defined from each other. You'll use this copy of your music for several more exercises coming up.

A closer look at the chorus

Since the chorus is the most musically distinct part of the song and because it often contains the most substantial dramatic material, we will take a closer look at it.

The chorus of the traditional theatre song is most often thirty-two bars in length. That thirty-two bar musical unit is usually divided into four phrases, each of which is eight bars long. Listen to Irving Berlin's '*I Got the Sun in the Mornin' and the Moon at Night*' from *Annie Get Your Gun* to illustrate this idea.

As you listen to the chorus of this song (which starts with the phrase, "Got no diamond, got no pearl"), notice that the first, second and fourth musical segments all sound the same (or close to the same). They share a common musical theme, are rhythmically consistent and even use the same lyrical device of listing things that Annie lacks and doesn't miss having in her life. But, the third section is musically different, with an entirely new melody being introduced, a different rhythmic quality and a different way of talking about her life (things from nature that she does have). This is also the only time in the chorus that we hear this melodic material. Those two different musical themes are called the "A" and "B" sections of the song. The A section is the theme that we hear in the first, second and fourth eight bar segments. That B section of the song serves an important purpose; it provides some musical relief to what could be monotonous repetition of the same thematic material. In fact, that B section is technically called the *bridge* because it connects the similar musical material of the front part of the chorus with the back part of it. But, it is also often called the *release* because it offers a release from the repeated musical material we've heard twice through already. Hum the song using only the A section four times. It sounds awfully repetitive, doesn't it?

The musical structure we've outlined above is the most common form used in popular music, even today. It is referred to as the AABA form. If you listen to your favorite songs on the radio, you'll see that there is still a strong reliance on this form. Some classic songs that fit this model are *'Oh, Lady, Be Good!'*, *'Almost Like Being in Love'* (*Brigadoon*) and *'I Remember'* (*Evening Primrose*). You will undoubtedly find many more examples in other shows and in popular music, such as Paul McCartney's *'Yesterday'*.

But there are a number of different structures for a chorus. The most common of these is the ABAC form. And, just as the name suggests, the songwriter has chosen to alternate the first two musical themes with a third theme at the end. Some well-known examples of this form are George Gershwin's *'Summertime'*, Jerome Kern's *'Look for the Silver Lining'*, and Irving Berlin's *'Alexander's Ragtime Band'*.

A less common variation is the AAA form. In form, the songwriter has chosen not to significantly vary the melodic material at all. You probably know *'Mary Had a Little Lamb'* as an obvious example of this form. As with all song forms, the writer chooses the right form for the right circumstances. One of the best-known examples of this form in musical theatre is Schmidt and Jones' *'My Cup Runneth Over'* (*I Do, I Do*). The simplicity of the idea and the gentle, heartfelt impulse behind the dramatic moment make that a perfect form for the song.

We mentioned that songwriters sometimes vary the A or B theme slightly with small modifications to the melody of one or the other theme. When this is done, the A theme may be referred to as A2, or even A3 if there is a third melodic variation. The most typical variations used are a slight change of the melody, choosing a higher or lower alternate note in the repeated phrase, or a modulation, raising/lowering of the song's key for one of the eight bar phrases. Songs will often end with a melodic variation in the last A section to give maximum power to the end of the character's experience.

The reason we emphasize these structural forms is that recognizing the themes and variations in your songs can help you to identify and express changes of acting beat or tactical variation in pursuing the objective, and inform your understanding of the accompanying lyric.

EXERCISE 4L   LEARN YOUR ABCS

Find songs that use the AABA, ABAC and AAA forms. Identify the A, B and C phrases and note where the composer creates A2, A3 and other variations.

Contemporary variations

UNIT 4.5

As the musical theatre has grown and changed, today's composers often choose to radically depart from these conventional song forms. Part of the reason for that is their desire to create a new style of writing to match the new set of ideas and themes they're exploring or to reject the certainty and comfort that many older shows and song forms seemed to affirm. Writers like Michael John LaChiusa (*Hello, Again, The Wild Party, Marie Christine*), Adam Guettel (*The Light in the Piazza, Floyd Collins*), Andrew Lippa (*The Wild Party*) and others often reject these forms for the majority of their writing, but will still allude to them. As you listen to these writers' shows in their entirety you'll discover that there are at least a few songs that do adhere to the older forms or partially observe these conventions. Even the most radical composers still utilize repetition and variations of musical motifs. You might discover that a song is A, A2, B, C, C2, A3 in structure. But there is still a distinct theme and variation going on that expresses an emotional journey.

Many contemporary writers like Elton John (*Aida, The Lion King*) Jeanine Tessori (*Caroline, or Change, Violet, Thoroughly Modern Millie*) and David Yazbek (*The Full Monty, Dirty Rotten Scoundrels*), Stephen Flaherty (*Ragtime, Once on This Island*) still frequently use the traditional forms from a century ago, though the melodies, instrumentations and accompaniment styles are all evocative of more recent popular music or other cultures.

A popular trend in musical theatre composition over the last thirty years is the *through-composed* musical, starting with *Jesus Christ Superstar* and continuing with shows like *Les Misérables* and others. This practice is similar to the tradition of opera, where even the dialogue is sung. In general, contemporary musicals include some portions of spoken dialogue between the songs, even in through-composed pieces. But, the inclusion of so much musical material can make it difficult to see the song structure clearly. In these cases, we need to identify when that musical material changes distinctly and when a new, important dramatic moment begins. This almost always signals a shift to a new song. In through-composed pieces, the writers will often choose a musical theme for each of the major storylines or characters. When one of these themes is utilized, it signals the audience to focus on that particular part of the story.

EXERCISE 4M   IDENTIFYING SONG STRUCTURE

1. Take the copy of your song that we began marking before and add divisions of the chorus. Mark the A and B sections of the song.
2. How does the B section lyric differ from the A section? Is there a relationship between the music and lyrics of each section?
3. Looking through a collection of songs, find the shortest and longest verses in the collection. Do the same thing with introductions and ride-outs.
4. Select a through-composed musical (*Les Misérables*, *Miss Saigon*, etc.) and listen to a long section of it to identify when the song moments begin and end. Identify how the underscoring and sung dialogue lead to the song. Once the song itself has begun, does it employ any traditional song forms (AABA, etc.) or does the composer observe a different formal structure? Can you chart the As, Bs and Cs of that song?
5. When you've mastered identifying A, B, C sections in traditional writing, move on to a song by a contemporary composer whose work you like. See if you can identify the verse, chorus and A, B, C components and variations for this song. It may give you a stronger appreciation of the technique behind that composer's writing.

UNIT 4.6   ## The musical "voice" of a song and of a character

Just as the people we encounter in life are all different, with variations in dialect, intelligence, verbal skill, regional identity, wit, sense of humor and so many other qualities, so are the characters we play. In plays, these qualities are expressed solely through dialogue. In a musical the music itself can reflect all of these qualities, as well. Let's take the example of three women from musicals in different periods. Compare Ado Annie from *Oklahoma!*, Marion Paroo from *The Music Man* and Mimi from *Rent*. All three are single women and are about the same age (early 20s). But, the apparent similarities end there. You could go through and make a detailed character analysis of each woman based on the script to identify these differences. But by listening to each of their main songs you'll get an immediate sense of the differences between these women. Ado Annie sings '*Cain't Say No*', which is bouncy and innocent, with a hint of a country quality. Marion sings '*My White Knight*', which is sweepingly melodic and richly varied in musical texture and moods. Finally, Mimi sings '*Out Tonight*', which is appropriately a driving rock song with seductive musical qualities – just right for a dancer in a strip club. Each of these songs reflects a very different kind of person. The quality of their music is what we call their *musical voice* – the way each character sings compared to all the others who surround her. And this is just the music alone. We haven't even looked at the lyrics yet.

Sometimes *what* a character sings (the lyric) is not as important as *how* they sing it: her musical voice. If you don't believe this, try listening to selections from an opera in a language that you don't speak. Regardless of the literal meaning of the words you're hearing, the emotional quality of the music and voices will probably affect you. And this is without your understanding a word they sing. Music sung in your own language can be just as effective.

Occasionally, a composer chooses a musical voice that we associate with a famous person or different style than he has used for the rest of the show. In the case of *Follies*, Sondheim chose to imitate particular songs and composers from the great age of *The Ziegfeld Follies* to help place the characters' past in that time period. In the case of *Chicago*, Kander and Ebb wanted the entire show to reflect actual performers and the types of acts that were famous in the days of vaudeville. This kind of *reference* and *allusion* can be useful for the audience and actors to place the musical and performing style of a piece.

Evaluate the musical voice of your role by looking at these issues.

Musical voice reveals character function   UNIT 4.6.1

Differences in musical dialect and style can help us see the nature and function of a character within a show. In *Oklahoma!*, Will Parker is probably best defined by '*Kansas City*'. Musically, it is a raucous and freewheeling two-step. The tempo of this song is bouncy and it is scored with lots of brass and percussion. This is in total contrast to Curly's '*Oh, What a Beautiful Mornin'*', a lyrical, folksy and poetic waltz that is scored richly with strings and woodwinds. The third major male character is Ali Hakim, who sings the vaudevillian '*It's a Scandal, It's an Outrage*', a bumptious oom-pah march. Finally, listen to Jud's '*Lonely Room*', a deep, brooding and driven tragic aria. Those four very different songs help to define four completely different characters, each with a different function in the show: Curly is the romantic love interest whose story is complicated by Jud (the other male singer of dramatic music). Will Parker is the comic love interest and carries the secondary plot. Ali Hakim is the other male comic character, and he complicates Will's secondary plot. The two storylines are matched in musical styles and we intuitively sense which characters belong together because of the qualities of the music that they are associated with. Notice that no two characters from these divided storylines ever share a musical moment. These are strong differences in musical voice that guide us.

UNIT 4.6.2 *Musical style reveals character status*

As you listen to a song for a specific character, compare it to other places in the script where the same character also sings. Examine how it is different from or similar to those other moments. Still looking at *Oklahoma!*, compare how Laurey sings in '*People Will Say We're in Love*' with her musical style in '*Many a New Day*'. She is a principal character in both songs, but uses two very different sets of musical tactics. In the first, she is flirting with and courting Curly. So, her musical style is romantic and whimsical. But, in the second song she is curt and defiant in response to the news that Curly is taking someone else to the dance. She never leaves the romantic vocabulary set up by the authors in either song. Yet, simply listening to the music of both songs, we can sense a strong difference in her from one to the other.

UNIT 4.6.3 *Voice type can reveal a character's nature*

We are given subtle information about a character by the vocal register they sing in. For instance, a lyric soprano voice is rarely associated with a brassy tramp. We normally identify lyric voice types with romantic stories and relationships and with the more serious aspects of a musical's storyline. The tramp/hussy is often sung in a belt register. Composers used to follow a set of tacit rules that told us which voice types went with certain character types. This is still mostly true.

Bass: Older characters and villains. Less used in contemporary writing.
Baritone: Romantic and mature male characters.
Tenor: Younger male and comic characters (in more traditional musicals). Now the dominant male voice type in contemporary musicals.
Lyric baritone (sometimes called *bari-tenor*): The more recent voice type for romantic male characters, most often used in rock musicals and poperettas.

Legitimate lyric soprano: Almost exclusively the province of romantic female roles in traditional musicals. Much less frequently used in contemporary writing except for deliberate choices of color and character type.

Pop soprano: Ingénues and romantic characters in contemporary musicals often sing in a light, high belt with strong mixing of soprano and belt qualities.

Belt or *mezzo soprano*: Strongly associated with comic characters or with secondary romantic storylines. As musicals have come to include rock and other top 40 styles, this voice type has come to cover a much broader range of character types. We see it used in two major ways.

> *Broadway belt*: This type of belt voice is commonly associated with singers like Ethel Merman, Judy Garland and other women of their eras. It is roughly the vocal equivalent of the brass section of a band.

> *Rock belt*: This women's voice type includes almost all colors of vocal expression in popular music since the mid-1960s when female singers began singing almost exclusively in their lower register, leaving the soprano (falsetto) range behind. This has now become the dominant range for most musicals since about 1980.

For validation of these guidelines, simply look at the principal characters in almost any classic musical comedy, operetta or even the more recent *A Little Night Music* or *Les Misérables*. You will see the character types align almost exactly with these voice type. Shows like *Spamalot* play with these vocal range associations for comic effect.

A final thought on musical analysis

UNIT 4.7

While everything we've looked at here can be understood through careful listening, there is no question that the more information you have about the musical aspects of *musical* theatre the better prepared you'll be. Study basic music theory and read music well enough to learn your material on your own. In the process, you'll develop an instinct for the musical structure of your roles. Does this mean you need to become a concert pianist? No. But taking piano lessons for a while, enrolling in a choir where you'll do some sight singing, taking up guitar or getting some self-teaching books from the library will certainly be a good start. If you discover that you like making music with an instrument, so much the better for you. But the first goal would be to gain a fundamental musical literacy.

Once you've gotten the music under control, you're ready to start looking at the words.

SECTION II: SCORE AND LIBRETTO ANALYSIS AND STRUCTURE

CHAPTER 5

WORKING WITH WORDS – THE LANGUAGE OF THE LYRIC AND LIBRETTO

Wadoo!
Zim bam boddle-oo!
Hoodle ah da waah da!
Scatty way!
Scatty wah!
Yeah!

'It Ain't Necessarily So', Porgy and Bess

Blah, blah, blah, blah, moon,
Blah, blah, blah, above;
Blah, blah, blah, blah, croon,
Blah, blah, blah, blah love.

'Blah, Blah, Blah', Delicious

Popitschka, Momitschka,
Now I can laugh and singitschka.
Since Katink, Katink, Katinka has a wedding ringitschka!

'Katinkitschka', Delicious

They're writing songs of love, but not for me.
A lucky star's above, but not for me.

'But Not for Me', Girl Crazy

Words. What words those are. From scat, to spoof, to slapstick, to simple sentiment, that's all Ira Gershwin. His work exemplifies one of the things audiences
love best about musical theatre: brilliant lyrics that make us laugh, touch us, and
amaze us with their apt, insightful dexterity.

In contrast to other kinds of theatre singing, like opera, where a beautiful sound
is more important than a clear lyric, musical theatre depends a great deal on words.

Think of the scope of lyrics in musicals. At one end you have art songs ('*Think
of Me*' from *Phantom of the Opera*), where the words are intended to be pretty
but insubstantial. In another direction there is the rough, character-driven, half-
spoken, hip-slang scramble ('*Officer Krupke*' from *West Side Story*). There are
deceptively simple soft-shoes of tender wit ('*Tea for Two*' from *No, No, Nanette*),
and complex psychological trios ('*Soon, Now, Later*' from *A Little Night Music*).
Lyrics cover the range from aria to anthem and psychology to pslapstick. Whether
sparkling, lyrical, intricate or simple, the musical libretto will demand as much
from an actor as the score.

UNIT 5.1   Acting through language

Camera acting has had an enormous influence on what young actors have come
to identify as truth in performance. Film is intimate, favors a naturalistic acting
style, and is a visual medium where what you see is more important than what
you say. If you think of the hours you spend watching camera acting versus the
time you spend seeing shows, it is not surprising that your notions of good acting
will be heavily influenced by the work you see on screen. This shows up in one
area more than any other: language.

In life, and in highly naturalistic scripts intended to mirror life, when we pursue
an objective and encounter an obstacle, that problem tends to leave us inartic-
ulate. How many times have you had an argument and only after stomping away
have thought of all the great things you could have said? The French have an
expression for this: *l'esprit d'escalier*, or the spirit of the stairs. This is the inspiration that visits you just when it is the least helpful – while you're storming down
the stairs. Afterwit.

Characters in musicals don't generally have this difficulty. Instead of being
verbally flummoxed, they respond to adversity by becoming extraordinarily articulate. They start singing in complex rhymes with alliterative virtuosity and deep
insight. Characters in musicals experience many frustrating obstacles, but
language isn't one of them. They have presentwit.

Since characters regularly ascend to these verbal heights, musical actors need to inhabit their language with equal skill and with no hesitation. We need to find the acting truth in these characters *through* their words.

To help get in touch with the words we'll set up some different ways to encounter the text. Sometimes we need to look at words from several angles in order to get inside them. As we take the next steps, carry with you the thought that as interpretive artists, actors are in service to the text. Though you will need to make strong choices in shaping the role, that isn't always the best place to start. Sometimes you need to hold off on interpretive choices, and begin by letting the words move you – rather than you trying to move the words.

We'll use a song from Sondheim's *Evening Primrose*, a musical he wrote for television. Ella, who has lived in a department store as one of a hidden society since she was six, sings it. When Charles, the man she is falling in love with, learns this, she says, "Don't pity me – I have my memories," and sings '*I Remember*'.

Lyrics as poetry

UNIT 5.2

We learn songs as words and music together. The lyrics aren't usually presented independently. Music can tend to dominate our attention so it's helpful to get the words off by themselves to make sure we have plumbed their possibilities. If you don't already know this song, it would be an interesting experiment to approach it from the lyric first, since that is not the typical way we learn a song.

Using the musical themes to divide the stanzas and the author's capitalization (an indication of where he thought each poetic line should start), here is this song as a poem.

(1)   I remember sky,
       It was blue as ink.
       Or at least I think
       I remember sky.

(2)   I remember snow,
       Soft as feathers,
       Sharp as thumbtacks,
       Coming down like lint,
       And it made you squint
       When the wind would blow.

(3) And ice, like vinyl, on the streets,
     Cold as silver, white as sheets.
     Rain like strings
     And changing things
     Like leaves.

(4) I remember leaves,
     Green as spearmint,
     Crisp as paper.
     I remember trees,
     Bare as coat racks, spread like broken umbrellas.

(5) And parks and bridges,
     Ponds and zoos.
     Ruddy faces, muddy shoes.
     Light and noise and bees and boys and days.

(6) I remember days,
     Or at least I try.
     But as years go by
     They're a sort of haze.

(7) And the bluest ink
     Isn't really sky,
     And at times, I think
     I would gladly die
     For a day
     Of sky.

There are seven units in this poem. Notice that some stanzas have a different number of lines? What do these structural elements tell you about the journey of the character? What is the progression of her experience through each stanza?

EXERCISE 5A   PLAYING THE POETRY

Choose a song to work on for all the exercises in this chapter. If you are with a group, it can be interesting (though not essential) to all work on the same piece.

It will make the exercises more interesting if you don't know the song beforehand. If you want to work on multiple pieces, have members of the group bring in beautiful lyrics they don't think anyone knows and give them to each other to work on.

Using the clues provided by the capitalization and the musical structure, write the lyric as a poem.

Speak it out loud. Don't work to interpret the piece, let the poem speak to you.

Poetry versus prose

Though the verse form can reveal certain things about the text, most of us are more familiar with reading prose. Look at the text that way to see if you get fresh insights. Write the text as a series of sentences.

(1)   I remember sky, it was blue as ink.
(2)   Or at least I think I remember sky.
(3)   I remember snow, soft as feathers, sharp as thumbtacks, coming down like lint, and it made you squint when the wind would blow.
(4)   And ice, like vinyl, on the streets, cold as silver, white as sheets.
(5)   Rain like strings and changing things like leaves.
(6)   I remember leaves, green as spearmint, crisp as paper.
(7)   I remember trees, bare as coat racks, spread like broken umbrellas.
(8)   And parks and bridges, ponds and zoos.
(9)   Ruddy faces, muddy shoes.
(10)   Light and noise and bees and boys and days.
(11)   I remember days, or at least I try.
(12)   But as years go by they're a sort of haze.
(13)   And the bluest ink isn't really sky, and at times, I think I would gladly die for a day of sky.

There are thirteen sentences in this version. How is that progression different from the seven stanzas of the poem? How is this flow of ideas different from that presented in the poem? What can you learn from the sequence of ideas in the run-on or short sentences?

EXERCISE 5B PLAYING THE PROSE

Rewrite the text separating it at full-stop sections.

Read this out loud, again, not focusing on interpretation. See how this way of understanding the text is different from the poetic version. Discover what the author is saying without imposing anything on it.

UNIT 5.4 ## Lyric rhythm

Musical rhythm is one of the most prominent features of a song. It is so prominent we can forget there is also information in the rhythmic speech cadence of a lyric. This comes in several forms.

Sound length creates texture. Notice the different syllable lengths in the words "heat" and "heed"? Say them a couple of times and you'll notice that "heed" is longer. In this lyric, compare the difference in "streets" and "sheets" with "leaves." Or contrast "lint" and "squint" with "strings" and "things." Short and long sounds have different emotional qualities. In poetry these differences are used in a pattern to establish the meter and to deepen the image or feeling. Skillful lyricists also use them to point up meanings and to set an emotional and sensory tone.

Syllable stress establishes rhythm. Observe the stressing in "re-*mem*-ber" and "um-*bre*-lla." This lyric sounds childlike (perfect, since she's recalling a childhood memory) and simple (deceptively) because there are only two words with more than two syllables. Compare that to the joyful doggerel of '*Supercalifragilisticexpealidocious*' (*Mary Poppins*), rhyming polysyllabically with "atrocious" and "precocious." In lyrics, the simpler the language is, the more complex the underlying emotion is.

Rhythm is established through phrase length. A poetic line has a certain number of syllables in it. Compare that to the prose sentence to get a feel for the rhythmic differences. These two structures package the ideas and feelings

differently (see Table 5-1). In encountering the text through these forms, let the
form lead you. Follow what you see.

Table 5-1

Verse	# of syl.	Prose	# of syl.
I remember sky,	5	I remember sky, it was blue as ink.	10
It was blue as ink.	5		
Or at least I think	5		
I remember sky.	5	Or at least I think I remember sky.	10
I remember snow,	5	I remember snow, soft as feathers,	
Soft as feathers,	4	sharp as thumbtacks, coming down	
Sharp as thumbtacks,	5	like lint, and it made you squint	
Coming down like lint,	6	when the wind would blow.	28
And it made you squint	5		
When the wind would blow.	5		
And ice, like vinyl, on the streets,	8	And ice, like vinyl, on the streets,	
Cold as silver, white as sheets.	7	cold as silver, white as sheets.	15
Rain like strings	3		
And changing things	4	Rain like strings and changing things	
Like leaves.	2	like leaves.	9
I remember leaves,	5	I remember leaves, green as	
Green as spearmint,	4	spearmint, crisp as paper.	13
Crisp as paper.	4		
I remember trees,	5	I remember trees, bare as coat	
Bare as coat racks, spread like		racks, spread like broken	
broken umbrellas.	11	umbrellas.	16
And parks and bridges,	5	And parks and bridges, ponds and	
Ponds and zoos.	3	zoos.	8
Ruddy faces, muddy shoes.	7		
Light and noise and bees and boys		Ruddy faces, muddy shoes.	7
and days.	9	Light and noise and bees and boys	
		and days.	9
I remember days,	5	I remember days, or at least I try.	10
Or at least I try.	5		
But as years go by	5	But as years go by they're a sort of	
They're a sort of haze.	5	haze.	10

Table 5-1 continued

Verse	# of syl.	Prose	# of syl.
And the bluest ink	5	And the bluest ink isn't really sky,	
Isn't really sky,	5	and at times, I think I would gladly	
And at times, I think	5	die for a day of sky.	25
I would gladly die	5		
For a day	3		
Of sky.	2		

In the comparison above, notice how the short thoughts of the verse compare to the, often, longer flow of the sentences.

Deviations in cadence are significant. In the verse form of this song there seems to be a five syllable unit that establishes the norm. Even the prose sentences, though longer, are usually in multiples of five syllables. The most interesting places for an actor to ask, "What's happening?" are when the phrase goes to four, three or two syllables (something halting, or missing?), and when the phrase runs over its banks with eight, seven, eleven(!) or nine syllables (something too large to contain?).

Tiny differences in rhythm matter. Look at the first ten lines. Only two are one syllable short of the normal five syllable pattern. This suggests a missing syllable on those two lines. Try speaking them with a sharp breath occupying the missing first beat. What happens emotionally when you do this? Try fitting the eleven syllable feeling into a five syllable line. It isn't necessarily about racing through. It might be about taking flight, soaring with the feeling. Don't look for "right" ways to speak the text. Look for how this stimulates your feeling.

Departures from that norm are clues to the character's experience. Once you identify what the author has established as the normal meter, look for variations. Can you see where Ella has to work to pull up a memory and when she becomes flooded with them? Can you see them fade in the end – all by looking at rhythmic clues?

EXERCISE 5C   POEM RHYTHM VERSUS PROSE RHYTHM

Compare the number of syllables in the verse and prose versions of your song.

Speak each version and explore what happens when you let the length of the phrase dictate the reading. How do you feel when speaking the short phrases of the verse and the longer phrases of the sentence? What does this rhythmic structure do to your emotional state? How does it affect your overall pacing, and how does that make you feel? What happens to the organization of the ideas?

What do the varying or regular lengths of the poetic line tell you about the character's experience? What clues can you glean about the character's journey from the rhythmic structures?

Rhyme

UNIT 5.5

Characters know they're rhyming. But they employ rhyme for different reasons. It will be up to the actor to discover the reason for the rhyme in the specific moment of the song. For example ('*Tea for Two*'), "Darling, this place is a lover's oasis, where life's weary chase is unknown." This multi-layered rhyme is a clever, persuasive marriage proposal, relished by the character and handed like a box of bonbons to his bride. In '*I Remember*', the rhymes come as Ella recalls childhood impressions and the images cohere into her awareness. In both cases the rhymes are present as part of the character's tactic or discovery.

Rhymes can be obvious or subtle. Finding rhymes involves more than just looking at the last word in a line, though end-rhymes are significant. You need to investigate the lyric for embedded repetitions of sound and then, when you find a match, see what kind of relationship it has to its partners. A traditional way of doing this is to assign a letter to each rhyming word in sequence (AABAB). In the table following we have (a) identified the most important rhymes, (b) in the second column listed the words in each rhyme set, and (c) underlined the end-rhymes to help you locate them. Remember that English spelling is not phonetic. Rhymes are about matching sounds, not letters.

I remember sky,	A, A
It was blue as ink.	B, C
Or at least I think	D, C
I remember sky.	A, A
I remember snow,	A, E
Soft as feathers,	
Sharp as thumbtacks,	F
Coming down like lint,	A, G
And it made you squint	H, G
When the wind would blow.	G, E
And ice, like vinyl, on the streets,	A, A, A, D
Cold as silver, white as sheets.	E, A, D
Rain like strings	H, A, I
And changing things	H, I, I
Like leaves.	D
I remember leaves,	A, D
Green as spearmint,	D, G
Crisp as paper.	H
I remember trees,	A, D
Bare as coat racks, spread like broken umbrellas.	E, F, A, E
And parks and bridges,	
Ponds and zoos.	B
Ruddy faces, muddy shoes.	J, H, J, B
Light and noise and bees and boys and days.	A, K, D, K, H
I remember days,	A, H
Or at least I try.	D, A, A
But as years go by	E, A
They're a sort of haze.	H, H
And the bluest ink	B, C
Isn't really sky,	D, A
And at times, I think	A, A, C
I would gladly die	A, A
For a day	H
Of sky.	A

Rhyme key

(Every occurrence of a rhyme in the entire lyric. End of line rhymes are underlined)

A

I, sky, I, sky, I, like, ice, like, vinyl, white, like, I, I, like, light, I, I, try, by, sky, times, I, I, die, sky

B

blue, zoos, shoes, bluest

C

ink, think, ink, think

D

least, streets, sheets, leaves, leaves, green, trees, bees, least, really

E

snow, blow, cold, coat, broken, go

F

thumbtacks, coat racks

G

lint, squint, wind, spearmint

H

made, rain, changing, paper, faces, days, days, they're, haze, day

I

strings, changing, things

J

ruddy, muddy

K

noise, boys

Read the list of rhyming words aloud. Then read the whole lyric again. What kinds of information can you get from an awareness of the rhyme patterns? What feelings does it evoke? What images? What does it mean when the last word in a line doesn't rhyme (feathers, umbrellas, bridges)? Did you notice that one of the non-rhyming words contains Ella's name: umbrella? What is happening when the rhymes come in a rush (ice-like-vinyl-streets and cold-white-sheets, and ruddy-faces-muddy-shoes-light-noise-bees-boys-days)? How do the rhymes reflect Ella's journey through the song?

EXERCISE 5D   RHYME SCHEME

Analyze the pattern of rhymes. Label each different rhyme with a letter. When the same rhyme reoccurs later in the song, use that same letter so you can see the pattern of internal rhymes as well as those that come at the end of lines.

List just the end rhymes. Then notice the more complicated internal rhymes and how a later end rhyme is set up from an earlier internal vowel. You may not have realized just how many rhymes there were.

Speak only the rhymed words. Then speak the whole lyric. Discuss how rhyming supports the character's journey through the song.

Vowels have tonal and emotional characteristics. If you look in a mirror, you'll see your face takes on a specific shape with each vowel. Say "street," "day," and "sky" and notice that your face is different from when you say "home," "law," "do." Ella's rhymes are mostly on bright vowels. Her song is written in a different vowel tone than the grieving reverence of 'Bring Him Home' (Les Misérables), with its chorus of long "oh" sounds. Ella's rhymes are a clue to her emotional state. She's longing for a "day of sky," not obsessing in a 'Lonely Room' (Oklahoma!). There is an affirmative absence of self-pity in her remembrance, even though her memories are slipping away. When you study lyrics, notice how the sounds make you feel when you speak them. Writers don't pick those sounds by accident. The choice of vowels is a window into the lyricist's imagination and the character's world.

UNIT 5.6   **Alliteration and consonance**

- **Alliteration** is the repetition of consonant sounds at the *beginning* of words. Initial consonant repetition tends to stick out noticeably in much the way end-rhymes draw attention.
- **Consonance** is the repetition of consonants *within* words. Like internal rhymes, they are complex and affecting, but not always as noticeable.

As with rhymed vowels, characters know when they are repeating consonants. They do it for a purpose. It will be up to the actor to spot the repeated sounds and to discern how the character can use them tactically.

Consonants have qualities that affect our senses. Notice the sharp percussiveness of p-t-k, the heavier bangs of b-d-g, the buzzing vibration of v-zh-z, and the hissing f-sh-s. These sounds have a sensory effect on both the speaker and the listener. There are no firm rules about how you should employ alliteration. It isn't formulaic. But it is a potent tool for you to explore. For example, the b-w-ch-t/b-th-d/b-w-l-d-d alliteration of '*Bewitched, Bothered and Bewildered*' (*Pal Joey*) is a lip burr of erotic reawakening, whereas the b-ng/b-ng/b-m sequence in "Bing! Bang! Boom!" ('*Snuff That Girl*', *Urinetown*) is a violent jazz pistol-whipping. Both are launched from an initial "b" alliteration. And they are completely different.

Words are sensual, not just intellectual. The sound of a word reflects the essential nature of the idea or feeling, not just its meaning. Try this experiment with several people to see what you find: tell them in your left pocket you have a rock and in your right you have a stone. Ask them to describe what they saw when you said that. Rock and stone are synonymous, but only at the intellectual level. At the sensory level, "r-ah-k" and "st-oh-n" are completely different.

All words are like this. They are made up of associated sensory information that far exceeds their literal definitions. When you clue into that consciously, you can play words with more skill.

EXERCISE 5E   CATCHING THE CONSONANTS/VOICING THE VOWELS

1. If you're working in a group, give each person a single line from '*I Remember*', or another song you want to explore, keep going around until the whole lyric has been assigned.
2. Take a moment for everyone to identify the individual sounds in their line. If you have been trained in phonetic transcription, write the line out in phonetics to get all the details.
3. Start at the top, and speak only the vowel sounds in sequence, going from line to line.
4. Start again. This time, speak just the A rhymes from the rhyme scheme analysis (I, sky, I, sky, I, like, ice, like, vinyl . . .), then the B rhymes (blue, zoos, shoes, bluest), etc. Make sure you haven't missed any.
5. Go around again, discussing the consonants. Look at the lines close to yours and identify patterns of consonant use nearby. Note the

> difference between initial alliteration (like-lint, when-wind-would) and internal consonance (the M pattern in "remember," the K sequence in "sky-ink-think" . . .).
>
> 6. Go around again and speak the lines, overworking the consonant patterns to bring them forward in your awareness.
> 7. Do one final round, without leaning on any sounds. Just let the feelings, ideas and words express themselves.
> 8. Discuss your observations.

Sharp, clear consonants are the primary way to maintain a grip on patter songs and rapid passages of dialogue. They require exceptional consonant dexterity. Try saying this *'Witch's Rap'* three times quickly: "He was robbing me, / Raping me, / Rooting through my rutabaga, / Raiding my arugula and / Ripping up my rampion . . ." (*'Prologue'*, *Into the Woods*). If you want to get your third encore on *'The Major General's Song'* (*The Pirates of Penzance*) – a song traditionally done several times with increasing acceleration – the best way to get there is to divide it into small phrases and drill them over and over like a pianist doing finger exercises. Feats of articulation are as thrilling for an audience as a complicated tap-dance sequence, and they take as much practice.

UNIT 5.7   **Rhetoric**

Rhetoric is both the way a character makes his argument and the argument itself.

So far you've been concentrating on rhythm, poetic and prose structures, and the small sound units of consonants and vowels. You've been encountering the text through each of these as a way of engaging the sensory experience of the words. These various encounters with the text are designed to reveal dimensions and perspectives we might miss otherwise.

Next we'll look at ways of discovering meaning in the words. It isn't that we need to explore meaning because the sense of the lyric is obscure. Most musicals have librettos that are easy to follow. So, meaning in this case isn't about understanding in an intellectual way. It is about finding an emotionally evocative connection with the text through the *argument* of the piece.

Every lyric has a rationale. Even when a character is completely befuddled and banging around blindly in unreasoning confusion, there is still a logic to her experience. Sometimes, to sort things out, it helps to reduce what she's saying to the simplest level. At its most basic, every sentence has a subject, a predicate (verb), and sometimes an object (the thing the subject acts on).

In this next encounter with the text, we'll take the original sentence (being guided by the punctuation the author has set up) and derive a simple sentence from it. Since he is writing character thoughts, not a formal paper, the rules of grammar are frequently not observed. That will mean we have to make some judgment calls about the exact structure. As usual, don't get caught up in needing to be correct. There are many right ways to do this. Asking the question is more important than finding the perfect answer. Follow the example in Table 5-2 [below] to see one way to investigate the simple sentence structure. (Items in parentheses are implied but not stated in the original text.)

Table 5-2

Original sentence		Simple sentence		
	Conjunction	*Subject*	*Predicate*	*Object*
I remember sky, it was blue as ink.		I	remember	sky
Or at least I think I remember sky.	or	I	think	(that) I remember
I remember snow, soft as feathers, sharp as thumbtacks, coming down like lint, and it made you squint when the wind would blow.	and	I (I)	remember (remember)	snow (that) it made you squint
And ice, like vinyl, on the streets, cold as silver, white as sheets.	and	I	remember	ice
Rain like strings and changing things like leaves.	and	(I) (I)	(remember) (remember)	rain changing things
I remember leaves, green as spearmint, crisp as paper.		I	remember	leaves
I remember trees, bare as coat racks, spread like broken umbrellas.		I	remember	trees

Table 5-2 continued

Original sentence	Simple sentence			
	Conjunction	Subject	Predicate	Object
And parks and bridges,	and	(I)	(remember)	parks
ponds and zoos.	and	(I)	(remember)	bridges
	(and)	(I)	(remember)	ponds
	and	(I)	(remember)	zoos
Ruddy faces, muddy shoes.	(and)	(I)	(remember)	faces
	(and)	(I)	(remember)	shoes
Light and noise and bees		(I)	(remember)	light
and boys and days.	and	(I)	(remember)	noise
	and	(I)	(remember)	bees
	and	(I)	(remember)	boys
	and	(I)	(remember)	days
I remember days, or at least		I	remember	days
I try.	or	I	try	(to remember days)
But as years go by they're	but	they	are	a haze
a sort of haze.				
And the bluest ink isn't really	and	ink	is not	sky
sky, and at times, I think I	and	I	think	(that) I would die for a day of sky
would gladly die for a day				
of sky.				

Speak the simple sentences (including the parenthetical words) three times through without stopping:

> I remember sky. Or I think that I remember. I remember snow and I remember that it made you squint. And I remember ice. I remember rain and I remember changing things. I remember leaves. I remember trees. And I remember parks and I remember bridges and I remember ponds and I remember zoos. And I remember faces and I remember shoes. And I remember light and I remember noise and I remember bees and I remember boys and I remember days. I remember days or I try to remember days. But they are a haze. And ink is not sky and I think that I would die for a day of sky.

Then go back and speak it three times without the words in parentheses:

> I remember sky. Or I think I remember. I remember snow and it made you squint. And ice. Rain and changing things. I remember leaves. I remember trees. And parks and bridges ponds and zoos. Faces shoes. Light and noise and bees and boys and days. I remember days or I try. But they're a haze. And ink is not sky and I think I would die for a day of sky.

How do these simple versions of the lyric affect you? Remember, the goal of these various encounters with the text is to allow the words to move you just by speaking them. When you are touched by the text, it is much easier to find the character's experience, and it doesn't feel like you have to generate feeling or need to fill the line. Feeling comes from the words themselves.

In most lyrics there is a lot of literal and implied repetition. Speaking those repetitions can be quite moving, and can get us closer to the character's reasoning. The name given to repeatedly using the same phrase with slight differences is "climactic parallelism." It is a rhetorical device that carries a great deal of emotional power. You might recall Dr. Martin Luther King, Jr. using it in his historic "I Have a Dream" speech. Lyricists revel in this strategy, so you'll encounter it a lot in musicals.

EXERCISE 5F   SIMPLE SENTENCES

Use the sentence (not verse) version of the lyric.

Identify the subject, predicate and object of each sentence, and any conjunctions (and, or, but). Organize them so you can see the sentences. If any of these elements are implied put them in parentheses. Follow the punctuation from the author.

Place yourself imaginatively in the circumstances of the character and speak the simple sentences as text. For the moment, don't aggressively push into your objective. As before, allow the words to work on you. Try this three times in a row, starting over as soon as you've gotten to the end, without stopping.

What did this version reveal? How did the words make you feel?

Since every lyric is different, there are a couple of other tricks that can be useful in whittling it down to its essential message. Not every approach will work on every lyric, so pick the one that seems to work best for your song.

Sentences can have primary and subordinate ideas. If you look at the sentence version of the lyric, you'll see there are parts of each sentence that are primary and some that comment on the main point, or are a parenthetical sidebar. Put parentheses around the subordinate phrases. In cases where you think there might be parentheses within parentheses, use hard brackets to make that clear.

> I remember sky, (it was blue as ink).
> Or (at least) I think I remember sky.
> I remember snow, (soft as feathers), (sharp as thumbtacks), (coming down
>   like lint), (and it made you squint [when the wind would blow]).
> And ice, (like vinyl), on the streets, (cold as silver), (white as sheets).
> Rain (like strings) and changing things like leaves.
> I remember leaves, (green as spearmint), (crisp as paper).
> I remember trees, (bare as coat racks), (spread like broken umbrellas).
> And parks and bridges, ponds and zoos.
> Ruddy faces, muddy shoes.
> Light and noise and bees and boys and days.
> I remember days, or (at least) I try.
> But (as years go by) they're a (sort of) haze.
> And the bluest ink isn't really sky, and (at times), (I think) I would (gladly) die
>   for a day of sky.

Then strip those subordinate sections out.

> I remember sky.
> Or I think I remember sky.
> I remember snow.
> And ice on the streets.
> Rain and changing things like leaves.
> I remember leaves.
> I remember trees.
> And parks and bridges, ponds and zoos.
> Ruddy faces, muddy shoes.
> Light and noise and bees and boys and days.
> I remember days, or I try.
> But they're a haze.
> And the bluest ink isn't really sky, and I would die for a day of sky.

Speak both of these versions cycling back and forth between them until you feel at home expressing the primary and subordinate ideas with a clear distinction.

EXERCISE 5G SIMPLE TO COMPLEX SENTENCES

1. Use the sentence (not verse) version of the lyric.
2. Identify any text that seems parenthetical or that isn't necessary to the direct meaning. If there seems to be more than one level of subordinate phrase use hard brackets to distinguish that.
3. Take out the subordinate phrases. Act this version of the piece. Run it three times without stopping, until you feel like it is the real version.
4. Put back the missing words, but keep them in parentheses.
5. Speak this version, making a deliberate distinction between the main ideas and those in parentheses.
6. Try this with two partners, A and B. Place them in front of you. Think of them as two versions of one character. A is interested in the primary message, and B needs more explanation. Make eye contact with A on all the primary thoughts and with B on all the subordinate ideas.

Every lyric has a point of view or an argument. You can take this as a given because every character is pursuing an objective. Rhetoric is the name applied to the persuasive devises writers and speakers use to carry their arguments. The way characters use words to push for their ideal outcome is their specific form of rhetoric. Looking at sentence structure is one way to reveal the argument or reasoning pattern. You might have a tendency to think of rhetoric as something rational. Actually, most arguments are a struggle between feeling and reason. Rhetoric is most persuasive when it appeals to the emotions (an explanation for why we have a paucity of reasoned political debate – it doesn't move people).

Rationale is revealing. Looking carefully at a character's primary and subordinate thought organization can give you insights into her personality. Notice how often Ella interrupts herself to qualify or excuse what she is saying. She interrupts herself with, "at least I think," "sort of," "at least I try," "at times," and "I think" – all marks of her lack of certainty and confidence.

If you try this with Henry Higgins' songs in *My Fair Lady*, you see he rarely equivocates. He is an articulate, reasonable man who knows how to frame a cogent argument. That is until he gets completely blindsided in the emotional–

rational struggle of *'I've Grown Accustomed to Her Face'*. Then his effort to master his emotions through force of intellect fails again and again as he swings between the rational, the vindictive and the desolate. His character's arc is beautifully reflected in the structure of his language.

You might not have noticed this feature as strongly if you hadn't deliberately separated out the implied parenthetical phrases.

As you do the sometimes heady work in this chapter, always link it back to feeling. Sentence structure is the scaffold for both our thoughts *and* our emotions.

UNIT 5.8   ## Simile and metaphor – telling you how I feel

It isn't easy to understand our own emotions. Much of what we feel is chaotic and incoherent, even to ourselves. So, it is a real challenge to find the right words when we need to explain our feelings to someone else. Simile and metaphor are the tools we often reach for.

*   **Simile** is finding a comparison. *'I Remember'* is filled with similes. Watch for the key words "like" or "as" to signal a simile. "It was blue *as* ink."
*   **Metaphor** is the figurative made literal. It isn't a comparison as much as saying something *is* something else. "Love, you *are* love, better far than any metaphor could ever, ever be" (*'Metaphor'*, *The Fantasticks*). "You *are* the promised kiss of Springtime . . . " (*'All the Things You Are'*, *Very Warm for May*). Look for a central use of the verb "to be," as in "you are," "love is." Metaphor is so important to lyricists that many songs, like the ones just named, have the metaphor directly in the title: *'A Woman Is a Sometime Thing'* (*Porgy and Bess*), *'I'm a Brass Band'* (*Sweet Charity*).

You can learn a lot about a person as he struggles to translate his abstract feelings into something tangible. Metaphor and simile are reflections of what that person knows and what he approves or disapproves of.

Let's review the similes Ella uses as she tries to express her memories.

> sky – blue as ink
> snow – soft as feathers, sharp as thumbtacks, coming down like lint
> ice – like vinyl, cold as silver, white as sheets
> rain – like strings
> leaves – green as spearmint, crisp as paper
> trees – bare as coat racks, spread like broken umbrellas

Ella's only frame of reference to explain the natural world is the synthetic one she knows in her department store. We can see her struggle to not only remember the world outside but to even comprehend it. One of the most notable moments in the song comes when she talks about "changing things / Like leaves." This is not a simile. It is a sudden recovered memory of things that change, and leaves are the example (so "like" doesn't always indicate a comparison, especially, like in contemporary conversation, fer shur). This discovery kicks her into an accelerating chain of memories culminating in "days" – the most potent and bittersweet memory of all. In the end, now that she knows what she has been missing, she has to reject her similes, "And the bluest ink / *Isn't* really sky." At this moment she understands what she has been cut off from for the last thirteen years.

There, right in the rhetoric of the textual argument, is the chain of discoveries you'll need to turn this from a sad, moody, wistful song into an active, forward-moving, objective/discovery-driven journey.

EXERCISE 5H   I'M A METAPHOR (OR LIKE A SIMILE)

Search out and list all the comparisons and metaphors in the lyric.

Ask what these tell you about your character.

Speak each of these metaphors until you can see, smell, taste, hear, and touch them. Then get a partner and speak the whole lyric with the intent to make the other person experience these as richly as you do.

Changing lists into ladders

UNIT 5.9

When Ella's mind opens to her repressed memories, a flood of images swamps her. She remembers sky, snow, ice, rain, leaves, trees, parks, bridges, ponds, zoos, faces, shoes, light, noise, bees, boys, and days. Lyrics abound in lists. One of the most common song forms in musical theatre is the list song and was mastered by Cole Porter, Noël Coward, W.S. Gilbert, Stephen Sondheim, and many others.

The problem with lists: they're flat and one-dimensional. They don't have forward motion – something essential to keep your character in pursuit of her objective.

Rethink the list into a ladder. Then look at the last item in the list and recognize that, since the author has placed it at the end, it must be the most important discovery, the one driven by all the others. Put that at the top of a ladder of ascending need, or as the last in a line of snowballing revelations. Sometimes the discoveries pull you up the ladder. Sometimes you'll drive your partner in front of you in an aggressive ladder of rage. (Sometimes you'll tickle them up the ladder into the bunk bed.) In Ella's case, she is being pulled upward by a dawning sense that there is one essential thing she must remember: a day with a sky. Her ladder is emerging out of a fog as she climbs.

A rant song has a particular kind of ladder structure. In a rant, the character arrives at what he imagines to be the top of a ladder, and says, "There. Now, that's the last word on the subject." The satisfaction he feels at nailing that last point makes him want to do it all over again, plus more. So he charges up another taller ladder in the next verse. There is usually a series. *'Hymn to Him'* (*My Fair Lady*) is a classic rant, as is *'Guv'ment'* (*Big River*). Unless the actor finds a progressively strong need to fulminate at higher and higher levels, the song can be earthbound, boring and repetitive.

UNIT 5.10 ## If–then, either–or, yes–but, not this–but that

Small words are the fulcrum on which our reasoning balances. Even though the words in the title of this unit are exceptionally common and you certainly know their meaning and function, look consciously for them in your lyric and recognize how they operate for your character to make his argument.

If–then. This is a proposition–conclusion statement. The "if" states the hypothetical situation and "then" asserts what will happen in those conditions. In *Big River*, Huck Finn is told, "If you don't learn to read then you can't read your Bible / And you'll never get to heaven cause you won't know how." It's interesting to notice how often only one of the words is used, and the other is left for the listener to fill in. In *Gypsy*, June and Louise sing *'If Mama Was Married'*, thinking how their lives would change *if* their mother had a husband. But, the "then" is missing in the lyric, "If Mama was married, [then] I'd jump in the air . . ." If you see an "if," find a way to rhythmically let us hear the "then," even if it is missing.

Either–or. This is a way of narrowing down the future to two possibilities. Usually one character is coercively limiting the other's choice by presenting a good/bad scenario. It shows up powerfully in ultimatums.

Yes–but. Try saying these two sentences and see how you feel. "I love you, but you drive me crazy." "I love you, and you drive me crazy." They feel different, don't they? "But" functions to selectively negate part of the previous statement. I love you, but . . . means I don't really love you all that much, now that I think about . . . It forms an exception, undercutting the truth of what you just said. So when someone says "yes, but" those tiny words mean something important is coming next. When Ella sings "But as years go by / They're a sort of haze," we know that all the memories she has just listed are slipping away. They aren't as clear now as she felt them to be only a moment ago.

Not this–but that. This structure reveals an argument made through contrast. The actual words "not this, but that" are rarely used, but the energy of the line is just that sort of "thesis–antithesis" organization. When characters are weighing the consequences, or reasoning a course of action, they will use this structure. Look at *'Good 'n' Evil'* (*Jekyll and Hyde*). As the title suggests, the opposites are laid out for contrast as Lucy makes a choice between them. When rehearsing this kind of reasoning, explore putting the choice in your body by feeling yourself pulled in two different directions.

In rhetoric, small words are the pivot points of the argument. An actor needs to spot them and consciously recognize what they stand for in order to make the argument have force and clarity. The words themselves rarely need to be stressed (and often they're only implied in the text). It's really just like operating a lever. People rarely notice the fulcrum. It's the lever that gets all the attention, but it can't work by itself.

Punctuation

UNIT 5.11

Some lyricists are highly detailed and intentional in their textual notation. An inspection of their writing can show an artful use of both verse structure and punctuation. In *'I Remember'*, the published manuscript is filled with important clues to phrasing the flow of ideas. Sondheim's verse is different from what you might expect if you were to write it by just listening to the music. So is his sentence structure.

An interesting way to reveal important clues the author has provided is to put all the lyric words down in a string without any punctuation, capitalization or specific line breaks. Have a friend dictate it word by word, so you won't be influenced from looking at the page.

i remember sky it was blue as ink or at least i think i remember sky i remember snow soft as feathers sharp as thumbtacks coming down like lint and it
made you squint when the wind would blow and ice like vinyl on the streets
cold as silver white as sheets rain like strings and changing things like leaves
i remember leaves green as spearmint crisp as paper i remember trees bare
as coat racks spread like broken umbrellas and parks and bridges ponds and
zoos ruddy faces muddy shoes light and noise and bees and boys and days
i remember days or at least i try but as years go by they're a sort of haze and
the bluest ink isn't really sky and at times i think i would gladly die for a day
of sky

Then, using your own sense of what feels right, punctuate it, and put it into verse
form, yourself. Set that aside, and repeat the process, this time by listening to a
recording of the song and marking what you hear. When you're finished, set
those two versions side-by-side with the original one written as verse (see the
beginning of this chapter), and compare them.

The author's version is the one we'll use as a standard. Assume that any time
there is a difference in the versions, the author is telling you something you don't
instinctively know or haven't understood yet about what they were writing. You
just found some important clues to understanding the piece.

Next, take the author's version and speak it, placing attention on expressing the
punctuation through your voice. Don't focus on interpretation per se, just on
speaking the structure of the piece the way it was written. When you arrive at a
comma, give your voice a little lift, so the conversational ball stays in the air.
When you hit a full stop, firmly plant your voice, definitively ending the thought.
If there is a question, make it a genuine one. Speaking the end of an unpunctuated
verse line is subtler. Don't "end stop" the line. Instead, use what verse speakers
call an enjambment. That's where you gently link through into the next verse
line.

With a little bit of practice you can put the author's visual instructions into sound.
Here's a way to test that. After you've rehearsed a few times, hand a friend the
unpunctuated version and ask them to punctuate it as you speak. In addition to
normal punctuation, use "/" to mark verse line endings. Go slowly. When you get
your friend to put in all the punctuation correctly, you've mastered the author's
version. What did you discover about the run and flow of the ideas? How did this
feel?

Period

We've run through a series of encounters with the text. Each one is designed to bring a different perspective into view. There are likely to be too many approaches to do every one on every song you learn. Try one or two each time you work on a new piece, or to give a fresh insight to a song you know so well you have stopped making discoveries. You'll probably find that you click with some approaches more than others, so have fun, but be rigorous about your development. Push yourself to master new or difficult techniques while enjoying those that are more instinctive. As with all the encounters we've made with the text, internalize this information, but don't be rigid or ruled by it. This is homework, and informative play. Bring it with you at the subconscious level and it will show up in your work. But don't make your performance about demonstrating your homework.

SECTION II: SCORE AND LIBRETTO ANALYSIS AND STRUCTURE

CHAPTER 6

ELEMENTS OF STORYTELLING

Musical theatre, like most forms of theatre, is fundamentally about storytelling. That means the basic elements we find in classical, modern and contemporary drama are also present in musicals. We meet distinct characters that engage us in a compelling story, rich in conflicts, themes and action; all played out through interesting dialogue. This is true from Aristophanes to Mamet to Berlin to La Chiusa.

Know what story you're telling

When you play a role, you act as the voice of the author focused through the perspectives of your character. You are telling a specific dimension of the story. If you're going to be an effective storyteller, it helps to know the story you're telling. This section is about analyzing and understanding the author's theme, the structure of the piece, the way the overall theme is told in the moment-to-moment interactions between the characters, and finding useful clues to acting your role that are embedded in the text.

An actor can often make perfectly reasonable and carefully thought out choices about her character but if she hasn't thought about the relationship her character has to the larger story, those choices can lead away from the point of the play. A smart actor will analyze a script and score for ways to build a powerful, personal and intelligent performance that is congruent to the story being told.

We'll create a questionnaire that will help you identify useful information about your show and your character's place in it. Look for these questions at the end of this chapter. They are flexible enough to apply to individual scenes or to a complete script and score. You'll probably find that, at different times, some of these questions are more relevant than others, depending on the show. But, it's important to ask and answer all of them since we never know where useful information might come from.

For this section, we'll focus on a number of classic Golden Age musicals to explore and illustrate our points.

UNIT 6.2 **Divide and conquer your text**

Read the entire script and listen to the complete score to get an overall sense of the story and characters. Then, if we want to look at a text with closer scrutiny it becomes necessary to divide and conquer. The general impressions you get on the first read/listen are useful because they represent an intuitive response and will form the basis of much of your investigation. But any complex text becomes clearer as you look more closely at the individual elements that comprise the whole.

Many musicals are written with distinct and obvious structural divisions, while others play in nearly continuous time in the same location, with no discernible breaks. In both cases, creating smaller, more digestible units will help you understand the whole more clearly.

Divisions of the script are best defined by identifying the beginnings and endings of important story events. As you read/listen to a show the second time, keep a pencil nearby and simply mark the page each time you sense something important has happened. Later, as you go back over the script, you can see where that event began.

UNIT 6.2.1 *Story events*

Table 6-1 looks at the story events in the opening section of Rodgers and Hammerstein's *Oklahoma!*

Altogether there are probably ten story events in Act I, scene i, of *Oklahoma!* Have a look at the script and see how we made our choices. You might make different selections. You'll also notice that Hammerstein wrote small transition

Table 6-1

Act I, scene i   The front of Laurey's farmhouse

Characters	Story event begins	Story event ends
Aunt Eller, Curly, Laurey	Aunt Eller is discovered on the porch churning butter.	Curly: Whew! If she liked me any more she'd sic the dogs onto me.
Aunt Eller, Curly, Jud, Laurey	Curly: I'll ketch up with you.	Curly: (singing as he exits) Fer that shiny little surrey with the fringe on the top –
Aunt Eller, Curly, Ike, Fred, Slim, Will Parker, Cowboys	Ike: Y'git the wagon hitched up?	Ike: Come on, Curly.
Aunt Eller, Laurey, Ado Annie	Aunt Eller: Hey, Curly, tell all the girls in Bushyhead . . .	Laurey: Not to a peddler it don't!
Aunt Eller, Laurey, Ado Annie, Peddler	Peddler: All right!	Peddler: I didn't say nothing!

scenes to bring an end to one story event and introduce another. Those could be set as distinct scenes unto themselves or appended to the one before or after. See how you would break it up.

French scenes

One of simplest ways to find story events is with *French scenes*. This term originates with plays from the French neoclassical period (mid-1700s), when each entire act of a play ran in continuous time in the same location. A new French scene begins with the entrance or exit of a character. This method of dividing a script implies that any character entering brings a new pressure on the existing situation, causing something to change. The exit of a character also shifts the energy through resolution of some objective or the suspension of unfinished business. So, in any play, a change in the number of characters onstage is a significant clue to alert you to a change in the scene. This doesn't mean that internal scene changes can only occur when a major character enters or exits. But, these are signals to take seriously.

Looking at Lerner and Loewe's *Brigadoon*, the milkmaid Meg Brockie offers us a perfect example of a character who brings a strong personal agenda with her wherever she goes: to find a man! She has decided that Jeff Douglas, a cynical New Yorker who has happened upon this magical village, is the perfect mate. So, after their initial meeting she plagues him for the rest of the musical. Every time she enters, we know that she will pressure him for sex. Her entrance, the beginning of a new French scene, signals the beginning of a new set of pressures and the pursuit of her single-minded agenda. When she exits, the pressure subsides and allows other pressures to rise.

UNIT 6.2.3   *Musical moments*

Another way to divide a musical theatre text is by the occurrence of songs and musical sequences (including dances) within the story. Just as entrances and exits signal important story events, so do these musical moments. A truism of musical theatre is that songs occur at the most important moments in the characters' lives, and these moments can only be fully expressed in song and/or dance. If there's a song or dance, we can assume something important is happening.

Let's use the first major scene in *Brigadoon* to identify a structure using both French scenes and musical moments. After a prologue scene where we meet the two modern-day hunters, Jeff and Tommy, we arrive in the town square of the ancient Scottish village of Brigadoon. The very long scene that follows actually contains many smaller internal scenes.

A quick list of these internal scenes is:

1. *'McConachy Square'* – A musical number that is actually a series of vignettes introducing us to many of the important characters in the town and the basic nature of the village on an average day.
2. Entrance of Mr. McLaren and his daughters, Fiona and the soon-to-be-wed Jean.
3. Harry Beaton, in love with Jean, rejects her offer of friendship.
4. Fiona shares her philosophy on love in *'Waitin' for My Dearie'*.
5. Tommy and Jeff arrive in Brigadoon to the amazement of the villagers.
6. Meg Brockie takes a shine to Jeff – he rejects her interest.
7. *'I'll Go Home with Bonnie Jean'* – Charlie Dalrymple arrives to celebrate his imminent wedding to Jean.
8. Tommy and Fiona explore their attraction to each other in *'Heather on the Hill'*.

9.   As Tommy and Fiona leave to gather heather, a rainstorm descends and the scene is over.

This one scene is actually made up of at least nine distinct internal scenes. The structure we identified reveals the sequence of story events. Now you can see how important moments stand out as different from each other and the story unfolds to set up the remainder of the show.

EXERCISE 6A   DIVIDE AND CONQUER

Choose a musical to study. Select an act to break down into divisions. Answer these questions:

1.   What divisions did the author set up? (acts, scenes, etc.)
2.   Have major characters come or gone? (French scenes)
3.   Were there songs and/or dances that caused major changes to the story? (musical moments)
4.   Was something significant completed or deliberately tabled?

Plot

UNIT 6.3

Understanding the simple story you're telling and the actions of the characters that drive the story forward is an essential starting point for developing a role in a musical.

Plot is, simply put, the story: a list of the events in the order they occur. This only includes the events that are presented, not background events or what we know happens after the play. Write a bare-bones plot synopsis, listing just the incidents that occur in the section you're studying. Keep it simple. The whole first scene of *Oklahoma!* is quite long, almost forty minutes of stage time, and contains a number of smaller scenes within it. So, for our purposes, we're focusing on just the first section rather than an entire major scene.

In that first unit the plot is:

*   Curly comes to Laurey's farm.
*   Curly asks Laurey to the Box Social.
*   Curly invents a surrey to take her in.

- Laurey finds out the surrey is fictitious.
- Laurey accepts an invitation to the dance with Jud.

There is very little subjective, interpretive work in the above synopsis. There is also almost no narrative, exposition or sub-plot. It really sticks to the facts of the scene and the skeleton of the story. When identifying the plot, resist imposing judgments about the characters or reasons for their behavior. We'll get to how actions, objectives and obstacles play into your analysis later. For now, we're just creating a list of the basic events of the story.

EXERCISE 6B   PLOT OUTLINE

1. If you're working alone, write a plot outline for the first scene of your musical. Start with the first event, then ask yourself, "and then what happens?" Once you've completed your draft, go back through and cut out anything non-essential. See how thorough, yet sparing, you can be.

2. This is often a group activity, since the shared wisdom and obser-vations of the full cast and director can be needed to make sure nothing is missed. If you're working in a group, sit in a circle. Take ten minutes for each person to privately write down what they think the plot is.

3. One person tells the first event and hands the story to the next person by saying, "and then . . ." If anyone notices that something has been skipped or feels that the detail just mentioned doesn't rise to the level of an essential plot point, then discuss it until there is consensus. There are many right answers in this process. Focus on "who," and "what." Part of the game is to see how briefly and simply the story can be told, so find out how much you can cut without loosing anything crucial.

4. If the director finds it helpful, you can track sub-plots separately, or cut them out of this version and come back to them later. A good example of a sub-plot in *Oklahoma!* is the Ado Annie/Will Parker/Ali Hakim story.

5. Have a designated scribe write down the plot points. A stage manager works well for this. It can be helpful to use a board so everyone can see the plot as it is revealed.

6. When you get to the end, have the scribe read back the plot. Compare your initial plot analysis to the one the group developed. If there is a difference, how does this change your understanding of the story and your role in it?

The work you have done so far is a product of asking, "What happens?" If you are really strict, a two-hour show can be reduced to a few sentences. A reading of that story may feel less than satisfying. Just to help you stay connected to the magic of the tale, expand the plot a little, but still keep it in the realm of a story.

EXERCISE 6C FAIRYTALE-ING YOUR STORY

Fairytales are among the simplest kinds of stories. They often contain only the essentials with a minimum of dialogue and events.

1. Tell the story of your musical as a fairytale. Imagine you are speaking to a child. In this iteration, your story can have more detail than the bare-bones plot. For instance, "Once upon a time, there was a cowboy named Curly who had fallen in love with an orphaned farm girl named Laurey. On the day of the big dance, Curly comes to Laurey's farm to ask her to go with him. He pretends to have a wonderful carriage, which makes her want to accept, but then he tells her that it's all made up. To get even, Laurey decides to go to the dance with the dangerous farmhand, Jud, instead." You can continue the story in this way.
2. Notice what additional details you included to make your story interesting to a child. How important are they? In what way are they important?

In the last exercise, the kind of detail needed to dress up your simple plot is usually made up of *exposition* (the set-up for the story) and *narrative* (necessary details that aren't shown).

Events seen (and unseen)

UNIT 6.3.1

Which events the author shows and the arrangement of those events are significant choices that reveal the point of view of the musical. Dramas don't attempt to include all events in a character's life. Rather, the selection of events guides the audience on a specific journey. In *Oklahoma!*, Hammerstein doesn't include the events prior to the day of the Box Social. We find out about Curly and Laurey's past relationship when they sing, *'People Will Say We're in Love'*. But those events are only referred to, not shown. This is an important day in the lives of these characters. It is the day Laurey and Curly admit they're in love and decide to get married. We meet these characters at dawn, spend much of the day with them, and finally take a break from their lives at dusk when it's time to leave for the dance. We rejoin these characters later that evening as the dance is in full swing with most guests already there (but not Laurey and Jud). We spend most of the second act with Laurey and Curly, up through their engagement announcement and Jud's threat of revenge. Hammerstein doesn't bring us back into their lives until after the wedding. And then we only spend about twenty minutes with the newly married couple as they are given gifts, Jud returns and is killed, Curly is acquitted of the death, and they start their life together.

We only know these characters during two days of their lives, and only for selected periods of those two days. The careful selection of events tells you what the authors really thought were the important moments.

UNIT 6.3.2 *Your character's events*

While it's easy to see the shape of an entire story, it may be harder to recognize what part you play in it. An easy and important step in your analysis is to make a list of every scene you're in and identify what plot points you are involved in and which you witness. You'll also spot those your character may be unaware of for the entire story.

Table 6-2 is an example of Jud Fry's event list from *Oklahoma!*

Table 6-2

Characters involved with Jud	*Jud's events*	*Plot*
Act I, scene i Laurey's farmyard, summer, morning		
Curly, Aunt Eller	Jud enters carrying firewood, exits into house.	We meet Jud.
Curly, Aunt Eller, Laurey	Jud enters from house with Laurey, announces he is taking Laurey to the Box Social, exits.	Curly loses his chance to take Laurey to the dance.

Characters involved with Jud	Jud's events	Plot

Act I, scene ii   The smokehouse on Laurey's farm, later that morning

Characters involved with Jud	Jud's events	Plot
Curly	Curly comes to Jud's room to confront him; song: *'Pore Jud Is Daid'*. Curly tries to convince Jud to commit suicide. Jud alludes to a dark past and violent compulsions. They argue. Both fire their pistols – but not at each other.	Curly confronts Jud.
Curly, Aunt Eller, Peddler	Aunt Eller and Peddler come in response to gunshots. Aunt Eller exits. Curly exits. As he does so, Jud threatens violence if Laurey doesn't go with him to the dance. Peddler stays to make a sale.	Jud threatens Curly.
Peddler	Peddler tries to make a sale, fails. Jud asks for a long knife, or better, a "Little Wonder." Peddler exits.	Jud tries to buy a weapon.
(Jud is alone)	Jud sings a personal lament: *'Lonely Room'*, decides to stop suffering and act on his desires.	Jud decides to act.

Act I, scene iii   A grove on Laurey's farm, later that morning

Characters involved with Jud	Jud's events	Plot
Laurey, Ado Annie, Girls from Bushyhead	Laurey's dream reveals deep fears about Jud. She is woken from this dream by the real Jud who has come to take her to the dance.	Jud wakes Laurey and takes her to the Box Social.

Act II, scene i   The Skidmore ranch, late that afternoon

Characters involved with Jud	Jud's events	Plot
Will, Peddler	Jud enters looking for Laurey, buys "Little Wonder," leaves to go to the auction.	Jud gets a weapon to kill Curly.

Table 6-2 continued

Characters involved with Jud	Jud's events	Plot
Full Company	Jud and Curly fight a symbolic duel over Laurey's hamper. Curly wins. Jud loses.	Curly wins the auction. Jud loses.
Curly, Peddler, Aunt Eller, Skidmore	Jud is forced to shake Curly's hand, and with false camaraderie tries to show Curly the "Little Wonder." Alerted by the Peddler, Aunt Eller interrupts them. A dance begins. Jud interrupts a dance between the Peddler and Laurey and sweeps her offstage.	Jud almost kills Curly, is deflected, and takes Laurey off to be alone with her.

Act II, scene ii Kitchen porch of Skidmore Ranch, immediately after

Laurey	Jud dances Laurey on, stops, tries to embrace her, is rebuffed, woos her, and is rejected. She fires him. He exits threatening her.	Jud gets Laurey alone to court her. He fails, loses his job, and leaves issuing threats.

Act II, scene iii Back of Laurey's house, three weeks later, the evening after Curly and Laurey's wedding

Full Company	Jud interrupts the shivaree, confronts Curly. They fight. Jud draws a knife, falls on it in the fight and is mortally wounded.	Jud returns to seek revenge and dies in a fight with Curly.

EXERCISE 6D MY STORY

Choose one character in the show you're studying and identify when he's onstage. Create a chart like Jud's.

1. List who your character interacts with.
2. Describe the story events in each scene.
3. Summarize the plot.

Backstory

UNIT 6.3.3

In order to create a pretext for their character's behavior and relationships, and because authors don't put everything into the script, most actors create a *backstory* for their role. A well-constructed backstory can answer questions about the circumstances of the characters before we meet them, their personal interconnections and motivations. But be careful. Keep your backstory rigorously congruent to the facts the author has put before the audience and make sure your invented history serves the plot.

In *Oklahoma!*, Laurey Williams' parents are nowhere in sight. Aunt Eller Murphy is the only adult living with her and the location is set as "Laurey's farm." That leaves some unanswered questions. It might help the actresses playing Laurey and Aunt Eller to fill in the blanks with a backstory that deepens their relationship and establishes a bond between them. Keep it simple and direct. Maybe Laurey's parents died in a cholera outbreak when she was 14 and her lonely spinster aunt came to live with her and run the farm. They both found family and a female friend just when they needed it the most. That gives them a strong emotional connection and a history. It would be a huge mistake to get creative and say that Laurey's parents were killed in a terrible accident in which they were run down by a surrey with a distinctive fringe, driven by a handsome cowboy who was kind to the infant Laurey, but this now leaves the adult Laurey conflicted over her simultaneous attraction and revulsion to good-looking but dangerous men . . . Stop! You're in a musical, not reclining on a Freudian couch.

EXERCISE 6E   BACKSTORY

Use the character you made the chart for and create a backstory that leads to her first entrance. Clarify and establish important relationships and life circumstances. Answer questions the author has left open about your character's past, making sure your story agrees with the author's.

UNIT 6.3.4   *What happens?*

We've broken the plot down into small story events. Now ask, "What happens within the story event?" and "What do the characters do that moves the story forward from the beginning to the end of that event?"

For instance, in *Carousel*, in the story event we'll call Billy Loses His Job, when you ask, "What happens?" you could say: Mrs. Mullins pressures Billy to choose her. Billy rejects her and her job. She fires him. That's what happens.

EXERCISE 6F   WHO DOES WHAT TO WHOM?

Choose one story event from Exercise 6B Plot Outline and give it a title. Now make a list of who does what to whom. Table 6-3 is an example using the first story event from *Oklahoma!*

Table 6-3

Story event: Laurey chooses Jud

Who	Does what	To whom
Curly	comes	to Laurey's farm.
Curly	asks	Laurey to the Box Social.
Curly	woos	Laurey with a story of the surrey he will take her in.
Curly	admits	to Laurey that the surrey is fictitious.
Laurey	accepts an invitation	to the Box Social from Jud.

How does this change your perception of the way your character functions as an aspect of the plot?

What happens . . . to me?

Let's be honest, it's all about you! But, we've resisted letting you look at it that way up until this point. You have a job to do in the story and its time to identify it. Let's imagine you're playing Curly. In *Oklahoma!* the action of the entire musical could be expressed as movement from territory to state, or frontier to farm, or wilderness to civilization. Viewed from the perspective of the whole show, Curly's journey in *Oklahoma!* is from bachelor cowboy to married farmer. That mirrors the arc of the play in a personal way. Curly becomes civilized and moves from independence to interdependence with a wife and a connection to the land and community. Here is Curly's journey through each of his scenes:

My journey from bachelor cowboy to married farmer

Act I, scene i	I woo Laurey. Laurey rejects me and chooses Jud.
Act I, scene ii	I confront Jud. It ends in a draw.
Act II, scene i	I compete with Jud for Laurey's hamper. I win but Jud forces me to sacrifice my saddle, horse and gun. In the process I give up my livelihood as a cowboy.
Act II, scene ii	I discover Laurey after Jud frightens her. We kiss. I ask her to marry me. I embrace my future as a farmer, a husband and father.
Act II, scene iii	I celebrate my wedding night. I fight Jud and in the fight Jud is mortally wounded. I go with Jud to try and help him. I return, surrender to the Judge, am tried and exonerated. I prepare to depart in the surrey for my honeymoon.

EXERCISE 6G MY STORY, PART 2

1. Give your journey a title like we did with Curly (My journey from bachelor cowboy to married farmer).
2. Ask whether your journey mirrors the arc of the entire show or runs contrary to it. Some smaller characters don't have a complete arc.
3. Break down your journey by scenes.
4. Describe what you do in each scene.

You know what you do in each scene, each story event and, in fact, the entire story. Now you can be confident that your acting choices will fulfill your obligations to the story. You may have noticed that a lot of the forward motion in the story was driven by characters wanting opposing things: conflict.

UNIT 6.4   **Conflict**

In our daily relationships with friends, family and loved ones, we often seek to avoid conflict. But in the theatre, conflict is a good thing. Conflict between characters, between ideas or philosophical perspectives, and between the great forces of human experience can operate on multiple and simultaneous levels.

UNIT 6.4.1   *Thematic conflict*

Thematic conflict expresses the major ideas at play in a story. In *Fiddler on the Roof*, we could say the struggle is one of tradition versus change. Although there are many smaller struggles that permeate this story, the most important conflicts between characters include an element of this thematic idea in which a central character fights to hang on to his traditions as his family and the world he lives in seek, or are forced, to change.

While this thematic conflict encompasses the entire story, we can also see it played out in relationships. In *Fiddler on the Roof* the protagonist, Tevye, has personal struggles that reflect the broader thematic conflicts: Traditional Tevye versus his Progressive Daughters, Authoritarian Tevye versus his Disobedient Wife, or Tevye versus God (with whom he has a very personal relationship). Understanding this is useful to actors. If you're playing Tevye, part of your job is to be traditional and to characterize your daughters as progressive. Then you'll serve the themes of the musical through your acting choices.

For every musical there may be a wide range of valid thematic conflicts that you can identify. You'll find numerous choices on which to build your performance. Below, we list a range of thematic conflicts that doesn't begin to include all the possibilities for those shows. But, it will give you some ideas to think about:

faith vs. reason	logic vs. feeling	chaos vs. order
true love vs. obligation	independence vs. belonging	law vs. morality
fear vs. courage	innocence vs. corruption	vitality vs. repression
dreams vs. reality	freedom vs. control	image vs. reality

As you read that list (incomplete as it is) you may have recognized some thematic conflicts for shows that you've worked on. Make a choice about what you think the most important ideas are in your text and see how they conflict with opposing ideas.

If you're working on your own, the decision is yours and you can make an independent choice for the thematic conflict. But if you're in a production with a director, decisions about the thematic center of the story have probably already been made. If this isn't clear to you by the time you've gotten through a couple of rehearsals, be sure to ask the director. It's important that you hitch your horse to the director's wagon on this issue. While you might think there are better possible interpretations of the show, everyone in an acting company must be on the same page and in the same production for good or ill.

EXERCISE 6H FINDING THE THEMATIC CONFLICT

1. Make a list of single words or short phrases that express all the themes of the musical you can think of.
2. Draw lines between the themes that seem to conflict with each other. Here's a list of possible thematic issues in *Oklahoma!* you can play with.

willfulness	interdependence	community	individuality
wildness	independence	conformity	sexuality
love	family	commitment	fencing in
roaming free	civilization	frontier	territory

Next to each word on your list of themes, write a word (or series of words) that seems to oppose the first. Now place the phrase "versus" between the first word and the others. Refine the oppositional phrases to express the thematic conflicts of your musical. Feel free to rearrange different ideas to get to the heart of your interpretation.

Possible thematic pairings for *Oklahoma!*

territory vs. state	roaming free vs. fencing in
sexuality vs. love	independence vs. interdependence
pride vs. commitment	personal willfulness vs. devotion
farmer vs. rancher	frontier vs. civilization

UNIT 6.4.2 *Personal conflicts*

Personal conflict is often an expression of the thematic conflict that we just discussed. Principal characters usually embody one side or another of the thematic conflict. This is absolutely the case in *My Fair Lady*, where the theme of intellect versus feeling is embodied by the central characters, Henry Higgins and Eliza Doolittle. These two are in clear conflict with one another for most of the musical. Higgins fights to actualize Eliza's potential, while Eliza fights against his dehumanizing exercises and expectations. Later, she fights for respect from him, while he fights to keep her as a student and scientific subject. Eventually, she fights to make him love her against his insistence on keeping their relationship purely platonic. This list of evolving personal conflicts reflects the changing nature of the relationship between these two characters. You can view this personal level of conflict as a collision between shifting and developing objectives. The central characters never really end their conflict until the end of the story. Only when that central relationship has resolved its conflict can the show end.

Virtually all characters have some kind of personal conflict with all the other characters, even those characters who appear to be friends. For instance, two characters may agree about a point and compete with each other to prove the point best, as in the title song from *Guys and Dolls* where Nicely-Nicely Johnson and Benny Southstreet try to one-up each other with stories about how men lose their power to women when they fall in love. Benny and Nicely are buddies who agree on the issue, but they fight to find the best illustration of it. This is still conflict because they are fighting to win a friendly competition.

Probably the most personal level of conflict is *internal conflict*. As we studied objectives and obstacles we learned that not all obstacles come from other characters. In some cases the obstacle is within the character. He feels or needs something that conflicts with another need or feeling. Looking at the monumental *'Soliloquy'* from *Carousel*, we see Billy Bigelow wrestle with his own anticipated fatherhood, his expectations about having a son and, eventually, with his inadequacy to raise a daughter. Billy never interacts with another person for the entirety of this twelve-minute song, during which he makes a complete reversal of his position from swaggering braggart to tender caretaker to fierce protector. Billy's own internal obstacles prompt these changes one step at a time.

Conflict in musical comedies

In more contemporary dramatic musicals it is often clear what kinds of conflict we're dealing with. *Les Misérables, Aida, Rent*, etc. all involve strong thematic and personal conflicts. Even in texts from the early years of musical comedy (*Anything Goes, Lady, Be Good!, Pal Joey*, etc.) and even recent comic musicals (*The Producers, Dirty Rotten Scoundrels, Urinetown*) these conflicts still exist and fuel the action of the story. The difference between more dramatic works and their comic cousins often lies not in how seriously the characters take these conflicts, but in how the creators intend an audience to take them. For Billy Crocker in *Anything Goes*, winning the hand of the girl he loves is no less important or filled with personal conflict than for Eponine in *Les Misérables* as she fights to gain the affection of Marius. The difference has more to do with the dramatic tone of the two shows and with how seriously the dramatists frame the conflicts. Billy's struggle is punctuated with overtly silly mistaken identities and witty songs, and a gallery of broadly comic characters surrounds him. But, the character's goals and struggles are no less life and death from his point of view and the conflicts he faces from opposing forces no less fierce than those of characters in shows with a more dramatic tone.

Look closely and you'll see that *Urinetown* and *The Producers* embody the individual versus society. You could make a strong case for romantic love versus family responsibility in the Gershwins' *Lady, Be Good!*. The tone of your production and the levity of the script and score will affect how you express these high-stakes conflicts, which are still desperately real for your character.

Characters carry the argument

Every piece of dramatic writing expresses ideas that the writers want to explore. These can be as profound as questions about the human experience or they can be as simple as affirmations of the joy and silliness of life. Musicals address every aspect of our lives. All themes are persuasive arguments to shift the audience toward the writers' point of view. One of our jobs as actors in a musical is to identify what the creators wanted to say, or what they might want an audience to walk away thinking or feeling. Since the actor is the main communicator of these ideas and themes, we ought to know what we're really singing and dancing about. Failing to identify these central issues in your text can lead you to build a performance that is fundamentally at odds with the rest of your production.

The questions the composer, lyricist and librettist want to address are played out by individual characters that function to bring the argument into relief by opposing it, representing one dimension of it, personifying it, or otherwise serving the main theme rhetorically. So, the personal conflicts between various characters are often an expression of the broader thematic conflicts at the heart of your show.

UNIT 6.5.1   *Characters embody values*

Central characters embody different sides of the thematic argument. Identify what those characters stand for and how your role relates to it. We often see the central characters in a musical taking action based on a strong set of beliefs, prejudices or attitudes. In *Carousel*, Billy Bigelow believes that those around him will betray him, so he acts out against society and those who try to get close to him. In his worldview, other people are out to get him. Julie Jordan, his eventual wife, loves him immediately and unconditionally. In her worldview, other people are worthy of love. The central characters embody two different sets of values about love and acceptance. Their worldviews are in conflict. It is only when Billy accepts Julie's love and finally returns it, in his afterlife, that their relationship can come to resolution and he can ascend to heaven. So, the theme of the redemptive and healing power of love runs strongly through *Carousel*, and it is played out through the conflicts in the values of the central characters.

Another set of ideas that runs powerfully through *Carousel* is the right to the American Dream for some and disenfranchisement for others. Billy and Julie live on the edges of that dream at the beginning of the show and are exiled from it on the night they meet, when both sets of employers fire them for associating with each other. But Julie's best friend, Carrie Pipperidge, dutifully obeys her boss and is engaged to an ambitious young fisherman named Enoch Snow. While Billy and Julie fall further into economic and personal distress, Carrie and Enoch's fortunes rise according to his plans. The theme of haves versus have-nots is vividly expressed through this secondary couple, and it contrasts with Julie's troubled life. The actors playing that secondary couple need to understand that their roles are written to stand in contrast to the central couple. Acting choices can help support those contrasts in creative ways: physical behavior, vocal colorings, choices of relationship, values to embody, etc.

This I believe

One of the most common song forms is the statement of a character's philosophy. We see this in almost every musical. Henry Higgins has at least three such songs in *My Fair Lady*: *'Why Can't the English?'*, *'I'm an Ordinary Man'*, and *'A Hymn to Him'*. Each of these songs exposes a different aspect of his critical and self-celebrating personality and strongly expresses one side of the central ideological tensions in the script and score. Higgins represents an inhumanly rational view of relationships. Eliza Doolittle has her own, much simpler and more sweetly melodic expression of philosophy in *'Wouldn't It Be Loverly'* where she fantasizes about a few simple comforts and tender love. She represents all the things that Higgins is not: feeling, sentiment and intuition. Eliza's unrepentantly amoral father, Alfred P. Doolittle, embodies a third part of the ideological equation in this musical. He sings *'With a Little Bit of Luck'* as an expression of his hope that he can have all the benefits of polite society without any of the responsibilities. Each character represents an important set of values in *My Fair Lady*, and the songs each sings describe that point of view.

As we continue to explore different aspects of dramatic structure, you'll probably begin to realize that theme and idea are woven into all of them. The great value of investigating theme and idea is that it can ensure that you build a performance that supports your production rather than fighting against it.

Dramatic function

Every scene and musical moment is created to help tell the story in a way that is compelling, interesting, entertaining, structurally sound or one of many other valid reasons. Authors, composers and lyricists have multiple agendas to serve as they craft a musical. Even as the writing choices are motivated by the characters, situations and conflicts, each musical moment often has several functions. For instance a song may convey necessary exposition. It may reveal the nature of the character singing it or chart a change in that character. It may afford the stage crew the opportunity to change the set behind a backdrop or allow an actor to make a costume change. Even practical considerations need to be dramatically justified. Every moment must have a *dramatic function*. The questions to ask are:

UNIT 6.6.1 *Why is it there?*

Every song is essential on multiple levels. Late in Act I of *Fiddler on the Roof*, in 'The Dream', Tevye tells his wife, Golde, of a dream that he's had which foretells a terrible tragedy if she allows their daughter, Tzeitel, to marry the butcher, Lazar Wolf. As Tevye recounts the dream (which he has made up), it comes to life onstage. This *musical moment* has a number of important functions. First, it allows Tevye to convince his wife to abandon the firm tradition of having her daughter pledged in marriage through a matchmaker. Second, it shows us how superstitious Golde is and reveals her respect and reverence for her deceased relatives. The number also provides the audience with a full-company spectacle sequence that is dramatically different from what has come before. Variety matters in this type of musical. As staged by director-choreographer Jerome Robbins, the number displayed a great sense of humor and reflected the visual world of painter Marc Chagall, whose work inspired the scenic design and the title of the show. Additionally, no other sequence in the show has this degree of fantasy and sustained humor. It builds the mood of the show in a positive direction that leads beautifully into the romantic, then raucous, then tragic wedding sequence. So, this one number does an awful lot for the show in terms of dramatic function.

UNIT 6.6.2 *Dramatic function of reprises*

Reprises depend on the audience's familiarity with both the musical and emotional contexts of a song they've heard before. When creators choose to repeat a song, it is done in reference to that first appearance, and with the idea that something has changed. A character may be reflecting on an earlier moment of joy in a relationship that has now gone sour, or echoing the feelings of the character who first sang the song. He may be commenting on himself at an earlier point or on the object of the song when he first sang it. Variations in the musical or lyric information of the reprise can tell you what the point of this reprise is. It's safe to assume that any time a song is repeated there is a conscious choice by the creators; they didn't just run out of tunes.

We're going to continue exploring the dramatic function of the first few songs in *Fiddler on the Roof*. Notice how many purposes each piece serves and how effectively the creators achieved these purposes.

Table 6-4

Musical moment	Characters	Dramatic function	What happens
'Tradition' (robust, uptempo, Freygish-scaled song)	Tevye and all the Jewish villagers, plus Constable and Priest	• Establishes the roles of each segment of Jewish society in Anatevka: what is expected of each and how they relate to and depend upon each other. • Introduces most of the secondary characters quickly and with humor. • Establishes Tevye as the protagonist and the audience's surrogate. • Sets the convention of Tevye talking directly to the audience.	Roles are fortified. Beliefs are affirmed. Nothing changes – that's the point!
'Matchmaker' (moderate waltz)	Tzeitel, Chava, Hodel	• Reveals the yearning of the young girls to receive romantically appealing matches, and their fear about what could happen if they don't. • Reveals how powerful and important the matchmaker, Yente, is in their lives – setting up her entrance in the next scene • Plants the seeds for all of the girls' later decisions about choosing their mates and taking charge of their futures. • Establishes the girls' worldview before change begins.	Tzeitel wakes Hodel and Chava up to the reality of their circumstances as victims of Yente's questionable taste in husbands. The girls go from adolescent fantasy about their mates to fearful young women.
'If I Were a Rich Man' (moderate Yiddish folk song feeling)	Tevye	• Reveals Tevye's priorities and his philosophy. This is an important character exposition song because we will follow Tevye through the entire story as our protagonist.	Tevye fantasizes about his life as a rich man.

Table 6-4 continued

Musical moment	Characters	Dramatic function	What happens
		At this point in the show we need to really meet him. • Develops the dramatic device of him talking to God on a casual first person basis.	
'Sabbath Prayer' (strongly Jewish prayer, with echoes of Cantorial singing)	Tevye, his family, Motel, Perchik, the rest of the Jews of Anatevka	• Establishes the importance of faith in the world of the Jews of Anatevka. • Completes the exposition phase of the show. Until now, we've spent much of our time learning about the world of the show and the given circumstances of the characters. • Provides the last element of revealing the status quo, and one of the most important given circumstances – the town's fundamental belief in God and His relationship to their lives. • It is an affirmation of the basic values of the faith, family and community. Every element of this song will be tested over the remainder of the show.	Tevye's family, his guests, and the entire village of Anatevka, in fact the whole world of faithful Jews, affirm their faith through the traditional lighting of Sabbath candles.

You can see how this kind of examination of the function and action of a song can put it into a different perspective from what you might have considered before.

If you were playing the role of Tevye and you knew that a song contained critical exposition you might make singing and acting choices that helped illuminate those important points. If you knew that a song was there to reveal Tevye's philosophy, you might heighten a range of personality traits that we don't get to see at other times, or that hint at qualities, events and actions yet to come. Since religion emerges as an important aspect of his makeup, you would probably treat those moments of deep faith with special attention. Understanding dramatic function can make you a valuable member of any company and the actor that directors want to cast again and again because of your instincts about how to serve an entire production with your performance.

Kinds of text

What a character says and *how* she says it are among the clearest ways that we understand and identify her. In a play, the term text refers to the spoken word. But in a musical, it also means lyrics, music, underscoring and even choreography.

The most critical part of a character's experience usually comes in the form of song or dance. In *Fiddler on the Roof*, the character of Tevye would be woefully ill-defined without the songs *'Tradition', 'If I Were a Rich Man', 'Sunrise, Sunset', 'Chavelah'* and *'Do You Love Me?'*. The book scenes he participates in are certainly important. But, it is through these songs that Tevye takes his greatest journeys and through which much of the story is developed and played out.

The more specific the characteristics of the various texts are, the sooner an audience can get to know and identify with a character. Speech patterns, dialect, voice type, movement, choreography and personal musical style all help to define character.

UNIT 6.7.1 *Spoken and sung text*

Dialect, lexicon (or vocabulary), grammar and idiom all reveal things like region, education, intellect, social caste, beliefs and overall worldview: the given circumstances of the character as revealed through voice.

In *The King and I*, the King speaks in a kind of broken English. He omits certain words, uses words in a slightly off-kilter manner, and grabs onto new phrases which he thinks will make him appear more civilized, intelligent and "scientific." So, the qualities of his dialogue tell us a good deal about his comfort with English culture, his ambitions for perception by others, and his ego. All of these are central to the story and this character. Conversely, in the same show, Anna Leonowens uses English with elegance and great facility. She has mastered the subtleties of the English language and is willing to explain them. She is highly intelligent, yet she uses that intelligence discreetly and with modesty. The contrasts between these two central characters' use of language are indicative of their differences and their conflicts. The actors playing these two roles gain a great deal by exploring these contrasts and heightening them.

UNIT 6.7.2 *Musical dialect*

Characters in musicals sound different from each other. In the same way the symphonic composer Tchaikovsky assigned a different musical motif and instrument to each of the characters in *Peter and the Wolf*, musical theatre composers create distinct musical "dialects" for their characters to distinguish them from each other and to help us identify them. The musical style and qualities of a musical moment tell you something about what is going on inside the character; it is her emotional underscore. Using our example from *The King and I*, we can see great contrasts in the central characters' musical dialect. The King sings in a set of Asian-sounding modes. The rhythms of his songs echo his spoken style completely and are almost exclusively comprised of spoken, patter songs. Anna, by contrast, sings in a fluid, gentle fashion – nearly all ballads, or gently brighter tempi. Her precise diction is reinforced in the music. The musical "voice" of the characters is in complete agreement with their spoken text. These two characters have distinctly different ways of seeing the world and of expressing themselves, and the musical information provided by Richard Rodgers makes this clear. A sensitive actor can pick up on the musical and linguistic differences between these characters to express the contrasts between the power and arrogance of the King and the grace and poise of Anna.

Physical texts

Dance can be a powerful and specific form of text in a musical. In *Brigadoon*, two characters are developed almost exclusively in danced text. Harry Beaton (who does have a few spoken lines, though no sung dialogue) and the totally mute Maggie Anderson. This storyline offers a different form of dialogue and requires physical specificity and expressiveness, but all characters have the requirement to be defined through movement. Just as everyone in a story doesn't talk and sing alike, they also don't need to move alike. Think how odd it would be to see Henry Higgins, Eliza Doolittle and Colonel Pickering all dancing in perfect, anonymous unison in *'The Rain in Spain'* from *My Fair Lady*. The point of the song and the dance within it is to allow them to celebrate Eliza's victorious mastery of proper spoken English in their own individual ways. Heighten those differences or defeat the purpose of the song. When you play an ensemble role, however, the choreographer may ask you to dance just like all the other people in the ensemble. This makes sense because, as a member of the ensemble, you are often really just one part of a collective character; the chorus. So, you share a common physical identity. Compare the little old ladies in *The Producers* to Leo Bloom's fantasy chorines, to the homogenized Arian storm troopers in the same show. Each group shares a distinct character identity expressed with uniform physicality.

Location, location, location

In the first scene of *Oklahoma!* the location is Laurey's farmyard. Aunt Eller is on the porch. She is the regent and the determiner of status for all visitors. It is also, significantly, a farm, and Curly is a cowboy. He doesn't belong on a farm – his very labor is socially and practically antithetical to farming. That undercuts his right to be there and to date Laurey. Curly has come there to ask Laurey to the dance. The farmhouse is not just a short ride for Curly; he must travel across pasture and farmland at dawn to get there. It is Laurey's territory; she has the upper hand on this turf. Aunt Eller favors Curly enough to give him some power here, though. Because we soon discover the story is really Laurey's, it is important we be on her terrain. The authors might have chosen some place else, but it would have had to favor her equally or better to make it a good choice; by placing this on neutral territory (like a store in town), we could weaken the story. This location is also a central meeting place for most of the characters in the story by virtue of its distance from the Skidmore Ranch where the dance will be held that night. So others congregate here over the course of the day as well. But, Laurey always maintains high status over the others because it is her home.

Later, when we go to Jud's Smokehouse, we have a whole new location dynamic in play. This is Jud's private domain. It is also the only interior location in the entire musical. That alone sets it apart. The darkness, sooty walls, lewd postcards and claustrophobic quality are metaphors for Jud's inner life and stand in stark contrast to the open, natural exteriors of the rest of the show. Importantly, this scene is the one time in the entire show he is in control. Otherwise, Jud is primarily an outsider fighting to be let into the group. Jud's domination of the space is a major obstacle to Curly's success. The location, secluded and private, puts Curly at a disadvantage. In his soliloquy, *'Lonely Room'*, Jud describes the space in powerful detail. So, his territory is clearly important to him and the dramatists. At the end of this scene, Curly attacks him by using Jud's living conditions as ammunition.

UNIT 6.9 **Time**

Time of day, season and historical period are important given circumstances that must be contended with. In our example of *Oklahoma!*, the play begins the morning of the dance. The choice to keep the action on that day heightens the pressure on everyone to fight for their desired outcomes, and to make quick (sometimes rash) decisions. If Laurey had several days to think about her decision to go to the dance with Jud, she might have changed her mind, he might have quit in frustration, or Curly may have had time to propose to her before the dance. Time pressure conspires to make things harder for the characters to react rationally and more interesting for the audience.

Time also includes year and season, which can have a subtle but potent effect on the characters. Curly tells us, "The corn is as high as an elephant's eye." So it must be that time in summer when corn is at its highest point before harvesting. There is also "a little brown maverick" in the pasture. So the calves are still young and frisky. This powerfully fertile time of year conspires toward romance and coupling up of these young people. For people who live on a farm, this is an important time of year.

Finally, there is the historical period. The authors have conspicuously set the piece just before the Oklahoma Territory became a state in the Union. In the show's first production, this would have been within living memory of many members of the audience. The show is set at a time of great hope and optimism for the future. Importantly, everyone in that first audience would vividly recall the ravaging Dust Bowl of the 1930s and the devastating effect it had on Oklahoma. So this show and the final song offer hope for the nation and for that state in particular. A word of caution for contemporary actors: this is an optimistic story from the 1940s. We need to understand all of that history and yet not indulge in the modern preoccupation with irony.

Sometimes a script like Meredith Wilson's *The Music Man* will give you a clear set of clues for using the element of time to great effect. The show takes place over the span of a summer in a year after 1907 and just before World War I. The historical time period is an important given circumstance for the show because audiences can identify this as the last days of America's innocence before the horror of our first modern war. For audiences that saw the show in its original production in 1957, this would have easily been within their childhood years. So, the choice of historical period would have been important to the show's original context, though that has changed now. *Grease* had a similar nostalgic association when it was written, just as the musical of *The Wedding Singer* did for its original audiences. Interestingly, all of these shows represent an idealized view of the past that doesn't reflect the political complexities, social difficulties or any of the darker aspects of their chosen era. These are carefully selected representations of a time period.

Another aspect for us to consider is the length of time the story spans. In *The Music Man*, the time between con man Harold Hill's arrival, when he sets the town ablaze with fear for their young boys' moral wellbeing, and the end of the first act when his band instruments arrive, is six weeks, compressed into a handful of scenes. But, the changes in his relationship to the town are significant. He has had time to build trust with some townsfolk, and to arouse intense suspicion from others. We can calculate that since he's been in town from July Fourth, summer is ending and the season is about to change. Hill has stayed in town long enough to risk being found out, and to form permanent attachments to Marian and her brother.

Time itself can form a valuable pressure on the characters. In *Brigadoon*, the alienated Harry Beaton has disrupted the wedding of Jean, the girl he loves, with a threat to leave Brigadoon and end the miracle that brings the village back to life one day every century. If the villagers don't stop him before night falls, they will all vanish in the mist, never to return. Time pressure here is vital.

A final consideration for any theatre artist is how your production relates to today. Are the themes and ideas being dealt with relevant to your experience? Can you find a personal connection to the characters, the conflicts and the message? While it may be fun to be in a show or important to have work as a professional actor, the most treasured experiences for any performing artist come from productions where we feel what we say as the characters speaks for us as artists, citizens and members of the human race.

Visual elements – how design affects your performance

Beyond creating an aesthetically pleasing frame for the story, design elements offer information about how to build a characterization. Pay attention when designers do their presentations at the beginning of rehearsals. If you're working on a scene on your own, research designs from past productions.

There are times where the script requires a scenic element. Tony and Maria must have a fire escape in *West Side Story* for their version of Romeo and Juliet's balcony scene. Huck and Jim spend about a third of their time in *Big River* on a raft. The physical shape of the playing space can add opportunities and obstacles to your performance. Props can have the same effect. Tevye hauls a milk cart around the stage for much of *Fiddler on the Roof*. Try playing Horton in *Seussical* and you'll soon discover the major scenic element you deal with is a rolling tree you sit on for almost half the show. These will affect your performance significantly, so it behooves you to include scenic elements in your creative process.

Design elements not only entertain and support the story, but also help us to know something more about the characters' world and their experience. Earlier, we talked about the time pressure in *Brigadoon*. There is a necessary visual element in the script that tangibly expresses the approaching end of their day: fog. As Tommy fights to decide whether to stay in Brigadoon or return to his modern life, he knows his time is almost up because the stage begins filling with a low, rolling fog, and he must make a decision immediately. The actor in that role knows this will fuel his performance and he must react to it. That fog also adds an element of real danger for the actors in the chase scene from the same show. Running around scenery, leaping off rocks, throwing each other around in choreographed stage fights all becomes exponentially more complex with wet fog onstage.

Imagine you've been hired to play Curly in a regional production of *Oklahoma!* You've researched the original production thoroughly and made clear decisions about how to move, sing and act in the role. On the first day of rehearsal you watch the design presentations where you discover that Laurey wears overalls and no shoes, the prop master offers to teach you how to hand roll cigarettes, and the set for Laurey's farmyard includes a rusting hulk of an old thresher. This is a radically different visual world than you imagined. But, it is the one that your production will live in. Think of the ways you will need to adjust your interpretation to harmonize with this production approach.

Designers and directors work to create a visual world that expresses their interpretation of the text. Those visual cues can tell you about the point of view of your production.

Designs for a musical often inform the audience about the world of the show more powerfully than anything else. Consider these elements carefully and use them to your advantage.

A review

This is a questionnaire you can use to incorporate the material from this chapter.

Divide and conquer your text

1. What internal scenes have you identified?
   a. Have major characters come or gone?
   b. Were there songs and/or dances that caused major changes to the story and action?
   c. Was something significant completed or deliberately tabled?
2. Are the internal scenes the same as the French scenes (a change in the number of people onstage)?
3. Do the musical moments form separate internal scenes?

Plot

4. What is the plot of this scene/unit?
5. Which story events does the author choose to show (or leave out)?
6. What story events am I involved with in the entire script and score?
7. What's my character's backstory?

What happens?

8. What is the action of the entire script and score?
9. What is the arc of my character over the course of the show? Does that match the arc of the show?
10. What happens to my character in each story event?
11. What does my character do in each event that moves the story forward?

Conflict

12. How are the themes of the musical expressed in conflict?
13. What are the personal conflicts for my character?
14. How do these conflicts change over the course of the story?

15. How do the personal conflicts propel the dramatic action?
16. How does the music reveal conflict?

Theme

17. What values do the central characters embody?
18. What is the writer's argument? What part of the argument do I carry?
19. Do the central characters sing any songs or make any speeches that express a strong perspective or philosophy?
20. How does that statement of belief reflect the themes of the musical?

Dramatic function

21. Why is the song or musical sequence included?
22. What does the song do for the show?
23. What does it do for a specific character?
24. Does the song, scene or musical moment facilitate some important technical requirement for the show? If so, how can I translate that into a character need?

Reprises

25. How does the song function in a reprise compared to the first time we heard it?
26. What does the reprise tell us about the character compared to the first time we heard it?
27. If the same character doesn't sing it in a reprise, then why did the authors give it to a different character?
28. Are the lyrics different this time? If so, what do they tell you about how the character has changed? If not, why is the character saying the same thing now?
29. Are there any musical differences between the first time the song is sung and in its reprises? (changes of key, tempo, melodic variations, emotional qualities)
30. Is there any irony in the reprised version?

Kinds of text

Spoken and sung

31. How does the way my character speaks reflect: education, intellect, values, region, caste and time period?

32. How is the character's way of speaking different from my own? And from the other characters onstage?

Musical dialect

33. Does the music my character sings reflect any given circumstances, like culture or temperament?

Physical

34. How does my movement or choreographic text reflect given circumstances, culture, temperament and dramatic moment?
35. Do I move as an individual or as part of a group character?
36. How do I infuse the choreography with character behavior?

Location

37. Where does the scene/unit take place?
38. Could the scene easily happen somewhere else?
39. Why did the authors choose to set it here?
40. Does the location tell you anything about the characters?
41. Whose "territory" is the location?

Time

42. When does the play take place?
43. Does time play an important role in the text?
44. What is the time span of the action?
45. How much time passes between scenes (and each of my entrances)?
46. How is the time period important?
47. When was the musical written and how does the cultural perspective of that time shape the values and viewpoints of the show?
48. How does the show relate to my own time?

Visual elements

49. What design elements does the script require?
50. How do these elements add to the story?
51. How do the designs for this production inform my work as an actor?
52. How realistic or stylized are the designs, and how do they suggest a performing style to me?
53. Do the designs suggest any adjectives to me? (romantic, disjointed, tragic, comic strip, etc.)

54. How do costumes and props inform me regarding personality, movement, social status, self-esteem, etc.?
55. How do the costume designs for my character relate to those for other characters? Do I look strongly similar to or strongly different from other characters in the show?

UNIT 6.12   ## How to use this information

We have discussed a wide range of ideas and information to be gotten from a musical script and score that can help you understand the text intimately as you prepare your role. But, how you choose to use this information is a personal thing and will not be the same for any two actors or any two roles. Like a detective, you've examined all the possible sources of evidence. Now, the job is to put the pieces together in a way that makes sense to you and agrees with the perspective of your particular production. We suggest you allow the most potent discoveries to guide you: those bits of information from any of these areas (and others) that seem most central to your role. We also suggest you give yourself time to digest the information. Rushing to quick judgments can lead you in odd directions if you're not careful. Also, be careful that what you have done doesn't simply confirm everything you wanted to feel about a role before you started the investigation. Your gut reaction may have been very accurate. But you may also have found new information that could lead you to a performance you never would have imagined.

SECTION II: SCORE AND LIBRETTO ANALYSIS AND STRUCTURE

CHAPTER 7

CHARACTER ANALYSIS

Introduction

For many actors, creating a character is one of the greatest pleasures of the rehearsal process. Deciding how to step into the imaginary shoes talented writers have cobbled can be fascinating, revealing, and intellectually and emotionally challenging. This chapter will help you build that character on a strong foundation of script and score analysis. As you begin combing through your texts for information about the character this is a good time to identify what will be useful to you and where to look.

"What is a character?" As much as we like to think of characters as having human qualities, it's important to remember a character is an "it," not a "who." Characters are invented by writers and don't exist independently of the writer or, later, of the actors who embody them on stage. Characters are limited in the scope of their actions to what the author wanted or needed them to do in order to make his point. Characters are unlike real people in a number of ways:

1. *Characters do not have the ability to act independently.* Human beings act autonomously with free will.
2. *Characters are highly predictable and consistent in their actions.* Human beings are unpredictable and behave in ways we cannot anticipate.
3. *Characters express themselves in carefully crafted forms of dialogue.*

Human beings are mostly unedited in their expression and often are tongue-tied or require extended, meandering discussion to articulate their ideas, needs and feelings.

4. *Characters in musicals express themselves through song and dance, as well as through speech.* Generally, human beings express themselves almost exclusively through speech and unstructured physical behavior.

The actor's job in interpreting a script is to take the information provided by the author and expand on it in ways that help an audience experience the character as human and real. Audiences must believe the behavior of the character to be spontaneous, truthful and consistent in order to buy in to the dramatic experience. Since no script is complete enough to answer all the questions you'll have, intelligent filling in of the blank spots is required. Rank your character choices and decisions in the following order:

1. *Information provided by the author.* This is non-negotiable and must be accepted as the foundation of all other choices. If the author says the character is from rural France, you must go along with that and not make other choices that negate or undermine this fact.

2. *Inferences based on the information provided in the script.* You need to make additional choices about the character based on the information in the text. If we know the story takes place in the poorer sections of Paris during the French Revolution, following your factual research, you can safely assume many things about living conditions, sanitation, hygiene, fashion, physical circumstances, nutrition, politics, etc. Even though the author didn't explicitly tell you all of this, you can infer specific character details from general facts.

3. *Fantasy and imagination based on the information and inferences you've drawn.* Imagination is your best friend. You need to imagine your character's experiences before and surrounding the action. But the cardinal rule of imagination and fantasy is that you may not invent anything that disagrees with either the *information* provided by the author or the reasonable and well-supported *inferences* you've made.

These three ways of arriving at your given circumstances are in order of priority because the first supports the second, and the first and second supports the third. If you place imagination and fantasy at the head of the list, ignoring the writers' mandates, you will inevitably start making choices that are inconsistent with the text and your other creative collaborators' well-founded choices.

Exposition

In an ideal world you could sit with the authors, or the character herself, and go down a list of questions that would tell you everything you needed to know about her life and her world. But, since that's really not possible, you'll need to do the next best thing. You'll fill out that questionnaire yourself based on these four means of *exposition*.

Characters tell us about themselves

Characters talk and sing about themselves a lot in musicals. Often you'll sing a song that serves the purpose of telling us all about your character. Songs like *'I Cain't Say No'* from *Oklahoma!*, *'Cockeyed Optimist'* from *South Pacific*, or *'My White Knight'* from *The Music Man* are *exposition songs* that tell us about a character. We find out how a character feels about herself and the people in her world, and what she hopes for. While characters assert a lot about themselves that is accurate or reliable, remember to question whether it is truthful, exaggerated or self-deprecating. The character may want to make a specific impression on the person they're singing to and choose to tell the truth selectively. Or they may be lying or exaggerating for another purpose. In *110 in the Shade*, Starbuck lies to the townsfolk about his ability to produce rain in *'The Rain Song'*. He makes false claims about his powers.

Characters tell us about each other

Characters talk and sing about each other in musicals and plays. *'You're a Queer One, Julie Jordan'* from *Carousel* is complete character profile by Julie's best friend. Remember to question the accuracy of and motives behind these statements. The classic example of this is in *The Music Man* when the "Pick-a-little" ladies tell Professor Harold Hill everything they think he needs to know about the town's librarian, Marion Paroo. Their assertions about her are actually nothing but innuendo and misinterpretation of Marion's past. Because these town gossips have a long-standing prejudice against her they have skewed every event in her life to support their beliefs. Later in the show, Hill discovers she is quite the opposite of the manipulative harlot they have accused Marion of being.

UNIT 7.1.3   *Authors tell us about characters*

You will sometimes be given important information by the author in descriptive passages and in stage directions. In *Carousel*, librettist Oscar Hammerstein II describes Julie Jordan as "more complex, quieter, deeper" than her friend, Carrie Pipperidge. Things reliable characters say about her, as well, support this.

UNIT 7.1.4   *The characters' actions tell us about them*

A character's actions speak loudly about what is important to him. This can be the trickiest way of finding out about a character because so much of the action we ascribe to characters in performance is decided in rehearsal between actor and director. But scripts do tell us important pieces of stage business, such as when Julie is riding the carousel for the first time in *Carousel*. When Billy Bigelow waves to her, Hammerstein tells us, "It means so much to her that she nearly falls off!" This is a good indication of her feelings and state of mind. In *Fiddler on the Roof*, Tevye shuns his daughter, Chava, because she marries a Christian. He says she is dead to him. Yet, when the family is preparing to leave their village forever, Tevye softens his position and passes positive messages to her through his wife and oldest daughter. His behavior (what he does) reveals he still cares for her and is beginning to accept her radical decision.

The next three units in this chapter will cover the facts, attitudes and ambitions of the character. Identify these useful types of information using the four means of exposition we discussed. You may not find all of it, and probably won't. But, you can begin creating a dossier on your character. Whatever you don't find out from the script, you can invent, based on what you do find.

UNIT 7.2   **Character facts**

Be a good detective. Put together a dossier on the character.

Name (full name, if possible): Characters often go by multiple versions of their name. Nicknames, affectionate shortened names, formal names, etc. In *Guys and Dolls*, Sarah Brown calls Sky Masterson Obadiah because it comes from the Bible and he has told only her it is his given name. All of his friends call him Sky. Lt. Brannigan, the policeman, calls him Masterson.

Age: Be as specific as you can. "In her 20s" isn't the same as "22." This some-times has to do with your assessment of the character's maturity given the historical period and your own understanding of the character. But specificity matters in building a character.

Height: Is she taller than you? Shorter? The same height? Does this matter to the author? Does it affect your understanding of the character and the important relationships in her life?

Weight: The same questions from above about height apply for weight. This may mean you behave or dress differently to help affect this change. Weight can affect relationships, self-perception, and the way other people treat your character. However, it doesn't mean you necessarily have to change your own physical makeup for the role. And if you do, it must be done in a healthy way.

Posture/physical stature: How does the character use her body? At ease, how does she stand? Qualities such as erectness, slouch, leaning into the pelvis, thrusting the chest, dropping the chin to avoid direct visual contact, etc. can be important keys to characterization. What is the relationship between posture/physical stature and her self-image and relationship goals?

General and specific health: Does your character have any illnesses or physical handicaps? Is she prone to any kind of weakness? Any physical manifestations of lifestyle? Playing many of the characters in *Rent* would require you to investigate the physical effects of drug use, alcohol, HIV/AIDS and the medication AZT (then the only available treatment for AIDS), etc. These are important aspects of the character that can't be overlooked because they are talked about in the script and are well known to many audience members.

Place of birth: In *South Pacific*, Nellie Forbush tells us she was born in Little Rock, Arkansas. This is an important fact of the character because of regional belief systems, her accent and behavior, etc.

Place of residence: For how long? Nellie is a transient. She has been stationed in the South Pacific on an island as a nurse with the US Navy. However, we know DeBecque has lived there long enough to build up a large and successful plantation, to have children with a Polynesian woman who has died, and to establish himself as an important figure among the planters on this island. His mastery of the island is a key factor in their relationship and in the action of the plot.

A character's reason for living where he does may also offer you useful information. DeBecque is definitely an expatriate, while Nellie's reason for being on the island is patriotic. The place they reside is the same, but their reasons are exactly opposite. (In fact, DeBecques transformation into a patriot is one of the important journeys of the story.)

Occupation: What does your character do for a living or as a daily activity? For how long? We know Nellie is a nurse, ranked Ensign according to the newspaper clipping she shares.

Income: This may only be a guess. But you can figure out a character's economic bracket and start to decide the economic class and the kinds of financial pressures being exerted on them. In *My Fair Lady*, Eliza takes the change she's been given for flowers and brings it to Higgins for speech lessons. He actually does the math and decides that, for her, this meager sum is the equivalent of a huge amount for his usual clients. His calculation is enormously useful to you in playing the role because it tells you how much she earns and what her economic status is.

Group identity: This is how your character sees himself as a member of an ethnic, racial, cultural or national group. What is your character's group identity? Is it different from your self-identification? Do other characters place importance on this aspect of your character? You may need to consider carefully whether you are required to make changes to your appearance in order to fulfill the specific obligations of the role. In some cases, it is now considered inappropriate to cast an actor from one ethnic or racial group in a role defined as being from a different one. In other cases, this is not an obstacle. This decision may also be influenced by the approach of your production. Be sensitive to the feelings of others. Know your community's standards. Have an awareness of changing theatrical traditions.

Dialect/diction/accent: Does the writing of the role express any distinct speech pattern? Many authors give an indication of a dialect or accent by employing an eye dialect (using respelling to make your eye hear a dialect). In *Oklahoma!* Hammerstein respelled words like can't (cain't) and forget (fergit) to help us hear the local lingo. Later, he has Bloody Mary in *South Pacific* use a kind of pidgin English, suggesting she has learned English informally and has not fully mastered its subtleties and nuances. Not every writer uses an eye dialect, though speech that reflects region, education, social caste, and sometimes original language, is essential to characterization. Even subtle choices about vocal placement or whether the character mumbles or over-articulates can be doorways through which we can enter that character's world. Be aware of times when the author has stipulated some vocal characteristic like Lina Lamont in *Singin' in the Rain*, as the silent film star who must have a dreadful speaking voice, or Winthrop in *The Music Man* who needs to have an extraordinary lisp, or Gertie Cummins in *Oklahoma!*, who needs to have a crazy laugh.

Social class and status: Aristocrat/peasant; lower-class flower seller/upper-class professor. Every character you play fits into some specific social ranking.

This affects how you may relate to others within and outside that group. In *My Fair Lady*, this is an obvious issue. But it is also one in *Carousel*, where Billy and Julie occupy a fairly low social status and make difficult, sometimes fateful, decisions as a result of their poverty. Class and status become pivotal in much of drama, and a character's struggle to elevate himself to a higher status can be a defining aspect of that character and a key motivator for his actions.

Social groups: Any group the character belongs to that shares a set of rules, standards or values – especially those groups that help to define him – are a social group. Cowboys, bachelors, married women, students, families, love relationships, gangs, congregations, clubs and cliques, etc. are all distinct social groups. In most cases you will discover that each character belongs to more than one social group. Identify which groups matter the most in a given scene. For Curly, being a romantic partner is the most important social group for him in the first scene of *Oklahoma!* But at the beginning of Act II, during *'The Farmer and the Cowman'*, being a cowboy is more important. At the end of the show, he is a new and jubilant member of the fraternity of married men. These changing social groups help define him from scene to scene.

Education (amount of formal or informal education, specialized training): Some characters display a high or low degree of education because of the way they speak or behave. The complexity of their language patterns and the formality of their behavior can reveal this. Different cultural and social groups place different values on formal education. Education and intelligence are not the same thing. In *South Pacific*, Emile DeBecque confesses he has almost no formal education, but has become "hungry to learn everything" and has an extensive library of great authors. He speaks at least two languages, and probably more. His curiosity about the world has led him to explore these things. So, while he lacks formal education, he has done a great deal to compensate for that.

Intelligence: The capacity for complex thinking, apparent aptitudes for different skills, and levels of intuition or sensitivity. Intelligence can be different from education, which is no guarantee of these qualities. Know where your character is on the IQ scale and what kind of intelligence he has. Oliver, for example, is innocent and so lacks the street-smart cunning the Artful Dodger has, but his emotional intelligence makes Fagin, and Nancy, and Brownlow (among others) all fall in love with him. Most characters have this sort of unbalanced intelligence. If they have one kind they often lack another. Henry Higgins is intellectually brilliant and a keen observer of human behavior, but completely blind to his own feelings.

Physical characteristics (exceptional abilities, physical attributes, handicaps): Some characters are defined by a specific physical characteristic. In *Once upon a Mattress*, King Septimus is unable to speak until the last moments of the show. So, he is defined largely by his silence and pantomimed dialogue. In cases where the author has stipulated some physical characteristic it often forms the center of the character. Think of Lucy Schmeiler in *On the Town*, who must sneeze and sniffle her way through the whole show. In *Once upon a Mattress* Winnifred is required to be strong, physically tough and clumsy. If your character is nearsighted, hard of hearing, limps, faints constantly or has uncontrollable flatulence, you had better make the physical obligations the author has given you the place you start building the character.

EXERCISES 7A GRAB BAG CHARACTER – PART I

For this set of exercises you'll need a song that is neutral, meaning that it's flexible in terms of character attributes and given circumstances.

Write a range of extreme physical circumstances on small slips of paper. Choose from this list and add some of your own:

facial twitch	rampant flatulence	leg falls asleep without warning
crossed eyes	uncontrollable sneezing	unable to hold your head up
hiccups	horrible congestion	random, unexpected cramps

Place the slips in a hat and have each actor select one. See what happens if you sing your neutral song with this one physical circumstance as the dominating given circumstance.

UNIT 7.3 **Attitudes**

What a character believes in and feels about himself and his world is a fundamental building block for character development because this motivates his behavior and actions.

Belief systems: Religion, spirituality, belief in higher powers (God or the gods). In *Carousel*, Billy Bigelow reveals his belief in the punishing hand of God that awaits him just after his death in *'The Highest Judge of All'*. He has never revealed a belief in God before.

Politics: Endorsement of any particular political or governmental structure. Politics are always an underlying aspect of the belief systems in a musical, even if they are not directly addressed. For most musicals, democracy is an assumption, but it may not always be. In *Les Misérables*, a fight for democracy is an essential part of the action. In *Of Thee I Sing*, a presidential election is the centerpiece of the story. But politics are not only the subject of musicals and plays. They are an expression of the belief systems inherent in the text itself. A character's preference for a certain kind of social organization tells us what their perfect world would look like. In the list of words rhyming with "ocracy," what would be your characters ideal? Meritocracy – Higgins; democracy – almost the whole cast of *1776* and half of *Les Misérables* (with Javert pushing for an autocracy); bureaucracy – Mayor Shinn; kleptocracy – Cladwell; theocracy, aristocracy, kakistocracy . . . pick your flavor. Consciously consider these attitudes. In some cases, a production is defined by its ability to reflect the implicit politics of the script, even though that may not have been the point in earlier productions.

Cultural attitudes: Cultural attitudes can be at the center of a character's struggle, as reflected in Lt. Cable's song *'You've Got To Be Taught'* in *South Pacific*. Cable reveals he is a victim of an underlying prejudice against non-Caucasian people, even though he is in love with a Polynesian girl. Cultural attitudes figure very differently in *Anything Goes* where Reno Sweeney catalogues the current social values of her time in the title song. She reveals her own attitudes about culture, sexuality, high and low art and so much more. This song overtly tells you almost everything you need to know about her and the world of this musical.

Occasionally a character will tell you about the social value system of a culture that is different from his, as in *'Trouble'* from *The Music Man*. In this song, Harold Hill perfectly captures the values and fears of the small Iowa town he sets out to exploit. We know he understands their values perfectly because of his ability to stir the entire town into action against the new pool hall in town: the purported source of youthful corruption. So, though it isn't his own value system, he has told you a great deal about the people and beliefs in this town. We have also learned that Hill's own values are flexible and self-serving. He is a con man. His moral code, however, undergoes a transformation through the show and he winds up a member of the community he earlier mocked.

Sexuality (sexual orientation, male/female role expectations, attitudes toward the opposite sex): Musicals often center on romantic relationships. So, the erotic presence, sexual attitudes and desires of the characters must be understood and defined, even if the character you play seems to be asexual, or if you have decided the show is so old-fashioned that sex isn't part of these characters. Although some characters don't overtly express sexual desire for others, romantic relationships almost always include a strong element of sexual attraction. Decide who you want, how you want them and how badly. Also consider what expectations your character has for the opposite sex or potential sex partners. Sky Masterson thinks women will behave in a certain way toward him, so he picks women who will do so. Only when he falls in love with a Christian missionary does he have to confront those expectations and, ultimately, change them in order to marry her. Suffocating gender roles are the primary obstacle for Mother in *Ragtime*. Father's expectation that she will be a dutiful homemaker conflicts with her deeper desire for self-determination.

Social mores and rules: All characters operate under a set of unspoken (or even very clearly spoken) rules of behavior. These moral and social codes determine what a character can and can't do, how he can relate to others, relationships he can enter into, and much more. A terrific example of a character that must confront a set of moral codes is Huck Finn in *Big River*. In this musical retelling of Mark Twain's novel, Huck is clearly told how he should behave, based on his aunts' interpretation of the Bible and his society's laws about slavery. Huck comes to question and reject these rules and laws after being severely tested. Research the moral codes of the society your character lives in and decide how firmly your character accepts or rejects those codes. The choice to accept or reject the moral codes is often the result of strong personal experience. Huck chooses to reject racism because his long trip down the Mississippi River with Jim brings him to the realization that Jim is a person whom he loves, not someone's property. On the other hand, Frankie Epps in *Parade* embraces racism because of his deep personal grief over losing his childhood sweetheart, Mary Fagin. Personal experience motivates the rejection or acceptance of social codes for both characters.

Temperament: Does your character have a general disposition? In *The Most Happy Fella*, Herman sings *'I Like Everybody'*. This is distinctly different from Jud in *Oklahoma!*, who distrusts everyone he meets. Temperament is like wearing colored glasses. Everything the character sees will be viewed through this lens. A timorous person will see everything as threatening to various degrees. A lonely person will see everyone in shades of separation. A trusting person will tend to assume everyone is honest.

Fears, phobias, obsessions: Occasionally, a character will have a strong psychological aspect that can color his behavior and guide his choices. Adelaide in *Guys and Dolls* has a psychological reaction to being engaged, but never married, to the same man for fourteen years. Nathan Detroit's resistance to getting married has induced a psychosomatic cold in Adelaide. Every character is afraid of something, whether it is growing old alone (Lizzie in *110 in the Shade*), being exposed as a fraud (Bialystock in *The Producers*), or letting go of childhood (Guido in *Nine*). They all fear something. Many characters are defined by an obsession. Finch is preoccupied with success (*How To Succeed . . .*), Javert obsesses about justice (*Les Misérables*), and Sweeney Todd is consumed with revenge (*Sweeney Todd*).

Catastrophic or defining events in the character's life: Does the author tell you anything significant happened to this character that has helped to define a major attitude? Does a significant, defining event occur during the course of the musical? Sweeney Todd's wife and daughter were taken from him and he was unjustly sent to the penal colony of Australia before the action of *Sweeney Todd* begins. This is the defining event of his past and colors every aspect of his being when the action commences. At the end of the first act of *Carousel*, Julie Jordan loses her husband while she is pregnant with their child.

EXERCISE 7B GRAB BAG CHARACTER – PART II

Use the same neutral song you used for the first grab bag character exercise. It is helpful to have an acting partner(s) for this exercise. Using slips of paper and a hat again, write the following phrases (as well as coming up with more on your own) on slips of paper and have each student in your group select one.

In love with yourself	In a class above your acting partner
Afraid of everyone you meet	Self-conscious about your complexion
Distrust everyone you meet	Attracted to everyone you meet
Sad about the world	Everyone's best friend

Sing the song using a partner, letting the attitude dominate your behavior. Keep it truthful, but powerful. Notice how that single character trait can stimulate you to other behavioral choices. How does it affect your vocal life? Physical responses? Relationship?

UNIT 7.4   **Ambitions**

Characters seek positive outcomes for themselves. This section is about what you are fighting for.

Superobjective. In a concise statement, say what your character wants on the largest, but still most specific level. Review the units on Superobjective in Section I if you are unclear about this concept.

Ideal outcome. At the start of *Sweeney Todd*, Sweeney's ideal outcome might be finding his wife and daughter waiting for him and discovering Judge Turpin has been sent to jail for corruption. As he slips into madness he wants to punish the whole human race by killing everyone. So his ideal outcome must be all of humanity dead. In contrast, Roger Debris (*The Producers*), the flamboyant director-choreographer of *'Springtime for Hitler'* aspires to a world of chorus boys sprinkling pixie dust on every street corner. Whether the character achieves the ideal outcome or not, it is still the pursuit of it that drives his actions. If I got what I wanted, what exactly would that look like?

Greatest fear. If the ideal outcome is what a character runs toward, then the greatest fear would be that possible future the character runs away from. In many cases, this is essentially a mirror image of the ideal outcome. For Laurie, in *Oklahoma!*, we get a clear vision of what that would be in *'Laurie Makes Up Her Mind'* (the dream ballet). She fears being taken away by Jud and forced to become one of the objects of his lust. In fact, her fear of losing her true love, Curly, to the physically brutish power of Jud drives her to attend the dance with Jud in order to spare Curly the possible repercussions (which turn out to be very true). Those fears are expressed through the original choreographic text. What's the worst that could happen?

Perception goals. We all wish to be viewed in specific ways by those around us. For some characters, the goal is to be seen as powerful, masculine and impervious to emotional contact (Billy Bigelow in *Carousel*). Others may wish to be seen as friendly and easily accessible (Nellie Forbush in *South Pacific*). This perception goal will help define how you move, speak, dress and behave. This also establishes your essential tactical vocabulary. If you are a person who sees yourself and who wants to be seen by others as nice, then most of your tactics will fall into the charm category. If you need to dominate through strength, control others and see life as a battle, then your tactics will be more aggressive. Groups also have perception goals. Notice the people around you. Do those in authority behave in ways that reinforce their power? Do the rebels in your crowd behave and dress in ways that help them be seen to reject the rules of good behavior? What groups is your character a part of? How do these groups achieve their perception goals?

Relationship goals. Every character has specific goals for each character he encounters. For Billy Bigelow, his initial goal for Julie is for her to fawn on him, sleep with him, or at least treat him to a beer and go dancing. His goal toward Mrs. Mullins, his boss, may be to have her accommodate his desire to see other women without a fuss. He will have a specific goal for each character, and often a new goal for each scene where he encounters that other character. What you're after tells us who you are. The careful selection and specific articulation of goals establishes character. The goal "I want you to propose to me romantically" comes from a specific type of person; "I want to rip your clothes off right here behind the bus station" comes from another. Both have consummation as their relationship goal, yet are antithetical characters. Be specific and detailed in expressing what your character wants.

Hierarchy of goals. Your character will want many things. It is up to you to decide what is most important at any given moment in the show. So, if Billy wants (a) to seduce Julie, (b) to keep his employer at bay, (c) to defend his character against the accusations of the police, (d) to put down the insults of Mr. Bascombe (Julie's boss), and (e) to figure out what is so different about Julie, then you'll need to decide how to rank these from moment to moment throughout the scene. The priorities for your character will change within scenes and over the course of the story. It is up to you to chart that change and to include it in the playing of your scenes.

EXERCISE 7C   GRAB BAG CHARACTER – PART III

Still using the neutral song from the earlier exercises, you'll write a range of Ambition aspects on individual slips of paper and have each actor in your group select one to use while singing the song. Try the following or add your own:

You want to be liked	You want to rule the world
You want to be your partner's savior	You fear that your partner will betray you
You fear being found out	You dream of being a star

| You want to please your partner | You want to make the world beautiful |

Allow these ambitions to totally dominate your behavior. Don't worry about rational behavior. Just go for broke with this. Notice that the more you submit to the ambition, the more you will discover other character traits. Try this a second time and add in the question, "What will happen if I don't get what I want?" Notice how this fuels you to fight both for the objective, and against the dire possibility of not having it.

EXERCISE 7D   GRAB BAG CHARACTER – PART IV

Have each actor select one physical trait (from Exercise 7A) and either one attitude trait (from Exercise 7B) or ambition (from Exercise 7C). See what happens when you attempt to commit fully to both of them. As silly as this can be, the great lesson is that only one or two strongly chosen character traits can define a character. Your job, especially with smaller roles, is to identify the heart of the role (the superobjective) and then find physical and behavioral traits to support and express that.

EXERCISE 7E   DATING SERVICE

Have a friend or classmate interview you as your character for a dating video. You'll have to talk about the facts of your life (as the character), your attitudes about men/women, past relationships, background. Be sure you dress, speak and behave like the character. If possible, do this on video to be viewed later.

EXERCISE 7F   EULOGIES

Imagine what happens after the script is done. Decide what the major achievements of the character's life were. Then, write two eulogies. The first is what the character wants people to say. "Governor Bigelow arose from humble beginnings to take his place among the most influential and wealthiest New England men; with his charming widow and beautiful daughter, now our nation's most loved first lady . . ." The second eulogy is what people might actually say. "Billy Bigelow was a rotten man, a violent criminal, and a deadbeat dad."

Archetypes, stock characters and character types

Writers often employ recognizable character types as models for the specific characters they create. These representative characters are called *archetypes*. Archetypes live in the collective unconscious. They exhibit physical and vocal behaviors related to a strong psychological and emotional predisposition. For instance, one well-known and easily identified archetype is "The Trickster" whose goal is to fool those in authority and to make them look stupid in public. We've seen variations on this model in almost every period and style of drama. In the *commedia dell'arte* he is Arlecchino. In Restoration drama he is Jack Horner in *The Country Wife*. In film he is Bugs Bunny. In recent television he is Bart Simpson. And in the musical theatre he would be Witty Watkins in *Lady, Be Good!*, Harold Hill in *The Music Man* and Freddy in *Dirty Rotten Scoundrels*. Although each of those characters is specific to the drama he was written for and different from the others, they all share a common archetypal root.

Writers employ archetypes because they allow quick identification of a character and eliminate the need for extensive exposition. We in the audience understand the behavioral expectations of these archetype-based characters and enjoy seeing familiar character types in new situations and in new variations.

There can be great joy in fulfilling the behavioral possibilities for a character that is based on a well-known archetype, and in doing so with imagination and creativity. But don't simply play the archetype as a cliché or stereotype.

There is a difference between archetype and stereotype, though they are related. A stereotype is a clearly identifiable character type that is played superficially, with attention on only the most obvious behavioral traits, often played without subtlety or nuance and as a negative comment on the character. This kind of limited, two-dimensional caricature is not good acting. It is simply playing at the character without finding his humanity. Stereotype acting is also a repetition or imitation of another actor's choices instead of a real inhabiting of the archetype's traits.

Some teachers call this "surface acting" or "playing the externals of a character." Because the musical theatre employs archetypes so strongly at times, it is vulnerable to clichéd or stereotyped acting. It is your job to fill the character's psychological and emotional life with a personal truth. With that strong caution, let's consider some common archetypes and talk about how to use them to your advantage.

UNIT 7.5.1 *Archetypal roots*

Look at almost any character in fiction or drama and you can find the archetypal root. Since understanding the conventions of behavior for each archetype is our aim, identifying an archetype and its antecedents is an important step in character analysis. We can look to a number of theatrical forms to trace sources of our characters.

UNIT 7.5.2 *Ancient Greek drama*

One of the earliest sources for character types is ancient Greek drama. We are fortunate that Theophrastus, an early disciple of the dramatic theorist Aristotle, noted many of the archetypes present in the drama of his time. Notice how many of these archetypes are still present in drama. Although these characters are called "men," they apply equally to women.

The Insincere Man	The Offensive Man	The Man of Petty Ambition
The Flatterer	The Officious Man	The Show-Off
The Boor	The Penny-Pincher	The Repulsive Man
The Complaisant Man	The Unsociable Man	The Coward
The Talkative Man	The Arrogant Man	The Slanderer
The Fabricator	The Faultfinder	The Lover of Bad Company
The Shamelessly Greedy Man	The Absent-Minded Man	The Superstitious Man

Each of these character types is initially defined not by physical or vocal behavior, but by a personality trait. It is your job to inhabit that trait in behavior. For instance, "The Flatterer" complements everyone around him in order to curry favor. He uses insinuating and overly solicitous physical and vocal behavior to achieve that goal, whether he is from working class Buffalo (*The Full Monty*) or medieval England (*Spamalot*).

Commedia dell'arte *characters*

A second source that still shows up actively in musicals is the *commedia dell'arte* of Renaissance Italy, whose roots are strongly in the ancient Roman comedy of Plautus. Most of the actors in this form of drama wore half masks and played the same role in hundreds of short improvised plays based on scenarios, or sketches of the story. The character type each actor played, sometimes for an entire career, was called a "mask" and had very specific and well-known attributes. The standard masks of the *commedia dell'arte* were:

Arlecchino (Harlequin). The central comic servant, usually working for Pantalone. He is illiterate, a fact that often causes amusement when a message arrives and Arlecchino pretends to read it. He is an acrobat and a clown, and carries a baton he sometimes uses to bash other characters for comedic relief, leading to the modern term *slapstick*.

Brighella. A fat, slow simpleton who is led by his hunger – a buffoonish clown.

Columbina. The smart maidservant to the female love interest. She is the lover and counterpart of Arlecchino, the go-between for the lovers and is a gossip. The prototypical saucy maid.

Il Capitano (the braggart warrior). Often from another country, he is a swaggering he-man soldier, but a coward underneath.

Il Dottore (the doctor). A teacher or authority on all subjects (though he often knows very little about any of them). Middle-aged friend of Pantalone.

Inamorata (the young female lover). The leading woman. She is lovely to look at, wears beautiful clothes, is fluent in poetry and music, and carries herself with great poise.

Inamorato (the young male lover). The leading man. He is handsome, dresses well, is fluent in poetry and music, and is poised and charming.

Pantalone. An older rich and miserly merchant who is frequently the father of one of the young lovers, or is pursuing an inappropriately young woman for marriage. He employs Arlecchino and treats him cruelly. Often the object of ridicule.

Prima Donna. A powerful middle-aged woman, often a wealthy widow being pursued by Pantalone and/or Dottore.

Pedrolino. A mild-mannered comic servant. He tends to be so kindly that other characters blame him for things he never did, and he accepts the blame.

La Ruffiana (old woman). Usually a mother or gossipy townswoman who intrudes into the lives of the lovers.

As you look at these character types, notice how present they are in contemporary stage and television writing. Stephen Sondheim's *A Little Night Music* and *A Funny Thing Happened on the Way to the Forum* use virtually all of these character types, as does television situation comedy.

UNIT 7.5.4   *Nineteenth- and early twentieth-century comedy, melodrama and minstrelsy*

Nineteenth- and early twentieth-century stage comedy, melodrama and minstrelsy created another set of archetypes, some of which are variations on the characters we've seen in earlier forms. (Note: Some of these archetypes are troubling or represent stereotypes or prejudices. But we include them here because we feel it is important to recognize these character types exist and still appear in new shows and in new productions of older shows.)

Female archetypes

Ingénue. A lovely, virginal girl who naively goes through the world being supported by powerful well-intentioned men, or being taken advantage of by powerful and evil men. A contemporary version of the *commedia dell'arte* Inamorata character.

Soubrette. A young female character who is attractive, but witty and spunky, as opposed to the pure loveliness of her friend, the ingénue. A soubrette is usually the companion to the male juvenile. A descendent of Columbina in *commedia dell'arte.*

Cinderella. A female character who appears to be poor and unattractive but who cleans up to be a beautiful and romantically ideal match for the male love interest.

Flapper. A perky young woman of good upbringing who wants to break out of the restrictive rules of her society and have fun. She never goes too far and usually returns to polite society.

Hooker with a heart of gold. A down-on-her-luck girl who has taken to a life of sin, despite her noble and heroic intentions. She sacrifices herself for others.

Gold digger. A young woman, usually from an urban setting (often a chorine), who seeks to gain upward social mobility by flattering and becoming romantically and sexually involved with a rich, older man.

Red-hot mama. A middle-aged, world-wise woman. Usually singing about the joys of a life of sex and sin.

Domineering wife (a.k.a. the battleaxe). Shrewish middle-aged woman whose main preoccupation is repressing her husband's pleasurable pastimes. Descended from Roman comedy and *commedia dell'arte*.

Femme fatale. A dangerous and alluring woman who tempts the central male character. He never stays with her.

Tomboy. A female outsider character who aligns herself with the protagonist. Can be either asexual or else an unrequited lover of the male love interest.

Bimbo. A gorgeous female character who is often pursued by one or more men. She is usually not very bright and frequently misses the point of a conversation going on around her. Completely unaware of the effect her sexuality has on men.

Male archetypes

Young male lover. The male counterpart and dramatic partner to the ingénue. He is often a hopeful, young man in search of his future. A range of secondary characters supports his central storyline. Descended from the Inamorato of *commedia dell'arte*.

Juvenile. A young male character who is full of energy and who supports the male lover in his romantic pursuits. The juvenile is the companion of the soubrette. They are often romantically involved. A descendent of Arlecchino in *commedia dell'arte*. This character is often a song and dance man in musicals.

Romantic hero. A man whose love or ambitions are unfulfilled or cannot be fulfilled because of circumstance. Sometimes also known as the Tragic Hero, because he often meets a fatal ending in pursuit of his dreams.

Noble Hero. A dutiful man with honorable intentions, often in love with the young, virginal heroine. Often a military man or involved with law enforcement.

Anti-hero. A bad boy who is still appealing to the mainstream because of his charm and non-traditional problem-solving skills. He often saves the day and joins conventional society.

Rebellious hero. A bold rejecter of mainstream society. Seeks to change society through defiant action. This can be a variation of the anti-hero. He can present a threat to the protagonists or act in support of them.

Lone wolf hero. A hero who lives outside of mainstream society, but works to help those who live in it, albeit using unorthodox means.

Happy slave. He is satisfied to serve his master and longs for the simpler times of slavery; derived from minstrel shows.

Uppity slave. He tries to elevate his position in mainstream society by acting like his "betters." He often wears exaggerated fashions of mainstream society and unintentionally misuses language. Later variations have this character adopting the culture of mainstream society, but surpassing the originators of that culture; derived from minstrel shows.

Foolish/ignorant slave. Often a grotesque representation of an ethnic type (usually African-American), who speaks and moves stupidly and is unable to solve even the simplest problems. A variation on Brighella in *commedia dell'arte*; derived from minstrel shows.

Hen-pecked husband. The much put upon, oppressed partner of the domineering wife. This middle-aged male character has strong antecedents in Roman comedy and *commedia dell'arte*.

Ethnic comic. A foolish character who cannot navigate the waters of mainstream American society; usually German or Jewish trickster, derived from vaudeville.

Noble savage (including servants and slaves). A stoic outsider (almost always from an ethnic group that differs from the central population of the story) who has a profound understanding of life, despite his lack of education and socialization.

Nerd. A character who doesn't fit into the mainstream of society. Frequently an intellectual and small in stature with one or more physical fallibilities (bad vision, sinusitis, allergies, etc.).

Nebbish. A whining, ineffectual, usually small male character who seeks to make an impact in the world, but has almost no effect. He is often a distant admirer of the female love interest. May or may not have strong intellectual capability. Often a lower-class New Yorker or Eastern European immigrant.

Jock. A male character who excels at athletics or any of a number of physical disciplines. Usually an ideal physical specimen, but completely lacking in intelligence and/or sensitivity. Often a tormenter of less physically able characters; derived from Il Capitano in *commedia dell'arte*.

Fop. A male character who seeks to be the last word in style, but fails because he overdoes the current fashion or misinterprets it. This is often accompanied by talkativeness, misuse of language and rural origins.

Country bumpkin. A naïve, gullible character who comes to the city or encounters city-dwellers. He is filled with wide-eyed wonder at the city. Often loud and bumptious. Also called a "hayseed" or "rube."

City slicker. A city-dweller who arrives in the country and is incapable of functioning in a natural, agrarian lifestyle; can be a carpetbagger.

Melodrama villain. A malevolent character whose intentions are to take advantage of weak or helpless characters, usually the ingénue. He seeks to exert financial or other pressure on her in order to force her into marriage.

The devil. An enigmatic, often sexy or appealing male character who tricks or seeks to influence the journey of the young male and female protagonists. While he must ultimately fail, this character frequently offers the most interesting plot complications and is given interesting songs.

The "queen." A flamboyant, caricatured depiction of a homosexual male. Often includes exaggerated feminine and "sissy-ish" behavior.

Unisex archetypes

Boy/girl next door. A middle-class, attractive romantic partner for the protagonist. Usually present in the protagonist's life in a non-romantic capacity for some time. Often employed for adolescent or young adult situations.

Sidekick (male or female). A close friend and confidant who supports the work or love interests of the hero or heroine. He/she often has a love interest of his/her own.

Trickster. The trickster's goal is to fool those in authority and make them look stupid in public.

Snob. An elitist who believes the protagonists are inferior. Often from the northeastern US or England.

Wise mother/father/mentor. An older character who advises younger characters about love and life. Often not actually a parent.

This list is by no means complete. See if you can identify other archetypes to add to the list.

As you looked at this list of archetypes, you may have noticed that many of these characters have contemporary variations or are present in a hybrid form, combining elements of two or more. There is no set of rules for portrayal of these characters. But tradition and frequent appearance make the behaviors and even their physical and vocal qualities so clear that we instinctively understand when we are on or off target with them. Here are some recent uses of these archetypes:

Mark (*Rent*) – Rebel/young romantic male
Mimi (*Rent*) – Hooker with a heart of gold/ingénue
Jean Valjean (*Les Misérables*) – Lone wolf hero/rebel/romantic hero
Eponine (*Les Misérables*) – Tomboy/Soubrette
Max Bialystock (*The Producers*) – Nebbish/ethnic comic
Leopold Bloom (*The Producers*) – Nerd/sidekick

Roger Debris (*The Producers*) – "Queen"
Ulla (*The Producers*) – Bimbo
Eugene (*Grease*) – Nerd
Rizzo (*Grease*) – Hooker with a heart of gold
Sandy (*Grease*) – Ingénue
Danny (*Grease*) – Rebel/young romantic male

UNIT 7.5.5 *Creating characters using archetypes*

We started this section by warning against playing these character types as stereotypes. That's a good caution to bear in mind, but how do you accomplish it? Actors often fear being trapped in a stereotypical characterization, so they stop short of fulfilling the archetype. If you find yourself saying things like, "My character is a hooker, but I don't want her to come off as hard and slutty," or "He tortures small animals but I don't want him to seem dark and evil," then you may be resisting a full commitment to the central, most compelling truth of the character. Be careful to avoid defining a character in negative terms: by what she isn't, rather than by what she is. A three-dimensional character isn't going to be found by simply watering down or stopping short of the character's essential archetype. Rather, fully embrace the rich, layered and elaborate truth of that archetype and find a three-dimensional character on the other side of that journey.

Notice that virtually all of these archetypes are based on a strong and specific superobjective, relationship goal or obstacle. It is the fight for that superobjective or against that obstacle that defines the character. A nerd is a very smart person who has myriad physical or emotional obstacles. Take away the obstacles and he is a well-adjusted genius; maybe even a leading man. But with those obstacles, we have a potentially wonderful character to watch as he fights to be taken seriously by the crowd. Asking some useful questions about the archetype will help you to start generating appropriate, but organic and original behavior.

Archetype questionnaire

1. What is my character's archetype?
2. What is the superobjective I associate with the archetype root of my character?
3. Does my character share that superobjective? If not, then you may have misjudged the archetype.

4. What physical or vocal behaviors do I associate with the archetype?
5. What is the specific physical, emotional or psychological source of those behaviors?
6. Is there a specific emotional or physical obstacle the archetype (and my character) must fight against?
7. How do I translate my archetype into the world of the musical? (style, period, nationality, etc.)

EXERCISE 7G IDENTIFYING ARCHETYPES

Look at the following shows and identify archetypes within them. Use the cast list for each as a checklist.

The Pirates of Penzance	Pippin
The Student Prince	A Little Night Music
Anything Goes	Sweeney Todd
Oklahoma!	Beauty and the Beast
The Music Man	The Producers
The Fantasticks	Urinetown
Hello, Dolly!	Wicked

EXERCISE 7H ARCHETYPE MATCHING

Copy each character type in the lists of archetypes we have provided onto a slip of paper. Place all of them into a hat. Separate your class into two groups. Each group draws an archetype slip out of the hat and identifies as many examples as possible of it in a range of musicals, plays, films, novels and television shows. Create a game out of this, giving each team a point for every example of the archetype.

EXERCISE 71 NAME THAT ARCHETYPE!

Select a song everyone in your group knows well. Now, draw from your hat full of archetypes. Sing the song using the behaviors of the archetype you've drawn and see if you can clearly identify and embody those behaviors. If you are in a group, have the group members identify the archetype. If your group is unable to name the archetype, tell them what it is and have them help you clarify the archetypal vocal and physical behaviors.

UNIT 7.6 **The world of the musical**

You will need to do research in order to place the world of the musical in its context. Here are some useful areas of inquiry.

Historical context. What historical period does your show take place in? How does that historical context affect the behavior, relationships and expectations of the characters? *Rent*, while considered a contemporary musical, is actually set in a very specific moment in time during the late 1980s. The politics of that moment in New York City toward the homeless, the pace of real estate gentrification, and the state of medical treatment for AIDS, are a given context for that musical. For each of the musicals we mention in this book, there is specific historical information available that can help you to ground your character in its context. Understanding the political system that fails to take action on the AIDS crisis or threatens you with eviction from your apartment will give you the rage you need to drive your performance in *Rent*. But that kind of rage would be oddly out of place in *No, No, Nanette*. This is set in a time when that kind of young adult rebellion was virtually unknown. How does the historical context of your show and role give you clues to possible behavior and attitudes?

Geographical/regional context. As we mentioned, *Rent* takes place in the Lower East Side of New York City. A few locations are mentioned in the script; enough to help you start to identify a finite world for your characters. There are ample photographs of those locations in the late 1980s to help you visualize that world.

Social contexts. The world of every musical comes with a set of rules for social engagement. We all observe written and unwritten rules of behavior based on the prejudices, fears and biases of our social groups. In *Parade*, even though Leo Frank is a successful businessman in Atlanta, Georgia, he is treated differently from others because he is Jewish and from New York City at a time when both of these things meant alienation from his new society. These facts are probably the defining aspects of Leo's story. Social rules like these can often be among the defining pressures on a character.

Fashion context. Different modes of dress and fashion correspond to every socio-economic group in a given time period and locale. Fashion is a way of expressing how we wish to be perceived by others, our social class and our values. Sky Masterson, in *Guys and Dolls*, wishes to be seen as the ultimate gambler and Man's Man. The suit he wears, the tie, cufflinks or shoes he chooses, can support his macho self-image. His hairstyle and even his cologne all help to convey a specific image to those around him. This will certainly be different from Emile DeBecque in *South Pacific*. Even though both shows were written within a few years of each other and both characters are romantic leading men, the fashions each wears will be markedly different because of how the two men wish to be seen and the specific given circumstances of their worlds.

Source material. Most musicals are based on source material from another medium or genre. Plays and novels used to be the primary source for musical adaptations. But, increasingly, films and even television shows have become popular sources. In all of these cases, the source material offers you detailed information on the character, relationships and original intent – even when your production may take an intentionally different route in telling the story. Audiences for *Les Misérables*, *Big River*, *My Fair Lady*, *Hairspray*, *The Producers*, *Showboat* and dozens of other musicals walk in knowing the characters beforehand because of their familiarity with the source material. The original sources contain obligations in characterization that may constrain the choices an actor can make, but also give him a terrific place to start.

Bringing all the character research together

If you have done all the research and analysis we recommend you'll have too much information to use well. You can't layer it all on. What you're looking for are only one or two critical circumstances or attributes that provide the key to your character. Once you've discovered those, you can play.

Some roles, especially those that are more slightly written, will give you almost nothing to go on. All you may have to define your role is the fact that the society lady you're playing in *Annie Get Your Gun* is an archetypal snob. From there you can make a wide range of choices about relationships, physical and vocal behavior, ambitions, etc. That one quality may be enough to help you create a fully defined character.

EXERCISES 7J ALIKE/DIFFERENT

As a way of making sense of all the character information you have gathered, ask yourself two basic questions:

1. How am I like this character? List all the ways in which you and the character are alike. Consider all the various categories within Units 7.2–7.4 on Facts, Attitudes and Ambitions. Now prioritize these similarities noting the items at the top of the list.
2. How am I different from this character? List all the ways you are unlike the character. This includes physical and vocal behavior, attitudes, ambitions, and facts of your lives. Now decide which of these differences are most important.

In aspects where you share qualities with your character, you can know what you instinctively bring to the process and can stand on this foundation. In facets where you are the most different, you'll know where to place your attention in order to find those in an honest way.

EXERCISE 7K VISUAL JOURNAL

Many actors respond to visual images as a way of stimulating character. Create a journal. Fill that page with photographs, magazine clippings, your own drawings, etc. that show your character and their world. You can include quotes from the text with those images to help clarify the connections.

EXERCISE 7L CARTOON YOUR CHARACTER

Even if you can't draw well, make several sketches of your character, then notice what you instinctively emphasized – like a caricaturist who focuses on defining features and blows them out of proportion. This will help you hook onto an essential insight into character.

Selective reality of your show

UNIT 7.8

Research is good. But it can confuse you. Musicals present a selective reality. For instance, the facts of daily life in New York City in the late 1940s may include difficulties with race relations, disparity in economic and social opportunities, changing roles for women and more. However, much of that is irrelevant to the world of a show like *Guys and Dolls* where Damon Runyon, Frank Loesser and Abe Burrows take a highly selective view of that period. In this "Fable of Broadway," as the show was originally subtitled, too much of the wrong kind of information can lead you to make choices that are fundamentally at odds with the style of the show.

All artists choose to represent some aspects of the world in their work and to exclude others. It is your job as an interpreter to identify what kinds of information you will pursue and how much of even that limited research will be useful to your development of a character. Artists of all stripes exaggerate certain aspects of reality to help make their point. So, two artists with different perspectives on the world may look at the same subject and end up with nearly opposite points of view. Neither is inherently more or less valid.

As a collaborative artist, the actor isn't always able to make completely free choices. Our profession is about actualizing the world the author, director and designers have chosen. If it is a world of light, we should make it brighter through our work. If it is a shadowy place, then we embrace the dark side. Sometimes we need to view our job as being like a carpenter's. The customer will say, "Give me kitchen cabinets in the French Provincial style." We go out and research that, discover cool things the customer never dreamed of and make just what they wanted, only more elegant than they could have ever imagined. But we don't put in fifties diner cabinets when they asked for French Provincial, even if we like them better.

Let's take two important Jazz Age works to illustrate this point. Written only a year apart, F. Scott Fitzgerald's *The Great Gatsby* (1925) and Youmans, Harbach and Caesar's *No, No Nanette* (1924) both look at New York society, but from radically different perspectives. *No, No, Nanette* is ultimately a light musical comedy emphasizing fun and frivolity with no lasting negative consequences from the actions of its characters. It is intentionally a diversion that looks narrowly at its contemporary society and is uncritical of their social mores and values. On the other hand, *The Great Gatsby* examines that same society from a much darker, more serious dramatic perspective. Corruption, the life and death struggles of the lower classes to gain upward social mobility, and the apathy and ennui among the privileged elite form the thematic center of that story. So, two works of art from the same time offer completely different views of the world.

As an interpreter of these two works it would be essential for you to understand the tone of these two pieces as different from each other, though much of the same research might be included in your inquiry. But the lens through which you view that information will be distinctly different. Imagine creating the dark and troubled world of *Gatsby* for your interpretation of Uncle Jimmy in *Nanette*! Trying to lace *'I Want To Be Happy'* with the psychologically complex feelings of Gatsby would be disastrous and even comical. Similarly, trying to make Gatsby a carefree optimist would be equally confusing.

So, your sensitivity to the kind of musical you are interpreting is the key filter in deciding how to select useful research for your character.

Finally

The development of a character is a process. Research, explore, fantasize, dream about and play with your characters. Take ideas into rehearsal and try them out with the director and your colleagues. Arriving at a fully realized character can be an unpredictable journey. Take it with an open heart and you may discover wonderful things.

SECTION III: THE JOURNEY OF THE SONG

CHAPTER 8

The Journey of the Song

THE JOURNEY BEGINS

While we may be tempted to think of a song in a musical as a snapshot of the character at a given time, it can be more useful to see that song as a *motion* picture. Rather than a static and unmoving two-dimensional image of a character having just one feeling for three or four minutes, a song in a musical is a dynamically changing experience a character goes through and we go through with him. We call this changing experience the journey of the song.

Four Journeys

A character goes on a journey within each song. A journey is something that has a beginning, a middle and an end. Along the way, many twists and turns occur, some of which the character may have foreseen and some of which are a total surprise. This unpredictability will be determined by your interpretation of the song, based on its musical and lyric clues, combined with your own instincts. Almost every theatre song has a treasure map folded inside, waiting to be discovered and followed. In some songs the outline of that journey is apparent, while in others the pathway may be more obscured. But with a well-trained eye and ear, you can begin to decipher the clues and plot your course.

All journeys don't result in forward progress, despite the character's best efforts. Sometimes we get where we're heading. But sometimes we get lost, distracted or detoured. Songs generally take one of four journeys.

1. **The winning journey**, where a character sets out to achieve a goal and is successful in doing so; she ended up where she wanted to go and won her battle. In *'She Loves Me'*, Georg discovers and confirms that Amalia loves him. Sky Masterson wins his battle for control over his relationship with Sarah Brown in *'I'll Know'* from *Guys and Dolls*.

2. **The losing journey**, where she may try to get to a specific place, but is unsuccessful. The attempt to gain territory is no less committed, regardless. If Sky Masterson won the battle in *'I'll Know'*, then Sarah Brown lost it. Henry Higgins fights to banish Eliza from his thoughts in *'I've Grown Accustomed to Her Face'*, and ends the song having lost.

3. **Serendipity**, meaning she begins with the intention of going one place but ends up somewhere unexpected. This isn't necessarily a bad thing. It's just a surprise. The singer in *'I'm Not Afraid of Anything'* (*Songs for a New World*) criticizes everyone in her life for their weaknesses, finally discovering she is really the one who is unable to love or be loved. She never imagined that kind of self-revelation at the beginning of the song. Billy Bigelow's *'Soliloquy'* in *Carousel* takes him on an unexpected and life-changing journey.

4. **The spiral journey**, in which the character begins trying to figure out a problem, goes on a long journey exploring all aspects of it, and ends up realizing she just can't solve it yet. Even a journey that essentially ends back where it began is still a valid one as long as the character has tried to make some progress. The character may have gained a deeper self-knowledge or important insights. One might think of this as a spiral. Seen three-dimensionally, she returns to the same point, but at a higher level. This type of journey includes songs that say: "This I Believe" (*'Why Can't the English'* from *My Fair Lady*), "Hooray!" (*'I'm a Brass Band'* from *Sweet Charity*), "I Feel Like . . ." (*'A Quiet Thing'* from *Flora the Red Menace*), "I Am" (*'I Cain't Say No'* from *Oklahoma!*)

In each of these four journeys, the character is trying to get to a desired destination, and the actor is looking for interesting terrain to travel over in performance.

EXERCISE 8A MAPPING THE TRIP

Answer these questions for each of the five activities that follow.

• What is the character's circumstance at the outset? Where does she think she is going? What does she want? What does she expect to find? What impulse is setting her on this journey?

- What important encounters does the character experience during the trip? What discoveries does she make? What obstacles appear?
- Where does the character end up? Is this where she wanted to go? Identify the kind of journey the character takes through the song: winning, losing, serendipitous or spiral.

1. Look at several filmed performances from a range of musicals. Compare your interpretation of the actors' work on film with your classmates. Discuss the differences in your reading of the performance. Section V of this book provides you with handy lists of representative musicals in different styles.

2. Listen to original cast recordings of songs from musicals you don't know. For each performance, decide what you think is the journey of the song. Now decide what you think the given circumstances of the song are in the context of the show. Then read the liner notes to compare your sense of what happened with the actual story of the show.

3. Have your class or a group of friends all listen to and read the same song. Each of you will write down which journey you think best describes the song. You'll probably find out you don't all agree. Find out why.

4. Identify four songs from musicals that fit each of the journey paths we've described. Do you find any songs you think can fit more than one path?

5. Take this to your own work. Look at a song in your repertoire and analyze the elements of the journey in that song. Try different journeys on for size.

A journey to where? Trip objectives

UNIT 8.2

You may have spotted a problem in the last exercise. In order to decide whether the journey is successful, you first need to know what the character wanted – the objective. If you don't know what you want, it is hard to know if you've achieved it.

Your character's superobjective is the force pulling him through the entire musical. The smaller objectives found at each level of his journey through the story all constitute steps in the direction of the superobjective. Songs come at critical moments when the character is about to take a big step forward and so they also have objectives that drive them.

Sometimes an actor needs to process his way to an understanding of the character's song objective. For instance, in *Les Misérables*, Inspector Javert isn't simply singing about lights in the sky as he sings *'Stars'*. He's singing to accomplish something. You might feel he is affirming his belief in the absolute righteousness of his quest to find and imprison Jean Valjean (objective: to prove myself right). Or you might say he is formulating a philosophy of life at that very moment for the first time (objective: to find a reason for my actions). You might even suggest he is fundamentally questioning whether he is truly justified in his pursuit of Valjean (objective: to justify my actions). The possibilities are numerous, but in each of them Javert is after something and expects a specific outcome.

How will he know he got what he wanted? For every objective we have an expectation of a result. This is the test of the objective. If your buddy Bob is taking a drive to Smallville to see his Aunt Minnie, he'll know he's arrived when she opens her door, and gives him a big hug and a slice of her famous apple pie. So, throughout his trip, even though he may tell you his objective is to get to Smallville, what he's really after is a hug from Minnie and a slice of pie. Every time he stops for gas, the things that get him back in the car are a hug and pie. Every time he has to take a construction detour, a hug and pie are what gets him back on the right road. Put that way, the actor can keep his focus on the simple outcome. That is much easier than chasing after an abstraction.

Notice that the hug and pie must come from Minnie. The test of an objective is usually in your partner's actions. We'll know we got what we wanted when she does it. What outcome is Javert expecting? He addresses God, and Lord, and the stars. The stars personify the deity, so let's make them his acting partner. This song has elements of a prayer ("Lord, let me find him . . .") and an oath made to God ("This I swear by the stars"). If his objective is "to prove himself right," the affirmation of his righteousness must come from his partner, the stars. He will be looking for a sign. Maybe he expects a star to blaze in a fireball across the sky. Then he'll know God has endorsed his mission and he'll be proven right. If you decide on that choice, the most direct objective you can have is: make God turn a star into a meteor. That will be something specific you can fight for.

To help process your way to an understanding of your song's objective, ask:

1.   What is the character doing? (story event)
2.   Who is he doing that to? (relationship)

3.   What does he want? (objective)
4.   If he got what he wanted, what would that look like? (ideal outcome)
5.   So, therefore I'm taking the journey of this song in order to have that person do . . . (whatever your ideal outcome looks like is your true objective).

In the same way that Bob is on a journey to get a hug and pie, Javert is on a journey to get a meteor. It doesn't matter at all whether the desired outcome is rational. It doesn't matter whether the audience could name your ideal outcome. What matters is a performance driven by strong, simple, specific needs.

Pursue objectives – don't play moods or states of being

UNIT 8.3

One of the most problematic issues of performing a song is the tendency of some actors to let the composer and lyricist do all the work. The singer has been handed beautiful material and all they may want to do is ride the wave of the melody on nice open vowels and punctuate it with some snappy alliteration. This will result in a general wash of feeling that makes for boring theatre.

"Fantine is lost," or "Fantine is sad." These phrases describe moods or states of being. This is useless to an actor because it is static and inactive – there is no "doing" involved in being sad. You are just sad. We don't need the journey of a song to get us into that state. There is no journey to go on. It invites you into solitary, isolated, indicative acting choices, rather than those that force you to work on, with or against others – or even on yourself. If our buddy Bob was in a mood state, he would probably just sit forsakenly in the car feeling sorry for himself and never even start the engine.

In almost all cases, the telltale signal of mood or state of being is some use of the verb "to be." When you say, "I am [——]," "He/She is [——]," you almost always reveal an inactive choice. The answer will be to convert these listless choices into active ones by pursuing an objective.

EXERCISE 8B   MOODS INTO OBJECTIVES

1.   Take the following state of being or mood phrases and revise them by providing a song objective for the character.

- In *'The Impossible Dream'* (*Man of La Mancha*), Don Quixote is heroic.
- In *'Defying Gravity'* (*Wicked*), Elphaba is determined.
- In *'My New Philosophy'* (*Charlie Brown*), Sally is mad.
- In *'This Is the Moment'* (*Jekyll and Hyde*), Dr. Jekyll is excited.
- In *'Not a Day Goes By'* (*Merrily We Roll Along*), Mary is sad.

2. Take a song you're working on and give it a descriptive mood phrase you might be inclined to indulge. Convert that into a song objective.

UNIT 8.4   ## Beat breakdowns

If our buddy, Bob is going to get his hug and pie, he needs to make the trip to get them. That trip will have several stages. Each stage will have its own objective. He'll need to take a couple of different highways (objectives: get to Topeka, then Kalamazoo), maybe suffer a detour (objective: solve being lost), have to stop for fuel (objective: get gas), need to ask for directions (objective: solve being lost again), and get coffee (objective: stay awake) – and the coffee will make him stop at least once more, too. He'll have a route planned, make discoveries, enjoy surprises and need to overcome problems. Though most songs are more inspiring than Bob's big adventure, they will have the same kinds of stages. As we chart our journey through a song, we'll need to find the smaller, incremental objectives that make up the stages of the trip. Those are beats.

In acting terminology, a beat is a unit within a scene where what you want changes, either because you have achieved, discarded or replaced your former objective. In plays, you look for clues to these scene gearshifts in the text, and sometimes there are many valid choices as to the exact location of beat shifts. A song is more likely to have beat shifts clearly planted by the composer and lyricist. In contrast to some play texts, these beat changes aren't obscure. They are more like imperatives. Deny them at your peril. A song may have as few as three or four beats, or as many as a dozen or more.

While there is no formula for the division of a song or scene into beats, there are a number of standard musical clues to look for as you read and listen. At each of these musical gearshifts, ask yourself, "Did I get what I wanted?" If so, "What do I want now?"

Clue 1 – Verse to refrain. When a song goes from the end of the verse to the beginning of the refrain or returns to the verse again, there is a good chance the character is looking at the objective in a new way. She may even begin a fresh objective at this point. This is usually the beginning of a new beat.

Clue 2 – Ending of one musical section. When a song moves from one melodic motif to another distinctly different musical theme, the character is often beginning a new beat.

Clue 3 – Musical modulation. When a song changes key there is often a new acting beat beginning. Key change is an indication of something changing emotionally. It often means that the character is dealing with the same objective, but in a more urgent way.

Clue 4 – Tempo change. As with musical modulation, the tempo of the song can change as an indication of the character's emotional shifts.

Clue 5 – Changes in accompaniment. When the qualities of the accompaniment change, even when you're singing the same melodic material, we know something is happening internally. This may mean more rapid or dense accompaniment, inclusion of other musical themes, counterpoint melodies, etc.

Now, look at the *beat breakdown* for *'I Dreamed a Dream'* from *Les Misérables* to see how we've broken the song into units based on the lyric and music clues we discussed above and in Chapter 3 Song Structure (Table 8-1).

Table 8-1

Lyric divided by beat	Lyric clues to beat division	Musical clues to beat division
There was a time when men were kind; when their voices were soft and their words inviting. There was a time when love was blind, and the world was a song and the song was exciting. There was a time . . .	• Fantine recounts her actual past.	• Steadily and insistently ascending accompaniment. • Melody is often on a steady, single note with only a melody at the end of the phrase.
then it all went wrong.	• "then" indicates a change. • The first mention of anything bad happening.	• First departure from the ascending accompaniment, open space instead. • First variation in melody from the steady single note.

Table 8-1 continued

Lyric divided by beat	Lyric clues to beat division	Musical clues to beat division
I dreamed a dream in time gone by, when hope was high and life worth living. I dreamed that love would never die. I dreamed that God would be forgiving.	• She begins recalling a dream of a better life. • Spoken in past tense, having "dreamed."	• Chorus begins. • Begins the thematic accompaniment for the song. New musical melodic motif ("A" theme).
Then I was young and unafraid, and dreams were made and used and wasted. There was no ransom to be paid; no song unsung, no wine untasted.	• She is talking about her behavior in her youth – what she did.	• Repeats the musical material, with slight enhancement.
But, the tigers come at night, with their voices soft as thunder, as they tear your hope apart and they turn your dream to shame.	• She uses present tense for the first time. • First use of metaphor – there aren't real tigers.	• New melodic material ("B" theme), the bridge. • Insistent, steady accompaniment. • Song is moving into a generally higher vocal range.
He slept a summer by my side. He filled my days with endless wonder. He took my childhood in his stride.	• First specific memory to be recalled. • First talk of her lover.	• Returns to the "A" theme.
But, he was gone when autumn came.	• "But" signals a shift in her thought process. • First negative memory admitted about him.	• More somber and spare accompaniment
And still I dream he'll come to me, that we will live the years together.	• "And still" signals another attempt at reversing her thought process. • She uses future tense "he'll come to me," "we will live the years . . ."	• Modulation to a higher key. • Music gets more insistent and complex, elevating the emotional tension.

Lyric divided by beat	Lyric clues to beat division	Musical clues to beat division
But, there are dreams that cannot be, and there are storms we cannot weather. I had a dream my life would be so different from this hell I'm living; so different now from what it seemed.	• "But," another change of direction in her thoughts. • She admits the futility of her dreams for the first time.	• Music is at its most driving, rhythmic state. • Melodic themes from earlier in the show are used as counterpoint in the accompaniment for the first time.
Now life has killed the dream I dreamed.	• "Now" is in present tense.	• The accompaniment becomes hollow and skeletal, with very little support for the melody. • Melody gets repetitive again, as in the verse.

Notice that the music changes and the lyric changes almost always support each other. Fantine's use of language, ideas and imagery in this song are all reinforced by a changing melodic and accompaniment structure. The result is a thoroughly integrated experience for the actor and the audience.

EXERCISE 8C   BREAKING IT INTO BEATS

For the next series of exercises, it can be a good idea to have one song that the group works on together. Then, each actor applies that work individually to one of the songs in his repertoire. Ideally, these are songs you know musically, but haven't yet worked on as acting pieces.

1. For this and upcoming exercises, you'll need several copies of your music that you can write on. You will also need to type the lyrics out on a separate page and have several copies.
2. Using the clues we've described above and in Chapter 1, break the lyric of the song into beats. Treat the song like a monologue and just look at textual information only. Where are there clear shifts in what you want, discoveries, ideas completed and new ideas introduced?

3. Look to the music for beat clues. Examine changes in musical theme, key, tempo, accompaniment and structural changes like verse, chorus, bridge.
4. Integrate the lyric and musical information. Separate each beat with a clear line on the page. Next to each beat, give both your musical and lyric reasons for the beat division.

UNIT 8.5　**Beat objectives**

Each new beat requires a fresh objective. This is the homework an actor does to transform a scene into an exciting chain of actions. When you have finished finding your sequence of objectives you'll have a kind of Mapquest guide that describes every step of the journey, just as you would if you were to go online to get travel directions to a specific destination. It tells you where to go each step of the way, and how long you'll be on that specific step of the journey and what arriving there looks like.

When Fantine begins *'I Dreamed a Dream'*, she has arrived at a situation where she must sacrifice herself to save her child. She needs to give up all her hopes and her personal dignity to enter a life of prostitution – a life she probably knows will destroy her spirit and ultimately kill her. At the beginning of this song, she stands poised at this threshold. She needs to cross it. She can't do that while she retains any hope of a happy life. We'll choose the objective: Fantine fights to destroy her hope. Her partners are herself and God. She will know she has achieved her objective when she relinquishes her humanity and goes numb – then she can go forward and sell herself. Horribly, this is a winning journey because she achieves her objective (Table 8-2).

The setting of objectives and the decision of what constitutes a test of each objective are so deeply personal and such an intimate product of the actor's artistic process that it is unlikely this exact explication would work for many individuals. The point isn't to take this as definitive. The point is to demonstrate that detailed decisions about beats can and should be made. Make the ones that move you. Notice how many of her objectives are failures? Notice how many could never realistically be achieved? Good. Hard for you is great for your audience.

As you create your objectives, enjoy finding multiple possibilities. When we look for a new car, it can be limiting to go to the dealer and tell them we want a specific

Table 8-2

Lyric by beat	What's happening?	Objective/discovery	Ideal outcome
There was a time when men were kind; when their voices were soft and their words inviting. There was a time when love was blind, and the world was a song and the song was exciting. There was a time . . .	Fantine reviews her past. How did her hope begin?	Objective: Fantine seeks to identify the origin and nature of her hope.	Fantine will know she has achieved this when she can see her younger self. She achieves this.
. . . then it all went wrong.	Fantine snaps back to reality.	Discovery: Fantine discovers the moment when her life went awry.	
I dreamed a dream in time gone by, when hope was high and life worth living. I dreamed that love would never die. I dreamed that God would be forgiving.	Fantine relives her naïve hope and belief in love and God.	Objective: Fantine wants God to make it true, to make her right about hope, love and His forgiveness.	God should reach down and pet her hair demonstrating his love and forgiveness. She doesn't achieve this.
Then I was young and unafraid, and dreams were made and used and wasted. There was no ransom to be paid; no song unsung, no wine untasted.	Fantine mocks herself for her failure to see the consequences of her actions.	Objective: Fantine seeks to punish herself for her naïveté and for wasting the promise of her youth.	God would slap her hard across the face. She doesn't achieve this.

Table 8-2 continued

Lyric by beat	What's happening?	Objective/discovery	Ideal outcome
But, the tigers come at night, with their voices soft as thunder, as they tear your hope apart and they turn your dream to shame.	Fantine succumbs to her nightmares. This is how her punishment arrives.	Objective: Fantine wants the courage to face what is happening.	That tightening of fear in her chest would release. She doesn't achieve this.
He slept a summer by my side. He filled my days with endless wonder.	Fantine relishes the memory of the love she once had.	Discovery: love and youthful hope are beautiful things.	(This is movement away from her song objective. So it is a large failure.)
He took my childhood in his stride.	Fantine understands for the first time that her innocence was stolen, not given away.	Discovery: I was undone.	(This is the turning point that makes her realize fate dealt her a cruel hand much earlier than she thought. Her lifelong hope has been false. This helps her because false hope is easier to let go of.)
But, he was gone when autumn came.	Fantine admits his abandonment.	Discovery: Fantine really understands how unfounded her hope has always been.	
And still I dream he'll come to me, that we will live the years together.	Fantine fights to hang on to her dream.	Objective: Fantine fights against the facts. She wants the dream to be the truth.	Her prince would sweep in and save her. She doesn't achieve this.
But, there are dreams that cannot be, and there are storms we cannot weather. I had a dream my life would be so	Fantine faces the facts of her life today.	Objective: Fantine fights to face reality and destroy hope.	The truth would hit her like a dash of cold water. She achieves this.

Lyric by beat	What's happening?	Objective/discovery	Ideal outcome
different from this hell I'm living; so different now from what it seemed.			
Now life has killed the dream I dreamed.	Fantine commits to doing anything it takes (including prostitution) to save her child.	Objective: Fantine needs to relinquish the last bit of feeling.	She would feel nothing. She achieves this.

make, model, color, etc. We test-drive what's on the lot. The same is true for objectives. Probably the best way of finding out which choice works best for you is to test each in rehearsal. We don't simply look at the brochure for our new car or even merely walk around it and kick the tires on the showroom floor before buying. We get in and drive it on city streets, highways and bumpy dirt roads. This is also true for test-driving the objectives you're considering. Only by trying them out with full commitment in rehearsal can you determine which works best for you. Since objectives are the vehicles that carry us on our journey through a song, be sure to choose wisely. And the wisest choice not only fits the context of the song and agrees with its musical quality and lyric information, but also stimulates you to your most exciting and engaged performance.

EXERCISE 8D   CHOOSING OBJECTIVES

1. Start by choosing an overall song objective.
2. Note who your character is addressing. Be clear about your relationship.
3. Using the beat breakdown you set up in the last exercise, add in beat objectives and note what constitutes the ideal outcome of each objective.
4. Try creating extra options for each objective. Use separate pieces of paper for each journey so you won't be influenced by your earlier choices. You may be surprised by how similar or different your ideas can be.
5. Reminder: detail each objective in sequence. For this first analysis, don't jump around or skip to the last beat with an end in mind. Allow

yourself to discover the journey. When you reach the end you may find you have a very different journey than you expected.

6. Which of the journey paths (winning, losing, serendipity, spiral) do you think best describes the journey you just chose for this song?

7. Now create two additional journeys for the song you've chosen. On these explorations try a couple of different approaches:

- For the first, start by choosing a different journey path from the one you just used.
- For the next, start by choosing a clear character objective for the song. Then set the place the character begins as far away from that end point as possible. Your journey is the tortuous trip between those locations. Remember that a short, direct and easy trip isn't as dramatically interesting as one that holds surprises, dangers and discoveries.
- Place all your analyses next to each other to see if you feel one best fits the song. Do you discover whether some objectives from different journeys might combine to create one you really like?

EXERCISE 8E REHEARSING WITH OBJECTIVES

Try acting the beat breakdown and beat objectives in rehearsal or class.

1. Speak the song as a monologue. Don't sing it.
2. Write each beat objective on a single sheet of paper or "cue card." Have your teacher or classmate sit with your beat breakdown and the cue cards.
3. Just before each new beat, have your coach hold up the matching cue card. Play these objectives in order and see what you discover about the song. Did you like what you chose? Are there others that might fit a specific moment better?
4. Try replacing weak objectives with new ones and explore again.

As you begin to navigate a song you've divided into beats, play only the objective for the beat you are in. Don't hang on to the last objective as you move into a new beat or anticipate the next one before you've gotten to it. By committing to and fulfilling each beat and action in sequence, you will discover what the journey of the song is for you.

Taking the journey in small steps

A key to believability in a performance is the truthfulness of every small moment. The next series of topics take us progressively into smaller and more detailed character moments. If your performance were a book, then these topics are the sentences, phrases, words, punctuation and even the spaces between the words – all of which need to flow seamlessly into an integrated whole.

Internal and external pressure

Think of the journey of a song as a ride in a bumper car at the carnival, where we ricochet from one collision to the next, helplessly shoved into another driver or deliberately guided by our own desire to smash someone else. Each of those collisions triggers others for the drivers we hit. The experience of living through a song is much the same. We are pressured by either circumstance or desire to react to the action that just affected us. And our reaction will cause another reaction from someone else or from us as part of a chain of pressures and counter-pressures that lasts as long as the drama itself.

Pressures can come from inside us (*internal pressure*) or from the actions of the other characters (*external pressure*). In *Les Misérables* Fantine's desire to be a good mother is an internal pressure because she pursues it without anyone forcing her to, based on her superobjective: protect Cosette. This internal pressure moves her to place her daughter with the unscrupulous Thenardiers. The same imperative drives her to take a factory job in town in order to pay for that care. Fantine is still responding to internal pressures. Once she has entered the factory, though, external pressures begin to build on her. The sexual advances of the foreman, the harassment of her coworkers, her ultimate dismissal from the factory, her eventual poverty and the ongoing need to keep sending money for her daughter's care are a series of overwhelmingly powerful *external pressures* that finally drive her to prostitution and ultimately kill her. All of Fantine's actions are driven by these two kinds of pressures.

If you'll review the beat/objective breakdown we made up for Fantine's song, *'I Dreamed a Dream'*, you'll see these pressures at work on her. Both internal and external pressure can drive her forward in pursuit of her objectives and they can also be the obstacles that keep her from getting what she wants. They advance her, pull her back, shove her onto false paths or stop her.

EXERCISE 8F   UNDER PRESSURE

1.   Make two lists: internal pressures and external pressures.
2.   In each list create two subcategories: objective and obstacle

Table 8-3

Internal pressures		External pressures	
Objective	Obstacle	Objective	Obstacle

- Looking at your practice role, identify major choices your character makes in the course of the story. For each of these, decide what the pressure is that moves her to take the action. Now, decide if that pressure is internal or external.
- Once you know if the character is responding to an internal or external pressure, ask whether that pressure is moving her toward her objective or is standing in the way of it. For example, if a character is ambitious, being drafted to run for president is a powerful external pressure pushing him on. If a character wants to be wealthy, but has guilty feelings about that, then that guilt is an internal pressure standing in his way. All pressures will either help or hinder.

Because your character is in single-minded pursuit of an objective, when confronted by anything other than a forwarding pressure she will need to devise some way of negotiating this immediate obstacle. She'll look for a tactical solution.

Tactical actions – verbs to do by

Tactics are verbs. They are the things you do in the moment-to-moment pursuit of your objective. You jab, block, punch, feint and body slam your partner in the sparring match that is your character's fight to overcome obstacles and have your way. (You might also stroke, embrace, soothe, calm or tickle to get what you want.) You're working with tactical detail toward some specific ideal outcome.

Many characters will habitually choose from the same set of tactics. Some shove, prod, nudge, push and batter their way toward their goals, like Bill Sikes from *Oliver!* Others might tend to flatter, charm, revere or coax, like Finch in *How To Succeed in Business Without Really Trying*.

Tactics will fall into two broad categories: intimidation or attraction. But there is a wide range of subtle shading within those. How you pursue your goals tells us a lot about you. That's because everything in your character's world is a reflection of his perspective. If you see problems as things that need to be hammered out or as things that need to be smoothed over, your tactical response is a window into your essential persona. So, in making tactical choices for your character, choose well.

To apply this to a song, start by finding the beats. Then, bearing in mind that every time you take a breath you're taking in a fresh thought, mark the places in each song beat where you breathe. Now your beat is phrased.

For each phrase choose a verb. Not just any old verb, though. Choose a verb that acts on your partner. Complete this sentence: I [——] you. This isn't the goal statement, it's the method statement – the way you're making the other person fulfill your ideal outcome. I seduce you. I caress you. I amuse you. I slap you. I fool you. I punish you. Etc.

Your tactical pathway toward your goal can be direct, or a crazy crabwalk past the obstacles placed in your way. Sometimes you'll select a sequence of tactics that are an undeviating intensification of the same approach: I nag you – I browbeat you – I bully you – I throttle you. At other times it will work to shift tactics, broadly: I reject you – I beg you – I ridicule you.

Resist making the basic sentence (I [——] you) more complex. It will only blur your tactic. Notice that the construction I [——] *with* you, or I [——] *to* you, or I [——] *your* [——], will remove the directness and immediacy. Be rigid about this guideline. It will require more thought and a friendly relationship with a thesaurus, but it will result in clearer acting.

Sometimes you are singing alone onstage. In that case you are working to change an imaginary partner or perhaps yourself. Imaginary partners function just like real ones in this game. Jesus talks to his father (God) in *'Gesthemene'* from *Jesus Christ Superstar*. If you're talking to yourself, you still have objectives and tactics, but now your ideal outcome might be up to you and your phrase tactics end in "me": I chide me, I cajole me, I attack me, I shame me, I punish me. Etc. Look at Dr. Jekyll's constantly evolving dialogue with himself in *'This Is the Moment'* from *Jekyll and Hyde*.

Operate from a straightforward template.

1. Divide your text into beats.
2. Determine your objective for each beat.
3. Identify an ideal outcome for each objective.
4. State that outcome in terms of your partner.
5. Break down the beats into breath units or phrases.
6. Apply a tactical verb to each breath phrase in the beat and use tactics to make that happen.

Table 8-4 **Tactical action phrases for the first beat of *'I Dreamed a Dream'***

Lyric by breath phrase	Tactics	Beat objective
There was a time when men were kind;	I search me.	Objective: Fantine seeks to identify the origin and nature of her hope.
when their voices were soft and their words inviting.	I lull me.	Test: Fantine will know she has achieved this when she can see her younger self.
There was a time when love was blind,	I hypnotize me.	She achieves this.
and the world was a song and the song was exciting.	I uplift me.	
There was a time . . .	I tantalize me.	
Then it all went wrong.	I puncture me.	Discovery: Fantine snaps back to reality. She discovers the moment when her life went awry.

In rehearsal, it is a good idea to try on as wide a variety of tactics as you can think of. From this you'll learn which expresses the inner truth of your character, stimulates your partner the most strongly and supports the moment the best.

Verbs can hurt or heal

Maybe you're looking for a way to specify the idea: I love you. Start by recognizing that love is a feeling or mood more than a thing you do. Here are some loving tactics you might do to someone.

accept	admire	adore	adulate
bless	beguile	bemuse	befriend
caress	cajole	chase	cherish
dazzle	deify	delight	desire
elate	electrify	embrace	enamor
favor	felicitate	flatter	fondle
gladden	gratify	grace	grope
harbor	hearten	help	hug
ignite	imbue	impassion	induce
jolly	jump	kindle	kiss
lick	lighten	lull	lure
magnetize	marry	massage	mesmerize
nibble	nip	nourish	nurse
obey	obtain	ordain	own
pamper	parent	pat	pet
ravish	receive	relish	romance
savor	seduce	shelter	spellbind
tackle	tease	thrill	titillate
undress	unite	uplift	urge
value	venerate	vibrate	vivify
warm	welcome	woo	wrap

Notice that all of these can inspire you to distinct relationship tactics. They are all things you do to your partner. So, they're much more active than: I dream about you, I sing to you, or I tell you about.

Let's play on the darker side. Actions can hurt. Imagine you're searching for ways to put tactics into the feeling: I'm angry with you.

abuse	afflict	aggravate	aggrieve
bedevil	befoul	belittle	bludgeon
castigate	choke	circumvent	combat
damage	damn	debase	defeat
efface	eject	eliminate	enslave
flagellate	flatten	flay	frighten
goad	gouge	grill	gull
hammer	harangue	harass	haunt
impale	impugn	indict	infest
jab	jeer	jeopardize	jolt
kick	kidnap	kill	knife
lacerate	lance	libel	lynch
malign	mash	maul	menace
nag	nauseate	negate	nettle
obliterate	offend	oppose	oppress
pelt	perturb	pester	pillage
ravage	refuse	reject	repudiate
sabotage	savage	scourge	seize
taunt	terrify	torture	tyrannize
undermine	unhinge	unravel	upset
vanquish	victimize	violate	vitiate
wallop	weaken	whack	wound

By now you may be finding that the structure of I [——] you holds a kind of magic. The direct link to your acting partner and the stimulating specificity of the verb can be inspiring.

Sometimes actors resist this level of specificity, wondering how they can be spontaneous and responsive to their partners if everything is planned. Correct. If everything is planned, and you stick to the plan no matter what, then you'll be denying your partner's responses and choices. Take this a step at a time, however. Initially, this is a training method designed to make actors gain a larger tactical vocabulary and to take more specific tactical actions at rapid, small levels of interaction. Find that first. Then, relax, and notice you have begun to habituate making tactical choices and can do them on the fly, based on the information you're receiving from your partner. Soon you'll be comfortable with both practiced choices and playing improvisationally.

EXERCISE 8G INTIMIDATING OR ATTRACTING WITH TACTICS

1. Start with the first beat of a song. Know what your song objective and beat objective are and identify the ideal outcomes of those objectives.
2. Break the beat down into breath phrases.
3. For each phrase, give yourself two general tactics, one that intimidates and one that attracts, like: I assault you, and I seduce you.
4. Use a thesaurus to come up with a list of more specific variations on each tactic. You're looking for transitive verbs. These are verbs that take a direct object and will fit in the sentence, I [——] you. Get a lot of them.
5. Organize them into a chart (Table 8-5):

Table 8-5

| Breath phrase | Intimidation tactic | | Attraction tactic | |
	General	Specific	General	Specific
Phrase 1 (put your text here)	I assault you.	assail	I seduce you.	allure
		attack		attract
		batter		beguile
		bombard		bribe
		bruise		court
		challenge		delight
		charge		ensnare
		combat		entice
		damage		entrap
		debauch		induce
		fight		lure
		harm		romance
		harry . . .		tempt . . .

6. Choose one specific tactic for each breath phrase. Keep this list in your hand.
7. Using a partner to play into, explore singing your first beat, changing tactics on each breath phrase with the clear intention of making your ideal outcome happen.

8.   Try shifting tactics by alternating between intimidation and attraction.

9.   Continue this process with succeeding beats.

What does this teach you about tactics? Do you find you're learning a greater tactical range? What did you find out about making a chosen tactic work for you in a specific situation?

UNIT 8.6.4   *Discovery*

As we've explored identifying and playing smaller units in the journey of a song, you may have found that a lot of choices in your moment-to-moment experience have been answered before you ever step onstage. And those choices, the plan you've outlined for yourself, provide you with a strong foundation for your performance.

But that reliable preparation can have one drawback – if you let it. You can find yourself going along a very planned pathway, on which everything makes great sense and you have lots of exciting actions to play that collectively add up to the kind of journey you want to take. But there may be little spontaneity. So, this brings up the question, "Does preparation make for dull performances?" Or even more extreme, "Shouldn't I just wing it in performance based on my instincts since I know that will always be exciting and unpredictable?"

The answer is neither rigidly adhering to a set plan, nor flying by the seat of your pants without any real preparation. There is a third option, and it involves *discovery*.

Discovery fills every minute of your onstage (and offstage) life. Consider a walk to the corner to drop a letter in the mailbox. As you get to the door you discover it is bright outside, so you grab sunglasses. As you get to the foot of the steps you see a child's toy in the way and step around it. There is a puddle at the end of the sidewalk to negotiate, a dog on a leash to veer around, a car approaching the intersection as you start to cross it, a pothole to leap across, chewing gum on the handle of the mailbox lid, a baseball being hit by kids playing in a yard to duck from, and so forth. Life is filled with all these little discoveries that alter our experience slightly and to which we are constantly adjusting.

Discovery for actors means pretending to encounter new information, experiences, feelings and needs as you live through the character's life onstage. This is what an actor does: pretends to live every moment as if for the first time. Even though you know in your rational mind what word, note and step of choreography is coming, you pretend those come to you spontaneously.

Onstage, we have constant stimuli to which we respond. Very often these come from the other actors we play with. No matter how well rehearsed a show or how long it's been running, no two performances are the same – thank goodness! Although you say the same words, sing the same notes and dance the same steps, you are different every night. The way you look at your partner, the way she responds to you, the tilt of her head, the intention and inflection in her voice, the pressure of her touch are all slightly different. This is part of what makes live theatre so exciting. These provide you with endlessly interesting discoveries to make.

One actor we know was performing in the ensemble of *Brigadoon* in a long run. During the second act of this musical a huge, drunken wedding celebration takes place, which is interrupted by the arrival of the town tailor, Archie Beaton, carrying the dead body of his son, Harry. Unbeknownst to most of the townsfolk, Harry has died when he fell on a rock in the forest as he attempted to escape from the town and end the miracle that preserves them forever in the past. During an early performance the cast onstage was raucously dancing when the bagpiper from offstage made his entrance followed by the actor playing the father carrying another actor playing his son. Our friend was so involved in the party that he didn't realize it was time for their entrance. He literally discovered Archie carrying Harry as they entered his field of vision. In that moment, he felt this horror as if for the first time. It was a chilling sight that was so compelling it changed the rest of the performance for him in wonderful ways. The gravity of the scenes that followed made such an impact on him that he decided to set himself up for that experience every performance. By engaging fully in the party, he allowed himself to "discover" the arrival of his fallen friend each night and experience the grief, blame and shame of that death. Not only was the performance made richer for him, it undoubtedly added to the texture of every performance for the audience and the other actors onstage.

This kind of planting of discoveries all along the journey of your role can make it an exciting one that feels surprisingly new for you and the audience at every step of the way.

Every duet in musical theatre can be seen as a chain of discoveries between two characters. Look at *'Take Me or Leave Me'* from *Rent*, *'Sun and Moon'* from *Miss Saigon*, *'If I Loved You'* from *Carousel*, or almost any other well-written duet. You see that each switch in musical dialogue from one character to the next happens because that character is responding to something that they've just discovered from the other character. The other character's actions and behavior are the reasons for the next exchange. Viewed this way, every scene is primarily about discovering things within yourself or in the other character.

EXERCISE 8H   PLANTING AND UNEARTHING DISCOVERIES

Go back to your tactic analysis.

1. This time, look at each tactic and decide exactly what is the discovery that stimulates this action.
2. Give yourself a very specific idea, image or inspiration to discover and it will shove you into the next moment. For example, in *'She Loves Me'*, it isn't good enough for Georg to remember generally that he didn't like Amalia. He brings up a *specific* memory of exactly what he thought. He smells her cloying perfume, despises the tiny tripping steps she takes, notices that her hair is always coming unpinned – and is deeply irritated by those things. The specific memory, attached to a specific image, or sensory experience (smell, touch, taste, sound, etc.), is what is key here. Later, he can eroticize those exact same things (her glorious scent, her delicate feet, her beautiful hair) as a way of specifying this complete reversal he is undergoing.
3. Create a list of each specific sensory discovery and spend some time clarifying and owning each one. If you are working with a partner, be sure to draw many of these discoveries from them, so you are invested and engaged in the relationship.
4. Practice going from one specific discovery image to the next, until the sequence is anchored.
5. Perform the same song with *every* beat launched from a discovery. See what happens when you don't know what the next moment is going to be and that you discover it in yourself or your partner.

A benefit of this kind of work is that, if you are deeply invested in evaluating the other person you're onstage with, it's difficult to worry about your voice, your looks or if the critics like you. This close investment in your partner can help narrow your circle of attention to what is most fundamental in your acting work.

EXERCISE 81   WHAT JUST HAPPENED?

1.   Looking at a two-person musical scene, identify the places where you do something to the other person. The scene will be filled with dozens of these. Speak the text and lyrics (without music) stopping at every action and saying aloud the action you took followed by the reason for taking the action (i.e. "I threatened you because you confronted me," "I flirted with you because you looked receptive," "I rejected your offer because you scared me"). This will require you to step in and out of the character.

2.   Another way of doing the same exercise is to have each character followed by an "alter ego" who says what action was taken and the reason. These alter egos speak for the actors onstage. After you've tried this, have the actors in the scene discuss whether your statements accurately reflected their intentions.

Evaluation and adjustment

For your performance to have verisimilitude, the audience needs to witness your process of going after something, discovering problems, attempting solutions, winning, losing, failing to understand, being blindsided by feelings, tripping by mischance into solutions, and bumping into all the happy and unhappy accidents of real life. Every time the smallest thing happens for good or bad, your character will need to comprehend it and cope with it. You will *evaluate* the changing situation and *adjust* your behavior to accommodate it. If you skip over or deny even the smallest shift in the changing dynamics of the scene, the audience will be instantly pulled out of their belief in the truthfulness of your acting.

Presented that way, believability in acting can be a daunting obligation. But it isn't so intimidating if you think of a performance as being more like a sporting match than a finished product. You drill all the fundamentals of the sport until you can throw, hit and catch with the best athletes, but when it comes to the game, you have to just play. In sports, playing means keeping your intention on the goal, reading the opposing players, making instant assessments about them and skillfully adapting your tactics. That's what believable acting is, too. There is a reason an acting troupe is called "the players." Our work combines childlike play with the adult passions of a competitive sport.

One of the things an athlete can't do in competition is say no. Whatever is coming at them, it must be dealt with. The same is true in a scene. Say yes to whatever is coming at you, evaluate, adjust and stick with your goal

EXERCISES 8J   REACTING AND RESPONDING

For this first set of exercises, you'll need to use a song you already know and have analyzed to understand the relationship with the character you sing it to. You'll also need a partner. It helps to have an observer. Describe the circumstances of the song and scene to your acting partner. He doesn't need to know every detail of the relationship, just the most important factors. He will also need to be familiar enough with the song to understand what happens from moment to moment. Give him an objective, such as "To get me to stay with you." Or "To get me to kiss you." This is something simple he can work toward. You will also need to remind yourself of the basic homework we've done already. Knowing your *objective* and the *specific relationship* are an important part of this exercise.

1. Begin the song with your active, living and breathing partner. When you do something, he will react to it based on his understanding of the relationship, his objective and the context of the song. He may begin to leave, so you'll have to respond to that. He may advance on you, and you'll need to deal with that, too. After you sing the song with his physical reactions, discuss with him and your observer what happened and which moments seemed to support the lyric and the action of the song as you understand it. Try the song again, asking your partner to continue doing the moments that worked and to experiment with new reactions around them. After each singing of the song with your partner, continue to build the framework of evaluations and adjustments. By the third time, you will probably have a strong framework established.

2. Try the same exercise again, but ask your partner to improvise short dialogue that will force the next phrase of the lyric to happen. He might say things like: "What?" "I don't believe you," "Please!" or "Really?" This dialogue should make sense in the context of the song. It will have the effect of turning your monologue into dialogue. See how this propels each new phrase and beat of your song, making it a necessary response. Again, try this several times until you've built up a strong

and logical dialogue that includes the movement and words that you discovered and selected together with the help of your observer.

3. After you've tried these two exercises, allow your partner to sit out and then try the song again, remembering his reactions. Can you relive that experience without a real partner? This may take some practice. But, it can make solo work come alive for you.

4. Try another song where you work without a real partner from the beginning. This time, as you sing, imagine a partner's reactions to you (both physical and dialogue reactions). How does this kind of imaginary reaction stimulate you to continue your song?

5. Try the same song again, but this time look at your song lyric sheet and decide on specific responses within the song from your imaginary partner. Write those lines on the lyric page and have it available to you as you sing. Once you know both sides of the conversation, put down the lyric sheet and act the song as a series of responses.

SECTION III: THE JOURNEY OF THE SONG

CHAPTER 9

WORKING WITH RELATIONSHIPS

The word *relationship* gets tossed around a great deal these days on afternoon talk shows and in self-help books dealing with romance or family problems. But, in acting, every relationship can be defined by how important the other person is to you; what he or she can do to help or stand in the way of what your character wants. Put another way, your character sees everyone else in terms of how they can help you achieve your objectives. That isn't selfish, it's human.

Any time you sing you are involved in an important relationship; the person you're engaged with matters at that moment. We don't generally waste time on unimportant relationships. So, if it seems unimportant, think again. In this next section, we'll explore some of the ways you can understand and take advantage of relationship in your acting.

Specific relationship

Every character has a *specific relationship* with every other character he encounters or talks about onstage. Even those characters in the chorus all have relationships to each other and to the more prominent characters in a show. The relationship is the *kind* of association between two people. The *significance* is the degree of importance carried by the relationship.

Let's take a look at several key relationships at the beginning of Rodgers and Hammerstein's *Oklahoma!* If you are playing the role of Laurey, you know that Curly, the cowhand who hangs around your farm, is important to you because:

- He is charming and likeable.
- He is physically attractive.
- We have been flirting with each other in many different ways for months.
- He offers protection from Jud, who scares me.
- He is the man I privately want to marry and spend the rest of my life with, but he is a cowboy and I need a farmer.

That escalating list makes some of the reasons why Curly matters to Laurey clear. It defines her specific relationship to him. He is important to her because he can help her get a range of things she wants. She wants visual stimulation from a man and he provides that. She wants to be charmed, flattered and flirted with, and he does that, too (on occasion). He is capable of protecting her when she is in danger; something else she wants. Finally, he might offer her love and lifelong companionship – probably the highest priority for Laurey. So, her specific relationship with Curly is defined by the ways he is important to her and what he can do for her.

However, if you're playing Curly, you have a different, though somewhat related, specific relationship. You might say Laurey matters to Curly because:

- She is attractive.
- She makes me feel calm and easy when I'm around her.
- I like her feistiness. She is able to resist my charm and put me in my place.
- I fantasize she will be my wife, but she will want me to settle down.

You can see that some of the reasons for Laurey mattering to Curly are the same as her reasons for caring about him. But there are different reasons that are specific to him alone, and that Laurey doesn't know about or share. Go through Curly's list and see how she stands to help him achieve his objectives and life goals. All of those reasons help define a relationship and make it important.

Each of these central characters has a pivotal specific relationship with Jud, the farmhand who lives on Laurey's farm and who takes her to the Box Social. From his perspective, Laurey matters because:

- She is attractive.
- She has nursed me in illness and showed me compassion – unlike almost everyone else here.
- She is young and inexperienced – something I like.
- She can help me fit into this town and finally be accepted.
- She is the woman I fantasize about being my wife and lover.

Those reasons define Jud's relationship with Laurey. But, he matters to her because:

- He is strong and powerful, and a little bit dangerous in an attractive way.
- He can help me make Curly jealous; something I want right now.
- He scares me and makes me feel that I might be hurt if I don't obey him.
- He is the man on our farm and keeps it running.

That is a markedly different relationship, and one that clearly changes throughout the show. For Curly, Jud matters because:

- He is a threat to my successful courtship of Laurey, the woman I love.
- He has Aunt Eller's confidence and I need her to support me as Laurey's winning suitor.
- He is menacing and dangerous and he scares me.

So, in just a few sentences, we have defined a series of totally different relationships between these three characters. All are intertwined, but each is specific to only one person and each provides the actor with strong reasons to care about the other characters. There are no weak or indifferent feelings between these three people.

By asking a few basic questions, we can define the specific relationship between the character we play and the others he encounters.

- *Who is that other person to me?* They are my [——]. This statement acknowledges that we are at the center of our own private universe and everyone in it orbits us. They all play roles and have functions strictly in terms of us. Feel free to be literal or create metaphoric relationships. Curly might be Laurey's savior or knight in shining armor or companion or romantic ideal.
- *Why do I care about them?* List the most important reasons why they matter to you.
- *What can they do to help or hurt my chances of achieving my goals?* I need [——] from that person. You need this for yourself. Try answering this using "me" or "for me." "I need you to love me." "I need you to be there for me." "I need you to stop Jud for me."
- *How important are they to me?* I would [——] if I were to lose that person. You don't know what you've got till it's gone. Ask what you have to lose.

EXERCISE 9A SPECIFYING RELATIONSHIPS

For the next series of exercises select a role you've never played before and you are appropriate for. It should also be one you're interested in and for which you can get a script and score (or at least vocal selections and a complete recording). Make sure the role is in the proper vocal register for your voice.

1. Identify two characters who have important relationships to your role.
2. Use the four-step inventory listed above to define and personalize your relationships with these two characters.
3. List at least five reasons for their importance to your character in the show. (Stay within the confines of the given circumstances of the show. Aunt Eller may remind Curly of his dead grandmother, but his grief over the loss of his doting grandmother isn't in the script and could be a distraction. It is okay for Curly to characterize her as "you are my grandmother" as a metaphoric relationship.)
4. Now, prioritize those reasons from 1 to 5 (or more). See how those reasons give you a personal stake in the relationships.

Does this list start to help you see what you want from each of these characters and why they really matter to you?

EXERCISE 9B WHEN I LOOK AT YOU

1. For the same relationships you worked on above, step into the other character's shoes and ask why you matter to him.
2. Answer each of those four questions about your character from the viewpoint of the other character.
3. Now that you know what the opposite character wants from you, you can make a decision about whether you can be or do that thing for him. Does your character recognize what he wants you to be?
4. Is this a unifying element between you or a source of conflict?
5. Should you play into his desires, or resist?

Changing relationships

As you read the list of reasons why Jud matters to Laurey, you probably noticed that her reasons appear contradictory. How could she find Jud strong and attractive, but also find him threatening and dangerous? Those reasons only seem opposed to each other if you insist they all occur at the same time. But, relationships change from moment to moment, and as important dramatic events unfold in the story you're telling. Feelings can also be irrational. It is possible to have two (or more) strongly contradictory feelings about someone or something at the same time. When asking whether Laurey feels turned on or disgusted and repulsed by Jud, an exciting answer is "YES!" Her way of framing the metaphoric relationship might be as her dark stalker – an object of nightmares, and her dark lover – the star of a very different kind of dream. Don't be bound by shallow rationality.

For Laurey, Jud presents a good way to get back at Curly for tricking her into believing he had a fancy buggy and helps her play hard to get. That is their relationship at the beginning of the script. But, as time goes by, she realizes what she's gotten herself into by agreeing to go to the Box Social with Jud. At that point he matters because she has to find a way to get out of her date without angering Jud. A new specific relationship has evolved. Later, when Jud threatens her at the Box Social, a more powerful relationship has developed between the two; he has become a physical threat to her. Finally, when he comes to Laurey's wedding celebration wielding a knife in a rage against her and her new husband, Jud matters most of all because their lives are literally in danger. Each of those relationships is distinct from the other, and yet all involve the same two people. It is the changed circumstances, the unfolding of events, the actions Jud himself has taken, and the new relationships with other characters that have all helped to make the specific relationship between Jud and Laurey evolve.

EXERCISE 9C   I AM CHANGING

1. Go through your script and list every scene your character is in and the other characters with you in those scenes. In order to visualize when you encounter different characters, create a grid with character names on the side and scene/song titles along the top.
2. For each of the two key relationships you've been working with (you can do this about lesser relationships later, if you have the time),

identify the places in the script and score where that relationship fundamentally changes.

3. Using the four relationship questions we have been building on, answer each of them again every time there is a fundamental shift in the relationship. This might happen in every scene.

4. For each of the key relationships, list the metaphorical relationships in a column, starting with the first scene at the top and the last encounter at the bottom.

5. Also note the cause for each shift. What was the discovery or the catalyst for this change?

6. Notice the relationship arc your character goes through from the start to the finish. What light does this shed on your character's journey through the show?

UNIT 9.3   ## Relationships as obstacles

Obstacles provide you with something strong to fight against and often come in the form of relationships. Laurey and Curly's relationship provides each character with obstacles to their goals. For Curly the relationship with Laurey is an obstacle because:

- She flirts with me, then plays hard to get.
- The thing I like most about her (her feistiness) makes me crazy. She's not submissive.
- Laurey wants me to be domesticated. I want freedom.

For Laurey, the relationship is an obstacle because:

- He could be a wonderful husband, but he's not a farmer.
- He makes me weak in the knees, but I don't want to give him control.
- He toys with my emotions.

As you look at defining your specific relationship to the various characters around you, see how they can become strong obstacles to your goals and how you might be an obstacle to their happiness. Without something strong to fight against, every problem is a small problem. Who wants to see that? We want to see people struggling to win the fight of their lives.

Some actors worry that using this high degree of importance in their work may force everything into a state of melodramatic hysteria. This is simply a question of degrees. Something can be vitally important to you without your needing to yell about it at all times. Indirect tactical choices are sometimes the most effective way to get what you want.

EXERCISE 9D   YOU ARE IN MY WAY (AND I'M IN YOURS)

Do this exercise using the detailed changing relationships in the relationship arc you created in the previous exercise.

1. Looking at the important relationships you've identified, define how those characters are each an obstacle to you getting something important. One way to do this is to make statements like, "I need [——] but you [——]."
2. Look at how your character is an obstacle to each of those characters. Come up with specific incidents where you see this obstacle in action. One way to specify this is to make statements like, "You need [——] but I [——]."

In real life, this sort of behavior (blaming the other person for your problems, and deliberately being a barrier to someone else) is not the path to happiness. On stage, however, it is the essential ingredient of dramatic conflict.

This is a good time to revisit our discussion of metaphorical relationships: those names we give to relationships that describe their essence. Rather than simply describing your relationship with your mother as "my parent," you can more specifically define it as "my jailer," "my nurse," "my banker," "my defender," and so forth. Look at Unit 2.3.3 Metaphoric relationships to remind yourself of this idea.

Don't stop at characterizing the other person. You can also do this for yourself. If your mother is your jailer, that makes you her prisoner. If she is your nurse, then you are her patient. By characterizing both yourself and the other character you instinctively fall into relationship behavior. If you were playing Laurey, consider how characterizing Curly as your Knight in Shining Armor defines a role for you. Are you his Damsel in Distress? What behaviors does that suggest?

UNIT 9.4 ## Relationship goal – I want more

If you look at your own life you'll see that very few relationships are the same from day to day. We characterize others around us in metaphoric relationships and then fight to make them accept the role and respond accordingly. Until that person embraces the role fully and behaves according to our specifications we aren't satisfied. But that's rarely enough. The minute she fulfills our expectations, we ask for more. We seek to redefine the relationship as one that is even more favorable to us.

If you were a new student at a school and didn't know anyone, they would all be strangers to you. For our purposes, refer to them as "My Strangers." But you'd probably encounter someone whom you wanted to make into "My Friend." In order to redefine the relationship favorably from your point of view you share homework tips, offer change at the vending machine or make small talk about the latest cast album you listened to – all of this in an attempt to redefine "My Stranger" as "My Friend." When that is reciprocated, you seek to make the friendship closer by inviting "My Friend" to lunch after class or to do homework together. You are now seeking to make her into "My Confidante" or "My Ally." If that works, as time passes you might see if she needs a roommate next year at school. You're seeking to make the friendship grow from "My Confidante" to the person whom you spend all your free time with: "My Best Friend" or "My Sister." These are all ways of upgrading and redefining the relationship in positive ways for you.

Look at the same relationship with "My Sister." Imagine you divulged a highly personal secret she shared with you. You've been caught telling the secret and she is angry with you. She redefines you as "My Betrayer." Perhaps you want to restore the trust and closeness you two have shared. Now, you are trying to redefine your role in the relationship from "My Betrayer" to "My Penitent" (a person atoning for some deep transgression). If your friend accepts your apologies, then you may be able to start redefining the relationship in positive ways and make everything right again. Relationships are in a state of constant redefinition.

Look at any set of important relationships in a musical or play and you'll see how the nature of those relationships changes throughout the course of the show. In *She Loves Me*, Georg first sees Amalia as "My Irritating Brat." When he discovers she is his pen pal, he redefines the relationship so she is "My Tormented Victim," and he takes pleasure in causing her suffering. But, when he discovers how lovable she is, she becomes "My True Love."

Constantly fighting to redefine important relationships is a useful string of objectives. It thrusts you into active response with your scene partners.

EXERCISES 9E   UPGRADING RELATIONSHIPS

1. Go back to Exercise 9C I AM CHANGING. This was where you specified the relationship arc of your character through the show.
2. Next to each metaphorical relationship, give yourself a matching (or reciprocal) relationship title. Fill in the phrase "He is my [——], I am his [——]."

Relationship goal – love me as I want to be loved   UNIT 9.5

In our earlier discussion of superobjective, you may have suspected that every character shares the same one: to be happy. On the most general level this is true. But what makes them different is that each individual has a personal vision of happiness. For Jean Valjean happiness may be living without the fear of Inspector Javert catching him: living as a free man. For Javert, though, happiness may be finding every criminal and putting him away forever: ensuring a secure society. Eponine sees happiness as spending her life with Marius. And Fantine sees happiness as finding safety and stability for her daughter, Cosette. So, as you seek to identify your character's superobjective, you're probably answering the question "What is perfect happiness *for my character?*"

Just as all characters want a personally specific version of happiness, they also want to be loved – and in a particular way. This is one of the basic human needs that fuels many of the most important relationships in drama. Characters don't seek to be loved in general terms. They want to receive love in the specific way they imagine perfect love should come from each specific person. In *110 in the Shade*, Lizzie Curry, a spinster from a small Texas town, has important relationships with several men. She requires each to supply her with a specific kind of love. She needs paternal love from Pop, her father. She needs filial love, support and confidence from her brother, Noah. The con man, Starbuck, must provide her with carnal love.

Even beyond those generic versions of love, characters have specific desires that need to be fulfilled. Characters will frequently articulate what that love they're seeking is; what it looks like to them. Lizzie shares her vision of perfect love in

'*Simple Little Things*'. She talks about a relationship with a man who trusts her and depends on her by asking "Lizzie, is my blue suit pressed? Lizzie, kinda scratch between my shoulder blades. Lizzie, are the children all in bed?" And, she'll simply say to him "My husband." That specific vision of happiness and love is Lizzie's way of saying, "Love me as I want to be loved." Any old love won't do. It must be in the specific way she has fantasized. In fact, finding that kind of love is her superobjective. When Sheriff File offers it to her, she takes it. Lizzie's dream of happiness would never work for Charity Hope Valentine in *Sweet Charity* or for Roxie Hart in *Chicago*. Those women have their own distinct ideas of what being loved is. Find that specific dream and you have something powerful to work towards. You'll also probably find you've humanized the character deeply.

Being loved as you want to be loved means not settling for someone else's version of perfect love. Although Burrs loves Queenie in *The Wild Party* in a passionate and all-consuming way, his version of love is so violent and suffocating that it drives her to find someone else. Burrs' need to be loved on his terms drives him to attempt murder because he isn't getting it in the way that will satisfy him. His struggle toward being loved as he wants to be loved is the powerful engine of that musical. If he were willing to settle for Queenie's version of love, there would be no second act.

The characters we most invest in sometimes do have moments of getting the love they want. Often this happens at the end of a show because the entire story has been built around central characters finding the right kind of love, as with Lizzie. But, in other cases, there are moments where it is nearly achieved, or achieved only for a moment, and then taken away or lost. In *Guys and Dolls*, Sarah Brown and Sky Masterson are an unlikely couple. He is a womanizing gambler and she is a religious missionary. But, they take a trip to Havana, Cuba and have what turns out to be a wonderful night. At the end of that night they stand on the street in front of Sarah's mission and share a moment where both characters are loved exactly as they want to be loved. In that moment, they sing '*I've Never Been in Love Before*'. That perfect moment is destroyed when dozens of gamblers come racing out of the mission, leading Sarah to believe that Sky took her out of town only to get a place to hold a dice game. For both characters, the remainder of the show and all of their subsequent actions revolve around being loved in that way again or fighting to forget it. But, both are still responding to the need to be loved as they want to be loved.

EXERCISE 9F   HOW I WANT TO BE LOVED

1. Using your study role, decide what that character's idea of being loved as he wants to be loved is. Identify moments in the story where he is working toward that or responding to it not being given.
2. Specifically note where the character says how he wants to be loved. Write these quotes down along with whom he is telling. Watch out for indirect or oppositional requests: don't throw bouquets at me, don't please my folks, don't laugh at my jokes, etc. or people will say we're in love, are all statements specifying exactly what love means to that character.
3. Look for places where your character identifies how he wants to be loved through his actions, not his words. Remember that most people do what they would like done to them. If someone sends you a love note or a card, then that is exactly the kind of thing he would most appreciate from you. That is the best kind of love in his world.

Find moments where your character does receive love as he wants it. What happens? Is it ever taken away? What happens then?

Power, control and status

UNIT 9.6

Every relationship is characterized by constantly shifting control, power and status.

Control refers to who decides what will happen in a relationship and when it will happen. Every event in the relationship (short of external events) is decided by one or another person in it. A king traditionally has total authority in determining the course of events for his kingdom as he pleases. He is the decider, therefore he maintains absolute control.

Power refers to the varying ability of a character to exercise control. In our mythical kingdom, the King's servant has very little say in what can happen, literally depending for his survival on the permission of the King. He has no control, and therefore no power. But once he takes the King's daughter captive at knifepoint the power shifts and the King is suddenly much less powerful. Because he can no longer decide what will happen, the King has lost power and control.

Status refers to the level of control one character has relative to others. Characters have differing levels of power and control at different times. Characters have either higher or lower status, depending on the amount of power and control over others they have at any given moment. Most characters spend a good deal of energy trying to raise or maintain their status. Generally, raising your own status means lowering another character's, causing conflict. In our kingdom, the King enforces his high status by threatening people with beheading or imprisonment. But, once his servant abducts the princess, the King's status is radically reduced and he must now negotiate and plead with his servant to get what he wants. That servant could have the King do or give anything because of the new power, control and status he has achieved.

Every story can be viewed as a constant struggle for power, status and control. The quintessential musical about power struggle, *West Side Story*, is a study in how to use these three ideas. As the story begins, the Jets street gang has control over their neighborhood. They are completely powerful because they have managed to intimidate everyone else on their turf into a position of low status (relative to them). As Jerome Robbins' danced *'Prologue'* proceeds we see that control threatened when a rival Puerto Rican gang, the Sharks, begins to successfully challenge the Jets' high status. The result is a gradual loss of control and power for the Jets, while the Sharks gain nearly equal degrees of power and control. Status is now only slightly higher for the Jets, and even then only because the ultimate power holders, the police, enforce that status for them. However, the Sharks are a real threat to the Jets' only slightly elevated status. Their thin margin of power creates a strong sense of urgency and immediate danger for the Jets. The rest of the action in *West Side Story* is stimulated by ongoing attempts between these two gangs to usurp power and control or to wrestle it back. Every character in *West Side Story* is profoundly affected by this high-stakes struggle.

By planting your desire to raise your status in another character or take power and control from them, you have given yourself a relationship goal. Putting the other character in his place will force you into action. The example above involved street gangs. But the fight for control exists in corporate boardrooms (*How To Succeed . . .*), in antebellum plantations (*Marie Christine*), and in most relationships between men and women (*Hello, Again*). Each of these scenarios involves different rules of engagement than those employed by street gangs. But, the fight for control is no less important to the characters.

An important phenomenon about status can be witnessed as we watch a parent trying to get a child to stop playing in the yard and come inside to dinner. The parent might seem to have higher status, but as the child refuses to come inside, notice who really has control. The parent begins with a command, "Come in to dinner." If the command isn't heeded, a threat is added: "Come in or no TV tonight." Still no response and the volume goes up as the threat becomes more extreme, with more dire consequences: "Come in right now or you'll be grounded for a week." If the child still refuses, the parent may be forced to go into the yard to physically remove the child. Parental high status is gone and it has become a test of physical strength. If a struggle ensues and the child writhes, kicks, screams and wrestles in front of the neighbors we can see that the parent has steadily lost control. Ultimately, she may get the child inside, but she has lost all dignity and barely won the fight for control. So, who really had power and control in this relationship? The parent lost status as she was forced into fighting for control.

EXERCISE 9G **PLAYING TO WIN**

For this exercise you'll need a musical scene between two characters.

1. Decide what it is you want from the other person (your objective). Now, play the scene as if it is a power struggle that changes with every step toward or away from your goal. You are fighting to win the control game. Have a classmate or teacher serve as coach to score the competition. For every win you get a point, for every loss to you the partner gets a point. Try using a whistle and have the coach blast the whistle and score the scene as a sporting competition. Notice how high the stakes become as you try to WIN the game.
2. Play the same scene with two chairs facing each other. As you gain or lose status, you either sit or stand in response. You can try to force your partner into her chair as you try to gain higher status, or be forced into your chair as she takes control. No physical coercion is allowed.
3. Play the chair game, but this time simply rise or sit as you feel your status change.

After each of these competitions, have a discussion about the tactics each character used to try and win. Limit your tactics to the verbal and psychological.

UNIT 9.7   **Alone onstage**

Many songs don't have a partner. Then, the character is alone onstage. There are four typical situations where this happens:

- Inner-directed songs
- Absent partner-directed songs
- Conversations with God
- Audience-directed songs.

UNIT 9.7.1   *Inner-directed songs*

In the inner-directed song a character tries to address a strong objective that is planted in himself. For this kind of song, we literally place another "self" in front of us. This is the "Me" that needs to change or help you in some way. You give yourself the same kind of objective you would with any partner. Most of us have lots of practice with this because we do it all the time as we talk to ourselves in our heads. You might even have had moments when you talked to yourself in the shower, in your car or as you jogged. On stage, we naturally accept the convention that characters talk and sing these inner monologues out loud as they work out a problem, weigh the pros and cons of a situation, punish themselves, or try to prod themselves into action.

In some cases, a character will be completely candid with himself, sharing all the pros and cons, self-criticisms and victories without hesitation. But other characters will lie even to themselves, hiding behind personal myths and avoiding painful truths. Decide how honest the character is with himself.

Examples of inner-directed songs are:

'Soliloquy' from *Carousel*
'This Is the Moment' from *Jekyll and Hyde*
'Stars' from *Les Misérables* (You could make an argument for this song being directed to God. Read on.)
'My Lord and Master' from *The King and I*.

Absent partner-directed songs

The second circumstance where we talk to ourselves onstage is the imaginary or absent partner-directed song, where we have a conversation with a person who isn't there. This is often the kind of conversation we wish we could have, but lack the courage or the opportunity. You might be addressing a boy you like, but are too shy to talk to, or practicing to tell a boss off. In these cases, you have an imaginary partner who reacts as you want him to. You are fantasizing as the character. Characters do rehearse winning great victories, but don't limit yourself to positive fantasies. We can also imagine awful outcomes. You might begin a conversation with one desired outcome and then fantasize the opposite happening.

Examples of imaginary or absent partner-directed songs are:

'Just You Wait' from *My Fair Lady*
'Shall I Tell You What I Think of You?' from *The King and I*
'Unworthy of Your Love' from *Assassins*

Conversations with God

A specific kind of absent partner conversation is one with God or any deity or supernatural force the character believes in. Remember we're embracing the character's theology and beliefs, even if they differ from our own. If you play a devout Buddhist, you must accept that reality while you are living the character's life. It isn't necessary to convert to Buddhism to play the role. An atheist can play a priest, and a Christian can play a Jew. Empathy and imagination are all that is required.

Be clear about which parts of the song are to God and which parts are to yourself. Decide what you want from God and how you'll know if you get it. When Jesus talks to God in *'Gethsemane'* from *Jesus Christ Superstar*, it is very different from Tevye's conversation in *'If I Were a Rich Man'* from *Fiddler On The Roof*. Different issues are at stake with differing degrees of urgency, and the characters have specific relationships with God.

Examples of talking to God songs are:

'Why, God, Why?' from *Miss Saigon*
'The Ballad of Booth' from *Assassins*
'Stars' from *Les Misérables*
'Bring Him Home' from *Les Misérables*.

UNIT 9.7.4   *Audience-directed songs*

The last circumstance where we are alone onstage singing is when the song is openly directed to the audience as the partner. This is sometimes also called direct address. In this case the audience becomes a sounding board for your character to say, "What do *you* think?" You are really characterizing the audience in a specific relationship with you. They may be your confidant with whom you share a secret, your fan club who you exhort to support you, your judge and jury with whom you negotiate for clemency, or some other equally specific relationship. We are pressing the audience to help us solve a problem, to offer advice on an important issue, to support our point of view, etc. The result may be great entertainment, but that is not the objective. Your objective will need to be stated in terms of something the audience must do for you.

The long tradition of actors selling a song across the footlights in vaudeville, revues and early musical comedies is evident in the continuation of this tradition. We still see songs like this in *The Producers*, *Dirty Rotten Scoundrels*, *The Boy from Oz* and *The Full Monty*. Even though the songs are addressed directly to the audience and often have a high entertainment value, don't step out of character. You are still the character talking to the audience. You may have seen performances where a well-known actor does step out of the role and acknowledge the celebrity relationship between himself and the audience. As much fun as this may be, it is almost always distracting and pulls everyone out of the story.

Examples of audience-directed songs are:

'How Lucky You Are' from *Seussical*
'It's Been a Long Day' from *How to Succeed in Business . . .*
'Greased Lightning' from *Grease*
'Anything Goes' from *Anything Goes*
'Magic To Do' from *Pippin*

EXERCISES 9H   YOU, ME AND GOD

For the following exercises you can use a song you know quite well. It's important to be able to let go of the original circumstances for the song. For now, we will be inventing relationships and objectives to apply to this neutral song to help explore each of these song circumstances.

1.   Sing your neutral song four times, using the following partners:

     •   Yourself
     •   An absent partner (ex-boyfriend/girlfriend, your boss/teacher,
         parent, etc.) whom you can have an imaginary conversation with
     •   God or some supernatural power you can imagine seeking help
         from
     •   An audience (classmates, teacher, etc.).

2.   For each performance, select a specific goal for yourself. What do you
     want that person to do for you? If you got what you wanted, what
     would it look like? (Your boyfriend asking you to marry him, God
     striking down your enemy with lightning bolts, the audience charging
     the stage and raising you onto their shoulders, etc.)

3.   Discuss the following questions about your work with this exercise:

     •   As you performed the song four different ways, did you notice
         that any of them fit the song better than others? Discuss why.
     •   How did you adjust your focus, physical movement and vocal
         choices?
     •   Did you feel more at home with any of these circumstances?
         Uncomfortable with them?

4.   Look at your repertoire of songs and see which if any fall into each of
     the four categories.

SECTION III: THE JOURNEY OF THE SONG

INTENSIFIERS

Much of what we do as actors is involved with personalizing our work. That is, making the imaginary leap into the character's shoes believable and important to us. So we seek ways to strengthen the given and invented circumstances and our involvement in the story. The techniques that follow are called *intensifiers* because they can help us take aspects of characterization and personalization that may seem only mildly important at first and make them critical in our experience. These are tools of the actor's trade that help us care more about our imaginary circumstances and character relationships. And if we care deeply about the circumstance and act on that amplified need, the audience will care about us.

This is the moment

In the Jewish religion, at Passover, the question is asked "How is this night different from all others?" That's an excellent question for you to ask about every song moment you encounter. How is this moment significantly different and important compared to the other moments in my life as the character? In reality, our daily lives are filled with mundane, uninteresting moments. We spend time filling our gas tanks and doing errands, waiting at stoplights or eating cereal. That is reality. But the pleasure of dramatic writing is that it usually skips those mundane moments and, instead, shows us the high points in the character's life. So, as actors, it is our job to make those moments important.

In *Carousel*, we only experience the critical moments and days in the lives of Julie Jordan and Billy Bigelow; even after he has died. Look at the first dialogue scene in this musical, sometimes called "The Bench Scene," and ask our question. This scene – this moment – is unlike any other in their lives because it is the moment in which Julie and Billy first meet, cautiously court each other and fall in love. It is the moment in which their lives are forever changed and placed on a tragic and painful path. And these two people realize they are experiencing a life-changing event. That is pretty significant! Recognizing how life-changing a scene, song or individual moment is for your character can help add a level of excitement and urgency to your acting choices. Think of all the moments in that day the authors chose to leave out. We don't see Julie leaving her job, making breakfast, running for the streetcar or dealing with her boss at the factory. Those are not essential or critical to her life story. Only her meeting Billy Bigelow, sharing her feelings with her closest friend, losing her job and joining her new-found love matter enough to be part of the onstage drama.

Following that musical further, the next scene takes place several months later. At the beginning of the day, Julie tells her new husband, Billy, she is pregnant. That same day he decides to steal money to provide for his family, fails in the attempted robbery, is cornered by the police, and commits suicide. Now, this is clearly an important day in their lives, and we get to witness a good bit of it. Each part of that day is critically important to each of the characters. Even for the chorus, it is the one day each year they get to cut loose and forget about work. It is a celebration of summer, freedom and love for them, too. But, here again, it is a series of carefully selected events during that long day and night. We don't see Julie wake up and get dressed, or make lunch for her husband (though we do see her give it to him), or sail across the bay to the picnic island, or even look for Billy on the island when he and his accomplice sneak away to commit the robbery. These are all less critical moments, compared to what we're shown.

Finally, Rodgers and Hammerstein show us one more day in these lives; a day that occurs sixteen years later as Billy and Julie's nearly grown daughter, Louise, is preparing to graduate from high school and become a young woman. This is also the only day Billy's spirit is allowed to return to earth to see his widow and daughter. It is his only chance to make things right with the most important people in his life. Lastly, it is the day he finally tells Julie he loves her and always has. That admission frees her from a lifetime of regret and wonder. So, for all those reasons, it is another hugely important day and series of events for each of the principal characters.

In that exceptionally well-written musical, Rodgers and Hammerstein chose to present a handful of selected events from only three days in these two lives (and afterlives). They give us a carefully selected two and a half hours out of a carefully selected seventy-two hours. And those seventy-two hours are chosen from almost seventeen years. So, when we look at the selection of moments we've been given, we can begin to realize that every musical is made up of a chain of the most important, life-changing events in the lives of our characters.

EXERCISE 10A   NOW AS NEVER BEFORE

For this series of exercises you'll need to have a song you know well, and the script of the show.

1. Look at the moment in the story where the song occurs and evaluate what the story event is.
2. Intensify the significance of that event by noticing things like "this is the first time that . . .," "this is the only time that . . .," or "never before have I . . .," or "out of nowhere, suddenly . . ." Why do you think that moment must be there? What would happen to the story and the characters if it were not?
3. Sometimes a character doesn't realize this is a significant event (though you and the audience should certainly see it). Sometimes these events are only known to be important in retrospect. Does the big moment happen before, during or after your song? How and when does your character understand the significance of this moment?
4. Identify three surrounding events in the lives of the characters that the authors decided *not* to include in the story.
5. What was the last important event in your character's life that was shown in the script? Why do you think the days, hours and events in between were not depicted?

Why must I sing this now?

One of the basic assumptions we've asked you to accept is that every musical moment in a show is there because that experience can only be expressed through song. But, we also need to ask ourselves why it occurs when it does. "Why must this song happen now?" "What makes this the only/perfect moment for the song to take place?" In our discussion of internal and external pressure we said that characters take action because of the things people do to them, or because of some internal response to events, thoughts, feelings or needs. Presumably, then, songs will be a response to the things that precede them: the events and pressures that force them to occur.

Returning to our metaphor of taking a journey, we know that following a map often requires us to identify the target destination and back up from there to find our way to it from our present location. The same thing occurs as you examine a script and score. If we know a song occurs at a specific moment, then there must be reasons it was pressured to happen where it does. If we can identify those reasons, we can build the performance so the eruption into song is a necessary part of the overall journey. Nothing is worse than getting to a song moment and being forced to start singing when there really isn't pressure to do so.

In *West Side Story*, Tony sings *'Something's Coming'* as a soliloquy after a conversation with his best friend, Riff. What happened that made him have to express the enormous anticipation he feels? Something between him and Riff and probably internally, as well, started him on the road to self-examination of his feelings. It becomes like an itch he simply can't avoid scratching any longer.

EXERCISE 10B   PRESSURE TO PERFORM

Answer the following questions for the song you're working on:

1. What just happened to make me do this now?
2. Is the pressure to act coming from an internal or external source, or both? What are those pressures? Do they conflict?
3. Why didn't I do this earlier?
4. Why can't I do it later?
5. What do I have to achieve right now that can't wait?
6. Can I avoid it? What would I lose by not acting at all?

UNIT 10.3   ## Backstory and frontloading

It is an article of faith for nearly every experienced actor that you must prepare yourself as vividly as possible for each entrance onto the stage by means of creative imagination and fantasy about the previous events in the life of the character. Nowhere is this more true than in the musical theatre because the script for a musical is often much briefer and less fully drawn than in a play, where a character may have pages of exposition and dialogue to build relationships and to find subtle character traits. In a musical, the scenes are often far shorter and lead directly to the songs, where those subtle characteristics are developed through music and lyrics. But for many scenes and songs, it is left to the actor to create a good deal of the previous life of the character, also known as the *backstory*. Using the given circumstances provided by the writers as the non-negotiable foundation for your imagination and inference, you can take the suggestion of past events and flesh them out.

A good example of how useful this is can be found in Maury Yeston and Arthur Kopit's *Nine*. Based on Federico Fellini's *8½*, this musical tells the story of world-famous film director/writer/actor Guido Contini, whose career is taking a decided nosedive. In order to help buoy up his current rudderless project, he calls on his long-time leading lady, Claudia Nardi, to act in the film. These two made many successful films together and were once lovers, though he was married. In this musical, we have spent the entire first act with Guido, his wife and the many characters who surround him as the pressure on him increases to begin shooting a film he hasn't even written yet. But we don't meet Claudia until the beginning of the second act. At this point, we have heard about her, but never seen her. The scene and song these two engage in is very different from the rest of the show. It is an extended dialogue scene between them that culminates in *'Unusual Way'*, a song that is almost entirely an inner monologue for Claudia. Guido never hears what she is thinking/singing. And the song is her confession of a deep and longstanding love for him, though she knows he will never leave his wife for her, and she herself has completely moved on. Aside from a few brief comments by other characters in the first act, we know very little about Claudia.

Up to this point in the show, these two characters have no onstage history together, yet the actors playing them must create the illusion of a deep, complex and long-term relationship. One of the most powerful means of creating that illusion is for the actors to conceive a past for themselves. A smart director may have the actors do some improvisations of past important moments. But often it is left to actors to do this for themselves. The actress playing Claudia can imagine her first meeting with Guido, their first day of shooting on a set, discovering his acute understanding of her, their first romantic flirtations, the first time they kissed, and so on. Importantly, she will need to imagine what made her decide to stop working with him. Was it romantic jealousy? Boredom with his repetitious stories? His intractable immaturity? Or something else? Going through the process of creating this backstory will greatly enhance the onstage life for these two characters. As she stands on that beach alone with him for the first time in years, their imaginary past will now inform her present behavior. All of this will convince an audience of the reality of a full-blown relationship that happened only in the authors' and actors' imaginations.

Not only must you create a rich past life for the character, but you also need to set up important expectations for your character's future. This means you prepare for each entrance by anticipating problems with the other characters you expect to encounter, or you remind yourself of important facts and feelings that give huge importance to those relationships. By doing this you are *frontloading* your entrance and creating the best kind of tension. You could do this in both positive and negative ways, anticipating success or defeat. Imagine a scene in which a young man goes to meet his ex-girlfriend. The actor playing the role needs to decide what that character expects to happen. In this case he frontloads the entrance by anticipating a joyous reunion with his old girlfriend. He might prepare by assuming she has asked for this meeting to repair their relationship and get back together. Now, imagine how interesting the scene might be if, upon meeting her, he discovered she was suing him and taking his house, his car and his bank account away. By frontloading the entrance with an anticipated outcome that is in stark contrast to what he actually does encounter, he's set the character up for a mighty fall. This is not to say the actor couldn't play the same scene with the anticipation of trouble with his ex-girlfriend. That might offer some good opportunities, as well.

We can see a good example of an entrance that needs frontloading in the last section of *Nine*, where film director Guido Contini's often-betrayed wife, Luisa, comes to her husband and ends their marriage in the song *'Be on Your Own'*. The actress playing Luisa must enter and begin singing immediately with no dialogue at all to help set up the confrontation with her cheating husband. It is a full frontal assault with no preparation. So, the actress playing this role must frontload her entrance powerfully.

Asking several important questions can help you create a strong entrance and beginning to a scene. First, ask what has just happened to you prior to your entrance. In the case of *'Be on Your Own'* the actress playing Luisa might imagine having coffee alone, bemoaning her fate, feeling sad and angry, or even talking to a friend. This might be part of a good preparation for the entrance. But it is generalized and doesn't give the actress anything specific to respond to. A more powerful previous moment could involve Luisa having visited her lawyer and filed for divorce. She could have just taken off her wedding ring for the first time since their wedding twenty years before. She could have seen him talking with both his mistress and his muse (which does happen in the musical) and correctly assumed he was trying to get each of them to stay with him. She might choose to specifically recall some of the many weak alibis for his continual infidelities. All of these more powerful choices involve recalling some of the backstory the authors have provided, and augmenting that with your own imagination and fantasy.

A second important reminder for yourself is to identify the specific relationship between you and the person you expect to meet. In Luisa's case, the man she is going to meet is her husband: a general relationship. But, more specifically, he is the husband who has flaunted his infidelities in her face for years. He is the film director who has chosen to make his career more important than his life with her. He is the man for whom she gave up a successful acting career and agreed not to have children with because of his career needs. He is her baby, her betrayer, her humiliator, her Peter Pan. This relationship backstory gives the actress playing Luisa plenty of emotional ammunition.

Finally, ask yourself what the character expects to happen when she meets her husband. Is she planning to deliver an ultimatum to her husband regarding his infidelities? Does she expect him to give in and admit his failings or to deny them? Does she plan to forgive him if he does apologize? Or, more powerfully, does she plan to end a long marriage to a man she is still in love with? Does she plan to tell him exactly what she thinks of him for the first time in her life? Is she going to reveal just how much he has hurt her over the years and, in particular, now? It's easy to see which of these choices is the strongest and most difficult for the character to go through. Even if most of those things don't end up happening, they help to fuel the entrance and give the entire scene a rich undercurrent of emotional energy and complexity.

This is a long list of possibilities to help you prepare – too many to use all of them. But rehearse them one at a time, identifying which elements of backstory and frontloading will set up emotional triggers you can use to quickly prepare. When you identify fantasies, images and experiences that work for you, they will launch you into the song.

EXERCISE 10C   USING BACKSTORY AND FRONTLOADING

Work with the same song and scene you've been using. Look at the start of the scene or the moment of your entrance into the scene.

1. Detail your backstory. Where are you coming from? What are your relationships and history with the situation you're entering? What just happened to you (as the character) before the scene began?

2. Frontload your action. What do you expect to find when you start? Who should be there and what do your think their attitudes will be about you? What are you entering in order to accomplish? What event do you think you are initiating? What does your character *know* and what does she *imagine* about the coming event? Imagine the dialogue: He'll say, "[——]," and I'll say, "[——]," etc. Actually speak this to yourself before starting. (Does this feel familiar? People do it all the time in real life!)

Remember that what you expect and what will really happen in the show can be very different things. Don't contradict any of the given circumstances, but also don't know what your character can't know ahead of time.

EXERCISE 10D   THREE THROUGH THE DOOR

Use the same material as in the previous exercise. Start the scene from an entrance through a door. (Even if, in the show, you are discovered onstage, for this exercise make an entrance.) Use the classroom door or a prop door.

1. Without contradicting any of the given circumstances of the show or your character, create three different sets of backstories and front-loaded expectations and intentions.

2. Make three different entrances through the door and into the dialogue and/or song. You don't necessarily need to do the whole song (unless you have the time). You could just take it to the end of the first musical unit.

3. Don't discuss your backstory or frontloading with your audience. Have them write down what they observed and understood from your performance. You can also ask for feedback from the other actors in the scene. The best way for them to comment would be to complete the phrase "When you did [——], I felt like doing or saying [——]." This tells you a great deal about how your audience is receiving you, and how you are affecting the other characters on stage. Resist the impulse to explain or defend your actions. Remember that the audience gets what it gets and your responsibility is to adjust to the feedback.

Invented memory

UNIT 10.4

In *The Scarlet Pimpernel*, Marguerite sings *'When I Look at You'* about her relationship with a man whom she once loved, and who loved her in return. But his feelings for her changed and she is now left coping with her memories of their past relationship. For some actors backstory can live at the level of information. That information needs to become memory. Those memories need to be invented by you.

One of the most useful tools any actor has is his imagination: the willingness to fantasize inventively for the purpose of filling out a script. Even the richest text and detailed backstory only give us hints and skeletal suggestions about our character's past. So, based on what information we do have, every actor must learn to fantasize constructively.

In the case of *'When I Look at You'*, she talks about specific memories. The actress playing that role needs to look at the nature of the relationship and begin inventing memories that are consistent with what she knows from the song. So she might begin asking herself questions, like:

*   When did I meet the man I'm talking/singing to?
*   When did I know I loved him?
*   Where were we?
*   What was the day like? Quality of the light? The time of day?
*   What was he wearing?
*   How did he look at me?
*   What did he say?

- What did he smell like?
- When did we first kiss?
- How did he taste?
- How did that event transpire, blow by blow?
- Who reached for the other one first?
- How did he react? How did I?
- Did we continue to kiss?
- And then what?

Keep going. You goal is to make this memory three-dimensional and five-sensual.

The more specific the invented memories are, the more they will affect you as you work. Specificity is the key. Don't let yourself off the hook by coming up with a generalized situation.

EXERCISE 10E CREATE A FANTASY MEMORY

1. Looking at the text of the song you've chosen, choose one specific relationship the song deals with.
2. Choose one key moment in that relationship that happens before the play begins.
3. (If it helps you to work with your eyes closed, it might be useful to record the following instructions so you can listen and be taken on a guided tour of that moment in your earlier relationship.)
4. Look around the imaginary room the event takes place in (see the window frames, the bedpost, the embroidered curtains).
5. Smell the scents (his aftershave, her cologne, the cookies baking, the flowers in the vase).
6. Hear the sounds (the birds singing, the clock ticking, the creek babbling).
7. Endow objects in that room with history and meaning for your character (the antique clock from your grandparents' home, the locket he gave you, the photo on the mantelpiece).
8. Listen to what is said, feel the contact, the touch. Let your mind create the entire encounter.
9. Linger in the important moments and relive them as if you're creating a three-dimensional multi-sensory filmed flashback. Take the time to really dig into the fantasy of the characters' relationship and past life, because this will allow you to react spontaneously as you work.

These invented memories will work for you as you return to the song you're singing if you take the time in advance to create vivid and specific memories. You don't need to labor over them as you work. They'll be there for you if you've done the homework of fantasizing.

Make this matter. Don't settle for a little peck on the cheek in this memory. Let it be a full-on-the-mouth, passionate kiss you feel deep down in your gut. That memory will affect you. Or let the moment he rejected you be devastating. Hear the specific words he spoke; let them burn in your memory with as much hurt as the character must have felt at that moment. And not just a general rejection, but also one played out with specific words and actions ("I never loved you!"). See the look of disgust and hate in his eyes. Feel the heat in your cheeks as you fight not to cry in front of him. See him slam the door as he leaves you for another woman (your best friend) in the carriage out front. Hear the horses pull away as you sink to the bed and finally let the tears flow. Those are some specific invented memories.

Creative fantasy is an actor's habit. Get used to it on a daily basis and enjoy the permission you give yourself to create vivid worlds to inhabit. You may ask yourself if this is all just an elaborate way to trick yourself psychologically? Yes! That's what acting is. And this is a much safer and more specific way for you to access emotion than digging up your own, possibly cherished and sacred memories. These invented memories exist only to serve your work as an actor. Your own memories about a failed relationship are often too complex and messy to work for you eight performances a week.

Some important guidelines to remember:

1. These memories are invented. They are not from your real life and shouldn't be. Have faith that you can specifically fantasize in a productive way. It does work.
2. You must take the time to get specific about details of the event. Relish the experience, fill it out and relive it a few times to get a full "memory" of the character's past critical events.
3. You do not need to share these invented memories with others. They are yours – your fantasies. You simply have to fulfill the exercise of creating specific memories. The test of any exercise is whether it works for you.
4. Trust your homework. If you've created the memories fully, they live inside you. You don't have to conjure them up.

EXERCISE 10F   CREATIVE FANTASY

1. Looking at the text of the song you've chosen, find out what information must be obeyed. (If the song says you're an orphan, then you must accept that.) So, come up with a list of all the given circumstances in the song.
2. Look at every suggestion there might be a memory or past experience referred to in the song.
3. Identify the key specific relationship(s) for the character who sings the song.
4. Now, see if the important memories and events are linked to that key relationship. Chances are good that this will be the case.
5. Select the key references from step 2 of this exercise and begin the process of specifically fantasizing those events. Look at the list of questions above to give you some ideas about how you might effectively fantasize as the character.
6. After you've gone through each of the specific memories, revisit the song and see what effect these memories have on your performance.

UNIT 10.5   The cost of failure – what's at stake?

What will happen if you don't achieve your objective through this song? What will it cost you *not* to sing the song – to *avoid* the conflict? A lot. Let's look back to our example from *West Side Story*, '*I Have a Love/A Boy Like That*'. This musical scene offers a high-stakes journey that begins with Anita condemning Maria for making love to her brother's murderer (Tony). By the end of the scene they have found consolation in each other. That passionate journey is fueled by two women, each of whom must get through to the other – or else pay a price that is too great for either to consider.

At the beginning of the scene, Anita must see Maria to vent her grief or else be destroyed by it. Then, she must shatter Maria's illusions about Tony or else allow her lover's death to be rendered meaningless. Maria, though, must convert Anita into her ally or else lose her only friend. Ultimately, Maria is successful in her quest to justify loving Tony and gains Anita's support.

Notice the constant presence of the words "or else" in each sentence. She must do this or else she will lose something gravely important. The cost of not getting what she wants is too great. So, she works like mad to achieve that objective.

What is at stake for each of these women drives them to work harder to make their points and win their battles. If they don't succeed in getting what they need, they will be settling for unacceptable circumstances – living with grief, loss of kinship, accepting meaningless death. These are tragically important costs. If these actresses make choices the characters can comfortably live with, the scene will be flat and uncompelling. We want to see acting gladiators enter the arena prepared to risk everything to get what they need or die trying. The cost of failure needs to be as high as you can get it.

EXERCISE 10G FINDING THE STAKES AND RAISING THEM

1. Looking at the text of the song you've chosen, examine the list of objectives you've created.
2. For each, ask yourself what you would lose if you didn't achieve your objective. Try phrasing it as "I must [——] or else I will [——]."

If your stakes aren't high enough to really drive you through the song, try raising them. With a little practice, nearly any potential failure can be felt to have devastating consequences. (You only have to watch a two-year-old not get a piece of candy to see that become the end of the world. Adults aren't so different. Only our desires are more sophisticated and we manage our expressions of disappointment more skillfully – sometimes.) You'll know you've arrived at appropriately high stakes when your earlier phrase reads: "I must [——] or else I will DIE!"

Journey's end

Just as the World Series of baseball is still only about hitting, catching and throwing, acting in a musical is also about fundamentals:

- See your song as a journey.
- Know where you're going and who you're going with.
- Make the trip important.

Now we'll look at how to take your work as an actor and put in onstage as a stageworthy performance.

SECTION IV: MAKING IT A PERFORMANCE

Making It a Performance

As we work onstage we need to develop two kinds of awareness. The first is what Stanislavski called the Perspective of the Role: what you want, do and react to as the character. When we pretend to be someone else and react as if we're that character, we are doing this from the perspective of the role: through the eyes and in the shoes of that imagined person. But, another important reality always exists for us onstage called the Perspective of the Actor. This refers to the part of our consciousness that is constantly recalling lyrics, staging, directions and choreography, melody, and is aware of whether we're in the light, what our fellow actors are doing, etc. These two realities must co-exist in balance for every successful performance experience. Too much attention to the inner life of the character and we may fail to bring the role to the audience. Too much stage awareness and we may become phony and performy, with no sense of the reality of the character.

We spent much of Sections I and III building a strong sense of your work from the perspective of the role. In this section we'll focus on learning how to bring your role to an audience.

As we perform, our audience perceives our experience in only two ways; through our vocal behavior and through our physical behavior. These are often the only aspects of the performance we have control of. The accompaniment or orchestra is in someone else's hands. The scenery, costume and lighting are also out of our control. And, no matter how good your analysis and emotional investment are, if they aren't clearly expressed in your physical and vocal behavior, it's all just an academic exercise. We've spent a lot of time talking about song interpretation and singing. So, we assume you're doing that work for every song you perform now. And you should already be spending a good deal of time on your vocal and dance training. Now we will focus on what you do with your voice and your body in performance.

CHAPTER 11 DISCOVERING YOUR PHRASING

One quality that makes some of the best singing actors stand out from the crowd is their ability to phrase a song well. In the hands of these singers we hear old songs as if for the first time, and new songs resonate for us with the beautiful and exciting interplay of words and music. But what is phrasing? Well, it's a lot of things. Many people understand phrasing as the relationship between the way you sing the melody and the way it is notated in the score. One performer may sing the lyric with absolute fidelity to the song as written, singing it pitch for pitch, rest for rest and note value for note value exactly as it is written on the page, while another singer may absolutely transform the same song through her variations in rhythm, timing and diction, and even by altering the lyric or melody. She might change a waltz into a bossa nova or a torch song into a lullaby. Whether strict or loose, phrasing is the singer's personal stamp on the song.

UNIT 11.1 Lyrics are dialogue

The major influence on phrasing in the musical theatre has to do with your expression of the lyric as sung dialogue. Songs in the musical theatre are musically vocalized expressions of a character's most important thoughts, feelings and needs. They are a critical portion of the dialogue in any show. The more that singers choose to honor the intention, meaning and emotional expression of the lyric, the more they may vary slightly from the exact written melody line. This is a trend in contemporary musical theatre performance where many composers recognize the limitations of musical notation in expressing phrasing. Also, some composers admire and seek actors who bring a strong interpretive perspective to their music. But it hasn't always been this way, and there are still many composers, musical directors and singers who do not wish to see any liberties taken with the score. Those variations all really boil down to taste and the agreed upon standards for the production you're working on. Be an actor who can do it all.

As you begin to approach phrasing, it's interesting to note that singing presents some challenges to discovering organic and expressive phrasing.

- Music is insistent and diverting. Music is so highly structured and can so totally dominate the artistic agenda that words and meaning can get lost in the process of developing a performance.
- Lyrics, as poetry, are a compressed and heightened expression. They can lack simplicity and directness. The presentation of the words as verse on the page can keep us from relating to them as dialogue.
- The technical demands of singing can be so extraordinary that they require all our attention. These demands can include: consciously controlled breathing, vowel modification, adjustment in tone or placement, and stylistic ornamentation. These demands can be so great that none of your energy or attention is left over for acting. In these cases, the experience of singing in a show is no longer about communication.
- The sound and feeling of singing can be so intoxicating, the singer can be lured into a dangerous indulgence that has nothing to do with relating to others onstage or communicating the character's need.

A curious irony is that the better the music, the better the singer, and the better the lyric, the easier it is to fall into these traps. Since these issues can be distractions, let's take them away for a bit. Let's work without the accompaniment. Let's turn the poetry into dialogue and the singing into speech. Then we'll reintegrate the ideas with the poetry and the music. The result will be phrasing that is musical, textually specific and personal.

We look at important words and decide what the main idea of a sentence or speech is. We use language to change our partners. We speak to their eyes, not their ears in an effort to make them see what we mean. We speak to their hearts to make them feel. We speak to their bodies to make them do.

EXERCISE 11A   LISTENING FOR EMPHASIS

For this chapter, pick a moderate to up tempo song from the mid-1930s through the mid-1960s. That period of music works well to begin understanding phrasing. Avoid frantic songs that you'll have to rush through or ballads that are so slow you must sustain words and ideas for long stretches.

1. Listen to the song's melody and accompaniment played together without any words being sung. You can have your voice teacher, coach

or accompanist provide you with a recording of this. As you listen, note on your score every place that gets strong musical emphasis for any reason. You don't need to worry about the technical musical reasons or techniques. All that matters is you hear a moment of emphasis. You can circle the place in your score, make a check mark, etc. to indicate where it happened.

2. Now look at the lyrics that coincide with those markings. Do you find that the words landing on or very near those markings are important? If they don't appear to be so at first, consider how they might be.

3. Look at songs from three different periods (Operetta, Musical Comedy, Golden Age, Concept Musicals, Rock Musicals, etc.) to see how the capitalization and punctuation are marked in the score or on the sheet music that was published. Notice where the lyric is punctuated in a way that makes sense to you and where it seems to be arbitrary or based on the rhyme scheme of the song.

Now we're going to explore a process for lifting a lyric from its normal place, surrounded by music, and help you see it as sung dialogue.

UNIT 11.2 **Monologuing the lyric**

This is the way *'Just in Time'* appears in the script of *Bells Are Ringing*. It is printed on the page to match the musical phrases and to emphasize the rhyme scheme in the lyric Betty Comden and Adolph Green supplied to composer Jule Styne.

Just in time
I found you just in time
Before you came my time
Was running low
I was lost
The losing dice were tossed
My bridges all were crossed
Nowhere to go
But now you're here
And now I know just where I'm going

No more doubt or fear
I've found my way
For love came just in time
I found you just in time
And saved my lonely life
That lovely day

EXERCISE 11B READING THE LYRIC

Try speaking this lyric out loud as it is written above. Notice how you end up speaking in erratic and illogical patterns.

If you spoke this lyric as written, the ideas and sentences were broken up into unnatural chunks of words. You were speaking word to word to word, not expressing ideas, needs and feelings. This has no relationship to the way we really speak or think.

Now, here is the same lyric written as a paragraph with the addition of punctuation that matches the logic of the dialogue. You might choose to punctuate it slightly differently, but the essential meaning of the lyric is clearly spelled out in this paragraph.

Just in time; I found you just in time. Before you came, my time was running low. I was lost. The losing dice were tossed. My bridges all were crossed: nowhere to go. But, now you're here, and now I know just where I'm going. No more doubt or fear: I've found my way. For, love came just in time. I found you just in time, and saved my lonely life that lovely day.

EXERCISE 11C MEANING THE LYRIC

Now, speak the lyric out loud again as it is written here. Read it from this page until you can speak it as sentences, free of the rhythm of the song. If you fall into the rhythm of the music, start the sentence again until you can do this without getting caught in the old musical rhythms.

Here are some helpful hints to look for:

- A period, exclamation point or question mark is a full stop: the complete end of an idea. Make it sound conclusive. *I was lost. The losing dice were tossed.*
- A semicolon is like a period, but doesn't have the same degree of finality. It rounds out something that is very like a sentence (with a subject, verb and possibly an object), but the idea isn't really finished. The next phrase will also be sentence-like, but the two parts depend on each other and cling together. Make us hear the relationship. *Just in time; I found you just in time.*
- A colon suggests "thus" or "so" or "therefore" or "because" – words that push you into the next phrase as a way of clarifying, detailing or explicating the earlier idea. Let's hear the need for the second phrase. *My bridges all were crossed: (so) nowhere to go.* You can practice saying this with the "pushing word" like "so," and then take the word back out but retain the energy of it.
- A comma is a way of defining the boundaries of a phrase. A phrase is just a part of the larger sentence. Let's hear the relationship of the phrases to the whole idea of the sentence. *But, now you're here, and now I know just where I'm going.* Many times a phrase can be deleted entirely. If you sense this, practice the sentence with and without the phrase to feel the balance and relationship of the ideas. *But, now you're here. But, now I know just where I'm going.*

Once you've got it punctuated, you can separate it by full-stop sections. Notice the relationship between the long and short ideas:

> Just in time; I found you just in time.
> Before you came my time was running low.
> I was lost.
> The losing dice were tossed.
> My bridges all were crossed: (so) nowhere to go.
> But, now you're here, and now I know just where I'm going.
> No more doubt or fear: (because) I've found my way.
> For, love came just in time.
> I found you just in time, and saved my lonely life that lovely day.

How does this change your sense of the lyric's meaning?

After a few tries, you probably noticed you were making sense of the lyric as a set of ideas, not speaking in blocks of words that are really small portions of sentences. This is the first step in developing your own sense of the song and understanding where you want to place emphasis in the song. These choices lead directly into phrasing.

The exercise you've just done is called *monologuing*, and it means you've turned the lyric into a spoken monologue that exists as a non-musical expression of the song. As you speak the lyric with its well thought out punctuation and normalized capitalization you can begin to apply all of the techniques you'd normally consider when working on a monologue. And you can see if there are important needs, thoughts and feelings expressed in that lyric. You'll need to get comfortable speaking the lyric without any of the rhythm of the song in it, and this often takes a little practice because those old rhythms can be deeply embedded in your way of thinking about the song. But persevere in temporarily separating the lyric from the musical structure. It will eventually start to come out as comfortably as spoken dialogue.

EXERCISES 11D LYRIC AS MONOLOGUE

Once you've become comfortable with the lyric as a speech, ask the fundamental questions you would normally ask of any dramatic moment.

- Who am I speaking to?
- What do I want from them?
- What am I doing to get it?
- What stands in the way of my getting what I want?
- How are they reacting from moment to moment, and how does that affect me?

Treat the lyric as you would any monologue. It will probably feel more like heightened speech or verse drama to you because of the rhymed or poetic nature of most lyrics. Don't hide the rhymes. Characters who rhyme know they are doing it, take satisfaction in it, and use it to make their points. Play with the rhyme. Use it.

Not only is this technique useful from a rehearsal perspective; you'll sometimes perform a song this way. There are a number of important cases where this is exactly what was done, and to great effect. In the original production of *My Fair Lady*, Rex Harrison "talk sung" virtually the entire role of Henry Higgins in just this fashion. He spoke on rhythm with the musical accompaniment, only rarely breaking into singing. And the original Musical Comedy Man, George M. Cohan, made a career out of talk singing all those patriotic songs we now sing with full melody. But, in most cases, the song is meant to be sung on pitch. You might gain great emphasis for an important word or phrase by dropping out of melody and speaking in rhythm for that section.

One general aesthetic unifying most styles of musical theatre is that the voice use is more speech-like than in purely musical forms. In an oratorio, like Handel's *Messiah* for example, it is less crucial that we focus on the lyric and more important that we hear a beautiful sound. The voice is an instrument and the words in their repetitive cycles, though meaningful, are a soundscape more than a dramatic playscript. In contrast, most musicals rely strongly on clarity of text and on a singing style that is more like speech and less like a musical instrument. The words, as dramatic script, matter a great deal.

Also, a musical theatre audience isn't usually supposed to think of the character as "singing." Instead, the character is so full of feeling that speech expands into song and normal movement into dance. We're meant not to notice when one becomes the other but to be carried smoothly along on the emotional flow.

Classical terms used to describe a speech-song quality are *recitative*, i.e. singing that is very close to speech, often with long passages sung on one note and in the free cadence of speech (*Jesus Christ Superstar*, Caiaphas, Billy Bigelow's 'Soliloquy' in *Carousel*), and *sprechstimme*, a vocal style in which the melody is spoken at approximate pitches rather than sung (the way Rex Harrison approached much of Henry Higgins in *My Fair Lady*). Through-composed shows like *Evita* employ these a great deal.

The issue for the actor is to make these transitions between speech and song with as little difference in vocal quality as possible. It isn't unusual for a person to have a speaking voice that is quite different from his sung sound. To avoid this difference, think of making both your spoken sound more 'sung' and your singing voice more 'spoken'.

EXERCISE 11E   SPEAK – SING – SPEAK

Pick a song with some sustained notes and lyrical passages. Work with accompaniment.

1. After every breath, explore speaking at least the first couple of syllables and bridging that into full singing.
2. When you're comfortable with this technique, reverse that and sing only the first few notes, then speak the rest of the section.
3. Explore this approach until you can comfortably switch in and out of singing and speaking. In every case find a vocal placement that blurs the line so the switches in vocal quality from speech to singing are as unobtrusive as possible.

EXERCISES 11F   EMPHATIC WORDS

After you've tried monologuing the lyric several times, take a moment to look at the lyric on paper again and see which words have become most important to you and have gained the strongest emphasis. Circle those words or phrases.

1. Sing the song and when you get to a word or phrase you circled, speak it. What did you discover as you tried this technique? Did the words or phrases become more or less important? Where there any particular phrases that you felt were helped by this technique?
2. Now try the same exercise in reverse, speaking everything else and singing the emphatic words or phrases. What did you discover?

Returning to music

Words and music are meant to be together. But let's reintegrate them carefully so you don't lose all the discoveries you've just made.

EXERCISES 11G RETURNING TO THE MUSIC

For this next set of exercises you'll need to get a recording of your song with just the accompaniment played. Leave out the melody and leave out your singing. This recording should sound exactly like what you'll hear underneath you when you sing the song. Using your "accompaniment only" recording, begin the music and, when the melody begins, simply speak the lyric over the accompaniment, letting it fall roughly where it would if you were to sing it, but still retaining the logical and emotional sense of the lyric as a speech.

You'll probably need to do this several times to get comfortable with it. Be careful not to abandon what you discovered while monologuing the lyric. Are you still able to retain the meaning of the words with the musical shape underneath it? Did you begin to sing-song the words or were you able to coordinate the words with music and still mean what you were saying and fight for what you wanted as that character? Did you keep the newfound emphatic words and depth of meaning you discovered earlier?

If you find you're having a hard time hanging on to the sense of the lyric, try monologuing the lyric again without music and then return to this exercise. There is no rush in your rehearsal process. Take as much time as you need to get comfortable with this technique.

UNIT 11.4 ## Singing ideas instead of notes and words

Now that you've mastered speaking the lyric over the accompaniment, you're ready to sing again. The purpose of this next exercise is to continue focusing on singing the lyric as dialogue, not on sounding beautiful. We are seeking to reintegrate the music with the dramatic event you've discovered in the lyric. Chances are you'll probably mess up a few musical passages, stumble here and there, and do a less than perfect job with the vocal aspects of your song this first time through. So what? That isn't the focus for now. Give yourself a break about the singing portion for a moment. You will certainly focus on that at a later rehearsal.

EXERCISES 11H SINGING YOUR OBJECTIVE

As you are about to begin, identify your partner (even use a live partner if possible) and your objective. Then begin *singing the ideas*. That's right. You're not singing notes and words, but ideas. After you've sung it once, take a moment to notice how the music and lyric relate to each other. Were you able to hang on to the understanding of the words and to fulfill your needs from the other character? As you did that, how did the music help or hinder you? Identify the places that are trouble spots for you. Go back and figure out why they felt awkward.

Phrasing with breath

This isn't about the technique of breathing for singing. You'll need to get one-on-one coaching to develop your skill for that. This is about the interesting fact that breathing has meaning, and is itself an important part of the performed text.

Have you ever been in the midst of speaking a line or singing a phrase and found yourself running out of air? Stand back and watch a casual conversation objectively. You'll notice that speakers in real life almost never have that problem. If you look carefully, you can see they take a breath that is the same size as the idea they're about to express. It is no accident that the word for taking a breath is the same as the one for getting an idea: inspiration.

If the speaker is in rapport with the listener, he will cede the conversation when the listener takes in a noticeable breath. Because we're looking to see how our message is being received, we notice the moment of inspiration to tell what struck home. Our partner's inhalation is a cue they want to speak, so we hand the conversation over. We also watch the speed, depth and relative freedom or constriction of the airway during that inhalation because it correlates to the imperative, size and emotional charge of the incoming thought. The information communicated via breathing constitutes an important aspect of the conversational text. Just like our conversational partners, audiences derive essential understanding about the moment in the show and the transaction occurring between the characters by noticing when and how they breathe. Breathing and meaning are powerfully linked. So, if you don't think carefully about where you breathe, you may be working against the text, and confusing your audience.

Using breathing to phrase ideas

Ideas can be big and small. They can be simple and short or simple but filled with a soaring emotion that makes them huge. They can be complex and come rushing out, or fragmented and frustrating. The possibilities are nearly infinite. But they all have one thing in common: all ideas initiate a breath.

Sometimes, in showing off their glorious voices, musical theatre actors will choose to locate breaths and sing through sections of a song for musical, rather than textual reasons. Look at this sentence from *Carousel's* reluctantly rapturous *'If I Loved You'*.

If I loved you, time and again I would try to say all I'd want you to know.

Speak it as a simple line of dialogue. Look where you naturally pause. Try it several times to see where the instinctive breaths will come. There is more than one right answer. Frequently people will choose: "If I loved you / time and again . . ." That's because there is a "then" missing in the lyric: "If I loved you, *then* time and again . . ." A breath at that point accommodates the change in thought present in an if-then statement. Singers, however, will sometimes fall in love with the ascending melody and link "you–time" without taking a breath. It is sweeping and musically showy, but doesn't express the text well. This decision also ramifies into the next phrase. In order to keep singing, a breath will need to be inserted soon, so the results will be: "If I loved you time and again / I would try to say / . . ." The odd breath choices have now made the text hard to understand. The breathing placement even changed the meaning to suggest that the question is how often they've loved, not whether they will love.

Sometimes you have to take a breath in the middle of an idea because the musical phrase is simply too long for you to sing. In this case, you need to take a catch breath to finish out the phrase. This is a short breath that will allow you enough air to complete the phrase before taking a full breath for the next phrase. Look for a logical place to do this within the long phrase. Place a mental tie-line in the gap and keep the idea going. As you practice singing with the catch breath, work to keep the idea and need continuous even if the breath isn't.

Now the dance between singing and acting begins in earnest.

Front phrasing and back phrasing

We can't prioritize the lyrics over the music or vice versa. Since lyrics transmit meaning and music conveys feeling, both of them work more powerfully together than apart. When we began this section we described singing with absolute fidelity to the music as it is written. Then we described singing with great liberties. This second approach employs the techniques of *front and back phrasing*. These techniques have to do with the singer slightly changing the written musical rhythms either by singing a word or phrase slightly earlier than it is scored (*front phrasing*), or by singing it slightly later than it is scored (*back phrasing*). Back phrasing is the most common of these techniques. It may seem that the singer is slightly late in starting, but by the end has caught up and is back in time with the accompaniment. In other cases, the singer makes the melody more elastic by stretching a word into the next bar or beat. These techniques are usually used with more contemporary theatre music, since about 1950. It would probably sound odd to hear music by Gilbert and Sullivan sung with much variation in rhythm (unless your production departed radically from the traditional approach). But, shows like *Rent*, *The Last Five Years* or *The Full Monty* almost demand this kind of interpretive latitude because they are so influenced by jazz and rock music styles. Composers like Cy Coleman, Jule Styne, John Kander and others from the 1950s and 60s wrote with the expectation that performers would employ these musical and stylistic techniques.

EXERCISE 11I   BACK PHRASING

For this exercise, continue using the song you've been working with. We're going to explore the idea of front and back phrasing.

1. Try delaying the beginning of each phrase of music by holding off on singing the first note for as long as possible before you begin and catch up to the music within that phrase. You can't be late at the end of the phrase.
2. Using a key phrase in the chorus of the song, experiment with that same phrase four times, varying the degree of back phrasing each time. The first time, sing it exactly as written. The second time, use a slight back phrase. The third time slightly more. The fourth time through should be the maximum amount of back phrase you can use while still maintaining a sense of musicality and the intention of the lyric.

EXERCISE 11J   FRONT PHRASING

Do the same exercises, but this time try anticipating the attack of the lyric slightly, using front phrasing. You'll probably find this much more difficult than with back phrasing. Most singers really find this difficult.

One survival strategy is to repeat a phrase. If you come in on the third or fourth beat of the leading measure, for example, you might find yourself singing, "Just in – just in time . . ." This repetition is a baby-step way to find front phrasing without losing track of the song altogether. Then you have to clip off the note value associated with "time" if you want to attack, "I found you . . ." early as well. For singers without a jazz background this can take a lot of practice before they can own it. However, it is absolutely worth learning. Another trick is to work with a friend who can conduct for you, maintaining a clear down beat and cueing you to initiate on the previous upbeat.

EXERCISE 11K   RESEARCH PHRASING STYLES

1. For research purposes, listen to mid-twentieth-century popular vocalists like Ella Fitzgerald, Billie Holiday, Sarah Vaughn, Judy Garland, Frank Sinatra, Al Jolson and Bing Crosby. Find examples of these singers varying the phrasing in songs. Identify examples of front and back phrasing. Since these singers seem to effortlessly rephrase their material, their application of front and back phrasing can slip by unnoticed. Try listening while keeping a strict beat by counting aloud and tapping your hand. This will make their phrasing choices even clearer. Discuss how you think the changes in phrasing enhance or detract from the meaning of the lyric. Listen for and identify any other variations in phrasing and melody that seem to stand out. Why did the singer do that?

2. Find the same song in recordings by three different popular artists from different eras. Compare how each treated the song, with special emphasis on their phrasing and their melodic variations from the song as written on the page. You'll need a copy of the sheet music for the song for this purpose. Songs like *'I Get a Kick out of You'* from *Anything Goes* or those by Harold Arlen, George Gershwin, Jerome Kern, etc. work well for this purpose.

EXERCISE 11L IMPERSONATING PHRASING

Using your song, or a song the artists you listened to were singing, try to imitate the musical phrasing of that singer. Don't worry about imitating their vocal quality or colorings. Simply try to emulate the phrasing. Regardless of your gender, try this out with several singers, both male and female. We'll explore another variation on this in Section V: Style in Musical Theatre

It's a musical, not a play-zical!

A lot of what you do as a singer is make emotionally evocative sounds. Your voice is a musical instrument. Play it.

We're going to offer a handful of simple exercises that will help you begin to explore the musical aspects of your songs.

EXERCISE 11M VOWELS ONLY

1. Sing your song on a single open vowel, such as "Ahh," "Ooh," "Ohh." Sing the entire thing this way, focusing only on the tonal qualities that you make. Did you find anything out about the musical shape of the song? Try it on other vowels.
2. Now sing the song again, but this time you'll sing all of the vowels in the song, with no consonants at all.

EXERCISE 11N I'M AN INSTRUMENT

1. Sing your song on any vowels or consonants you like as long they are not the actual words. As you sing, imitate one of the following instruments:

trumpet	bass
saxophone	violin
electric guitar	trombone

2. Now try other instruments or those that are not on the list. Have your group create a vocal orchestra. Each member selects an instrument. Have a jam session. Get a pianist to join you. Use your body for percussion.

EXERCISE 11O   SCAT SINGING

1. Sing your song using *jazz scat* phrases like "Ba dat do dah," "Zo be zo bah zo way." Sing like no one is listening. Many people find it easier to begin this practice alone. It can be a ball. Singers like Ella Fitzgerald, Sarah Vaughn, Mel Torme and Louis Armstrong were masters of this style. Listen to them if you want some ideas.
2. Separate into groups of four (or smaller) and take turns scat singing phrases from a song you all know. Each person will sing four or eight bars of the song before the next person picks it up.
3. Do the same exercise but bring a ball, a hat, a scarf or something light and soft that you can toss back and forth. One person starts scat singing the song, when he feels like it, he passes the ball to another person, any person in the group, and that person picks up singing immediately. Try this game with the instruments, as well.

EXERCISE 11P   REMASTERING

Remix a song you know using different musical styles, beats and meters. Change your song from 4/4 to 3/4 time. Or from a fox trot to a bossa nova. Explore each of these musical flavors:

waltz	tango	march	charleston
swing	pop ballad	hip-hop	

How many variations can you think of?

As you played with these exercises, you probably discovered you stopped worrying about what the lyrics were and began treating yourself as a member of the band. Relishing the act of vocalizing can be freeing and can inform the song within the context of the show, too. The job of the singing actor is to fulfill the music *and* the lyrics simultaneously.

SECTION IV: MAKING IT A PERFORMANCE

STAGING YOUR SONG

After all of our analysis, introspection and exploration, it is time to put your song on its feet. In this section we will deal with gesture and physicalization – issues that go to the heart of good acting. We'll explore ways you can address the challenge of staging a song yourself and ways to be an effective artistic partner with a director or choreographer.

You'll need the skills to generate your own staging for auditions and shows where either the style is naturalistic or there isn't the time to set every song on every character. You'll also need to be able to quickly understand and embody choreography and staging that is imposed by others. An actor who is self-sufficient and who can make abstract direction into concrete behavior is one who will work steadily.

A common language for working on the stage

Let's lay out some commonly understood terms that actors and directors use in referring to the playing space and how we move in it. This will give us a shared language and set of terms.

In almost all theatre spaces, stage positions and movement patterns are referred to from the actor's point of view. Therefore, the actor's right as she faces the audience is called stage right and her left is called stage left. Because stage floors prior to the twentieth century used to be tilted downward slightly toward the audience (called raked) the front of the stage is called downstage and the back

Table12-1

The back wall of the stage

(Upstage)

Upstage right	Upstage center	Upstage left
Center stage right	Center center	Center stage left
Downstage right	Downstage center	Downstage left

The audience or orchestra pit

(Downstage)

---

of the playing space is called upstage. We hang on to these terms even though stage floors are most often not raked anymore. Table 12-1 shows the various areas of the stage in a standard proscenium setting, where audience members sit in front of a rectangular opening through which they view the stage area, as in a movie theatre.

EXERCISE 12A   ONSTAGE TWISTER

1. Make multiple photocopies of the diagram above and cut the squares out. Drop all of the pieces into a hat. Use a large space, preferably a real stage space. Choose one person to play the director. Send all the other players to the stage. Drawing from the hat, the director orders individual players randomly around the stage.

2. To make this more competitive, the director can eliminate any actor who hesitates or goes to the wrong location.

3. To take this up one more level, have the director draw two slips of paper and send the player to a location by passing through another, as in, "Joe, cross through down left to down right."

4. Countering. The next level requires any actor already occupying the end location to leave that area before the next actor arrives and stops. Actors should make small adjustments to their positions to remain visible and not be obstructed by another player. They should also avoid standing in a line.

5. Increase the tempo of play by having more than one director. (It might be necessary to designate a referee, as well, because it can become chaotic.)

Body positions

Actors have a language not only for where they are onstage, but also for how they stand. These terms allow you and your directors to discuss staging without one person demonstrating the staging to another. As we look at these positions, think of yourself standing at the center of a large clock face with 12:00 directly upstage of you as you face the audience, and 6:00 directly downstage of you.

Full front. Facing directly downstage so the audience can see both eyes equally. You do not favor one side of the stage or the other. Your face is pointed towards 6:00.

Full back. Facing directly upstage so the audience sees none of your face. Your face is pointed towards 12:00.

Profile. Standing onstage so the audience sees only one side of your face, with only one eye visible. Profile right refers to your standing facing stage right, revealing only the left side of your face. Profile left refers to your standing facing stage left, revealing only the right side of your face. So, you would be facing either 3:00 (profile left) or 9:00 (profile right).

Quarter profile. Standing onstage facing one downstage corner so the audience can see all of one side of your face and part (but not all) of the other side. Quarter profile right means you are facing the downstage right corner of your playing space, toward 8:00. Quarter profile left means you're facing Downstage Left, at 4:00.

Three quarter profile. Standing onstage facing either upstage right (10:00) or upstage left (2:00), so the audience sees only a very small portion of your face from the audience

Stage positions and visual impact

Different stage positions give the actor differing visual impact. Directors and choreographers work to make stage pictures using actors and scenic elements as their compositional tools. You can help with this if you understand how you're being used and what part of the focus you carry. The terms *strength* or *power* and *weakness* here refer to visual impact in staging.

Center center is the most balanced position on stage. It implies stability.
Downstage center is the most powerful position onstage.
Downstage left and *downstage right* are the second most powerful positions

onstage, but they are not stable positions. They imply that there is a more powerful, more certain place for the character to get to.

Upstage right and *upstage left* are the weakest positions onstage.

EXERCISE 12B   LIVING TABLEAU

1.   If you're in a group, select an area of your studio space or use an available stage space. Have one member of your group stand in different areas of the stage, and at different angles. Decide which postures and positions have the greatest and least impact. Try this with two, then three members of a group to see how the physical relationships affect their power onstage.

2.   Classical master paintings. Looking at a book of classical master paintings, identify a number of images with several people in them. Treating the canvas as a stage, name the positions on the stage and their angle. Use the members of the class to reproduce the famous picture.

UNIT 12.4   ## Staging terms

Actors also share a specialized set of terms that describe how they move from one place to another onstage.

Blocking. Formalized patterns of stage movement and business, developed in rehearsal.

Enter. To walk (or arrive by some other means) onto the playing space.

Exit. To leave the playing space.

Cross. To walk from one place onstage to another.

Counter. To move in the opposite direction of another actor who is crossing past you. So, as she moves to the left of you, you would counter by crossing toward stage right a few steps. Countering is a way of keeping the stage picture balanced and avoiding all of the action becoming pushed to one side.

Onstage. Toward the center of the playing space.

Offstage. Away from the center of the playing space.

Depth/shallowness. This refers to how far away from the front edge of the stage you are, with *deep* being closest to the back wall of the stage, and *shallow* being closest to the audience edge of the stage.

Plane. If we drew a series of many right to left lines, running parallel to the

Proscenium Line, we would see planes on the stage. These planes mark the depth of the stage.

Proscenium line. The imaginary line that runs along the stage floor directly under the proscenium arch (the opening in the imaginary fourth wall that allows the audience to see that stage action).

Point of focus or anchor points. Where you look while you sing or speak. You may decide you need more than one point of focus to make your experience clear. You will probably not look exclusively at this spot. But, it is important for you to have selected it and to know who is supposed to be there in your imagination. This can include your partner (if you have one). But it often includes specific spots in front of you, over the audience, higher or lower in front of you, that you've selected to help tell your story.

Staging yourself

There are many schools of thought about what to do when staging a song. One says that you shouldn't stage it at all. People in that camp believe that simply playing your objective will be enough to create organic movement, and that anything extra will come off as phony or artificial. Others say that you need to plan every movement and gesture thoroughly to express your ideas about the journey of the song. Our opinion is that whatever your choice about movement and staging, it should be a conscious choice and should be appropriate for the song, the style and the circumstance. And no matter how heightened the theatrical reality of your song, it needs to appear to be a spontaneous experience for the character in the context of your production. Mature performers with years of experience learn to stage songs on their feet, as they are performing them, and develop instincts about when to move and when to stay still and let the power of their voice and the song carry the moment. But their instincts were developed over years of studying, experimenting and watching the work of others whom they respect. Chances are that you're not at that place yet. So, this is the beginning of your development of those instincts.

An external expression of the inner journey

As you watch actors perform songs in fully mounted productions you will probably notice that nearly every musical moment is staged in some way. Staging is a term we use to describe the movement patterns, physical shapes and gestures used by the actor as he performs the song. This may mean some kind of gently organized realistic behavior like walking from one place to another, sitting, standing, leaning, kneeling and so forth. But it may also mean specifically choreographed dance movement while singing, with a dance break in the middle of the song, or some other kind of stylized or heightened movement. No matter what the degree of realism or stylization, the staging of a song should be a physical expression of the character's journey. What we see onstage should be a manifestation of the song's dramatic action. And it's your job to create that physical expression. In the following units we'll discuss some frequently used tools and techniques for expressing that journey.

UNIT 12.7   Generating your own movement and staging

UNIT 12.7.1   *Impulse leads to action*

Every thought or feeling we have shows up somehow in our bodies. Breathe, bend, blink or bellow – some impulse made you do it, and that spontaneous action was the product of a flash of feeling or the spark of an idea.

This is a natural part of life and we are skilled at reading the behavior of others for clues to the underlying context and meaning. You could say that one of our first jobs as infants is parsing tiny shifts in facial gesturing, vocal tone and other behaviors. We get more sophisticated at this as we go through life. Audiences, in particular, are especially attentive to behavioral indicators because they are looking for those clues to help them understand the characters, their relationships and all the elements of the story.

The challenge for actors is that, unlike in real life, theatrical moments are rehearsed, planned and sometimes choreographed. In musicals, we have heightened periods of expression during songs where the way we use the body is often expanded beyond the casually pedestrian movement of daily life to something more evocative and emotionally specific. As we said at the beginning of this section, audiences only perceive our experience through our vocal and physical behavior. For the musical actor that physical behavior means the use of gesture and body shape: some of the most powerful tools we have to share our inner life with an audience.

Deciding on which gestures are appropriate or whether to even select gestures at all are common dilemmas for the musical actor. When we talked about staging songs, we told you that some actors (and productions) don't make conscious selections for staging, preferring to keep the process closer to realism, and allowing the actor to generate a physical life that is exclusively the result of playing actions and exploring the inner life of the character with commitment. In many cases, this is the ideal choice. But if you were to attend two performances of a production that was developed in this fashion you would probably discover that the actors were doing almost the same things physically at both performances. How can this be if the actors are inventing the movement spontaneously each night? The patterns you saw repeated were the result of unconscious selection of gesture and movement. In the process of repeating a series of psychological actions the actors arrived at a series of corresponding physical actions that best expressed the character's inner life. This happens in even the most realistic plays, as well, because our inner life and our physical life are absolutely connected to each other.

One of the boldest uses of gesture in recent years comes in the Broadway performances of the role of The Phantom in *Phantom of the Opera*. For anyone who has seen that production it is clear the actor playing The Phantom must be a master of gestural acting. As he seduces Christine, The Phantom uses his hand to hypnotize her, to lure her, to caress her. Each gesture is a specific expression of the tactic being played at that moment. Many roles invite this heightened use of gesture, and many more require the same specificity in a more naturalistic style.

Inhabiting gesture

Young actors often feel artificial when they begin working with the heightened physical aspects of musical expression. While singing, the practice of altering pitch, volume and duration of our vocal expression seems perfectly natural. Yet doing the same thing physically can feel strange. It's crucial we get used to this prime tenet of acting in musicals: our physical and vocal realities must match in style and intensity. If we remember this idea, it becomes infinitely easier to embrace the use of extended gesture and extreme body position.

Not only do we match expression with style and intensity, but we must also inhabit the gesture. This means that we express the psychological action through the physical action. So, if we're pleading for mercy and we've selected the physical action of kneeling and reaching up with both hands, then we also need to commit our full emotional energy to that plea. Again, the music will tell us the degree of physical intensity required to inhabit the gesture. Strong or brassy music will require movement to match. Gentler, more rhapsodic passages will invite more fluid, subtler movement.

UNIT 12.9   ## Illustration versus gesture

This is a good time to point out the important difference between a *gesture* and an *illustration*. We have all seen or maybe even made fun of the amateur actor who recites the line "Look, up in the tree, a beautiful bird" with the following movements accompanying it: "Look (*points upward*), up (*right hand indicates a great height*) in the tree (*hands make the shape of a round canopy of branches*), a beautiful (*hands clasped together on her chest*) bird (*hands flutter upward*)." This illustrates the danger of illustration. That is, carrying out movements that don't spring from your character, but rather serve to depict or enact the subject that the character is talking about. In the mid-nineteenth century, an acting teacher named François Delsarte created a system of gestures that were meant to represent specific emotions to the audience. Theoretically, if you saw the actor strike a particular pose, you would know it meant sadness or deep love. We see remnants of this kind of acting in ballets like *Swan Lake* or *The Nutcracker*. But on the musical and dramatic stage this kind of literal association between prescribed gestures and feeling is not considered the norm except in the most extremely stylized productions or when one is trying to invoke the spirit of this much older, melodramatic style of theatre. For most purposes, there is a huge difference between living through an experience as the character and demonstrating each image for the audience. While any of the above movements might become a justifiable gesture in the right context and with real commitment from a fine actor, illustration has very little to do with contemporary acting.

UNIT 12.10   ## Anchoring

UNIT 12.10.1   ### *Anchoring things – a 3-D map of your outer world*

You'll notice that we don't normally introduce a new concept with an exercise rather than an explanation. In this case, do the following exercise and use your powers of observation first. We'll explain the concept afterwards.

EXERCISE 12C   GIVING DIRECTIONS

Ask for a volunteer (#1) who lives at some distance from the building you're now in and who drives in regularly. It is important that the route is well known and routine and it's nice if it is a little bit complicated. Choose a second volunteer (#2). The first person (#1) is told that there is a party at her house and that #2 needs driving directions to get there from here. Send #1 out of the room where the next instructions can't be heard being discussed.

Spoiler Alert! #1 must not have read the remainder of this exercise or it will taint the spontaneous truthfulness of what is to come. If you have a large enough group, it can also be interesting to send a couple of people out of the room with #1, so you can have a set of unbiased observers.

Put two chairs up front facing the group. Sit #2 on the side that would be natural for a front-seat passenger in a car. Divide the group into four sections. Each will have responsibility for observing #1's overall behavior, but will focus primarily in one major area.

Group one – eye movement. Watch how the person will see things like stoplights above, stop signs to the side, freeway signs where they really are, the location of houses on their correct sides, etc. Notice how they might check oncoming traffic when turning or changing lanes, and how the conversational eye contact may be different because of the need to "see" the road and to remember and locate landmarks on the route.

Group two – weight. Watch how the driver will lean into turns, tilt with the angle of a curve or on-ramp, lean forward when coming to a stop, lean back when moving forward.

Group three – feet. Watch how the driver's right foot will subtly press the brake when stopping, shift slightly to step on the gas when moving forward, and both feet may brace on turns.

Group four – hands. Common gestures will be to occasionally grip the steering wheel, turn palm down and swing over the wheel when describing a turn, point directions, point at signs and landmarks.

Part 1. Bring #1 back into the room. #2 should adopt the role of a stranger in town and ask for specific, clear directions to the party. It is okay to interrupt and ask for details and clarification, but keep it simple; don't make this about #2.

Observers should note how #1 embodies the directions. This is often quite subtle, so watch carefully. Make notes on what is observed. (Note that it is possible for the person to make mistakes in giving directions, but that is still different from the errors that might show up in part 2, next.)

Don't discuss it yet.

Part 2. Ask #1 to now invent a set of driving directions. Say there is a circus on the outskirts of town. You need to give #2 driving directions to this circus. You must invent all the directions in a believable way, using no actual streets, highways or landmarks. As before, #2 may interrupt for clarification or additional details.

Observers watch as before, noting the difference between the remembered directions and invented ones. Be on the lookout for errors and incongruities. Notice if the person says "left" and gestures right, or changes directions. Notice how the eyes give away when something is being invented, and how the body isn't as deeply involved or betrays anxiety through breath-holding or rigidity.

Discuss.

Now, the explanation. When we have an experience, the physical details of that incident are anchored for us. All the features of the event live in our bodies and are reflected congruently in our behavior. The person we are speaking with will be able to see the matching overlay of our memories with multiple tiny behaviors. In real life those behaviors (little eye movements, subtle shifts in weight, minor indications of direction through head movement or arm gesture, etc.) are the product of an actual experience and so have congruence. The audience can recognize that it all matches up.

How we know someone is lying: as you will have noticed in the exercise above, we always instinctively attempt some form of anchoring, even when we are making things up, because it helps to keep the invented facts organized. This is true for both improvised and memorized material. You will notice the person fabricating directions will still point broadly and do indicative physical behaviors. But since the speaker wasn't actually present for the events, the description just won't have the congruence of an authentic experience. The audience will recognize that for some reason it doesn't make sense and lacks the consistency of truth. (They will often not be able to identify this feeling and may even blame themselves for not understanding. This is particularly the case in situations where the speaker is an authority.)

Improvisers, actors (and liars) are the most successful when their invented world is woven in with actual experiences. So if, in the exercise above, the invented directions are overlaid on top of real streets and existing landmarks (renaming Main Street as Maple Street and switching the church on the corner for a school), the description will be more believable for the audience. You might try this version to see. This is a fundamental premise of acting and the reason many acting methodologies rely on sense memory and personalization to make an authentic connection. A lie is more believable if it is 99 percent truth.

Occasionally directors will have a cast improvise an event that occurs offstage, or before the play begins, such as a party. This isn't an idle exercise or something that is vaguely about character or relationships, though it can help with those things. The payoff in this kind of improvisation is that everyone now has the same set of real experiences with each other so their performances will subtly have the same anchor points. The references to that party don't have to be created but can have the force and detail of actual memory. It isn't practical for a director to arrange an improvisation session for all the events referred to in a script. Yet, it is essential for an actor to have imaginatively created and lived in these events with all the richness of detail and sensory stimulus possible, as we did with Invented Memory in Chapter 10.

Different actors in the same show may unwittingly present an incongruity if the cast hasn't agreed on the map of the world. For example, if in a production of *West Side Story* one person refers to the Sharks and glances off left, then another looks in the same direction for the Jets, or someone inadvertently gestures up right for Maria's apartment when the wagon with her fire escape on it is planned to come on from down left, the audience will become unconsciously confused. Wise directors talk these things out in rehearsal and smart actors seek out this information without being told. The principle here is that audiences unconsciously search out the anchors or references in order to understand what is being communicated. If the anchors are missing, incomplete or contradictory, the audience will be perplexed and spend time sorting out the map of the play instead of being fully engaged.

Actors need to create anchors that are detailed and internalized in order for the audience to follow the meaning and accept the truthfulness of the performance. You'll need to anchor concrete facts and abstract ideas.

Situations that call for anchoring concrete people and places fall into two main types: facts that are *remembered* and facts that are *imagined* by the character.

1. Remembered anchoring – serves to bring the offstage world onstage, to pull the past into the present, to warn of an approaching problem, or to justify this character's choices and to enroll the listeners in ratifying them. Think of *'Kansas City'* from *Oklahoma!*, or Noël Coward's *'I've Been to a Marvelous Party'*. This message is usually, "It happened this way."
2. Imagined anchoring – the character is usually saying, "Envision it like this." Think of songs like, *'If I Were a Rich Man'* from *Fiddler*, *'Just You Wait'* from *My Fair Lady*, *'Melisande'* from *110 in the Shade*, or *'Pretty Little Picture'* from *A Funny Thing Happened on the Way to the Forum*.

EXERCISE 12D   PICTURE IT THIS WAY

1. Take a song like *'Pretty Little Picture'*. List all the nouns, in each verse and chorus.

    Verse: Tiber, boat, bow, picture, boy, side, rail, bride, bed, sun, sea
        tide, boat, bed, boy, bride
    Chorus: picture, picture, picture, I, Pseudol-iddle-us, you
    Verse: waves, sails, slaves, picture, it, cares, sight, mind, buoy, bay,
        sea, spray, night, moon, arms, below, behind, day, bong, bell,
        buoy, bay, boy, bride, boat
    Chorus: picture, boat, sea, trip, air, freedom, me
    Bridge: worries, bothers, captains, fathers
    Verse: ocean, island, lemons, nuts, dates, picture, cottage, trees,
        seashells, door, boy, bride, life, nothing, what, night, stars,
        nothing, shore, lovers, sand, sea, stars, sky, sound, sigh
    Chorus: problems, blessings, family, picture, masterpiece, picture

2. Choose a specific location for each noun. See it. Engage all your senses. Give it colors, smells, sounds and even a tactile feel.
3. If the noun changes (moves, acts in some way) identify those changes

and see them happening. In the song above, the couple boards the boat, goes below to the bed; the boat sails away and arrives at a tropical island where they get off the boat and start a family. Work out the specific progression mandated by your song. Be alert to repeated nouns. Does the vision intensify, clarify or evolve with each repetition?

4. Remember that one of the objectives of songs like this is to make the others onstage see what you're describing and be persuaded to act because your depiction is so compelling. Do whatever is necessary to make the listener enter into your vision.

5. Have observers give you feedback on what they understand and anything that looks vague or contradictory. Make adjustments.

Don't be shy about making broad, illustrative gestures when working out the anchoring. Depending on the style of the show, expansive, sweeping physicality might be an appropriate performance level. In cases where the acting style is more internalized, start with broad, specific gestures, then relax them back to an internal place. As you will have observed earlier, in real conversations we anchor with everything from tiny muscular movements to huge gesticulations.

Anchoring ideas – a 3-D map of your inner world

We not only anchor concrete things like people and places. We also anchor ideas and concepts. The two forms this typically takes are the *ladder* and the *contrast* or *antithesis*.

In the ladder, ideas are stacked and built one on the other. Think of *'The Impossible Dream'* from *Man of La Mancha*. Look at the sequence of actions: to dream, to fight, to bear, to run, to right, to love, to try, to reach . . . It is a series of noble attempts that builds to an actual accomplishment: reaching the unreachable star. These abstract ideas need to live specifically in Don Quixote's mind. They aren't abstract to him. He knows exactly what it means to do each one, and doing each one makes it possible to dare to do the next in an ascending ladder. A ladder can also take the form of a proposition–conclusion, "if this – then that."

When a character is wrestling with a choice or having an internal conflict and working that out through the song, the ideas are usually presented in contrast to each other (antithesis). Typically, there is a premise and its direct opposite. This takes the forms of either "this versus that" or "not this, but that." Think of *Jekyll and Hyde's 'Good and Evil'*. Lucy grapples with the two as she justifies her journey from the light to the dark. She doesn't think of these abstract concepts abstractly, however. She has specific examples that are concrete in her mind. They need to be anchored in her physical behavior as well. Let's walk an actor through the process of making abstract ideas into physical actuality.

Whether the idea is presented as a ladder or an antithesis, the actor needs to take the seemingly philosophical and make it real to the character and the audience. One way to get this out of the intangible into the three-dimensional is to attach an idea to a specific location. Start by finding the ideas.

Take a song that is mostly about ideas rather than about people or things. *'There's a Fine, Fine Line'* from *Avenue Q* is a good example. Make a list of the nouns, paying particular attention to those that contrast: lover versus friend; reality versus pretend; love versus waste of time; fairy tale versus lie; "You're wonderful" versus "Goodbye"; love versus waste of your time.

Notice that the bridge of the song is a ladder: I don't have the time (and) I don't think you know (so) I've got to close the door. Then the lyric returns to the antithesis pattern: together versus not; what you wanted versus what you got; love versus waste of time.

Don't worry about doing this in a realistic way at first. Set each idea in a specific place on the stage or in your studio, with the antithetical points on opposite sides of the space. For the bridge, place each idea in steps going downstage away from you. Now, try the song making bold crosses to each area as you sing (or, if you like, speak it). Do this a couple of times until it feels coordinated and organized.

Once the large crosses are in your body, take them away. Stand in one place and just feel the internal impulse toward those crosses. Notice how your body still retains and expresses all the organization and clarity of the ideas.

Frequently, ladders and antitheses are combined. The reasoning or argument a character makes is usually established through contrasting ideas and building on them. This argument needs to live in the actor's body in order to make it clear and compelling.

EXERCISE 12E **FIND AND ANCHOR THE ARGUMENT, PHYSICALLY**

1. Start by identifying the argument the character is making. What is the essential question or persuasive point being made?
2. Simplify and paraphrase that argument.
3. Look for contrasting or antithetical ideas (not this, but that).
4. Look for ideas that repeat and intensify (ladders, or this plus this).
5. Find places to anchor the antithetical ideas and places to build the ladders.
6. Decide how your character feels about each idea. Sometimes characters are torn between two opposing things that they want. Sometimes they are repulsed by one thing and drawn to another. Make a large physical commitment to each idea to intensify the physical impulse toward the action underlying every idea. Go over the top.
7. Get feedback to see whether the show requires a large physical action or if you should take the large physical impulse and pull it back in to a more naturalistic expression. In general, because songs are more heightened than text sections they will ask for a larger physical commitment.

Often, you're talking to yourself. So, you're placing another "you" in front of the real you. That other self is the one you're working on, seeking advice from, convincing, etc. And you'll place her clearly in front of you as you do these solo songs. Look at her (the other you) as you make an emphatic point, seek clarification, plead for validation, chastise her, or any of the other important actions you play. The anchor point is a visual marker you return to as you pursue the objective. However, you're not obligated or expected to look *only* at your other self. Just as we do in life, you can search for ideas elsewhere, avoid contact when it's awkward, or get distracted by other things (which you'll anchor in distinctly different places).

In fact, staring catatonically at your anchor point appears strange in most cases. It's as though you have seen some bizarre creature and can't look away or as if you've been hypnotized. The audience will want to see what you're seeing and concentrate on that instead of what you're doing and saying. So, an easy contact with this anchor point is preferable.

Guidelines for anchoring

1. Use your imagination to create the events just as if you were actually there.
2. Whenever you speak about a person, or thing, see it, feel it, smell it, and make specific choices about exactly where everything and everyone is. To help you with this, speak the text while actually pointing to these people or things in a large and committed way.
3. Do the same thing with any ideas or intangible things. Place antitheses, ladders and other parallel devices in actual physical space.
4. Let the style determine the level of physical amplification. After you have really owned these things through large gestures, you can relax and not actually point (unless you want) but allow the clear experience of these ideas or things to live in subtle movements and in your voice. Don't start subtly, though, even if your goal is to end there.

Finally, be critical of your choices. Make sure they make sense. Have someone who understands your process listen and watch and investigate your choices. It is easy to make inadvertent errors and place anchors in illogical places.

UNIT 12.11   ## Playing multiple roles in the same song

Occasionally you'll be asked to play multiple roles within the same song. These are often more comic moments in a musical and allow you to show off your strengths in characterization. The techniques for doing this effectively relate to the issue of clear physical reality and anchoring, once again.

A perfect example of this kind of song is *'A Trip to the Library'* from *She Loves Me*. In it, the somewhat naïve Ilona Ritter recounts the events of the previous evening to her close friends at the parfumerie where she works. Over the course of the song Ritter actually plays three roles: (1) Ritter as the narrator of the events (in the present moment), (2) naïve Ilona in the story (the night before), and (3) Paul, the optometrist she meets on her maiden voyage into the library (also the night before). The actress singing this delightful song must help the audience understand when she is in each of these three roles.

Your first job in a song of this type is to identify when you're playing each role, even going as far as highlighting each character's dialogue with a different color pen.

To understand when Ritter is in each of these three roles, we must see her change in specific ways. Each role will have a specific posture (which can change as the story unfolds) and anchor point (which probably won't change). The narrator role is the one that talks directly to Ritter's friends in the present moment. Naïve Ilona, from the night before, must be clearly different from the woman she is today. So you need to ask yourself how does she now see the girl she was before (ignorant, shallow, gullible, unenlightened) because that is how she is going to physicalize her characterization of her old self. For the third role, Paul, Ritter must find a clearly contrasting anchor point that allows us to see him talking to her. The actress can then clearly alternate between these three characters. She will anchor Paul in one place, naïve Ilona in another and the narrator's focus to a third place. The library will need a very specific location, as well.

Since the narrator knows that the story ends happily, she is at ease while she reveals the rollercoaster ride of events. But, as naïve Ilona, the actress must embody the cold-sweat anxiety of entering the intimidating library, the fear of being approached by a strange man, her coffee with this nerdy bookworm, and his transformation into a handsome savior for her. Likewise, as she personifies Paul, she must embody his transformation from a library-haunting wolf, to harmless geek, to his final status as knight-in-shining-armor.

An important aspect of this kind of song performance is the transition from one role to the next for the actor. Particularize the physical life for each of the multiple roles you play. Things such as posture (rigidly upright, slouched, seductively curved, etc.) and vocal mannerisms (dialect, timbre, nasality, etc.) tell your audience when you've moved from one character to the next. In combination with the shifting anchor points, this kind of physical and vocal adjustment must happen in an instant.

This sort of song can be fun for everyone, but it requires a great deal of accuracy on the part of the lucky actor in that role.

When to move

UNIT 12.12

You are probably familiar with the experience of standing in an audition or classroom performance in a state of near paralysis because you're unsure of when or how to move. Rather than make a wrong move you simply avoid the problem by rigidly standing stock still like a ladder in the garage. This obviously isn't helping you tell your story or feel at ease onstage.

Simply put, the answer to this question is that you move or make some kind of physical change in your body or behavior every time you experience a new step in the journey of the song. For each new thought, discovery, pursuit of an objective, or encounter with an obstacle, you will have physical movement or reaction of some kind to express it. Evocative and meaningful gestures most often result from your following the good acting choices you've been developing using the tools we've covered earlier in this book. You might need to take organic gestures and heighten them or make conscious selections from among them to tell your story. What will appear spontaneous to your audience will actually be chosen and rehearsed.

When we see a dynamic or deeply affecting performance, we rarely remember the staging, unless it is highly choreographed or unless it gets in the way of the performer. We'll talk about choreography later. For now, let's focus on how to create appropriate and transparent staging.

We've defined blocking as the formal patterns of stage movement and business, developed and set in rehearsal. Many directors define blocking as moving the actors around the stage. Regardless of whether the director has a focus toward organic movement or only an interest in framing a masterful stage picture, an actor should define blocking as the physical expression of his character's pursuit of an objective through tactics and in response to obstacles, discoveries, failures and victories. For instance, if you want something from someone, you go toward him to get it. If you encounter an internal or external obstacle, you stop or move away from it. If you're afraid of something or put off by it you definitely move away. Staging is really that simple at its heart. Of course, there is a lot of nuance and subtlety involved. And there are more and less interesting ways to tell the same story. But, at its essence, good staging follows the logic of your inner journey.

You'll recall in Chapter 8 you broke your song down into units that lined up with the various musical and lyric clues. These units give us a framework for staging a song.

Let's pretend you've arrived at the following beat breakdown for 'Lost in the Wilderness' from Children of Eden. Cain delivers it to Abel. Your objective is to get your brother to join you as an ally and leave your parents. This chart breaks the song into beats and tells you what happens in each.

Each of these phrases represents one acting beat. You (as Cain) do something in that unit, so let's express it physically. In this example, we are going to have nine specific movement changes, physical shapes or pieces of staging because there are eight beats in the song.

Table 12-2

Unit	Lyric	What happens?
1	(*Musical introduction*)	I figure out how to begin changing my brother into my ally
2	*I never made this world,* *I didn't even lose it.* *And I know no one said it was fair,* *But they had a garden once.* *They had the chance to choose it.* *They gave it away, including my share.*	I blame my parents for their failings and mistakes
3	*And now, we're lost in the wilderness.* *Lost, crying in the wilderness.* *And if anyone's watching,* *It seems they couldn't care less,* *We're lost in the wilderness . . .*	I accuse God of not caring what happens to us
4	(*Musical interlude*)	I assess whether I've changed my brother and discover I haven't yet
5	*You follow all the rules,* *You swallow all the stories* *And ev'ry night you wish on a star,* *Dreaming your day will come, trusting in* * allegories* *And ev'ry morning, boy, look where you are!*	I ridicule my brother for his groundless faith
6	*And now, we're lost in the wilderness.* *Lost, slowly dying in the wilderness* *With no chance of living, boy,* *Until you confess, you're lost in the* * wilderness . . .*	I expose the hopelessness of our situation
7	*Don't ever watch the eagle fly to the sun,* *And wonder how he got to be so free?* *If you ever have, you know your journey's* * begun.* *Hey! What have we to lose, boy,* *When already we are lost in the wilderness?*	I press my brother to question his faith
8	*And where we are headed, boy,* *I couldn't even guess.*	I plead for him to join me

Table 12-2 continued

Unit	Lyric	What happens?
	But off we go, without a warning, Running as we hit the ground. Where our future lies a borning, Where our hearts are outward bound . . . Till one bright and distant morning, We may stop and look around and there, In the wilderness, fin'lly we'll be found.	
9	(Ride-out)	I wait to see if he will join me

EXERCISE 12F ACTION FIGURE STATUES

Use nine other actors. You sculpt a set of Cain action figures. Make each actor into a statue that embodies what's happening in each unit. Remember, all levels, shapes and positions are possible. Any child playing with these toys should instantly recognize what's happening with each. Don't forget them. We'll play with them again.

UNIT 12.13   ## Relating actions to anchors

Although this song is addressed *to* his brother, Cain doesn't only talk *about* his brother. He refers to his parents, to God, to an eagle, to the wilderness around them, as well as to his brother. He has relationships with all those things. Before you begin staging this song, you'll need to anchor each person, place or thing referred to.

For our staging of *'Lost in the Wilderness'* we have decided on the following anchor points. Notice they are all assigned logically and to allow the audience to see the performer.

* The Wilderness is all around the singer.
* The partner, Abel, is imaginary for this performance (though he would be present in a full production) and is in front of You/Cain, slightly left of center.

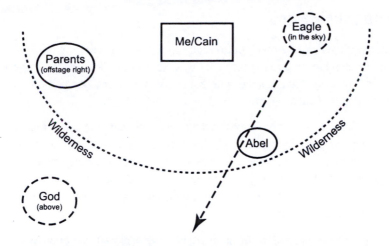

- God is placed at a 45-degree angle above the audience, downstage right.
- The eagle will fly across the sky from stage left on your plane, over your brother toward down stage center over the audience and off into the distance.
- The parents' home is offstage right. (They are far enough away that Cain doesn't need to fear they will overhear him.)

Once you've decided on anchor points, you can play your objective through a clear relationship with those places, things and people, and in turn be affected by them. It will become natural for you to point or gesture offstage right as you blame your parents. You'll automatically see the eagle above and watch it fly past you (just over the orchestra seating). You will look to God as you accuse him, and receive his judgment in return. And we in your audience will never notice these were choices. We will simply know what you know. You've built a set and peopled it with your mind. The audience will follow you with their own imagination.

EXERCISE 12G   ACTION FIGURES: THE SEQUEL

1. You've got an imaginary world. Now, place your nine action figures in it where they belong. Stand back and see the whole journey.
2. Stand behind each action figure in order. Adopt their shape.
3. Send the other actors away, and you become all nine figures in sequence.

Scoring your staging

Now that you have your world, you're ready to move in it. That means we're going to develop blocking to express your inner journey. This process is called *scoring your staging*. You'll literally write out every movement, gesture, change of level, moment of stillness, etc.

Before you decide this feels too formal, old-fashioned or rigid, remember that you are exploring this technique as one part of your total skill set. Recognize that what you're doing here is no more formal or inorganic than what a director or choreographer would do to stage you in rehearsal. And you'd probably accept their staging directions without question. Someone has to make the physical decisions. In this case, it's you.

Using the previous rehearsal for the song in which we explored anchoring, we've arrived at the following score for the staging of *'Lost in the Wilderness'*.

I have decided that my starting position is slightly to the right of center center. I'm standing at a slight angle (about quarter profile) toward my brother, Abel, whom I imagine is standing just past the edge of the stage at down center left.

Table 12-3 is a detailed plan for the physical behaviors that express the character's psychological and dramatic action. You might think this is too detailed and specific – *until you try it*. If you do so, you'll discover gestures and stage movement that expresses a direct and passionate encounter between two brothers. As importantly, your inner life will both support the staging and be fortified by it.

Dance movement

Many songs in musicals are so clear and driving in their rhythmic beat that we are almost required to dance as we sing. Other songs provide passages of music without lyrics where the characters are clearly expected to dance. In some cases, the lyrics, dialogue or stage directions tell us the characters must dance. This presents a whole range of opportunities and requirements for you in the role. In most cases, you will be provided with a choreographer whose sole purpose is to create dance movement for you. But this isn't always the case. Sometimes you are left on your own to create the movement, or you're lucky enough to be invited to participate in the choreographic process. If so, consider how dance functions in a musical.

Dance and movement form an entire type of dialogue in a show. While dance may serve as a kind of spectacle in some cases, it is usually much more than that. It

Table 12-3

Unit	Lyric	Tactical actions	What's happening	Physical actions
1	(Musical Introduction)	I ponder Cain I investigate Cain I dissect Cain	I figure out how to begin changing my brother into my ally	I stand at a 1/4 angle toward my brother, sitting into my downstage hip, and shake my head slowly in disbelief at him.
2	I never made this world. I didn't even lose it. And I know no one said it was fair, But they had a garden once. They had the chance to choose it. They gave it away, including my share.	I enlist Cain I deprecate my parents I buddy Cain I scorn my parents I deride my parents I condemn my parents	I blame my parents for their failings and mistakes	I begin addressing my brother directly without any specific gestures. As I refer to my parents I cross to Stage Right, just past Center toward them (offstage). I gesture sharply toward them with my Right hand, and then sharply throw it down, dismissing them harshly. My focus alternates between my brother and my offstage parents.
3	And now, we're lost in the wilderness. Lost, crying in the wilderness. And if anyone's watching, It seems they couldn't care less, We're lost in the wilderness . . .	I pity me I enroll my brother I accuse God I indict God	I accuse God of not caring what happens to us	I spread my arms wide and refer to the vast wilderness surrounding me, looking first to the right then panning my focus to my left. I shift my focus toward my "God Spot," referring to Him with my Right arm, making a fist when I'm at my most vehement, still looking at my brother at will to make my points as needed.
4	(Musical interlude)	I assess Cain I reinvigorate me	I assess whether I've changed my brother and discover I haven't yet	I cross downstage toward Center as I assess my brother. When I discover that it hasn't worked yet, I cross Upstage just Left of Center Center with my back to him until I'm ready to begin my next action to him.

Table 12-3 continued

Unit	Lyric	Tactical actions	What's happening	Physical actions
5	You follow all the rules, You swallow all the stories And ev'ry night you wish on a star, Dreaming your day will come, Trusting in allegories And ev'ry morning, boy, look where you are!	I shame Cain I ridicule Cain I mock Cain I deride Cain I taunt Cain I incite Cain	I ridicule my brother for his groundless faith	I now turn to him and squat down to address him personally and more gently.
6	And now, we're lost in the wildnerness. Lost, slowly dying in the wilderness With no chance of living, boy, Until you confess, you're lost in the wilderness . . .	I frustrate me I abandon me I challenge Cain I confront Cain	I expose the hopelessness of our situation	I rise as I sing the title line of the song again, my arms stretching out, referring to the wilderness we are in.
7	Don't ever watch the eagle fly to the sun, And wonder how he got to be so free? If you ever have, you know your journey's begun. Hey! What have we got to lose, boy, When already we are lost in the wilderness?	I inspire Cain I amaze Cain I exhilerate Cain I galvanize Cain I propel Cain	I press my brother to question his faith	I cross to just downstage of Center Center, using very little gesture. Follow the eagle's flight with my eyes.

8			
	And where we are headed, boy,	I excite Cain	I cross Downstage Center slowly with a rising gesture of reaching to him (stepping on the first beat of each bar). As I get to my final spot my arms are stretched out again. I slowly spin once toward my Right looking slightly upward, finishing looking at him.
	I couldn't even guess.		
	But off we go, without a warning,	I hearten Cain	
	Running as we hit the ground.	I inflame Cain	
	Where our future lies a borning,	I motivate Cain	
	Where our hearts are outward bound	I spur Cain	
	Till one bright and distant morning,	I brighten Cain	
	We may stop and look around and there,	I excite Cain	
	In the wilderness,	I enspirit	*I plead for him to join me*
	fin'lly we'll be found.	I promise Cain	
9			
	(ride-out)	I await Cain	My arms drop to my sides and I stand with one foot slightly in front of the other, looking at him, awaiting his reply.
			I wait to see if he will join me

is an extension of the music, lyrics and character journey. One of the best examples of how this works is in the title song from *Singin' in the Rain* (both the film and the stage musical) in which Don Lockwood celebrates his newfound love for Kathy Selden. He essentially says, "I'm the happiest man alive even though it's raining outside." His objective is to make the world as happy as he is. Then he proceeds to celebrate this great joy in the middle of a rainstorm. It is entertaining. It is diverting. It is spectacular to see rain pour down onstage. But, most importantly, it is completely driven by that character's feelings and needs at the moment. This illustration goes to show what dance in a theatre song can do. It helps take a character to the ultimate level of expression. If we agree that singing is a level of heightened expression beyond dialogue, then we can see dance as an extension even beyond singing.

We aren't going to begin to teach you how to choreograph theatre dance here. But what we will do is remind you that even the dances in a musical are part of the character's journey. Therefore, every moment of a dance sequence is part of the story you're telling. The steps each have an objective, tactical choice, obstacles, etc. If we return to *'Singin' in the Rain'*, we can see that choreographers Gene Kelly and Stanley Donen built that dance to reflect Lockwood's growing glee. He begins under the umbrella, but quickly decides it will hamper his celebration. He then begins playing with his environment: the sidewalk area. The downspout, the metal fence and then a lamppost provide him with a chance to improvise on a theme of joy. He playfully riffs on various conventional dance forms (soft shoe, eccentric dance) until, finally, he can no longer contain his ecstasy and he leaves the traditional territory of the pedestrian for the unexplored landscape of the street itself. Like a kid who can't (or won't) follow the rules of conventional society anymore, he joyously splashes in puddles in the middle of the street before being discovered by a passing cop. Suddenly aware of how he must appear, he begins to justify his behavior, but quickly decides not to even bother, and gives his long since pointless umbrella to a dripping passerby and jauntily walks home in the downpour. That is a character driven story with distinct beats, tactical phrases and everything else a good actor plays with in any text. The song and dance together form a single integrated journey.

It is essential to do choreographic text accurately and with good technique. But, as an actor, *how* you do the movement and *why* you do it are equally important. Whenever you are given choreography, don't wait to assign it motivations and make tactical choices, such as "I tease her," "I challenge him," "I seduce her," "I reject him." These will probably be suggested by the music or movement quality. They may be discussed as you learn the steps. If you don't understand what story is being told, discuss it with the choreographer. Make the dance as integral a part of your story as the singing.

In most cases, the danced text serves to reinforce the ideas of the song surrounding it. So, if you're flirting with someone in the song, then you break into dance, you are probably going to try more ways to flirt that are primarily physical. You might be celebrating new love, a great victory or a wonderful idea. Dance will extend each of those ideas. Tell your story through every kind of text.

Sharing your performance with the audience

UNIT 12.16

At some point every actor deals with the question of how to share a private experience in a public forum. So, we're laying out some guidelines to consider.

Show your eyes. If we can't see your eyes, we are cut off from your experience. This doesn't mean you have to look directly at the audience. But allow them access to your experience. Closing your eyes while you sing is selfish. Performance is inherently a shared and public event. Even when the experience is deeply personal, the point of putting it onstage is to make it available to the public. So shutting your eyes repeatedly or for extended periods of time during a song can close the window we need to see inside you.

Show your face. If the audience can't see your face, they can't share your experience. You are only rarely allowed to hang your head low while singing. This can occasionally happen between phrases. More contemporary styles sometimes invite this kind of singing. But be careful you don't rely too heavily on it. Don't hide.

Show yourself. Facing upstage during intimate moments denies the audience access to your performance. Share important moments in the life of the character. Facing upstage to protect yourself from vulnerability hides the good stuff from the audience. If you need to hide or protect yourself from another character, do it in a way that denies them access, but opens you to the audience.

Scale

UNIT 12.17

A note about scale is appropriate here. Every performance you give must be tailored to the size and shape of the space. Your performance in a 1,500-seat arena theatre with a full pit orchestra is probably not the same one you'll give in a small audition room with only an accompanist and a casting director. If you don't adjust the size of your performance to the space, you'll either blow your very small audience out of the water or you'll appear invisible on a larger stage. The same song can be performed in many different ways by the same performer, depending on the circumstances. Regardless of the size of gesture, the volume of singing, the length of the stage cross, and so forth, the physical expression of your journey will spring from the same character truth.

EXERCISE 12H   CALIBRATING THE SPACE

1. Stand either onstage or at one end of the room. Place four other actors at regular distances between you and the back of the house or the end of the room. Think of these actors as defining the far edge of your "performance envelope."
2. Start singing your song using all the staging, anchoring and focus points you have worked out.
3. Begin your performance reaching only the first helper. When they feel the size fits, they'll raise their hand. That's your cue to expand to the next helper, and so on. Calibrate the scale of your performance to the appropriate size.

UNIT 12.18   ## What is a "button"?

. . . an ideal way to close out this chapter. . .

At the end of many theatre songs, particularly those from before about 1980 and those from shows that want to sound as if they're from that period, we hear a distinct musical ending on a single note or unsustained chord. This strong musical accent may feel like the accompanist is slamming her hands down on the keyboard to make the chord, it could be a long glissando down the keyboard, or simply a single bass note gently tapped. This undeniable musical information tells us we have reached a definitive conclusion to the song and the dramatic journey. It is over!

When we have a strong musical accent to end a song, the composer is often telling us the character has arrived at a definite decision about something, or has great certainty about his feelings. The music tells us, "I mean it!!!" So we want to match our movement to the music by creating a snapshot of the character in that moment. The physical shape we create is called a *button*. This tells the audience the song is done, the character has arrived at the place he has been going, and it is time to applaud. If the idea of using something so old-fashioned and corny as a button feels artificial to you, try doing the same song without a button on it, then again with a clear physical button. Notice how much more definitive the ending is, and how much more readily your audience responds.

Because this final musical accent is among the most heightened moments in any song, it will probably need to be matched by a heightened physical choice. Not all buttons are signaled by trumpets and a cymbal crash. Many are quite the opposite, offering a gentle tap of the piano key or grace note by some quiet instrument in the orchestra. The degree of musical emphasis will determine the size of the gesture or physical shape that you adopt for that moment. A gentle musical button needs to be matched with something subtler. Look at the end of Leonard Bernstein's 'A Little Bit in Love' from Wonderful Town. There is a quiet and simple musical button on the song that might be matched by just resting your head on your hand at the exact moment the musical button occurs. Or you might just sit back in your chair or easily fall back on your pillow in bed. On the other hand, the end of 'Trouble' from The Music Man involves an entire chorus of townsfolk fervently agreeing with Professor Harold Hill that their town is in trouble. That song has one of the most emphatic buttons in any musical. In the original staging, Prof. Hill had mounted the base of a statue and, as the musical button occurred, he posed exactly like the statue while everyone else created a dynamic physical tableau pointing toward him. That is an appropriately strong button on the number.

Not only does the button put an end to the song, it should tell the audience in one snapshot how the character feels at that moment. By looking at your beat breakdown, you will know what you want and how you feel about it at that point in the song. You may have achieved your objective and want to celebrate it. Therefore, a physical shape that shows celebration, victory or affirmation would be perfect. Arms thrust into the air with both fists clenched, as if to say "I did it!" tells this story. So does slam dunking an imaginary basketball or pumping your fist into the air on the last beat. The possibilities are endless and should reflect not only the character's feelings at the moment, but also the given circumstances. Think how anachronistic it would be for Harold Hill (circa 1912 in Iowa) to do the basketball "whoosh." His victory pose must be appropriate to that show, that time period, that particular circumstance and your sense of his feelings at the time.

Other songs and circumstances will require different kinds of buttons. If the last moment says to you, "I don't know what to do," then the button should reflect it. If you think the last moment would be titled, "I'm lost and afraid," then the button should look like that.

. . . there, I've said it!

. . . and that's the last word on the subject!

SECTION IV: MAKING IT A PERFORMANCE

CHAPTER 13

REHEARSAL INTO PERFORMANCE

Every exercise in this book is intended to help you develop and perform a role through some kind of rehearsal process. This may only consist of several rehearsals alone or it may be a full, multi-week rehearsal experience. Or it may be somewhere in between those two extremes. In every case, though, you are going through a *process* to arrive at the performance. That process is another journey of its own, where you experience artistic victories and personal defeats, and synthesize all the elements of your very personal technique.

No two rehearsal processes are the same. No two actors follow the same road to their opening night performance. Your rehearsal process is guided by a director, musical director, choreographer and, most significantly, your own intuition. The strange alchemy that goes into a successful rehearsal process differs for every actor. There are a number of habits you can develop to make it easier.

Begin at the beginning

There is often a great temptation to start the rehearsal process by trying to do everything at the same time. We often feel a pressure to do it right the first time and to come in with a finished role. But imagine you're playing the role of Eliza Doolittle in *My Fair Lady*. To successfully perform this role an actress must fully master two extreme British dialects, and get comfortable singing in both a legitimate soprano register and a lower, nearly belted register. She must develop two opposing sets of physical behaviors and, oh yes, then she must also address the acting questions! Given those requirements, how could she possibly do it all on the first day of rehearsal? Even for the diligent actress who has done the work of learning the score beforehand, coached in advance with a professional dialectician and analyzed the script for acting beats, changing relationships and the rest of the preparation one might do, there is still an enormous amount to do with the rest of the cast and creative team. For every process there is a beginning point and it is up to you to determine where that is. For some actors it is simply mastering the musical elements of the role; learning the songs exactly. For others, it might involve listening to as many different interpretations of the songs in the show as possible, or viewing other performances. Still other actors might feel the need to articulate the character's journey by carefully annotating their script. Though very different, all are valid places to begin. You will ultimately need to cover all those bases before you're done. But trying to do them at the same time is guaranteed to confuse and frustrate you.

UNIT 13.2   ## Layering

For all of the elements we described above, there are many others you might also do, including applying many of the exercises and techniques outlined in this book. You and the people you trust to guide you will decide what needs to happen next. Just remember that once you've mastered one set of challenges, the mastery will stay with you. For instance, when you've learned and mastered the choreography to a dance, you can move on to investing the movement with your character's physical attributes and attitudes toward the people she's dancing with. Then you might begin to integrate the vocal aspects of the character. Finally, you might decide you simply need to share your joy in doing the song and dance with the audience. And you might need to review and brush up on various of these along the way. That's a lot of phases. But layering them on, one by one, gives you the best chance of building a confident and cohesive performance.

UNIT 13.3   ## Setting goals

In any task that really challenges you, the end can seem unachievable at first. Simply looking at the mountain, it may feel unscalable. But once you break the journey down into shorter legs and give yourself reasonable goals along the way, reaching the summit is much more achievable. So, for each rehearsal, set just a few clear goals for yourself. On one day you might decide you simply want to be off book with your dialogue and music. The next day, you might decide you want to fully incorporate the dialect training you've done. Next you might focus on the changing relationship with your principal counterparts, or clarify and intensify your objectives. Of course, your personal goals need to coordinate with the overall rehearsal plan. Often, discussing these goals with your director and acting partners will help rehearsals go smoothly for everyone. Otherwise, if you have one set of goals and the director has a different set, you're both bound to end up frustrated. Setting attainable goals is a way of layering the rehearsal process so you build a performance step by step.

Exploring and experimenting

UNIT 13.4

One of the best reasons to rehearse is to discover possibilities. We don't rehearse to simply nail down our first and only idea and slowly drain it of any hint of spontaneity. Rather, rehearsal can be a blend of exploration of the possibilities, experimentation within a set of boundaries and, finally, a selection of the best elements from a wide range of possibilities. This scenario may sound idyllic, or even frightening. You may be used to going in to a rehearsal hall and being told where to go, what to do, how to say it or sing it, and then drilled on that until you repeat it exactly like the director has told you. So, the notion of trying something different time after time could be intimidating to you and threatening to your director. But get in the habit of trying new things without fear of ridicule or "making a mistake." You may need to talk to your director and explain that you're trying to explore things for a while, to find some options and possibilities, and that you will settle into a consistent performance as you and she make selections. Find out when the deadline for experimentation will pass and when you need to have made your selections with the director. You may discover you have much more latitude than you thought.

Room for failure

UNIT 13.5

In every rehearsal process there comes the day when you feel like a complete failure. It seems you can't act, sing, dance, connect with anyone else in the company, or even care about the show. This day will pass and you'll regain the life of the role and your confidence and enthusiasm for the project. In each rehearsal along the way you will also have moments of great insight where you and the rest of the company recognize something wonderful has just happened. But the expectation that you will always be so inspired is unrealistic and puts too much pressure on you. You'll be much happier if you accept that building a role is like shooting a film. For every shot that ends up on screen, the actors and director may have tried dozens or even hundreds of others that weren't as good. The challenge of performing live is you have to attempt that entire selection of "best takes" every night. Doing so requires a lot of skill that must be built over a rehearsal process, not overnight. Learning how one moment follows another and finding the internal logic and emotional throughline takes time and experimentation. Beating yourself up because you didn't get it right the first time or every time is almost always counterproductive.

UNIT 13.6 ## Changing venues

One of the most fragile times for any production is when you move from the rehearsal studio onto the stage. Suddenly, you're in a much larger space with different acoustics, greater distance between you and your audience, a different sense of height and space and many other variables you aren't used to. Most often, the goal for those first rehearsals is to get acquainted with the new space and then to regain your sense of the show you rehearsed. This means you're going to include an awareness of all the new physical differences in your environment (which will hopefully help you in the long run) while you reconnect with your fellow actors and the heart of the show you're doing. Don't panic because things feel different. Take some time to figure out what those differences are and how you can adjust to them.

UNIT 13.7 ## Adding elements

When you begin adding costumes, wigs, orchestra, lighting, moving scenery, amplification, quick changes and the need for all of those different crews to master their jobs around you, the opportunities for derailment are enormous. Before you break down in tears, remember that each of those new elements needs to be incorporated into the overall performance. It will not go perfectly the first time you add those elements. Repeat. IT WILL NOT GO PERFECTLY THE FIRST TIME YOU ADD THOSE ELEMENTS!! Know that going into this part of the process and accept that a lot of people, including you, need to learn to work together to solve the problems as they come up – and they always do. No doubt Sophocles sat in the Theatre of Dionysus with his head in his hand at the first technical rehearsal of *Oedipus Rex*, sure it would never work. Of course it did. Almost all rehearsal processes are made up of three steps forward, followed by at least one step back. The recovery from every new onslaught of technical elements is relatively short. Learn to work with those elements and get back to acting as soon as is reasonably possible. If you can focus on just those problems that affect you, work to find a solution and disregard unnecessary distractions, you'll have the greatest chance for success during this part of the rehearsal process.

Previews and opening night

UNIT 13.8

The final addition to any production is the audience. And when the throngs arrive, the electricity level for everyone jumps. Everyone reacts differently. Some people overact, while others get self-conscious and forget everything. It's all due to nerves, which stem from the desire to be liked by the crowd and the fear you won't be. And that desire can override two months of rehearsal if you're not careful. Accept that you want to be liked and to do well. But trust that the work you've done for all that time is really the best route to the success you deserve. Stick with your plan, focus on your fellow actors and your objectives, do the show you rehearsed and the rest will follow.

Advice

UNIT 13.9

Immediately following every first performance you will be approached by parents, friends, boyfriends and girlfriends, teachers and critics who all have advice for you about how you could do better in the role. And try as you might, you can't avoid this or ignore it. The advice is often well meant (though sometimes not). But it is not given with the same awareness you have of the goals of the production and the interpretation you've developed over a long process. So, as you hear the advice, resist the urge to scrap all your hard work simply to get a laugh or a standing ovation. Instead, consider what your friend is saying and decide if the point has merit. Then you can decide if you want to take action to address it. If you are going to consider outside advice, you must do so only with the consultation of the director, choreographer, musical director and whomever else it may affect on stage. It is not professional or acceptable to simply change your performance without discussion because it can derail an entire production that may simply need time to get used to an audience.

Hits and flops

When a show is a success there is almost no way to understand why it went so well and we were all so lucky. It all seems to flow together as if that were the natural order of things. But when a show goes poorly, for whatever reason, the fingers start pointing and everyone has a reason, an excuse or a blame to lay for the failure. As a member of the acting company you can only be responsible for your part of the equation. Do your work as well as possible, bring positive energy and good will to the rehearsal room every day, and work constructively to find solutions to problems as they affect you. Beyond that, you can't rewrite a show, redirect it, redesign it, act for other people or otherwise change any other part of the complex puzzle that makes up a show. Enjoy the successes with humility while they last and endure the failures with grace. There will always be another show.

Your evolving technique

Besides the programs and memories, you can take something more valuable away from every work experience: an awareness of which parts of your process worked well and what you'd do differently. Each actor's technique is really a collection of habits that work effectively for him. And every work experience offers you a chance to refine that collection of habits by adding new ones and evaluating old ones.

EXERCISE 13A   REHEARSAL JOURNAL

On your next project, start a rehearsal journal as soon as you've been cast. Let the first entry be your analysis of the audition and what you did to win the role: preparation, selection of material, your behavior in the audition, etc. Then begin laying out a strategy to prepare for the role. Make a list of the kinds of preparation you'll want to do so you can logically organize them and take them on one at a time (layering). Take notes on your progress, the obstacles you encounter and the victories you enjoy. Starting with the first day of rehearsal, outline a set of goals for each rehearsal before the day begins. Then, at the end of the day, take some notes on how you did with those goals and whatever else you feel is important to remember or acknowledge. This can be anything you feel like writing. Some actors take their notes from directors and other creative staff in their journal with the day's entry. Other people use the journal to vent their frustration or celebrate a breakthrough. By the time you've finished the rehearsal process you'll be able to look back at your journal and recall the ups and downs of your process with amazing clarity. So, the next time you're cast in a role, you can look back on this journal and conspire to succeed by embracing your best habits from each rehearsal process and avoiding those that undermined your best work.

SECTION V: STYLE IN MUSICAL THEATRE

CHAPTER 14

Style in Musical Theatre

Working in a style that differs from contemporary acting means entering a complete and fully dimensional theatrical world. We will spend the next section of this book helping you identify and enter the worlds of style with clarity and confidence. Much of what we'll do is akin to working like an anthropologist studying a foreign culture. This is not a recipe book or set of formulas, but rather a system for investigating the world of each style and the conventions associated with it.

WHAT IS STYLE?

Good acting is good acting is good acting. We all agree with that. But we probably also agree that good acting in *The Merry Widow* is different from in a production of *Anything Goes*, and that would be different from good acting in a production of *West Side Story*, or *Dreamgirls* or *Rent*. What is the difference? Aside from the specifics of characterization, that difference is called style. We will define style as the agreed upon rules of performance behavior associated with a particular genre, type or period of theatre. Style is not different from acting or instead of acting. It is a way of acting. You still pursue objectives, specify characters, create relationships, etc. But style work allows you to place your role in the world it is supposed to inhabit, and in a way your audience can identify and understand.

Evolving notions of style

Style is not a fixed idea or set of rules that were established at some point in history, and which we must reference as gospel each time we perform a role from a particular genre. Rather, each style is an evolving performance tradition that simultaneously refers to its origins while mingling with current acting conventions. Style is a highly selective intersection of the past and the present. While one generation may identify a particular style by their own standards, subsequent generations will probably see it differently. As long as there is living memory of a style in the form of artists who performed it we are more likely to see it presented closely to its original fashion. But as that memory fades, we depend on successive generations to pass on their understanding of that style until, eventually, our perception of what is authentic about that style has changed. We are influenced not only by the power of new interpretations and performers, but also by new acting styles, new technologies and new trends in writing. In fact, seeing filmed records of original performances in a particular style may offer a shocking surprise for audiences that think they know that style. What that audience sees may seem foreign, stilted or overblown, and inauthentic. So, while that performance may be historically accurate, it carries no power for a contemporary audience.

As important as that gradual evolution of styles is, an equally powerful force helps to nudge performance tradition away from its origins. This pressure is our changing sense of ourselves in society. Certainly the social conventions and modes of behavior our parents or grandparents lived with in 1932 have changed. We are more permissive in certain ways, less so in others. We carry ourselves differently, dress differently, speak with a different vocabulary and slang, and view ourselves through a different set of lenses than we would have then. These pressures have a great influence on how we adopt style. The degree to which we adhere to those early modes or to which we incorporate our current behaviors will fundamentally influence our presentation of style.

To see this in action we only have to look at the portrayal of Curly in the 2003 revival of *Oklahoma!* starring film actor Hugh Jackman. His interpretation probably more resembles Michael Ball in *Les Misérables* or Larry Kert in *West Side Story* than Alfred Drake's original Curly, because the tradition has evolved and performance conventions have changed over the sixty-five years since *Oklahoma!* was first produced. Though you might feel comfortable watching the recent revival, compare it to footage of the original production to see how significantly performance conventions and our understanding of the style have changed.

In the case of Curly, the new performance conventions reflect a great many factors, including: a more relaxed attitude about the ways that men and women court each other, an openness about sexual attraction, a broader acceptance of female authority and independence, contemporary modes of physical behavior (certainly more casual than onstage in 1943!), a greatly changed approach to stage singing, the use of electronic amplification, a revised idea of how cowboys and frontier women dressed, and a greater sense of responsibility to historical regional accuracy regarding dialect. These influences have helped create a new sense of the appropriate style to perform the show.

But there are at least as many factors that remain indelibly stamped on the show from its earliest productions. Remnants of operetta, adherence to many of the acting conventions associated with the first productions, the sense of optimism and joy, pure romance and flirtatiousness, swagger and longing all remain – though expressed differently today.

When an actor successfully integrates the traditions associated with a musical or role with more recent conventions, the tradition is revised. Anyone who sees that new interpretation will be affected by it and may even decide that it is the new "right way" to perform the material. This evolution is inevitable and necessary for these older shows to maintain relevance for new audiences.

Audience awareness of style

Whether we know it or not, we each carry an unconsciousness understanding of prototypical styles of music, art and theatrical performance. This has been passed on to us through television reruns of old variety shows, repetitions of older performance traditions by younger artists in music videos, cartoons and films, easy listening radio stations played in elevators and doctors' offices, and many other stimuli we constantly encounter and which reinforce our under-standing of styles. The result is, without ever trying, we are highly sensitive to the accuracy and authenticity of the performances we see in a given style. Referencing a particular performer, such as Al Jolson, Ethel Merman or Bing Crosby, can be deeply evocative, even if the audience has never actually seen them. Even today, their essence is pervasive through imitations and references. So it is our job to invoke these memories intentionally and specifically. We want to trigger an audience to receive our performance on the same terms that we offer it, without mixed messages or inadvertent references.

UNIT 14.3   **The human truth of style**

Working in a style that differs strongly from contemporary acting can feel false. Just because these characters don't live in your world doesn't mean they live in a phony world. Kneeling at a woman's foot to beg her affection is as potent a tactic as leaning against her at the bar and sticking your tongue in her ear. If you recognize this, regardless of style, period or genre, we will believe your performance. Without the ring of truth, all the careful study of style will be a wasted effort because you will not have engaged our audience's basic desire to identify with the experience of the characters. The mask of style must have a human face.

UNIT 14.4   **Fundamental assumptions about style**

As we begin looking at style work, we want to offer some basic assumptions that underlie all of the work we'll do as we move forward.

Theatrical style is recognizable to the audience. Even if they don't know all of the specifics of a style, audiences will identify enough features of that stylistic world to quickly categorize the experience. Circuses have rings, trapeze, clowns, gymnasts, sawdust, etc. These tell us it's a circus. Musical comedies have comics and romantic characters mixed in with each other. The comics deliberately share their humor with the audience, the songs tend to be very hummable and clearly structured, and the scenery is often a cartoonish version of reality. These are some of the ways we know it's a musical comedy. On the other hand, in rock musicals we see deliberate use of realistic acting conventions, vocalists emulate popular recording artists from the 1960s and 70s, there is almost no comedy, the voices and instruments are heavily amplified, and so forth. These hallmarks of style help us to quickly classify the event. Then we adjust our expectations and measure the success of the production against those expectations.

Theatrical style should be applied consistently throughout a production. We will propose a range of factors to consider as you approach different styles. But the answers you arrive at for each will not be as absolute as you might think. Though some central aspects of a style will probably remain constant for any production of *The Drowsy Chaperone*, at least as many will vary from one production to the next. This is because style is as much an agreement among theatrical artists as it is a fixed notion. The stylistic agreement reached for any production will affect every aspect of design, the orchestral performances, choreography and certainly the actors and director.

Some productions consciously arrive at shared assumptions, with a director articulating how everyone will express the style. In many cases, these performance guidelines will be conveyed more subtly, but everyone involved will nonetheless mutually understand them. Unfortunately, many other productions neither discuss nor share a common set of assumptions about style. These productions become a hodgepodge of different approaches, leaving the poor audience wondering what world they are supposed to be in. The collision of contemporary realism and old-fashioned "selling it to the back row" can result in a schizophrenic production. Much of that chaos can be avoided if some basic decisions about style are examined and agreed upon.

Style is associated with a particular genre of musical, not necessarily just with a historical period. A genre is a category of art, such as operetta, musical comedy, rock opera, etc. Although each of these categories began in a distinct historical period, the genre continues to be used well past that time. So, although true musical comedy reached its peak in the 1920s, the genre has continued to be actively employed since then with great regularity. Shows like *No, No, Nanette* (1924), *Guys and Dolls* (1950) and *The Producers* (2001) all belong to this same genre. An audience member seeing each of these shows will recognize similar qualities in acting, composition and orchestration, and even design. The genre determines the stylistic conventions that will be employed, not the year a show was written.

Theatrical conventions

UNIT 14.5

The musical theatre is a highly artificial environment full of ritualized behaviors in acting and writing that both theatre artists and audiences readily accept. These behaviors are called *conventions*. We'll define conventions as agreed upon models, manners or traditions associated with a specific style. Conventions tell us what is normal. Some musical theatrical conventions that we all accept as normal are:

- Characters sing to express their feelings.
- Actors face the audience when singing certain types of songs.
- Actors break into dance part way through songs.
- Large groups of people spontaneously break out into songs they all know the words, music and movement to.
- Certain character types only sing specific types of music, while other characters will only sing other types.

Table 14-1

Golden Age musical drama	Rock musicals
The presence of musicians in an orchestra pit to deny their presence.	Musicians frequently onstage and intentionally included in the action.
A break in the continuous series of scenes after about an hour that we call intermission, allowing the audience to use the restroom, stretch our legs or get a drink.	Many rock musicals intermissionless.
The playing of a medley of music from the show before the action begins, and another at the halfway point, just after intermission.	Few rock musicals with a formal overture or entr'acte.
Scenery highly stylized and painterly, and leaving a framed opening for the audience to look into.	Rock musicals frequently avoid scenery that looks cartoonish or unrealistic. Scenery often looks industrial.

- Audience conventions include periodically clapping our hands together to show appreciation after a song or scene and sitting quietly in a cavernous darkened room while observing people pretending to be someone other than the people we rationally know them to be.

An unfamiliar anthropologist could have a field day noting the absurdity of these behaviors. Yet, we embrace them as normal when viewing a musical.

Different styles have different theatrical conventions. Compare the theatrical conventions for Golden Age musical drama and rock musicals (Table 14-1).

These are the broadest examples of theatrical convention. But, the idea of conventional behavior doesn't stop there.

UNIT 14.6   ## Conventional behavior

Without becoming formulaic, we can safely say that each character type in a genre behaves in ways that are consistent with other characters of a similar type. For instance, the ingénue characters in Golden Age musicals are remarkably consistent in their conception. Place Laurey in *Oklahoma!*, Fiona in *Brigadoon*,

Julie in *Carousel*, Hope in *Anything Goes*, Amalia in *She Loves Me*, Marian in *The Music Man*, and to some extent Guinevere in *Camelot*, all next to each other and see how similar these characters are. They are all written in the same vocal range, they all convey a strong quality of hopefulness and determination, they are all the romantic center of their respective stories, they are all intelligent (regardless of their formal education), they are all roughly the same age (approximately 20–30 years old), they are almost all unmarried, they are all lovely and lovable, but with emotional complexity. Each of these characters behaves with a grace and dignity that differs from other characters in the same show.

We could do the same exercise with each of the character types in any genre of musical and you'd also see similarities. This isn't meant to imply that each of these characters can't and shouldn't be specifically drawn by the actress playing them. There is no formula for playing within a character type, and no one-size-fits-all approach to these roles. But understanding conventional behaviors allows you to decide how closely you're going to adhere to audience expectations, and the ways in which you'll deviate from them. If you do choose to reject the conventions of a style you may send a set of signals to your audience about the character that are contradictory to the world of the musical you're in. There is no law that says you can't play with these conventional behaviors. But doing so by choice instead of by accident puts you in control of your performance.

Analyzing the worldview of a style

UNIT 14.7

The acting conventions we associate with any style are the extension of a way of seeing the world. Each style has a unique worldview. We'll articulate some aspects of what a worldview is and then help you to particularize the worldview of the styles you're likely to encounter.

Value systems

UNIT 14.7.1

Implicit in every musical is a value system: a set of beliefs about the ways people deal with each other and the social structures in their world. Every style is informed by a different deeply embedded value system and is an expression of it. The value systems we're talking about can include faith in God, relationships between men and women, visions of beauty and fashion, and ideas about our relationship to authority, family and community. In Chapter 7 we talked about some of these same ideas in relationship to character. But we are not just talking about value systems of the individual character here. Rather, we're talking about the value system a musical advances as desirable for its audience. No value system is inherently better or worse than another. These are just worldviews that represent different ways of placing one's self in society. Since each style carries an implicit value system, understanding and embracing those expectations and assumptions will help you place yourself in the correct world for your musical and to make choices consistent with that worldview.

UNIT 14.7.2   *Romance and sex*

Most musicals concern characters that are engaged in romantic pursuit of each other. The stories in musicals almost always begin close to the time a romance begins or reaches a crisis and conclude when the romantic crisis is resolved. Even when other important issues dominate the story, romantic coupling is typically the excuse to address these ideas.

Because romantic love is such a central aspect of the musical theatre, it begs us to address a variety of related issues. Each genre of musical conveys its own assumptions about how men and women should treat each other. Issues of respect, formality, physical contact, courtship and whether sex will even be mentioned are fundamental aspects of behavior for characters in any musical. *Oklahoma!* and *Rent* communicate nearly opposite romantic and sexual values that reveal the worldview of each musical. In *Oklahoma!* Curly and Laurey coyly court each other in *'People Will Say We're in Love'*. They talk of early flirtations and indirect romantic encounters, like her giving Curly a rose and a glove, the two of them standing in the rain together, his throwing bouquets to her and laughing at her jokes. They are even indirect in the way they sing about courtship. Telling each other that "People will say we're in love" is not the same as saying "I love you." And forget about sex! For them, holding hands is the height of physical romance. This relationship is on a path toward marriage, not just sex. The values of this genre don't permit a different set of relationships, though we can infer a deeper longing and physical attraction between these two. Notice that the obstacle to getting married is the internal obstacle of pride for both Curly and Laurey.

Now, compare that scene to *'Light My Candle'* between Roger and Mimi in *Rent*. These two characters occupy the same central romantic position as the lovers in *Oklahoma!*, but they deal with romance and sexual attraction in a completely different way. Far from being a shy farm girl, Mimi is a stripper in an S&M club. She is the aggressor toward Roger, repeatedly blows out her candle to maintain his attention, overtly flirts and attempts to seduce him. Mimi's phrase "light my candle" is a double entendre inviting him to have sex with her. She talks about having "the best ass below 14th Street," and says she was "born to be bad." The oblique discussions of love from *Oklahoma!* are replaced by overt sexuality and aggressive female seduction. Marriage isn't the goal here, but a quick and dangerous fling. And the obstacle to their coupling isn't pride, but Roger's fear of infecting Mimi with HIV/AIDS and of being emotionally hurt again.

Two songs from different genres, each introducing the central romantic relationships in these shows, reveal completely different ideas about how men and women relate to each other.

Relationship to authority

UNIT 14.7.3

One of the central ways styles differ from each other is in the ways they view authority. Authority certainly refers to royalty, political officials and governmental representatives. But it also includes captains of industry, teachers or anyone in power. In some cultures or social moments these figures are treated with great respect and are strictly obeyed, as with the absolute reverence for the Queen in Gilbert and Sullivan's *The Pirates of Penzance*. Other sectors of society view these figures with suspicion, as with the almost total disdain for government and big business in *Hair*. Each of these shows conveys a different relationship to the authorities of its world.

Social ideal

UNIT 14.7.4

Because the musical theatre often reflects the values of mainstream society, the ways in which that part of society wants to (or wanted to) see itself are often mirrored in characters written for the musical stage. We call this positive self-image a social ideal. As that phrase suggests, it is the idealized, commonly held vision of what a perfect man or woman will look, dress and behave like. This varies from sub-culture to sub-culture (age group, social group, ethnic group), and it evolves as society changes through time and social pressure. Impossible to really live, it is the image we aspire to and it is reflected in advertising, popular entertainment and popular art. The value systems we talked about earlier are deeply embedded in this social ideal. Each sector of society may have a different social ideal.

The central characters in most musicals are the normative characters, representing the mainstream social ideal for their segment of society. Let's look at the central male figure in five musicals from different styles to illustrate this.

Pirates of Penzance (1879) *Frederic* – Earnest, devoted, dutiful to a fault, charming and innocent; all central Victorian virtues. The musical itself is written with a great deal of literacy and wit, as well as a gracious and classical tunefulness. Frederic is a perfect, if comically exaggerated embodiment of the social ideal of his time.

Lady, Be Good! (1924) *Dick Trevor* – A wise-cracking, tap-dancing young man of leisure. In a devil-may-care world where everything turns out all right, Dick ends up with the girl he loves after a string of improbable comic misadventures. Carefree 1920s America loved this jazzy score and story.

Oklahoma! (1943) *Curly* – Hearty, physical, steadfast, optimistic and forward-looking, he is independent, with a sense of responsibility for his family and his community. The score is unpretentiously poetic and musically simple and direct. These are exactly the values of mid-century America.

A Little Night Music (1973) *Frederik* – He is witty, wistfully cynical to cover a vulnerable heart, acerbic and slightly self-deluding. The unsentimental score is sophisticated and complex with a deep emotionality. This is how the cosmopolitan audience for an early-1970s musical wanted to see itself.

Rent (1996) *Roger* – A deliberate outsider from mainstream society. His highest value is artistic integrity, and he desperately wants love despite the tragedy that colors all of his experiences. For a youth culture that faced AIDS and felt that government had failed them, the anti-musical theatre rock score for *Rent* was a perfect fit and Roger was the perfect hero.

As an actor in a musical from any of these styles, it is your job to identify the corresponding physical and vocal behavior. That means you'll research and identify ways of standing, sitting and moving, of speaking and singing, of behaving, that express the value system and social ideal your character embodies.

Each sector of society has commonly understood social ideals, but not every character embodies a positive expression of those values. Some characters live outside mainstream values, embrace only a limited aspect of them or have beliefs that are contrary to them. Each of these differing points of view is still a response to or expression of the values of the style. So, you don't need to make every character in a show the same, or to have them express the culture in the same way.

Identifying the social ideal

As you begin identifying the social ideal for a character, you have a number of useful resources. Create a portfolio of research material and spend the time needed to truly inform yourself. You can't rely solely on your impressions of a style or character type. You need to actually research it to have a concrete starting place. Thankfully, we live in an age where films are readily available, visual images can quickly be researched on the internet or in libraries, and recorded music is more obtainable than ever. Add to that popular magazines and books, advertisements (a highly useful resource), fiction, radio and television from a specific period, and you've got a broad base to draw from.

Our earlier discussion of character types in the musical theatre from Chapter 7 is important here because, in order to research and identify appropriate models for a character from any style, we have to also identify which character type he is. Ultimately, the research you access and the way you incorporate it in your process will affect how you stand, speak, move and sing. Understanding style and character type provides you with the tactical range for your character. *What you want* becomes clear once you've investigated your character's objectives. But, *how you get it* is colored by social guidelines for how you are permitted or expected to behave. Desirée Armfeld wants to have sex with Fredrik Egerman (*A Little Night Music*), just as Mimi wants to have sex with Roger (*Rent*). The underlying need is the same. But how each goes about getting what she wants is defined by the rules of her society.

Beauty and fashion

Analyze images of ideal male and female beauty for the time a style originated in and deduce the values that those images project. Once you understand the culture your role emerges from, you can translate that culture into your behavior.

Among the most obvious ways we identify different styles of theatre is through the clothing or costume associated with each. The physical shapes or silhouettes created by these different clothing styles often reveal how each theatrical world defines physical beauty. For instance, current images of female beauty often emphasize low body fat and a high degree of muscular fitness in women between the ages of approximately 15 and 30. This has been increasingly true since the mid-1970s when low-calorie, healthy food and fitness became status activities. But if we look back one century to the late 1800s we'll see that images of feminine beauty reflected a much higher amount of body fat. At that time, thinness and muscle tone betrayed that a woman was part of the working class. She couldn't afford enough food to maintain greater body weight because of the high degree of physical labor required to work in factories or on farms. So, higher weight and soft muscle tone were status symbols, and therefore considered beautiful.

Beyond actual physical shape, fashion has a magnifying effect in representing social values. Values such as independence, weakness, ability or inability to work, and the desire to accommodate or reject traditional gender roles are all reflected in fashion.

Clothing fashions tell us what beauty is at any given time. And beauty is a tool for characters because it can get you what you want, whether a romantic partner, an advantage in a contest, or power of some other kind.

UNIT 14.7.7   *Performance tradition and style*

The way musical performers act, sing and dance has changed significantly over the years. Identifying the right performance tradition can be the key that unlocks a style for you.

Performance tradition is the way that musical performers relate to each other and their audience. Changes in musical style, technology and acting conventions have resulted in constant redefinition of this tradition. What we may now identify as a highly theatrical style was once accepted as realism by its audience. No single tradition dies out completely in the musical theatre, but instead it simply takes its place in the continuum of performance traditions.

When we step into the world of a style, we adopt at least some elements of the performance tradition that it belongs to. This can even be the case with an individual character or song in a show that, otherwise, belongs in a very different tradition. Look at *'Herod's Song'* from *Jesus Christ Superstar*, *'All For The Best'* in *Godspell* or *'Glory'* from *Pippin*. Although these shows are all rock musicals, these individual songs recall the vaudeville performance tradition. Accordingly, the actors singing and dancing them adjust their performance conventions to remind the audience of this stylistic quotation. They will probably even heighten certain elements of the older style to make their point. This self-conscious use of performance conventions helps illustrate how sensitized audiences, writers and performers are to the evolving performance traditions we associate with different styles.

The buffet of styles and influences we draw from and seek to become familiar with includes the following popular musical performance traditions:

- Opera
- Vaudeville
- Operetta
- Minstrel show
- Ragtime/early Jazz
- Folk songs
- Big Band singing
- Early use of microphones (crooners: Frank Sinatra, Ella Fitzgerald, Bing Crosby, Al Jolson)
- Early Rock and Roll (Elvis Presley, Chuck Berry)
- Mature Rock and Roll (The Beatles, U2, The Sex Pistols)
- Pop music/Top 40 (Carole King, Elton John, Billy Joel, Carly Simon)
- Rhythm and Blues
- Gospel
- Country Western
- Motown/Soul

Many non-musical dramatic and comic acting styles inform musical theatre performance, as well. Among these acting styles are:

- Shakespearean acting (both early twentieth-century and current)
- Early Modern (Ibsen, Chekhov, Shaw)
- Vaudeville and Burlesque comedy
- Screwball comedy
- Farce
- Mid-century ("kitchen-sink") Realism
- Radio drama
- Film and television (including soap operas and situation comedies)

Mixing performance conventions and mingling traditions is typical and can be useful as you begin to address style choices for your role. By invoking the performance conventions of an earlier style, the audience is signaled to treat that character in a particular way.

We see this technique used to great advantage in what many critics consider the first modern musical, *Show Boat*. The stage adapters created a wide range of musical voices to dramatize the many different characters and storylines in Edna

Ferber's sweeping novel. Kern and Hammerstein associated each set of characters and storylines with a different set of performance traditions to help their
audience identify and place those characters accurately. So, the romantic couple,
Magnolia and Gaylord, is written in the European operetta tradition. The song
and dance couple, Frank and Ellie Mae, is written in true vaudeville song and
dance style. The tragic heroine, Julie Laverne, sings torch songs, as one might
find in cabarets or saloons. The former slave couple, Joe and Queenie, sings in
a hybrid of black spiritual and plantation song styles, appropriate to the post-Civil
War American South. Finally, Magnolia's parents, the Hawkses, come straight
out of vaudeville comedy. He is the henpecked husband, she the shrew. This
technique has become a presumption about musical theatre characters ever
since *Show Boat* first premiered.

UNIT 14.7.8   *Self-conscious use of performance traditions*

Writers sometimes draw on our associations with and memories of a specific
tradition to call attention to their ironic use of the style. *Follies*, *Chicago*, *Forty-
Second Street*, *The Wild Party* (LaChiusa) and *Hello, Again* all contain what
Stephen Sondheim calls pastiche songs. These are songs that consciously mimic
the writing conventions of another time or a specific composer or performer.
Alerted to this kind of quotation or reference we are able to have a simultaneous
experience of seeing the current performance and remember a past one. So,
when the Leading Player in *Pippin* drops to one knee at the edge of the stage and
says, "You ain't seen nothin' yet!" we see his performance and remember Al
Jolson's famous pose and line.

UNIT 14.7.9   *Historical accuracy and modern perceptions
of style*

Historical accuracy is not an end in itself. Audiences must be touched by the
performances. While abundant records of film and audio exist to document
almost every period we study, these records are of only limited value as we arrive
at our sense of the best way to represent a particular style to our audience today.
These historical artifacts offer useful insights into a past performance tradition
and, as importantly, the values that underlie the styles we work in. So, they are
a valuable point of departure. But they don't necessarily help us bridge the
gap between the performance conventions of that time and ours. Merging what
are sometimes disparate traditions is critical if our audience is to receive the

performances we create as both authentic by contemporary standards and still evocative of a specific past performance tradition. The next chapter will help you do that.

SECTION V: STYLE IN MUSICAL THEATRE

CHAPTER 15

STYLE TAGS

We have said that, for style to be effectively played, it must be recognizable and it must be applied consistently throughout a production. In addition to understanding the world of the style you're entering, you must also manifest those values and worldviews in performance behavior. How does it make you stand, sing, move and talk?

EXERCISE 15A   POP MUSIC STYLE-GO-ROUND

Take a song that everyone in your group knows, like *'I Got Rhythm'* or *'Popular'* or *'I Dreamed a Dream'*. If you know a classical aria or art song, try that too. Have each person in the group sing that same song, but in a different style. Video tape this for later. Try these styles for starters (though you can certainly add your own):

grand opera	country western	punk rock	lounge singer
blues	1990s power ballad	big band crooner	Elvis Presley

Without too much effort you were probably able to make the necessary adjustments to the song so that you could adopt the style fully. If you're like most people, you changed not only the way you sang, but also the way that you stood, gestured, and used your entire instrument. You instinctively changed your vocal and physical behavior to fit the attitudes of the style.

UNIT 15.1   **What are style tags?**

That last exercise demonstrates how adaptable and transformative most actors are, once they understand the attitudes and performance conventions associated with a style. When playing Elvis, most of us instinctively know to lower the key, curl our lip, adopt a slurred Southern dialect, and live within a very tightly prescribed set of physical shapes and movement options. To a large extent, we do just that as we approach playing different styles in musical theatre.

The list of vocal and physical changes you underwent as you stepped into the style exercise above are the telltale symptoms of that style. We call these vocal and physical behaviors *style tags*.

> **EXERCISE 15B   NAME THE TAGS**
>
> 1.   Look back at the performance you gave in the last exercise. Take a moment to quickly list the vocal and physical changes and choices you made to step into that style. Share the list with the other members of your group and see if they can help add to the list or to specify and clarify it.
> 2.   Trade lists with someone else in your group and, using the tags that your partner defined, try to step into that new style. Let them coach you on the style tags that they identified. Can you make any suggestions about how to specify the style through vocal and physical behaviors? Try to identify the specific attitude or worldview required to succeed in that style. For instance, Elvis knows everyone thinks he's sexy. Is the punk rocker yelling at the world? Or the power balladeer super-serious about love?

After having gone through this last exercise, you probably saw that style tags fall into two categories: vocal tags and physical tags. We will identify a handful of vocal and physical areas that most styles are expressed through.

UNIT 15.2   **Vocal style tags**

If you've ever studied singing before, you know that you learn by imitating a sound and then figuring out what physical changes you made in order to achieve the desired outcome. This is what we'll do as we explore vocal style tags. From the outset we want to remind you that vocal manipulations that feel abusive probably are abusive. This includes scratching, tearing and grating sounds. These are not acceptable choices, even if you get laughs or it seems stylistically appropriate. These are the rough equivalent of a dancer walking on broken glass in bare feet in order to achieve an artistic goal. It might be interesting for the moment, but he'll never dance again. Don't do it. Look to the essence of the vocal quality you want to imitate and see if there are elements you can appropriate without including the abusive behavior. In almost every case this is possible. With that having been said, let's proceed.

By listening observantly to recordings in the styles that you seek to enter, you can usually identify the vocal qualities that help define that style as distinct from others. Those qualities usually fall within these categories: diction, tonality, vibrato and phrasing.

Diction

UNIT 15.2.1

One of the central premises of Shaw's *Pygmalion* (and *My Fair Lady*) is that the way a person speaks "absolutely classifies him." It tells us his education, social caste, region and personal aesthetic. So we might know, by listening, *where* the person is from and where they're coming from philosophically. We can also tell *when* the person is from. Tastes in speech reflect time as well as place. If you watch a film from the 1940s you can hear a definitive pronunciation, a faster more machine-gun rhythm, a different sense of what constitutes formality and slang, even a different melodic pattern – all adding up to that recognizable way they talked. It is this essence we look to identify through studying the diction associated with a style. Diction includes:

Articulation. The formation of small detailed sounds, especially consonants (notice the way the s-t-r consonants in "street" have evolved to sh-ch-reet in many modern dialects).

Enunciation. Broader than articulation, this is the larger issue of word clarity (compare "probably" spoken with all the consonants present, versus "prolly" or frequently even "pry").

Pronunciation. A concept of the "right" way to say a word (tune as "toon" or "tyoon").

Dialect. The sounds and speech patterns associated with a particular region, culture, caste or time.

As you listen to source recordings, note how important precise diction is to that world. If you hear elaborately rolled Rs, deliberately popped final consonants or the word "been" pronounced as "bean," then you know you're in one kind of world. But if you hear the word "I" expressed as "ah," or "going" as "gohne," then you're in a very different world. In rock music from virtually every country in the world, there is a heavy emphasis on adopting a relaxed American diction, with a slight Southern dialect. This is central to stepping into the relaxed, slightly rebellious belief system that rock music embraces. The relationship between the central values of a culture and the way that its inhabitants speak is powerful. Listen to Nelson Eddy and Jeanette McDonald's operetta-style *'Indian Love Call'* then switch to Mick Jagger hammering out "ah caint git no sadisfaction." Jagger's performance is an especially interesting study in style, since his rock/ R&B dialect is spot-on, but miles away from both his middle-class British roots and the Cockney working-class-rocker persona he created.

UNIT 15.2.2 *Tonality*

As we address tonal quality, we are asking you to listen for and experiment with resonances, vocal coloration and degrees of breathiness. Learning to deviate and modify your habitual tonal quality in a healthy way is a necessary skill for all singing actors.

Every period and style has a set of vocal colors and values that are favored over others. Think of the nasal twang of a bluegrass singer contrasted with the dark roundness of an operatic coloratura. It's moonshine and merlot. Each has its special kick.

When you sang in the exercises that began this chapter you probably realized the silliness of singing *'I Dreamed a Dream'* as an operatic aria because the tonal qualities favored in opera are the opposite of those favored in Broadway pop singing.

Vocal quality is sometimes described using musical analogies, like trumpet or cello, or adjectives like warm, bright, dark and rich. The evocative words that inspire you and help you identify a vocal color with specificity are the terms to cling to. Terms often heard to describe tonal quality are:

warm	bright	brassy	rich	dark
velvety	metallic	round	cello	trumpet
clarinet	reedy	thick	breezy	pure
violin	operatic	belty	growl	floaty

You can certainly add your own adjectives to develop this list. Gathering a vocabulary to help you do this will become an increasingly valuable part of your arsenal of skills.

EXERCISE 15C   PAINTING WITH VOCAL COLORS

Choose a vocalese that you're comfortable with. With each repetition or modulation, apply a different vocal color. Use the list from above or create your own. If you're in a group, have each person select two contrasting vocal colors. Everyone stands in a circle. As you all take a breath for the next repetition, the next person in line calls out the vocal color you'll all explore.

Vibrato versus straight

UNIT 15.2.3

One way to understand vibrato is to notice how a violinist uses it. In order to make the tone of a sustained note more beautiful, they rock the finger holding the string back and forth. This action slightly sharps and flats the pitch. A straight sustained sound can be piercing. Vibrato mellows that stridency and produces a richer tone.

Like a string player, singers need to make skillful choices about how to employ vibrato and straight sounds. Both are useful. As you listen to songs from different styles and periods, make a point to spot how the original performers used them. There are distinct preferences in when they use vibrato, how wide the pitch change should be, and the speed of the vibrato.

Notice your own preferences in using vibrato. Then learn to play with it as one of the many style elements you can change like hats.

EXERCISE 15D   RATE OF VIBRATO

1. Taking a full, healthy breath, begin singing a note that sits comfortably in the middle of your range.
2. As you begin singing, slowly change the rate of vibrato you apply. Start with it at what you feel is a moderate rate and gently explore faster

and slower rates of vibrato. This may take some time for you to get comfortable with.

3. Try changing pitches on this exercise. Do you notice any difference in ease as you do so? Be careful not to overdo this. If you begin to feel vocal fatigue or distress, stop!

EXERCISE 15E   VIBRATO ONSET

1. Again, picking a pitch that sits comfortably in the center of your range, begin singing a sustained tone. Try to sing this without any vibrato, what some people refer to as straight tone. Try this on several different pitches. Can you sing with no vibrato at all?
2. After you've mastered singing with straight tone, slowly allow vibrato to begin. Try this several times on different pitches with early and late onset of vibrato. Can you decide when to apply vibrato? If not, explore gaining control of the onset of the vibrato. Many pop singers from the 1970s and 80s made great use of late onset of vibrato. Some big band crooners used wide and slower vibrato as a central feature of their singing, often with a late onset.

EXERCISE 15F   COMBINING VIBRATO SKILLS

Now, try the same exploration of different pitches, but this time decide in advance the point of onset (early, middle, late) and the rate of vibrato (slow, medium, fluttery fast).

UNIT 15.2.4   *Phrasing*

We have already explored this idea in Chapter 11: Discovering Your Phrasing. We suggest you look back at those exercises as you consider this aspect of style. The degree to which you sing the music exactly as it is written on the page with strict adherence to all the note values and dynamic markings can be highly expressive of the stylistic world you enter. The kinds of flexibility that performers in rock musicals explore are very different from the close adherence to written notation that composers like Richard Rodgers or Frank Loesser insisted on. Listening for back phrasing, spoken passages, punching of words and notes, instrumental imitation and so forth will connect you with the phrasing conventions of the style you're exploring.

An area of phrasing that we didn't cover in Chapter 11 is the use of vocal ornamentation. In most styles singers adorn the basic melody with improvised or carefully developed variations. Each period and style has its own set of ornaments, such as Bing Crosby's "Boo-boo-boo"s or Rudy Vallee's "voh-doh-dee-o-doh." You have only to look to *American Idol* on television to see how important ornamentation can be in defining a performance. Singers on that show are encouraged to make ornamentation the central aspect of a performance, with the melody, as written, a distinctly secondary concern. As we look back on popular music from the early twenty-first century we'll undoubtedly see a heavy reliance on vocal ornamentation as a hallmark of the style.

For the purposes of our study of style, we need to become sensitive to the kinds of ornament that each style embraces and learn to comfortably include them in our performances without making the performance about the ornamentation. The focus is still the dramatic circumstance and your pursuit of an objective. It is almost never simply about the style and the ornamentation – even in musicals that seem to be about style, like *The Wedding Singer*, *Dames at Sea* or *Grease* – although the awareness and amplification of style elements is often higher in these shows.

Researching vocal styles

Getting to know the vocal world you're entering involves listening and research. Finding period recordings to help you create a vocabulary of vocal choices is a great practice. We encourage you to listen to a wide range of sources for the style you're approaching. Don't limit yourself to listening just to the show you're working on. You might choose to spend more time listening to other recordings than dwelling on the original, lest you find yourself imitating someone else's performance of your role. But, as we have said, style is an evolving notion. So listening to subsequent performances of the music from your show or by the same composer and lyricist will often help you understand how the style has changed. The older the show, the more likely a change will have taken place. We also recommend listening to iconic singers from the period and style you're working in.

EXERCISE 15G BREAK DOWN

Have each member of your group bring in a song from a range of different popular singing styles. Listen carefully to identify how the singer used style tags in the performance. Assign each person to focus on a different vocal style tag. One person will listen for vibrato, another to tonality, and so forth. Be precise. Try imitating those tags. Some distinctive singers include: Billie Holiday, Louis Armstrong, Nell Carter, Judy Garland, Michael Jackson and Tony Bennett.

UNIT 15.3 **Physical style tags**

UNIT 15.3.1 *Posture and silhouette*

Finding the body shapes that support the worldview for each style does wonders for helping you and your audience step into that world. When we talked about fashion we said the value systems of any given society are reflected in its fashions. But reinforcing those values doesn't stop at the cut of the coat. The person wearing it creates postures that reinforce those values. The combination of the physical body shapes made by the actor and the assistance of the costume is called the *silhouette* of the character. The term literally means the outline of the person or garment. Every style and each character type within that style has a silhouette that would have been considered ideal. It is your job to identify and adopt that set of shapes comfortably. Just as we learn a dialect for a role and then speak almost unconsciously in it, you will also adopt a set of physical shapes and ways of moving that are appropriate to the style world you enter. For example, the gentility of the feminine ideal at the turn of the twentieth century is reinforced by soft shapes and delicate, curving postures. Contrast that with the defiance of the feminine ideal in the late 1960s. In rebellion against the polite and obedient image of femininity in the 1950s, women adopted masculine shapes, and the silhouette of this new ethos was slouchy and intentionally casual. These shapes match the worldview of the time.

UNIT 15.3.2 *Formality of movement*

Unlike the static fashion photos and period advertising in your research of the silhouette for each style, you will be moving onstage, not just standing in pretty shapes. So, finding ways of living comfortably and moving flexibly within the period style will be important. Again, we return to the worldview and values of the time. We seek to understand how a character might move, but still within her social station and in the specific circumstances of the script.

Looking back at our previous example, a young, upper middle-class woman at the turn of the twentieth century would probably aspire to movement that was fluid and graceful, suggesting conformity and obedience. But her counterpart in the late 1960s sought movement that was shambling, bobbing and intentionally bumpy as a way of expressing an easygoing rebellious and "groovy" lifestyle.

Understanding the permissible relationships between men and women and the social expectations of relationships between classes will give you the clearest sense of how your character would behave around the other characters in your musical. Men and women had a highly formal public relationship in Victorian England. Accordingly, relationships in the operettas of Gilbert and Sullivan will require great deference on the part of the actors toward each other. Bowing, keeping plenty of distance, and measuring the amount of direct eye contact between potential lovers will all support that value system and help create a set of movement rules to follow. If we look at guidebooks for social behavior (such as Emily Post's *Etiquette in Society, in Business, in Politics, and at Home*) it's astounding to see how many actual rules for social interaction people were expected to follow. These modes of behavior quickly help to dictate your movement qualities.

Fashion and movement

It would be hard to overemphasize the influence of fashion in each style and period. For today's young woman, performing in a corset and high heels may be a foreign skill. But, the roles you'll play and the audience's awareness of silhouette and movement patterns requires absolute freedom in garments and accessories you may find personally uncomfortable. Young men may consider wearing a suit and tie unnaturally formal. But, until about 1960, this was the most common form of dress for almost every class of society. Get past that awkwardness. Learn to work with freedom in this part of your given circumstances in the earliest stages of rehearsal. Waiting until the first dress rehearsal to deal with these fundamental issues may destroy your performance, while including these elements from the outset may give you unexpected insight into the character and help you to create a role that surprises even you. So, acquire and wear appropriate rehearsal clothing early on.

UNIT 15.3.4   *Gestural vocabulary*

We spent a good deal of time looking at ways to organically and specifically create gesture and movement for your songs in Chapter 12: Staging Your Song. Creating and using gesture within a style is simply an extension of that work. In the case of style, we'll often find patterns and shapes that are the result of social convention and custom and of performance conventions. Turn down the volume on any music video channel to look at contemporary hip-hop performers. Without paying attention to content, you'll quickly see a clear gestural vocabulary being employed. Notice how the thumb, index and middle fingers on both hands are extended (or some other very deliberate combination of several extended fingers). Do you see repeated circular thrusts using one or both hands at about waist level? You probably notice the performer tipping from his waist slightly to the right and left as he gestures. These are all part of the gestural vocabulary associated with rap and hip-hop performance. They work comfortably within the fashions and silhouette of the style and adhere to the highly informal worldview associated with this music.

In the same way you looked at the hip-hop videos, you can research gesture shapes for every world you seek to enter. Looking at performances by different actors in the same way that you listened to influential singers will help you accumulate a gestural vocabulary that helps to place you into that world. Pay attention to these elements in particular:

- How does the actor stand? Where is his weight placed? (In one hip or the other, on the balls of the feet, with one foot in front of the other, in a wide and firm stance, etc.)
- What physical shapes does he make? (Postures, silhouettes.)
- How fluid is the use of gesture? (Do you see thrusting or stabbing gestures often? Do hands and arms move smoothly through space?)
- How wide a range of motion is permitted? (Does the actor frequently move above the shoulders or below the waist? Are his arms locked at the sides? How athletic is the motion?)
- Do you see the same gestures used by different performers? (This can be a good indication that the gesture is typical of the period, not just that actor.)

Once you've established a palette of gestures to work from, try singing from your own repertoire while using these gestures. This can feel a little awkward at first. But what you'll quickly discover is you're simply channeling expressive impulses through these gestures. After a while, you'll feel completely natural living within this set of options.

Attitudes into actions

As interesting as understanding the world of a particular style may be, it is of little use to us as actors unless we can convert the attitudes and values implicit in that style into objectives and tactics. This is most easily accomplished if we remember that those attitudes motivate us to characterize ourselves and others in specific ways. For instance, in European operetta, male lovers usually subscribe to an attitude of chivalry and pure romantic love toward their female counterparts. So, how would he characterize her? Look at the lyric of *'Rose Marie'* by Rudolf Friml and Herbert Stothart to get an idea of how we might make this attitude active and actable.

> Oh, Rose Marie I love you.
> I'm always dreaming of you.
> No matter where I go I can't forget you.
> Sometimes I wish that I had never met you.
> And yet, if I should lose you
> 'Twould mean my very life to me.
> Of all the queens that ever lived I'd choose you
> To rule me, my Rose Marie!

In this lyric, the singer literally characterizes Rose Marie as his queen and ruler. And, by extension, he has characterized himself in the role of servant, supplicant, knight or idolater.

Taking this direct cue, we could employ the following tactics as we relate to and pursue Rose Marie.

> "I worship you."
> "I deify you as my goddess."
> "I revere you."
> "I glorify and honor you."
> "I cherish you."

Or, from a slightly different angle:

> "I submit to your will."
> "I grovel before you."
> "I lower myself."
> "I obsess over you."

The great value of understanding style tags is that those customary behaviors will provide a tactical range specifically suited to the world of the style.

In European operetta, the codes for behavior between men and women were chivalrous and courtly. Knowing this will allow the singer to treat Rose Marie appropriately by bowing before her, lowering himself, deferring to her physically. His worship of her will provide him behaviors that elevate her in a chaste fashion. Having discovered a vocabulary of movement and vocal possibilities, you can work freely within them to play these actions and win your fight for her love.

Fashion, physical and vocal behavior, and attitudes give you ways to work toward your objectives. If the character you're pursuing subscribes to a particular world-view with identifiable male ideals, your character can use these as a model for his own behavior. Think of phrases like, "You want me to act like [——], so I will do that to please you." Or "You desire men who look like [——], so I will try to look like that to win you." These codes and modes give you ways of pursuing your goals.

UNIT 15.5   **Style and truth**

Working within a style also includes bringing your own identity as an actor to the table and incorporating significant elements of what you understand to be truthful acting. Without that, this all becomes a phony experience. Your job is to identify the style tags that feel most appropriate and to assimilate these into your sense of the role and your current technique. Remember, you were cast for who you are in the role, not because you could impersonate someone else. Even the most chameleonic actor is still that actor.

Style is the mask you wear to tell your truth in. It is not an end in itself.

SECTION V: STYLE IN MUSICAL THEATRE

CHAPTER 16: STYLE OVERVIEWS

STYLE OVERVIEWS

Over the next five units we will apply the style skills that we've explored to a range of musical theatre styles. You'll see how the worldview and cultural perspective of the world a style emerged out of colors how you act and sing in it.

European operetta

Background and worldview

Viennese, German and French operetta (and its later American and British antecedents) create a fantasy world of elegant courtiers, aristocratic nobility, exotic locales and mistaken identities. Although these operettas were enormously popular among all classes, they told stories that focused almost exclusively on the lives of royalty. In a world where the many duchies and ethnic states of the Austro-Hungarian Empire were under threat, these entertainments ignored that reality in favor of stories depicting young noblemen falling in love with beautiful peasant girls and gypsies (who turn out to be princesses!). These operettas were filled with sweeping waltzes, romantic songs, handsome young men, glittering young ladies and buffoonish comic characters. Reality was not the point here, nor political correctness. Instead, romance, lush orchestras, beautiful voices and visual spectacle were spun into gossamer confections. Another typical early operetta conceit was to lampoon stories from classical mythology as a way of veiling criticism of current political figures, or to place well-to-do cosmopolitan Europeans in faraway exotic locales.

European operetta reigned as the most popular musical theatre form from roughly the 1850s through about 1914 when American composers took over the form and modified it to fit the anti-German tastes of the United States during and after World War I. It continued to be produced regularly on Broadway into the 1930s.

Although early operettas were full of comic characters and situations, eventually the romantic stories and songs came to exemplify this form. Today, it is this deeply and unapologetically romantic influence that we most associate with European operetta. And it is this emphasis on earnest romance that has continued to be a powerful performance influence. As actors in contemporary musical theatre, we are wise to become familiar with this legacy, since it still defines at least some part of every musical.

Social ideal and values

UNIT 16.1.2

The social ideal in European operettas comes from the world of aristocracy and nobility. Both men and women were expected to maintain the appearance of noble motives, dignity and poise. This expectation and the resulting behaviors, attitudes and fashions are all inherently related.

Men were members of royalty (often dukes or princes) or at least moneyed aristocracy in small, usually fictitious Eastern European countries. The men were typically military figures with a great sense of duty to their country. Women came in two flavors. The first was a virtuous young woman of noble birth being courted by the men we just spoke of. These women were elegant, sometimes betrothed to the wrong man, and they prefigure the ingénue of early musical theatre. The second kind of female character was an exotic or dark gypsy figure that tempts the central male character. As gypsies were simultaneously figures of revulsion and attraction for European society, these characters offered forbidden, exotic temptation. In America, these figures became native Americans or mulattos.

In the end, chivalry, noble motives, virtue and pure romantic love always triumph. Order must be restored by aligning the heroic leading man with his true love.

Romance and sex

As we've said, romantic love was this culture's most prized virtue and the central engine of these operettas. Despite any of the many improbable complications of the plots, there was never a question for the audiences devouring these musical entertainments that true love would win the day. The casual ways of touching between men and women that we take for granted today are unacceptable in this world. Physical contact between the sexes always carries important meaning because physical intimacy is not part of any premarital relationship. The highest form of physical love between unmarried men and women is a kiss (with lips closed!). The "bad women" who tempt good men in these operettas never triumph. Their very sexuality marks them as secondary characters.

Beauty and fashion

Typical of the fashions represented were men in full Hussar military regalia or formal tail suits, women in full evening gowns (complete with enormous foundation garments), or stylish fantasies on gypsy peasant garb. Our traditional wedding gown with a train offers us a good way of imagining this style of dress. In the late nineteenth and early twentieth centuries the idealized image of both male and female beauty was older than today's and was somewhat more heavy-set. We would probably find the slightly portly man in tight pants and high boots and the full-figured lady with overflowing décolletage an incongruous romantic pair. But this was the physical ideal of the time. Most modern productions modify this early image to accommodate current tastes.

Relationship to authority

The central figures in these operettas not only showed total and willing obedience to authority; as members of the aristocracy, they often *were* the authorities in society. In Sigmund Romberg's late-period operetta *The Student Prince*, the title character is torn between his obligations as future king of his nation and his desire to live the carefree student life. His chaste but passionate love affair with a beer hall waitress, Kathie, comes to an end when he is called home to succeed his grandfather, who unexpectedly dies. Accepting his responsibility as heir to the throne, Prince Karl can only look back on the *'Golden Days'* of his student life while he sacrifices love for duty.

Performance tradition

Because operetta is such a close descendent of grand opera, the performance tradition is strongly built around the voice (*la voce!* as the Italians might say). Pure bel canto singing for men and women, with only limited physicalization, is typical. The sound of the voice *is* the emotion.

Although operetta is roughly contemporary with vaudeville and musical hall entertainment, it represents a very different performance tradition. Unlike vaudeville, where direct address to the audience is expected, operetta places the imaginary fourth wall up to allow the audience to observe but not participate in the performance. Actors in operetta treat solo songs as soliloquies or monologues to other characters onstage.

While later musical theatre forms convey a heavy dose of cynicism and biting humor, European operetta eschews this for a lighter touch. Bumbling comic characters, ethnic satires and silly drunks form the basis of the humor here. The comic tradition leans more heavily on oversized caricatures, rather than verbal wit or subtle characterization.

Style tags

Vocal style tags

Tone: Pure bel canto in the opera tradition. Round, rich tone for men. Pure legitimate tone for women.

Vibrato: Early onset and steady use of vibrato. In period recordings we often hear what some refer to as a "flutter vibrato" in high sopranos. The application of this rapid vibrato has fallen out of fashion, but a steady vibrato is still typical. This is one of the areas you'll want to experiment with to find a good balance.

Diction: Since many of these shows take place in European countries, the use of a mid-Atlantic dialect (not British but also not American, and high class) is the standard even for later shows set in the USA. Formal diction is required. Today, we typically expect that all words will be understandable, but, as in grand opera, vocal production of the beautiful sound will usually win out over clarity of the word, if necessary. Early on, we typically heard things like tapped Rs ("very" would sound more like "veddy"), and words like "ask" shading toward "ahsk." There are virtually no contractions or casual modifications of the spoken or sung text.

Phrasing: Strong emphasis on musicality and lyricism of the phrase. Beauty of the musical line and tonal purity are the primary concerns. Many lyrics and translations are essentially strings of open vowel sounds that allow singers to emote through sound. Phrasing is more emotionally indulgent and sentimental than in any other style.

Physical style tags

Posture/silhouette: The world of operetta requires actors to adopt an upright, perfectly aligned posture. Men must be able to carry themselves with an obvious but invisible dignity that believably supports the wearing of ornate dress military uniforms, fine suits, top hats and canes. Actors can imagine that the shoulders and spine form an invisible cross that doesn't twist or bend, unless the character is involved in physical combat. The chest remains lifted in a healthy (not hyper-extended) posture. In our society, the military is probably the last place where this type of posture is still expected. Modeling that type of posture and silhouette without the insistent rigidity will offer male actors a useful starting point. Rehearsing in a fully buttoned jacket, dress pants, a shirt and tie, and hard-soled dress shoes will begin to prepare you for the costumes that we most often see in operettas. Men will want to be sure that they are shaved and their hair is groomed for every rehearsal.

Women in operettas are almost always corseted underneath tight bodices, very large floor-length dresses and full wigs. Negotiating this amount of clothing and accessories requires an upright, but not rigid, posture. As with the male silhouette, women will need to become comfortable with a fully erect and aligned posture. Rehearsing in a corset (preferably one that still allows you to breathe), shoes with a medium heel, and a full-length rehearsal skirt with several layers will offer you the best preparation for working in this world. Women will want to use basic make-up and a floral cologne as part of rehearsal practice.

Degree of formality: Custom and tradition for the world of operetta require the highest degree of formality of any style we will study. Because respect for authority, femininity and our elders are central to the worldview of this style, we must always employ the good manners that our parents probably wished we had in public.

Gestural vocabulary: All movement and use of gesture in the world of operetta must be filtered through the requirement that the characters maintain dignity and poise. So, retaining the upright and elevated postures we've described in the upper torso is a given at all times, even while sitting or kneeling. Actors will want to get used to sitting on the edge of the seat, allowing the majority of the thigh off the seat. Slouching while sitting, though comfortable, is not part of this physical world.

Gestures in the world of operetta are typically fluid, sometimes containing a bit of flourish. Flicking, tossed-away or busy gestures and movements are not part of this world. In general, the body and arms are less active in operetta than in other styles.

Contemporary behaviors that include slouching into one hip, leaning on walls, hooking a thumb in a pocket or waistband, standing with legs crossed over, sitting with knees apart or slumping in the upper torso are not part of this world.

Examples from the style/genre

Orpheus in the Underworld – Jacques Offenbach (the first successful operetta)

Tales of Hoffman – Jacques Offenbach (his final work)

Die Fledermaus – Johann Strauss II (still among the most produced operettas)

The Gypsy Baron – Johann Strauss II

The Merry Widow – Franz Lehar (a breakthrough in its time)

The Student Prince – Sigmund Romberg

Rose Marie – Rudolf Friml

The New Moon – Sigmund Romberg

Naughty Marietta – Victor Herbert

The Desert Song – Sigmund Romberg

Research resources (film/audio/visual)

There are many good recordings of operettas available. Of special interest are a series of early recordings released by Pearl Records that reveal just how much our conception of operetta performance has changed. Be sure to listen to a range of recordings from both early and recent productions. No period of musical theatre performance has evolved more than operetta.

The series of films that Jeanette McDonald and Nelson Eddy made during the 1930s offers a valuable, if narrow, view of the performance tradition. These include:

Naughty Marietta, 1935
Rose Marie, 1936
Maytime, 1937
Sweethearts, 1938
The New Moon, 1940

Mario Lanza had a brief film career as the great tenor hope for operetta on film in the late 1940s and 1950s. His voice appears in the film of *The Student Prince*. He also stars in *The Great Caruso* as legendary tenor Enrico Caruso. Although his career was brief, this marks the last time traditional European operettas were filmed. As such, these films have an important place in your research.

Among the best ways to fully appreciate the tradition of operetta is to view the Walt Disney cartoon *Snow White and the Seven Dwarfs*. In that film's earliest scenes, the peasant girl, Snow White, first meets her Prince Charming. Their physical and vocal behavior are so typical of the performance conventions of operetta that one can instantly get a sense of the style.

For a later interpretation and evolution of the operetta worldview, see Disney's *Cinderella*. Again the heroine and her prince carry on the tradition, but from the vantage point of the 1950s.

Rodgers and Hammerstein's first made-for-television *Cinderella* is also a great model for this style. The more recent version of the same story is somewhat less useful as a model for operetta because it intentionally blends styles and cultural behaviors in a way that departs from this tradition.

Public television in the USA and the UK has frequently broadcast operettas over the years. Many of the performances are available on video. These are of great use to your research as well, because they are the most current record of the tradition as it exists today.

UNIT 16.2 **Gilbert and Sullivan operetta**

UNIT 16.2.1 *Background and worldview*

We will look at the operettas of Gilbert and Sullivan as a separate style, although they have a good deal in common with their contemporary counterparts, the European operettas. But there are sufficiently different conventions associated with these "G and S" operettas that a separate study is warranted.

William Schwenck Gilbert (lyrics and libretto) and Arthur Sullivan (music) were arguably the most influential artists in English-speaking musical theatre. Their work combines high and low literary and musical influences with keen wit, a brilliant sense of parody that continues to resonate today, a delightful sense of the absurd, and great skill and artistry in scripting and composition. The result is some of the funniest, most charming, tuneful and lovely musical theatre ever created. Gilbert and Sullivan worked together most productively under the producer Richard D'Oyly Carte at the Savoy Theatre in London. For this reason we often refer to their works as the Savoy Operas.

Gilbert coined the phrase "Topsy-Turvy," which expresses his artistic point of view perfectly. It means to take a normal situation and spin it upside down, inverting the logically expected social responses by pushing them to their illogically absurd extreme. This results in characters who embody ridiculously opposing values, such as members of parliament masquerading as pirates who won't kill anyone claiming to be an orphan, admirals who know nothing of real naval operations, condemned men who are appointed royal executioner, and so forth. One contemporary critic said that Gilbert had "a piercing vision of the insanity of reason."

Employing tightly plotted and composed operas, every tier of society and every character type in it were the target of Gilbert's skewering wit. Yet the satire is not mean spirited. Since everyone is fair game for satire, they are all treated equally and everyone's silly imperfections are ultimately forgiven. Gilbert and Sullivan were content to hold a mirror up to their society and laugh even at themselves, while striving for moderation, reason and common sense. This generosity and even-handedness made them popular in all circles of Victorian society.

W.S. Gilbert continued a tradition in English theatre and literature of verbal play – an exploration of the comic, ironic or satiric possibilities of language that dates back to before Shakespeare's time. Gilbert refined a lyric and libretto tradition that leads directly to P.G. Wodehouse (1910s and 1920s), Ira Gershwin, Lorenz Hart, Cole Porter and Noël Coward (1920s to 1950s), and Stephen Sondheim (1950s to the present). It would be hard to imagine shows like *Avenue Q* and *Urinetown* without the precedent of the Savoy Operas. The use of witty wordplay and complex rhyming, satirical characterizations and affectionate absurdity are all part of this tradition.

UNIT 16.2.2 *Social ideal and values*

Gilbert and Sullivan were well versed in the rules of polite Victorian society because they were members of its top echelon, both eventually being knighted. At the heart of their best works is the lampooning and satirizing of the social institutions and conventions of proper Victorian society (1837–1901), such as honor and duty, England's social class structure, the absolute superiority of the British military, respect for the monarchy and its right to rule the empire, chivalry and romantic love.

In order to act well in the works of Gilbert and Sullivan you need to grasp the underlying formality and rigidity of Victorian society so you can poke good fun at it. The social ideal was one of absolute propriety, respect and obedience in every facet of behavior. Obedience to all social institutions underpins the ethos of this world. Hard work, self-sacrifice and pious virtue were the guiding principles by which everyone was expected to live. Yet, underneath virtually all of these works is the notion that everyone in proper society takes himself far too seriously. These operettas are filled with examples of Victorian values gone awry. For instance, in *The Mikado*, Koko has been condemned to death for looking at a woman who wasn't his wife. The commandment not to covet your neighbor's wife has been taken to its absurd extreme. In a spoof of the value of absolute honor to commitments, Frederic, in *The Pirates of Penzance*, has steadfastly stood by his promise to fulfill an apprenticeship to a group of pirates until the age of 21, even though it was based on his nanny misunderstanding the word "pirate" for "pilot."

As an actor in any of these operettas, your job is to understand which values from this culture are being lampooned and to emphasize where you fit into that value system. Are you a dutiful person or one who will abandon the commitment? Are you trying to uphold the value or are you trying to knock it? This is often central to the identity of your character.

UNIT 16.2.3 *Romance and sex*

Romance and virtue were central values in Victorian culture. A woman's virtue was to be protected and worshipped, even into marriage. Gilbert and Sullivan make fun of the repressed desires of some of their characters, but traditionally don't descend into ribaldry or raunchiness. The lovers, like Frederic and Mabel in *The Pirates of Penzance*, are often naïve to the point of near idiocy, and their inconceivable innocence is part of the fun.

True love with impossible romantic complications is fundamental in these stories, with young lovers trying to connect, but being prevented until the last minute (and even then only through absurd and extraordinary measures). Marriage was the ultimate romantic goal. Premarital sex, though rampant in Victorian England, was never spoken about and its mere mention was considered taboo.

Romance is a frequent source of fun for Gilbert and Sullivan. Especially when playing the romantic characters, it's important to identify how your character feels about love. Frederic (*The Pirates of Penzance*) has no experience with women at all. So he is innocent and gullible. On the other hand, Nanki-Poo (*The Mikado*) is the emperor's son and is smart enough to masquerade as a strolling minstrel in order to get near the girl he loves. He can manipulate the system.

Beauty and fashion

UNIT 16.2.4

The same dominant fashion ideals we observed in European operettas applied to Victorian culture, but with a somewhat more conservative approach for men. However, the exotic locations and circumstances of Gilbert and Sullivan's stories often place characters in fanciful costumes, which are now frequently combined with some aspects of Victorian garb to help anchor the stories in that cultural moment. For women, corsets, full-length dresses with many layers of underskirt (or, eventually, bloomers) and fully covered legs were the requirement.

The reality of male dress was a fairly unexciting gray, brown or black sack suit or frock coat with shirt and tie and an anonymous bowler hat. But stage clothing for these operas was much more interesting and frequently invoked seventeenth- and eighteenth-century modes of dress or was so distinctly specific to the character that current fashion was hardly the point.

The ideals of respect, politeness and virginity become active and actable for you if they are used to help you create stage behavior that acts on your love interest. You can use clothing and images of beauty and fashion, military superiority or menacing villainy to help you get what you want.

Relationship to authority

UNIT 16.2.5

There is perhaps no area of Victorian culture that was more absolute than the unquestioned respect for authority. The hierarchical class system placed the Queen at the top of the pecking order and moved down through the royal family and aristocracy into the upper class, and industrial and religious leaders. Further down the social ladder were the middle classes (a major part of the audience for these operas), and finally the lower working classes. Gilbert and Sullivan had a good deal of fun at the expense of this system of social ranking in many of their most famous operas. The pirates (of Penzance) are finally stopped from their attempts to exact revenge on Major Stanley and his daughters because of their obedience to the Queen. Order is restored when they are finally repatriated into proper society as the members of the House of Lords that they truly are. In the same opera, both the police and the military are far less worthy of respect than the supposed bad guys: the pirates. That's part of the point.

This use of social rank can define relationships onstage. By virtue of his military rank, Major Stanley (*The Pirates of Penzance*) should be treated with great respect. But once his lie about being an orphan is exposed, he can no longer rely on his supposed integrity to get him out of trouble. An absence of authority now defines him. Characters act out of respect for authority or in defiance of it, so authority is a key factor in your acting choices.

UNIT 16.2.6   *Performance tradition*

Gilbert and Sullivan's operettas were the prototype for later musical comedies. They are meant to be funny, the lovely songs for romantic characters notwithstanding. These stories rely heavily on clearly drawn and interesting characters in smartly laid out farcical plots. So, as you toil in the mines of style and acting, remember that your audience is meant to have fun at the theatre. This ain't Ibsen!

The dominant performance traditions of the time were melodrama and highly formalized acting styles like those espoused by François Delsarte. In both of these traditions, actors adopt exaggerated poses that indicate feelings and relationships. Gilbert was known to aspire to a more realistic approach than many of his contemporaries. But, nonetheless, this influence was still significant. As you approach acting in this tradition today, a little melodrama can go a long way. The other major influence at the time was the British music hall, which is the rough equivalent of American vaudeville. Pure entertainment, direct audience address, comedy and novelty were the rule in this genre.

Gilbert and Sullivan's operettas are now performed in two diverging traditions. The original stagings at the D'Oyly Carte Opera Company were scrupulously notated and reproduced for decades with very little variation from the originals, in much the same way that traditional Kabuki theatre is passed on in Japan. Although adherents to this first tradition insist that individual actors have latitude in adding business and redefining characterization, there is still a powerful pressure to stay fairly close to the original interpretation. As such, jokes are very clearly set up and responded to in a somewhat ritualized fashion. There are traditional ways of playing the Mikado, the Pirate King or Katisha accompanied by set pieces of business that all traditional Savoyards look forward to and appreciate. However, this is not a lot different from seeing a faithful recreation of *A Chorus Line* right down to choreography, direction, line deliveries, lighting and costumes. We can count on seeing the boy in a headband look down at the floor at the traditional moment in the opening audition sequence, and that's part of the reason to see it.

A different performance style is more prevalent in the US and has emerged most strongly since the early 1980s. In this approach actors play the roles much more like contemporary musical comedy (*Urinetown*, *Avenue Q*, *The Producers*) where anything goes in terms of characterization, irreverence, shtick, bawdy humor, and revision of the text to include contemporary references. Those who subscribe to this approach feel justified in doing so because it allows the delightful humor and music of these two geniuses to live for twenty-first century audiences. But although these new approaches are popular, they are still built on a foundation of the D'Oyly Carte productions. It is advisable to understand that tradition before you choose to reject it.

Style tags

UNIT 16.2.7

Vocal style tags

Tone: Sullivan's music is vocally demanding and requires strong technique from everyone who takes it on. But the current approach to singing these roles places less emphasis on beautiful sound for the sake of beautiful sound than does European operetta. Vocal character qualities are also more likely to carry into singing with this repertoire. Characters in these operettas are defined through vocal choices and a wide range of vocal colors as much as, or more than, in any other style of musical theatre. Don't be shy about making the character sound like who he is.

Vibrato: Again, a more relaxed attitude toward vibrato is allowed here, even in traditional productions. The romantic characters will probably sing with a more legitimate approach, while comic characters will allow the circumstance to dictate vocal choices.

Diction: You will rarely, if ever, have as high a demand placed on you for diction as when you approach one of Gilbert and Sullivan's roles. The words are paramount. These two geniuses invented the "Patter Song," in which a character performs astonishing articulatory acrobatics at breakneck speed. Numerous encores are usually provided to take advantage of the verbal gymnastics required. Originally, everyone involved would have spoken with an upper-class British dialect. Though this is still true of certain characters and in certain productions, the prevailing requirement is simply that every word and syllable must be completely understandable, regardless of character choice.

Phrasing: As with diction, the singer's flexibility in terms of phrasing is much more limited in the Savoy Operas than in European operetta. This has a good deal to do with how closely words and music work together in these scores. So, taking too great a liberty with musical phrasing, especially in quicker songs, will make the lyric unintelligible. Ballads and romantic duets allow for more stretch and rubato. But good taste and care are still highly recommended. Too much emotional indulgence is uncharacteristic of the style.

Physical style tags

Posture/silhouette: The physical life of these characters is influenced by the stage tradition of the time. Melodrama was a powerful acting influence that encouraged actors to strike physical shapes and poses that "indicated" a feeling or character type. Central to this type of acting is the idea that no character is so complex that he can't be understood at first glance. You really should judge the book by its cover, in this case. Images of nasty villains skulking across the stage, lovers reclining on tree trunks or kneeling with the back leg extended and arms toward each other are typical of this style. If you've ever seen nineteenth-century story ballets like *The Nutcracker* or *Coppelia* you'll recognize the pantomimed acting conventions. This is where period visual research will pay off for you. Also, looking at the acting in silent films (both comedies and dramas) will give you a good sense of the possibilities for this school of acting.

Degree of formality: Victorian society was a highly formalized culture, and this extended deeply into public physical relationships. For those normative characters in the Savoy Operas, this would be true, as well. But there are precious few "normal" characters in these operettas. So, modify the degree of formality to fit the character. Frederick and Mabel (*Pirates*) are about as close to normal as we get. So, their degree of formality would be quite high, especially toward each other and the figures they should respect. The Pirate King would be dramatically less so, except in special cases or for comic effect. Remember that Gilbert and Sullivan sought to juxtapose the social expectations of the time with the reality of responding to extreme circumstances. The obstacle of formality can be useful at times.

Gestural vocabulary. The gestures used in the original productions would be considered florid and exaggerated by contemporary standards. Because of the broadness of the characters, the range of gestures, shapes and movement qualities is more extended than in most other early styles. But with this broadness comes a clear requirement that you make all of your physical business clear and precise. Sullivan provides you with so much musical specificity that you must match your physical actions and behavior to that music as you pursue your objective. Sloppiness is simply not permissible with this material.

Examples from the style/genre

UNIT 16.2.8

The most popular examples of this limited canon include:

> *H.M.S. Pinafore, or The Lass That Loved a Sailor*
> *The Pirates of Penzance, or The Slave of Duty*
> *The Mikado, or The Town of Titipu*

Somewhat less performed, but still wonderful are:

> *Ruddigore, or The Witch's Curse*
> *The Gondoliers, or The King of Barataria*
> *Patience, or Bunthorn's Bride*
> *The Sorcerer*
> *Iolanthe, or The Peer and the Peri*
> *Princess Ida, or Castle Adamant*
> *The Grand Duke, or The Statutory Duel*
> *Utopia, Limited, or The Flowers of Progress*
> *The Yeomen of the Guard, or The Merryman and his Maid*

Research resources (film/audio/visual)

UNIT 16.2.9

These are a choice few of the many excellent books on Gilbert and Sullivan.

Bond, Jessie, *The Life and Reminiscences of Jessie Bond, the Old Savoyard (as told to Ethel MacGeorge)*, London: John Lane at the Bodley Head, 1930

Bradley, Ian C., *Oh Joy! Oh Rapture! The Enduring Phenomenon of Gilbert and Sullivan*, New York: Oxford University Press, 2007

Bradley, Ian C., *The Complete Annotated Gilbert and Sullivan*, New York: Oxford University Press, 2005

Gilbert, W.S., *The Bab Ballads*, Charleston, SC: BiblioBazaar, 2007

Goodman, Andrew, *Gilbert and Sullivan's London*, London: Faber and Faber, 2000

Filmed and videotaped performance resources abound for these delightfully silly works. Among the best records of the traditional approach are:

The Mikado – a 1939 film with Kenny Baker II and stars of the D'Oyly Carte Opera Company. This is a good record of the traditional approach. Image Entertainment.

The entire body of Gilbert and Sullivan's operas was filmed by British television and is available through Acorn Media.

There are a handful of wonderful and more irreverent productions available for viewing. Among the best are:

The Pirates of Penzance, *Iolanthe*, *The Mikado*, *The Gondoliers*: Stratford Festival in Canada created a series of outstanding productions that were filmed and are available through Acorn Media. *The Pirates of Penzance* and *The Mikado* are particularly fun.

The Pirates of Penzance: Starring Kevin Kline, George Rose, Linda Rondstadt and Rex Smith, this production in New York's Central Park sparked a revolution in US interest in Gilbert and Sullivan. Directed by Wilford Leach and choreographed by Graciella Danielle, it is raucous fun, if a little crudely filmed. Available through Broadway Theatre Archive.

The Mikado: Eric Idle (of Monty Python fame) stars in this distinctly British production by the English National Opera. A&E Home Video.

Another outstanding resource for understanding the performance world of Gilbert and Sullivan's London theatre is Mike Leigh's film *Topsy-Turvy*, which includes several extended segments of greatly detailed recreations of D'Oyly Carte productions. Polygram USA Video.

There are too many good audio recordings of Gilbert and Sullivan's operas to list here. But every one of the operas has been recorded many times over the last century. Listening to a range of interpretations will be enlightening as to the use of language, singing qualities and diction.

Musical comedy

UNIT 16.3

Background and worldview

UNIT 16.3.1

Musical comedy is a name that has been applied to musical theatre entertainment almost since its earliest days. But, what we currently think of as musical comedy began in the early 1900s and has continued, through constant evolution, to this day. This energetic form is an American invention, with lots of help from a number of British and European friends. Musical comedy has been remarkably durable, adapting to new values and musical idioms, and supporting any number of variations while still remaining clearly identifiable. It has been flexible enough to support frothy Cinderella stories, political commentary, fantasy, spectacle and parody. Consider the following lists of shows that all fall into the style we call musical comedy. *The Producers*, *Spamalot*, *Urinetown*, *Legally Blonde*, *Hairspray* and *The Full Monty* all belong in this category. Earlier generations will remember *La Cage aux Folles*, *Forty-Second Street* and *Chicago* as typical of the genre. And still earlier are classics like *Kiss Me, Kate*, *Guys and Dolls*, *The Music Man*, *Bye, Bye Birdie* and *Hello, Dolly*. And in the beginning were the Princess Theatre musicals (1915 to early 1920s), *No, No Nanette!*, *Lady, Be Good!*, *Anything Goes* and *Babes in Arms*, to name a small sample. There are many more shows we could list that fit firmly in this style and there are still others that use only some elements of the style.

What separates musical comedy from the major musical theatre forms that precede it is its focus on average working people and their values and entertainment interests. For the first time, shop girls and clerks looked onto the stage and saw images of themselves rather than the princes and peasant girls they were used to in operetta. By incorporating strong influences from vaudeville, minstrelsy and burlesque, and blending them with the fast-talking banter and repartee of turn-of-the-century comedy, writers like George M. Cohan and, later, Jerome Kern and his colleagues created a new kind of popular theatrical entertainment.

Musical comedy is the ultimate democratic entertainment form because it is insistently populist, incorporating and assimilating whatever the popular culture of the moment offers while maintaining strong elements of its tradition. It is typified by stories that center on working-class characters and situations, employ popular song and dance forms, and aim to tell simple stories with plenty of humor and sex appeal, and just enough romance to hold the plot together. Initially, musical comedy sidestepped nearly all of the elitist conventions of European operetta. The music came from Tin Pan Alley and was anything but refined. This was the music of the popular dance band, not the symphonic orchestra. Operetta's bel canto singing was replaced with the brassy belt of red-hot mamas and wisecracking singer-comedians. In many ways, personality overtook technical mastery as the primary requirement for musical comedy performers.

It is not accidental that this new form grew to popularity at the same time that New York City emerged as the popular cultural center of the Western world in the first decades of the twentieth century. The melting pot of Eastern European and Irish immigrants, rural blacks and other minorities that flooded into New York City at this time came together on the variety stage. The natural dramatic extension of this was the creation of a theatre form that hit its audience squarely between the eyes with energetic and catchy tunes, brash comic routines, frequent use of ethnic stereotypes and an underlying patriotism all performed by stars with outlandish personalities and charisma to spare. The energy of this most American of cities made its way into fast-paced productions with multiple storylines that all came together in improbable and satisfying resolutions.

UNIT 16.3.2 *Social ideal and values*

Musical comedy emerges from a culture that was radically revising its values to accommodate a more American sense of informality where the ideal was the middle-class, not the elite. In part because the middle-class had grown so large, and in part because of later failures of the upper classes to guide society effectively, a more common social ideal emerged. Brash at times, coarser, more familiar, and even comically subversive, this new common man was adaptable, quick-witted and jovial. His counterpart was a young woman who came to be known as the Flapper. She was more accessible than the refined heroines of operettas, with a fun-loving spirit and a hint of mischief and flirtation about her.

The new social ideals for both men and women skewed more toward youth than in the past. Central characters in their early twenties began to appear with increasing frequency. Because romance continued to anchor the plots of musical comedies, marriageable young men and women were the protagonists.

Romance and sex

Musical comedy emerged as a theatrical form just when American society was undergoing one of its greatest upheavals. And these social changes were nowhere more apparent than in attitudes toward sexuality and romance. Prior to the 1920s a young woman was expected to remain submissive and demure, projecting an image of modesty and virginity. But with the rejection of prim Victorian values came a new way of behaving. Sex was suddenly part of the cultural conversation, much to the dismay and shock of older generations. While statistics reflect that young men and women were engaging in premarital sex far more than previous generations admitted to, musical comedy didn't directly make this the subject of its shows. But the context of a more permissive society that allowed women to be increasingly aggressive did have enormous impact on the behavior of female and male characters in musicals. While strictly romantic characters still tended to embrace the value system of an earlier style, secondary characters often carried sexier, more audacious storylines. The Flapper became a charming and rebellious archetype in musicals. Nanette in *No, No, Nanette* resists marriage to her boyfriend so that she can live a little first. Suzy Trevor (*Lady, Be Good!*) is powerful, independent and manipulative in ways that could never have been imagined even in *The Merry Widow*.

As musical comedy evolved, writers like Cole Porter and Lorenz Hart delighted in writing slightly scandalous, progressive and titillating lyrics in their musicals. Have a look at Porter's lyrics for *'Anything Goes'* or Hart's for *'Bewitched, Bothered and Bewildered'*. By the end of the 1930s sex was a central part of the musical theatre.

Beauty and fashion

Modern society shed not only the musical forms and the social mores of the nineteenth century, but also the restrictive clothing that went with them. While the Victorian ideal was restraint, corseted curves and full-length dresses, the society that musical comedy emerged from favored straighter, shorter and looser cuts for women. Columnar dresses in the 1910s were soon replaced by much shorter Flapper dresses in the 1920s. The de-emphasis of extreme feminine curves for a more boyish look included cropped hairstyles and even the adoption of male-styled clothing for women.

The new feminine physical ideal was flat chested, had trim legs and bobbed hair, and lacked the distinct curves of older women. Physiologically, she was more like an adolescent girl than a grown woman.

Men were allowed some more ease in dressing, though the always practical suit coat, trousers, shirt and tie continued to dominate. An air of casualness entered the fashion ideals. Men could now wear golf, boating and tennis garb as part of social dress. The more casual tuxedo replaced full tails and top hats (except for formal occasions). Checked and patterned sports coats and coordinating trousers, straw hats, narrow brimmed hats and caps helped ease the stiff silhouette of the late nineteenth century into a jauntier, relaxed look.

The male physical ideal was trim, young, long-limbed, lacking any thick muscularity. Again, this physical ideal was more like a young college boy than a mature man. The evidence of a youth culture was present in its idealized man.

UNIT 16.3.5   *Relationship to authority*

Musical comedy generally takes two different approaches to authority. The first places authority figures like police officers and politicians as equals to the common man. So, the reverence and respect that the earlier aristocratic forms afforded these figures is tempered by a democratic sense of fellowship. The second, more prevalent approach to authority figures places them as objects of ridicule. Foolish cops, befuddled corporate moguls and bumbling politicians are standard characters in many musical comedies. Look at *Anything Goes* for examples of a ship's captain who is more interested in showcasing celebrity than in upholding the law and a Wall Street tycoon who spends most of the show drunk and in search of debauchery. The heroes of the show are the people who break the rules with flair. This irreverence for authority springs from the failure of the government and business to anticipate or prevent the Great Depression of the 1930s. George M. Cohan popularized this brash anti-hero character in nearly every role he played. But the archetype quickly became a staple of musical comedies and he (usually male) shows up in the form of Billy Crocker in *Anything Goes*, Sky Masterson in *Guys and Dolls*, Harold Hill in *The Music Man* and even Max Bialystock in *The Producers*. As Carolyn Leigh wrote in *Little Me*, "We'll break the rules a lot. We'll be damned fools a lot!" A creatively subversive disregard for authority seemed to fit the ethos of musical comedy.

UNIT 16.3.6   *Performance tradition*

It is impossible to separate the variety stage from the beginnings of musical comedy as a style because its performers and writers all got their start in vaudeville, burlesque, minstrel shows and revues. For the years when all of these entertainment forms coexisted there was a constant back and forth exchange between Broadway musicals and the variety stage. Eventually the variety stage died out, but its influence on musical comedy remains potent to this day.

Central to performing on the variety stage was establishing a clear and direct relationship with the audience. Unlike contemporary drama where we pretend the audience isn't there by utilizing an imaginary fourth wall, variety entertainers spoke and sang directly to the audience and gauged every aspect of their performance on their responses. Sharing the performance was key. So, facing front, singing in a loud and distinct voice, setting up jokes, hitting punch lines clearly, and allowing time for audience response, were central performance values, the measure of which was applause and laughter.

Songs from the variety stage and musical comedy were completely different than in either of the earlier operetta forms we've discussed. These new songs were shorter (roughly three minutes each), easy to learn on just one hearing and insistently rhythmic, and required a far smaller vocal range to perform. They were also, by and large, written by composers and lyricists from New York's Tin Pan Alley, the virtual factory of American popular music in the early twentieth century. Writers like Irving Berlin, George Gershwin and Jerome Kern all began in the music publishing houses of Tin Pan Alley.

The songs and orchestrations for musical comedies were created using the dance band model instead of the symphonic orchestras of the past. New instrumentations originating with military marching bands of the nineteenth century and reflecting the influence of ragtime and jazz music became the signature sound of musical comedy. A rhythm section of piano, bass and drums with trumpet, trombone, saxophone and clarinet support became the backbone of the new musical unit. Waltzes, polkas and other European song forms and dances were the structural basis for most operetta composition, but musical comedy embraced a very different set of composing conventions. The fox trot, a simple 4/4 meter, became the dominant song form for over half a century. Syncopated jazz-styled rhythms quickly found their way into popular songs.

And with this new instrumental sound came a new way of singing, as well. While operetta orchestrations with lush strings and cushioning woodwinds made room for singers, musical comedy required performers to sing over the band. So, the clarion sound of performers like Al Jolson and Ethel Merman became the new aesthetic. The marriage of these foghorn voices and the energetic nature of these new stories and characters seemed perfectly matched.

A new musical theatre form also required new dance forms. So, Black American and Irish tap dance, eccentric dance and American popular social dance forms replaced the aristocratic dances of the European operetta. New dance crazes emerged from and found their way onto the musical comedy stage.

The egalitarian worldview of musical comedy introduces a completely new dynamic to characterization. Our work with character types and stock characters from Chapter 7 will be particularly valuable to you as you work in musical comedy because quickly sketched, easily identifiable characters are central to this world. Believe it or not, an ideal resource for investigating the kind of broad characterization that this material demands is Bugs Bunny cartoons. The clarity and precision of the physical business, and the relationship between comedy and music in these cartoons are ideal models. And the characters act out of pure need for very clear objectives, utilizing any tactic available to get it.

Before musical comedy, ethnic characters were nearly always villains or objects of ridicule. But with the integration of vaudeville and variety stage character types, many ethnic characters became tricksters. Jewish and Irish immigrants start to appear as characters that can function in society in creative ways that allow them success. The Marx Brothers typify this kind of comic characterization.

Black characters rarely appear in mainstream musical comedy, except as servants or in disparaging roles (*Show Boat* notwithstanding). The overwhelmingly white audience was less sensitive to the impact of racial and ethnic stereotypes than audiences of today. For this reason, almost all shows with this type of characterization are now revised to exclude these depictions.

UNIT 16.3.7 *Style tags*

Vocal style tags

Before we start to articulate the style tags for musical comedy, we caution you not to be confused that some of the characters you'll play in this style don't seem to belong with the tags that we'll articulate here. Typically, romantic characters fall outside this description because they are most often modernized versions of the romantic couples in operetta. Although the musical structure may be more like musical comedy, the vocal and physical behaviors and the storylines and attitudes belong to earlier forms.

Tone: If the singer's tonal aesthetic in European operetta matched the oboe and violin, then the preferred sound for musical comedy emulated the trumpet and saxophone: bright and brassy. The placement is more forward in the head and engages resonators in the mask (nose, sinuses, forehead). Think of pingy, belty, shouted, brash, forceful and sassy to describe the sound. The singing style is much more speech-like. This is the period when belt singing was first refined and it remains an essential female singing style for this material. Modern tastes have modified the Broadway belt with a more classical approach and now singers often employ a mix of the two.

Vibrato: The more rapid classically oriented use of vibrato in the operetta styles is now widened for musical comedy. In general, vibrato onset is early, though some later period singers become "croonier" and add an intensifying vibrato after a period of straight tone. But the older convention is early onset of a slightly less rapid vibrato. Because the use of brighter vocal coloring and more frontal resonance can significantly change the quality of the sound, the vibrato may become more apparent.

Diction: As with Gilbert and Sullivan, the words in musical comedy must be understood. Lyricists like Ira Gershwin, Cole Porter and Lorenz Hart crafted such witty and touching lyrics that no one should miss a word. Clear diction, but not classical speech is the convention here. The rat-a-tat New York City dialect of so many of these shows allows for a crisp and percussive use of language to help carry the words clearly. The pitch range for most songs in musical comedy is narrower than in the earlier forms. Therefore, the modifications of vowels that are sometime necessary in classical singing are less frequent with this style.

Phrasing: Singing in musical comedies often privileges the cadence of natural speech over the longer, primarily musical phrase. If you listen back to period recordings from the early decades of this style you'll probably feel that the phrasing was fairly square and strictly metered. But, for its time, this phrasing was quite relaxed. In adapting this quality to productions for our time, explore how loose you want to be in terms of phrasing. If you're too square in your phrasing the sense of the words can be lost. But if you loosen the phrasing up too much it begins to sound like Las Vegas lounge singing. There is definitely an area to explore between these two extremes that will allow you to serve both the music and the lyric.

Along with a somewhat loosened approach to musical phrasing comes an invitation to explore rhythms. The 4/4 fox trot rhythm of so much of this music allows for syncopation and back phrasing that wasn't stylistically appropriate in earlier styles. In Chapter 11: Discovering Your Phrasing, we offer a range of exercises to help you expand that aspect of your work. This is a good time to revisit those exercises because much of the music in the style allows for flexibility in phrasing.

A typical structure for songs in this style is that the verse sets up a problem to be solved or an idea to be explored by the singer, and that the refrain (or chorus) will be the exploration of that idea. So, it is imperative that you clearly set up the problem and then work to solve it. This dramatic device is extraordinarily useful in keeping the song active because it allows you to constantly reexamine a problem or explore new facets of the subject of the song.

Physical style tags

The staging conventions for many songs in musical comedy are overtly performative; meaning, they are "sold" directly to the audience. The presentational quality of this style can seem uncomfortable for actors who are used to movement that is essentially just naturalistic behavior. But this style begs for clear staging and choreography. It may be useful to see how you can discover gestures organically and then isolate and amplify them to create the conventional size and flourish for this style. This is a case where blending the tradition with your own sense of contemporary acting practice can be useful. But first, we encourage you to try working in the bold pure performance shapes and movements of this style before you reject them. Try inhabiting the purely presentational gestures before you modify them.

Posture/silhouette: A new set of physical shapes accompanies the much more relaxed social attitudes of musical comedy. For both men and women, a sense of calculated energetic casualness pervades this style. Jaunty tilts of the head, hands in pockets, crossed feet for men. The youthful energy of popular culture encouraged a more physical presence for men. Shorter dress lengths invited women to adopt quirky shapes that feature interesting leg positions (one or both legs slightly turned in or crossed) for women. Legs are a central attraction for women, whether standing or sitting.

Degree of formality: A slightly more provocative sense of physicality allowed women to break the rigidly formal and upright postures of operetta. While men and women did not engage in overtly sexual relationships in musical comedy, flirtation and courtship are a strong part of most stories in this genre. Also, because characters tend to come from the middle class, the strict codes of aristocratic social conduct are freely rejected here. A far more realistic sense of youthful enthusiasm informs much of the movement and physical behavior for this style.

Gestural vocabulary: Use of the body in this style falls into two categories. The first is the overt performance where characters are unapologetically singing and dancing to and for the audience. The second is where songs are an extension of scenes the way we often see in musicals today. Since we have spent a good deal of time addressing that kind of singing and staging in Chapter 12: Staging Your Song, we'll focus on the pure performance songs here.

Gestures in the pure performance songs of musical comedy tend to be much more presentational and posed than in current styles. Some of the hallmarks of this style include: symmetrical use of hands and arms, offering and pleading gestures, kneeling on one knee, the creation of balanced and pleasing stage pictures, initiating gestures with a slight flourish (as a magician might do), and isolation and amplification of a single arm or head gesture while sustaining stillness with the rest of the body. In all cases, there is a sustained physical energy (even in stillness) that engages audience attention.

Research resources (film/audio/visual)

Essential films

(These include either period performances or authentically inspired performances by performers who understood the tradition.)

Animal Crackers, Duck Soup, A Night At The Opera – The Marx Brothers
The Gay Divorcee, Top Hat – Fred Astaire, Ginger Rogers
Easter Parade – Fred Astaire, Judy Garland
The Jazz Singer – Al Jolson
Singin' In The Rain – Gene Kelly, Donald O'Connor
Show Boat (1936) – Helen Morgan, Paul Robeson, et al.
Take Me Out to the Ball Game – Gene Kelly, Frank Sinatra
There's No Business Like Show Business – Ethel Merman, Dan Dailey, et al.
That's Entertainment I & II
Yankee Doodle Dandy – James Cagney
The Three Stooges short films
Bugs Bunny and Betty Boop cartoons
Films starring Bob Hope, W.C. Fields, Charlie Chaplin (for physical style) and Lucille Ball

Essential singers

Louis Armstrong
Fred Astaire
Irving Berlin
Eddie Cantor
Bing Crosby
Al Jolson
Gertrude Lawrence
Ethel Merman
Helen Morgan
Bessie Smith

Useful recordings

(Many of these are revivals because the original productions were not recorded at the time. In every case, get multiple recordings to compare if you can.)

Anything Goes – 1962 Off-Broadway, 1987 Lincoln Center revival, 1988 Studio
Babes in Arms – Original and 1998 revival
Crazy for You – 1992 Broadway
Lady, Be Good!, Girl Crazy, Strike Up The Band, Oh, Kay! – Nonesuch Records/Gershwin Estate Recordings
No, No, Nanette – 1971 revival cast
On Your Toes – Original and 1983 revival
Of Thee I Sing, Let 'Em Eat Cake – Studio recordings
Show Boat – Numerous recordings
Tintypes – 1981 Broadway Cast

UNIT 16.4 **Golden Age musical drama**

UNIT 16.4.1 *Background and worldview*

Although the musical comedy continues to be one of the most powerful influences in musical theatre style, its dominance of the stage has waned since the late 1930s. Its humor and tunefulness offer undeniable appeal, but there are some inherent limitations to the genre. For one thing, the sophisticated humor tends toward cynicism. An unrelenting diet of acerbic characters and double entendres can become tiresome. And the songs, while often appealing and exquisitely crafted, are tightly defined by the Tin Pan Alley song form. More expansive singing, complex harmonies and extended musical passages are just not part of musical comedy's stylistic conventions. Productions in the 1920s and 30s also relied heavily on star performers to carry a show and on the somewhat unmotivated introduction of leggy showgirls to buoy up the action. In the opinion of many artists, critics and audience members this more limited range of subjects, characters and music had begun to show signs of exhaustion by the early 1940s.

Not only had the artistic form begun to fail, but the culture it emerged out of had also fundamentally changed. America was no longer in the throes of the decade-long party of the 1920s or a period of economic distress and consequent escapism of the 1930s. With America's economy finally rebounding through hard work, and worldwide crisis arriving at her doorstep, the frivolity and cynicism of musical comedy seemed to say almost nothing about the reality of the 1940s. The times called for a musical theatre form that reflected an earnest concern for the rebirth of the nation and its revised values and culture. This is the world that gave birth to the Golden Age musical drama.

As we approach this style you may be surprised to find that almost none of the elements that we'll discuss are original to this form. There is still comedy (of a slightly different variety than in musical comedy), and there are still romantic heroes and heroines, though revised from the continental models we saw in operetta. And the music and lyrics are a curious hybrid and evolution of both the Tin Pan Alley song form and the more musically expansive operetta structures we've become familiar with. It is the reassembly of these parts in the service of new story and character types that really defines this style development.

Popular lore would have us believe that Richard Rodgers and Oscar Hammerstein II gave birth to a wholly new art form when *Oklahoma!* opened on Broadway on March 31, 1943, and that it was instantly recognizable. The show was an undeniable commercial success, but the indelible way in which Rodgers and Hammerstein subtly revised the priorities and artistic agenda of the musical theatre only became apparent in their own subsequent shows and in the nearly complete emulation of their work by other artists for the next thirty-five (plus) years. Because this subtle but critical shift in artistic expectations was so influential, we're going to outline some of the innovations of this new form.

Golden Age musical drama:

- places moral struggle as a central element in the conflicts of the musical
- is far more sentimental than musical comedy and emphasizes a belief in human goodness and faith over cynicism and trickery

- integrates the book, lyrics, music and dance into the storytelling more completely than in any other popular musical theatre form (except, perhaps, verismo opera like Puccini's *La Bohème*).
- uses dance as a fundamental storytelling element of the musical drama
- places drama ahead of comedy as the priority in writing; gag writing and vaudevillian comedy virtually disappear from the style
- makes songs extensions of the specific character in a distinct dramatic moment; less emphasis is placed on songs as stand-alone hits
- makes songs the primary element of action, creating character-changing dramatic journeys, not just static ruminations on feelings
- places the poetry of lyrics over the witty conceit of the lyricist
- includes lengthy passages of fully orchestrated choral music, accompaniment and underscoring, as well as wider vocal ranges and more complex concerted singing; the musical palette is nearly as expansive as that of operetta, though the styling is distinctly of the mid-twentieth century.

Just like all the other styles we've explored, the Golden Age musical drama continues to influence new writing. Recent musicals like *Les Misérables*, *Ragtime*, *Wicked* and *The Color Purple* all carry this agenda forward, incorporating new musical styles and cultural influences along the way. But the essential artistic form remains intact. This continuing influence is felt even in many of the transitional musicals of the 1960s like *Cabaret*, *Fiddler on the Roof* and *The Rothschilds*. How these shows differ is that they take a more skeptical view of the innate goodness of humanity and the affirming power of love.

The acting conventions we associate with this style are also perfectly suited to the more problematic new musicals we have seen since that time. Most of Stephen Sondheim's work can be approached with this same set of acting conventions, by simply honoring the complexity of the characters and their conflicting desires.

UNIT 16.4.2   *Social ideal and values*

The Golden Age musical drama places family, community, country, responsibility and faith as its central values. What many people now call traditional values are clearly articulated in this genre. Acting style choices are often an extension of this set of values. The earnestness and commitment with which characters pursue and support these values are often their central motivations. While you can't play a value or an attitude, you can certainly let those values motivate your actions. Look back at our discussions of conflict in *Oklahoma!* to see how important these central values are for Curly, Laurey and the members of their community. You can also see how important these same values are in *Brigadoon*, *Carousel*, *South Pacific* and many other examples from this style. The characters seek to protect their community, create a family, overcome prejudice, etc.

In addition to a new value system, the Golden Age musical drama shifts the center of attention away from New York City to rural locations (Oklahoma Territory, Maine coastline, Western mining towns). Look at the lyrics of Harry Warren and Al Dubin's 1935 hit musical comedy song, *'Lullaby of Broadway'* and compare it to *'Oh, What a Beautiful Mornin''* (*Oklahoma!*, 1943) to see how differently music from these two styles treats idealized locations. In the earlier rhythmically driving song Manhattan is the playground of the musical comedy Flapper who parties until dawn. But, in the Golden Age musical drama, hard-working farm women and cowboys rise before dawn to celebrate the quiet beauty of cattle in pastures, the simple sounds of the earth and the low mists hovering on fields as the sun rises. This waltzing celebration of the pastoral life is a very different ideal from what we've seen in other styles.

Alternately, we set Golden Age musicals in exotic locations (the kingdom of Siam, South Pacific islands, the Scottish Highlands) in something of a throwback to European operetta. But the stories that are being told are frequently morality tales and the characters are often solid citizens trying to overcome various forms of moral threat.

A third aspect of the Golden Age musical drama value system is the emphasis placed on hard work and the struggle of the common man or woman. Protagonists are cowhands, carnival workers, soldiers and teachers. Musical comedy often celebrated either the idle rich sophisticate or the smart-alecky huckster. Neither of those two types gets much play in this new style.

Many of the central characters in this style are defined by the certainty of their moral stance coupled with a clear understanding of the internal and external obstacles to achieving their goals. For the first time, we see emotional and psychological struggle in musicals that are expressed in the same way as they have been in film and stage drama.

Romance and sex

Marriage, monogamy and secure matrimonial happiness are the romantic and sexual focus of this style. Musical comedy and operetta certainly have their share of weddings at the end of the last act, but this is often more a function of wrapping up the plot than an expression of a value system. In the Golden Age musical drama we see characters struggling to establish secure marriage as a way of creating families, shoring up the community and expressing sustained faith in God. Tommy Albright transcends time and scientific reason to be with his true love in *Brigadoon*. Authoritarian Henry Higgins ultimately shows signs of marital need at the end of *My Fair Lady*, offering a glimmer of hope that his bullying can be tamed by love and eventual matrimony with his Cinderella, Eliza. And *Oklahoma!* is really the story of how Curly and Laurey get to the altar. When they ride off into the sunset (in their surrey with the fringe on top) it is toward a stable life as farmers in a brand new state. Even a show like *Guys and Dolls*, which seems to be a musical comedy at first glance, has the tricksters (Nathan Detroit and Sky Masterson) opting for marriage and traditional jobs. Masterson, once a sexual predator and inveterate player, is transformed into an honorable man who forsakes his former life in favor of joining the Save-A-Soul mission band as its new bass drum player, Mr. Sarah Brown. So, in the end, the Golden Age view of romance and marriage wins out over musical comedy cynicism.

In the Golden Age musical drama those characters that are overtly sexual tend toward the charming and innocent (Ado Annie in *Oklahoma!*, Carrie Pipperidge in *Carousel* and Meg Brockie in *Brigadoon*), rather than the voracious or vampy. This is not necessarily a reflection of actual practice in the social culture these musicals arose from, but an expression of the values it aspired to.

UNIT 16.4.4   *Beauty and fashion*

The men and women who populate Golden Age musical dramas look different from either those city slickers we saw in musical comedy or the aristocrats of operetta. Now we see strong women and corn-fed young men who are capable of rolling up their sleeves and working the land or protecting it, if need be. A more athletic look for men, and a more sensible and fresh-scrubbed look for women, is evident in virtually all Allied World War II propaganda of the time. Strength, stability, independence, capability and common sense all translate into the physical ideals of this style, even as it continues to this day.

Men no longer wear suits or tuxedoes, but opt for open-collared shirts with rolled sleeves, and slacks: evidence their manhood and physical power is attractive in this world. Women are fresh-faced with less obvious make-up. Domestic fashions, regardless of the period of the setting, tend to win out over fancy party wear. Sensible, but trimly cut, work dresses, aprons and so forth help to paint a picture of a perfect wife and mother. The sexy flapper, the exotic gypsy or the aristocratic princess are out of fashion in this world.

Men will still wear clean hair styles, though the vogue for lots of controlling hair product is let go of for a sense of engagement in the natural world. Attractively wind-tossed hair is appealing. Women will wear their hair in ways that allow them to get down to business, but still maintain an attractive presence. The comic image of a housewife in tasteful high heels, neat lipstick, pearls and a kitchen apron is iconic of the world that gave birth to this style. As silly as this may be to us today, it represents all of the values of the time.

Regardless of how the style is interpreted in your production, the sense of no-nonsense stability, responsibility and capability underlies all fashion choices. Recent productions of Golden Age musical dramas have tended to favor historical accuracy over the visual conventions of the 1940s through early 1960s (when these musicals were first produced) in order to escape the stigma of corniness these shows can sometimes carry. So, the period clothing styles are sometimes very different from those worn in original productions. Regardless, fashion is often all in the wearing. The values of the text will still be present in the way you carry yourself in the historically more accurate costume.

Relationship to authority

UNIT 16.4.5

Central characters in Golden Age musical drama are often authority figures themselves or agents of authority. Tommy aids in hunting down the renegade Harry Beaton in *Brigadoon*. Emile De Becque and Lt. Cable act as special agents for the Navy in *South Pacific*. The main guys are also the good guys. Because community and standing up against those who threaten society are so central to the beliefs of this style, authority tends to be part of the shared experience. Hardy women and steadfast men are essentially an embodiment of those values that authority seeks to uphold. Those who threaten society (Jud in *Oklahoma!*, Nazis in *The Sound of Music*, etc.) need to be repelled, and usually are by the central characters.

Even when an appealing character embodies values that threaten the stability of the community, he is expelled or reformed to fit into society. We've already talked about Sky Masterson's rebirth in *Guys and Dolls*. Lizzie passes over the dangerously appealing Starbuck in favor of stable Sheriff File in *110 in the Shade*. And the ultimate charming con man, Professor Harold Hill is reformed into a stay-at-home husband and solid citizen in *The Music Man*. They each capitulate to the needs of their society to partner with, rather than fight, authority.

UNIT 16.4.6 *Performance tradition*

The performance traditions that inform Golden Age musical drama were all still in active use when this style gained popularity. It is really an amalgamation of three distinct traditions that are modified to work together as a new tradition. The operetta convention of bel canto singing was still being celebrated in revivals and even occasional new shows in the early 1940s. The musical comedy performative tradition was still the dominant style. And the serious acting conventions that we now associate with mid-twentieth-century Realism were employed in most stage and film dramas, though they had been applied only experimentally in musical theatre. When Rodgers and Hammerstein, choreographer Agnes De Mille and director Rouben Mamoulian set out to create *Oklahoma!*, they unconsciously integrated a hybrid of traditions that would allow them to tell a different kind of story with serious emotional content and expressing a more relevant worldview. Following this practice, Hammerstein's protégé, Stephen Sondheim, would later articulate his own artistic credo as "Content dictates form."

Although the writing of the early Golden Age shows was singled out as different and exciting, critics and audiences wouldn't be able to identify a distinctive set of acting conventions for some years to come. In fact, even now, many people will identify the content and moral tone of these shows more readily than they might identify a particular acting style. But, as you have read, the worldview of this style is so deeply ingrained in the performance of it that they are impossible to separate.

UNIT 16.4.7 *Style tags*

As we begin to articulate the style tags for Golden Age musical drama, we will offer the same reminder that we did in the last overview. Many characters in shows from this new genre will still belong to an earlier style. Writers in this style were especially adept at utilizing character types and acting conventions from many traditions to give variety and range to their shows. So, you'll want to identify the nature of your character before you proceed. In *Oklahoma!*, Ali Hakim would be absurd if played any other way than in the musical comedy tradition with a strong understanding of the Yiddish Theatre variety stage. Trying to make him a Golden Age leading man would be hopeless.

The singing (and dance) approach that defines the Golden Age musical drama is that you are expected to have strong classical technique, but you must modify it so you don't seem to be working in a formal or elitist way. As we approach these style tags, you'll see how you can wrap your classical technique in a cloak of informality.

Vocal style tags

Tone: Dramatic characters in this style return to broader vocal ranges and more deliberate use of classical vocal technique. (John Raitt auditioned for *Carousel* with an aria from *Rigoletto*!) But unlike the operetta, Golden Age style doesn't make vocal flourish and the bel canto quality of the voice the center of the experience. Vocal strength and flexibility are now used to express strength of character. How you sound in this style tells the audience what your inner qualities are. In this respect, it is very much like opera. Singing in this style may require the most developed set of vocal colors and skill of any style that we've studied, because the relationship between vocal tone and emotional complexity is so direct. But we never want to be aware of the technique.

If operetta favored open vowels and beautiful sound, and musical comedy favored consonants and clarity of the words, the Golden Age musical drama requires both. A speech-like singing quality that matches the spoken voice of the character is an absolute necessity.

As you explore vocal tone in this style, you'll want to play with the degree of "covered" sound (focusing on the raised soft palette) you use and the other resonators in the mask. This mixing of the most legitimate sound and the musical comedy sound is characteristic of this style, and it will be something you need to explore for each production, character and song because the use of resonators and formality of sound is central to our understanding of style. The bottom line regarding tone with this style is that you must never sound classical, but you must have that classical technique as support.

Vibrato: For dramatic songs and ballads, the use of a steady vibrato with early onset and consistent application is really required. Again, depending on how your production defines the style, you may find that you back off on how present this vibrato is or when you initiate it. But you will almost certainly still use it and will rarely move to pure straight tone. Some comic characters, soubrettes and juveniles may use the vocal characteristics of musical comedy. This tag becomes much less an issue in up-tempo songs because they are simply too fast to use much vibrato in.

Diction: This is one of the most distinctive style tags for Golden Age musical drama because the General American dialect is used. The very New York-y sound of musical comedy is too street-wise, and the elitist vocal manner of operetta seems equally out of place. The deliberate ordinariness of the dialect in this style allows you to bring in a more classical approach to vocal production without it being obvious to the audience. It is the combination of classical vocal production and elitist diction that gives away true operetta, or reveals the grand opera singer who seems to be slumming in a Golden Age musical drama. General American is a transparent dialect, and aside from shows where the regional setting is itself a defining feature (*Oklahoma!*, *My Fair Lady*), the non-regional American-ness of the dialect makes the characters live where most of the audience does.

Phrasing: As we've said for several of the earlier styles, you must make sure that the logic and sense of the idea being sung is clear to the audience. Thankfully, the majority of shows that have survived to become part of the canon of Golden Age musicals were written by excellent composers and lyricists who knew how to turn a phrase. In current productions of these shows, the tendency toward taking some phrasing liberty is much more common than when they first appeared. Both Richard Rodgers and Frank Loesser were notorious for admonishing performers against taking any liberty with the phrasing of their songs. However, because of the influence of the great song stylists of the 1940s, 50s and 60s, where extremely loose phrasing is typical, we now have a much more flexible approach to phrasing, in general. That having been said, this style is notable for the cleanliness of the phrasing. This is not the same thing as rigidity or squareness of phrasing. But sloppy and emotionally indulgent or musically showy phrasing is not at all typical.

Physical style tags

As we approach the physical life of this style it might be a good idea to look at some of the dance from this period. Of particular value for men will be Gene Kelly, because he embodied the male ideal of the time so well and because movement was his primary means of expression. His meat-and-potatoes masculinity coupled with his willingness to access emotional and sensitive aspects of himself through movement is the perfect combination for this style. One of the iconic physical embodiments of this value system for both men and women came not from the musical theatre, but from the world of modern dance in Martha Graham's *Appalachian Spring*, which tells the story of a newlywed pioneer couple starting their life together on a small farm in rural Appalachia. Graham created an ideal study of the physical qualities and relationships between men and women for the Golden Age musical drama.

Posture/silhouette: We could best describe the physical presence for both men and women in the Golden Age musical drama as relaxed, but alert. Men in these shows were solid and stable. Their neutral stance in the style has the feet planted firmly on the ground at about shoulder width, with the chest lifted, head aligned comfortably over the spine and the energized arms resting easily at the sides. It may be useful to contrast this with the rigidity of the operetta silhouette or the herky-jerky shapes of musical comedy.

Because the clothing for men in this style is often more physically revealing (collars unbuttoned, sleeves slightly rolled), even those men who don't possess a powerful physique can project a sense of muscularity and strength as they engage the world of their musical. Look at pictures of John Raitt or Yul Brynner in their prime to see how the male ideal is embodied in solid posture and silhouette.

Women are similarly grounded, but not as heavy or solid. The goal is to project inner strength. Think of looking hopefully toward the horizon. Women were strong and feminine, not dependent or girlie. The pioneer spirit of Laurey in *Oklahoma!*, the independent strength of Marian in *The Music Man* and the courage of Julie Jordan in *Carousel* are typical of the qualities we associate with these women. There is an earnest simplicity in their shapes. The Golden Age leading lady stands solidly on two feet, but doesn't attempt to co-opt masculine silhouettes.

Men and women in romantic roles are often seen as heroic and unbroken by life's disappointments. Comic characters generally derive their humor from wide-eyed innocence, naïveté, or a desire for companionship from the opposite sex. Physicalizing these qualities without letting them get too "knowing" is central to the style.

Degree of formality: This world is relaxed, simple and deliberately un-formal. As we said, since these characters are often closely aligned with authority figures in their community, the necessity for formality is greatly reduced. These central characters rarely fear or reject authority. In cases where conflicts between classes are central (*The King and I*, *My Fair Lady*) you must honor the given circumstances of the script. The same is true for characters that are specifically outside the mainstream, like Jud Fry (*Oklahoma!*), Jigger Craigan (*Carousel*) or Harry Beaton (*Brigadoon*).

Gestural vocabulary: Simplicity is the key here. This style allows you to do almost anything you want to with gestures, but self-conscious theatricality or flourish is not typical for the normative characters (unless they are supposed to be performing as the character). Because the lyrics in many of these songs are so filled with specific imagery, your use of gesture can become a valuable part of manifesting those images. Use specific gestures to anchor images, ideas and actual things in your space for both your audience and the characters you're singing to. This style invites you to accent and punctuate your singing and acting with physical choices. But these choices must be motivated by the character's desire to illuminate the experience, not by the performer's desire to "show." This is a good time to review our comments about illustration versus gesture.

Rehearsal clothing: Try rehearsing for this style in khaki trousers that fit at your true waist, not the lower waist of current fashion. Wear a long-sleeved shirt that is unbuttoned at the collar and with sleeves rolled to the elbow. Get some casual lace-up shoes (not sneakers or dress shoes). Men will typically cut their hair over the ears and out of the face.

Women can work in a dress or circle skirt that comes to just below the knee, with short sleeves and an open neckline. No tight or mini skirts in this style. Whether you use a skirt and blouse or a dress, you need to be able to see where the waist is. Your shoes should have a heel (not stilettos or flats). Keep your hair out of your face. Getting comfortable with this type of clothing will help you find the right body to work within.

UNIT 16.4.8   *Examples from the style/genre*

Oklahoma!, Carousel, The King and I, South Pacific, The Sound of Music – Rodgers and Hammerstein
My Fair Lady, Gigi, Camelot – Lerner and Loewe
Guys and Dolls, The Most Happy Fella – Frank Loesser
The Music Man – Meredith Willson
Kiss Me, Kate – Cole Porter
The Pajama Game, Damn Yankees – Adler and Ross
Hello, Dolly, Mame – Jerry Herman
110 in the Shade, I Do, I Do, The Fantasticks – Schmidt and Jones
Ragtime – Flaherty and Ahrens
Les Misérables, Miss Saigon – Boublil and Schönberg
Finian's Rainbow – Harburg and Lane

Research resources (film/audio/visual)

Essential singers

Christine Andreas	Brent Barrett
Barbara Cook	Alfred Drake
Melissa Errico	Shirley Jones
Gertrude Lawrence	Rebecca Luker
Ethel Merman	Gordon MacRae
Mary Martin	Brian Stokes Mitchell
John Raitt	Vivienne Segal
Dawn Upshaw	Richard White

Essential films/video recordings

Annie Get Your Gun (1957) MGM – Hutton, Keel, et al.

Camelot (1981) Broadway revival – Harris, Bussert, et al.

Carmen Jones (1954) Twentieth Century Fox – Dandridge, Belafonte, et al.

Carousel (1956) Twentieth Century Fox, MacRae, Jones, et al.

Cinderella (1957 & 1965) – Rodgers and Hammerstein's groundbreaking television musical

Damn Yankees (1959) Warner Bros. – Verdon, Walston, et al. (good reproduction of the Broadway production)

Guys and Dolls (1955) MGM – Brando, Blaine, et al. (Vivian Blaine recreates her Broadway role and Michael Kidd restages his Broadway choreography)

The King and I (1956) Twentieth Century Fox – Brynner, Kerr (Marni Nixon sings), et al. (outstanding record of Brynner's performance and Jerome Robbins' Broadway choreography)

Kiss Me, Kate! (1953) MGM – Keel, Grayson, et al.

Kiss Me, Kate! (2003) London Production – Barrett, York, et al.

The Music Man (1963) Warner Bros. – Preston, Jones, Walston, et al. (good reproduction of the Broadway production)

My Fair Lady (1964) Warner Bros. – Harrison, Hepburn, et al.

Oklahoma! (1955) Hollywood film – MacRae, Jones, et al. (includes Agnes DeMille's Broadway landmark choreography)

Oklahoma! (2003) London Production

Several special video recordings are useful performance resources:

Broadway's Lost Treasures, Vols. 1, 2, 3 – Acorn Media
Broadway: The Golden Age (2003) – excellent documentary by Rick McKay
Les Misérables (in concert) (1995) – London Gala, Wilkinson, Solonga, et al.
The Best of Broadway Musicals (2003) – Selections from the Ed Sullivan Show

Broadway Cast Recordings for all of the shows mentioned in this section and many compilations and anthologies of good Golden Age musicals are available on high-quality CD. Many shows in this style have had credible (or better) studio recordings.

UNIT 16.5   **Rock musicals**

UNIT 16.5.1   *Background and worldview*

While the Broadway establishment continued to churn out hit shows following a form established by generations of Tin Pan Alley songwriters and the innovators who followed them, a different kind of music was beginning to dominate popular tastes throughout the 1950s and the 1960s: rock and roll. Strongly influenced by African-American blues music and incorporating elements of country swing, gospel and a range of other musical forms, rock was radically different from the popular music of the Broadway stage.

Performers like Elvis Presley, Buddy Holly, Chuck Berry, The Beatles and The Rolling Stones created an instrumental and singing style that overtly rejected the smooth crooning of big band, jazz and Broadway music. Those were seen as representing the attitudes and values of older listeners, the parents of the teens who listened to rock. This rejection was part of a much broader realignment of values and popular tastes that took place over the next two decades. Rock music became identified as the music of rebellion and was the soundtrack to a profound and far-reaching social movement in Western society.

As rock became the dominant popular music form, musical theatre grew increasingly isolated from the rest of the culture until a new generation of theatre writers embraced rock as a musical vocabulary that could convey dramatic content. Though rock and roll had achieved enormous popularity by the early 1960s, especially after the arrival of The Beatles in America in 1964, Broadway didn't know what to make of it. As a gimmick, an occasional pseudo-rock tune was incorporated in shows like *Bye, Bye, Birdie* and *Do, Re, Mi* to make the show seem contemporary. But no significant use of rock was attempted until almost the end of the decade. This wasn't only because Broadway writers tended to write in a wholly different musical language, but also because rock music itself was still in its infancy for much of the 1960s. Rock's simple and repetitive musical changes and limited stylistic range rendered it a weak vehicle for the stage because it didn't offer enough variety to express a range of different musical character identities.

But, as the decade progressed, rock artists were expanding the form at a breath-taking pace. The Beatles, who began the decade with simplistic tunes like *'Love Me Do'* and *'She Loves You, Ya, Ya, Ya'* were now working with symphonic complexity on albums like *Rubber Soul* and *Sergeant Pepper's Lonely Hearts Club Band*. Jimmy Hendrix had turned the electric guitar into a virtuoso instrument. Bands like The Beach Boys, The Doors and The Who expanded both the musical complexity and the subject matter addressed in pop rock music.

And, along with the main stream of rock and roll, several closely related musical styles emerged. Folk music became popular, with singer/songwriters like Bob Dylan, Judy Collins, Peter, Paul and Mary, and Joan Baez. Rhythm and Blues (also called Motown for the record label in Detroit that popularized it) emerged as the dominant musical sound of African-American culture. And singers like The Carpenters and James Taylor, among others, also popularized a mellower, main-stream sound that we'll call soft rock. By 1967, rock and roll was ready to handle the musical demands of character and dramatic situation that musical theatre required.

Hair (1967), generally considered the first rock musical, was quickly followed by a number of others including *Jesus Christ Superstar*, *Godspell* and *Pippin*. The rock musical has grown into one of the dominant styles in musical theatre writing, but it has not eclipsed the others. The influence of rock music is evident in many musicals that are more closely related to operetta and Golden Age musical drama, including *Lestat*, *Les Misérables* and *Jekyll and Hyde*. Some critics have called these shows "Poperettas" because they employ many of the thematic and writing conventions of European operetta with a contemporary, soft rock compositional style.

Social ideals and values

The 1960s were a time of tremendous social upheaval. The civil rights movement that began to take root in the fifties was in full force during the sixties when

Blacks and women were demanding equal rights and encountering violent, sometimes lethal opposition. The generational schism between young and old represented a shift in values and social ideals that many in the older generation simply did not understand, or were unwilling to accept. But young people believed they were rejecting a set of values they felt supported an imperial government, and the oppression of virtually anyone who was non-white, non-Western or non-male.

In the US, the traditional male obligation of military service faced open rejection, and religious ideas were being challenged on the highest level. Many people began to use mind-altering drugs as a way of seeing the world through a different set of eyes. Each of these rebellions represented an affront to established social norms and sent seismic shock waves throughout virtually every sector of the culture.

The new social ideal for this counter-culture was to create a world that lived in peace, where different races and genders treated each other with love and respect, and where race, gender and sexuality were not the primary sources of identity. Part of the rebellion was the result of what this generation saw as a widespread failure of central institutions (marriage, industry, the military and government) to serve the real needs of society. So, the youth movement created an ideal that functioned outside of institutional values by blending gender roles and identities, by rejecting traditional employment and educational conventions, by refusing to serve in the military, by seeking social change outside of traditional governmental processes, and by mobilizing many thousands of disenfranchised citizens to take action for change. This change manifested itself in behavior, fashion and every aspect of culture.

UNIT 16.5.3   *Romance and sex*

Among the most significant changes in culture that we see in rock musicals is the shift in attitudes about sex and romance. Until this time, sex was not openly discussed as part of the musical theatre. Even the most risqué songs of the 1930s only addressed it through naughty allusion. But, the counter-culture of the 1960s came about as female contraception became easily available and afford-able. For the first time in history, women could choose to have sex for pleasure without fear of unwanted pregnancy. This fundamentally shifted the dynamic between men and women, and the rock musical took note.

Romance and love are still central to the rock musical, but overt and aggressive seduction by either partner is now an acceptable tactic to achieving it. Because the Golden Age social ideal of a powerful and controlling man supported by a submissive woman had become problematic, rock musicals left the issues of sexual and romantic control up to the characters on a more equal basis. This release of the old male-pursuit model gave much more flexibility to creating stories and relationships in this style.

Sex is very much a subject in rock musicals. As taboo as it had been in the Golden Age, this new style brought sex out of the closet, in more ways than one. Whereas heterosexuality was the only romantic model allowed in previous styles, gay and bi-sexual relationships pervade rock musicals.

Beauty and fashion

UNIT 16.5.4

As an expression of their rejection of the "establishment" and mainstream values, many young people in the 1960s began experimenting with their appearance, their behavior, their language and almost every other aspect of social engagement. While long hair had always been reserved for women, young men now adopted it to signal a blurring of gender roles. Similarly, women began wearing men's clothing, especially denim jeans, as an expression of equality. They eschewed bras and other restrictive undergarments and began to flaunt their physical freedom as a form of social rebellion. Wearing parodies of vintage military garb, speaking with new jargon, openly rejecting traditional ideas of marriage, race, gender, educational and career expectation were part of the creed of what became known as the Hippie movement (taken from the word "hip," a term coined by members of the Beatnik movement of the 1950s). Jewelry appropriated from other cultures (India, Africa, the Far East, etc.) became popular for both men and women. The intentional neutralizing of male and female dress became one of the primary tenets of rock culture. However, this androgynous blending of genders is more of an ideal than a pervasive reality. Women also dressed in ways that were overtly sexually attractive, in keeping with a newfound sense of power and freedom.

Relationship to authority

UNIT 16.5.5

Rock musicals tend to treat authority with open skepticism and disdain that reflect the culture they emerged from. In the opinion of many in the counter-culture of that time, government and virtually all institutions of authority were corrupt and had failed the average citizen. So, "the man" (as authority was called) was an object of distrust and ridicule. This anti-establishment view of the world has remained nearly constant in this style.

UNIT 16.5.6 *Performance tradition*

The performance tradition that rock musicals reflect is one of the most distinct in all of musical theatre. It is a reflection of the various popular rock musical forms that we discussed, with much less infusion of Golden Age musical drama, musical comedy or operetta performance conventions (except for purposes of quotation). These popular rock forms all share a number of qualities that inform the rock musical style. First, they are all dependent on electronic amplification of voices and most instruments. Except for folk music, the idea of acoustic voices and instruments blending naturally is anathema to this style. Second, the instrumentation for these styles and shows is centered on a lead guitar, rhythm guitar, bass guitar and drum set, with occasional electronic keyboard or organ. Motown and softer rock influences also eventually include augmentation with horns and strings. But, the center of composition and performance is the rock band structure. A third consistent element is that both men and women sing in similar vocal ranges. Blending gender means that women and men sound more alike than ever before.

Performance in the rock tradition means singing in front of a band with a microphone on a stand or in your hand. Even as cordless miniature microphones have become ubiquitous, many rock performers still use handheld microphones. The size of physical expression is greatly reduced as the microphone allows a more intimate and internalized experience to become public. So, the performers own physical resources are no longer the central means of transmitting the performance.

Rock music favors vocal colors that are rawer, and emotionally and psychologically more violent, than in earlier styles and include musicalized screaming and wailing. This is another way of rejecting older musical theatre styles. In addition, the vocal stylings that we associate with gospel, blues, and rhythm and blues singers have been appropriated into the rock musical.

Some of the experimental theatre techniques of directors like Peter Brook and Jerzy Grotowski have been incorporated into the rock musical aesthetic, allowing for a more contemporary, edgy and overtly performative set of performance and staging conventions.

Finally, the kinetic direct-address aesthetic of rock concerts, where performers stimulate, agitate and respond to the audience energy and feedback has been absorbed into many rock musicals (though few allow the full range of freedoms many concert performers engage in).

Singing actors in this style may find themselves depending on pure emotionality to convey a character's experience, because lyric writing in rock musicals aspires to neither the wit of musical comedy nor the poetry of Golden Age musical drama. Opening your heart and singing your feelings with extreme passion, using vocal technique and color to convey tactical variation and evolving experience, is more the tradition.

Style tags

UNIT 16.5.7

Vocal style tags

It would be hard to overstate how important it is for you to listen to the seminal singers we list at the end of this unit. Singers from the 1960s and 70s continue to have an indelible effect on rock musicals because many of the composers and lyricists for rock musicals have been most deeply influenced by these singers and songwriters and openly acknowledge that debt.

Much of what we'll discuss here regarding singing colors and approaches is too technical to express adequately in this forum. Because this territory is largely explored through supervised imitation, it is essential that you learn to do so with care. If it hurts, stop! Some teachers will not touch this material because they don't know how to teach it (a good reason), don't like it (personal taste), or believe it cannot be sung without doing permanent vocal damage (not true in our experience). There are many excellent coaches and teaching approaches to this work that help students sing in a sustained and healthy way.

Tone: Rock musicals employ a wide range of traditional and less orthodox tonal qualities. Because we are talking about performing in musical theatre, the mixing of styles and genres continues here, as well. But the range of new and distinctive sounds that we hear in this style includes: wail, growl or rasp, falsetto belt (for men), stylized yodeling, belt mixing and other tonal qualities that are referred to by many different names. There is often an aggressive, angry or desperate quality to the singing that reflects the despair of the character in their circumstance. In almost no case will the "covered," highly rounded tonal quality of operetta or the bright and brassy belt of musical comedy be used in rock musicals. The mixed sound that we use in Golden Age musical drama is often employed in this style, though the dialect and diction are changed to fit the contemporary and casual nature of the music. Although many teachers caution against this, there is a fairly heavy use of glottal onset for vowels in this style. It will be important for you to learn to modify this to accommodate healthy singing.

Another important aspect of singing in rock musicals for women is that the legitimate soprano register falls into almost total disuse for most shows. The adoption of lower-register pop/rock belting as the dominant sound follows what most of popular music had already done. This is part of the gender blending that we've discussed. Women and men now frequently sing in a much closer match of ranges. There is increasing pressure for women to belt ever higher notes at full volume. At the same time, male singing is pushed into higher registers with the majority of roles being written in the tenor and high baritone range. This is often referred to as the bari-tenor range. The stratospherically high pitches that many women (and men) sing for what are sometimes thrilling technical effects are not really sung in the old soprano register, nor do men sing in a pure falsetto register. Very little "legit" sound is allowed.

Vibrato: Many of the singing styles within the rock musical genre use little vibrato. Straight tone is the dominant sound. Singers will sometimes delay use of vibrato until quite late in a sustained note, if they use it at all. This is a stylistic choice. But, many of the colors that we associate with rock musicals use straight tone with press or edge added.

Diction: The diction for much rock music comes from the enormous influence of rural American music; blues, black R&B, and gospel. So, the dialect substi-tutions that you might make if you were taking on a role in *The Color Purple* would be used to a greater or lesser extent when singing in rock musicals. This can be done subtly, as with the substitution of "ah" for "I," softening hard Rs, and so forth. Its interesting to listen to singers like Elton John speak with a Middlesex English accent, and then sing with an appropriated rural American dialect and diction. This is typical of many rock singer/stylists and carries into rock musicals, as well. But there should never be a distinct difference between the way you speak and the way you sing. These subtle modifications need to be modulated according to the specific circumstances of the character. Since rock lyrics often don't have a great deal of verbal complexity, articulation is less essential than passion. What you feel is sometimes more important than what you mean.

Phrasing: Rock phrasing is strongly influenced by two factors. First, the more dominant presence of the rhythm section in accompaniment and orches-tration tends to make singing more rhythmic as well, even in many ballads.

The second influence is a shift in the rhythmic underpinning of much rock music. In the fox trot of the Golden Age musical drama, the jazz influenced songs of musical comedy, and much of the music in operetta, the musical accent is on the counts 1 and 3 of each bar of music. But, rock shifts the emphasis to 2 and 4. So, this blues-based rhythmic structure realigns how we hear and feel the music. It adds a groove and syncopation to the music that we haven't heard in other styles. If you think back to the exercise you did at the beginning of this section where you sang the same song in a range of different styles you'll realize that one of the things you instinctively did in the contemporary styles was to shift the emphasis. Clap your hands along with George M. Cohan's *'You're a Grand Old Flag'* or Cole Porter's *'I've Got You under My Skin'*. Notice how you naturally fall into clapping on 1 and 3. Now listen to James Brown's *'I Feel Good'* or The Beatles' *'She Loves You'*. You have instinctively shifted the emphasis.

The flexibility in phrasing that we began to feel in the Golden Age musical drama is expanded exponentially here. Every aspect of phrasing can be amplified. Punching words for emphasis, back phrasing, emphasizing the underlying rhythm of the words, and creating melodic improvisations on the basic melody are all typical phrasing tactics. These must be developed through rehearsal and decided on with your musical director and director. But this is the tradition with much of the Rock Musical repertoire. Some composers in this style simply don't write all of the riffs and variations that they want to hear into the score.

Physical style tags

Posture/silhouette: Rock musicals ask you to get casual, informal, anti-establishment and as far away from the operetta shapes as you possibly can. This physicality is far more common today than any of the other physical behaviors that we've approached before. To get a sense of the typical posture and silhouette, sit comfortably into one hip (with your knee locked back and very little weight on the other leg), relax your chest and allow a slight droop of the shoulders, hook one thumb or hand into your pocket and allow your head to loll to one side or the other. This is probably a fairly typical posture for you as you wait in line at the grocery or stand casually talking to a friend, because most contemporary informal behavior comes from this worldview. This is as true for women as it is for men. The differences between male and female casual clothing today are minor compared to the other styles we've studied. Most women wear pants at least as much as they do dresses. For many, wearing a dress of any kind is a rarity. Loose shirts (t-shirts or buttoned) are the dominant fashion. And nearly everyone wears flat shoes, often sneakers or casual shoes, as their daily attire. This is true for casual wear. When characters are defined by strong qualities (Mimi in *Rent*, Jesus in *Jesus Christ Superstar*) you must serve the specifics of the character, but the relaxed and casual nature of this culture will probably still pervade.

As rock musicals have expanded their range of subjects and time periods, physical characterization has had to incorporate both the customs of the time period or culture being written about and the conventions of rock music. For instance, a musical like *Jekyll and Hyde* asks us to accommodate both the formality of Victorian England and the rock musical aesthetic. This requires you to specially address the physical life and dialect issues of your production so that you clearly understand how to negotiate these potentially contradictory value systems.

Degree of formality. Rock musicals generally adhere to the cultural values they grew out of. A conscious and intentional degree of informality is typical. Touching, sharing close personal space, and informality of address are hallmarks of this style. Again, modify this to accommodate the specifics of character relationships.

Gestural vocabulary. One of the reasons many young singers find working in earlier styles awkward is that the specificity of gestures in those styles tends to be more precise and exaggerated than with the rock musical, where these actors feel most at home. In truth, the gestural vocabulary of the rock musical is the least specific of any of the styles you've studied thus far. It is typified by the repeated use of symmetrical and balanced gestures; lightly tossing arms up from the sides and releasing them back down, extending the arms to the sides (crucifix-like), and reaching forward with one or both arms. Songs with lots of need or angst are often filled with touching the stomach or chest.

We recognize these gestures as typical of the style, but encourage you to continue specifying your physical life to particularize every moment of your work as the character. You will want to be sure the kind of movement and the way that you tailor it is consistent with the given circumstances of the role, your production's theatrical conventions and what you understand of the style.

Examples from the style/genre

There are many musicals that fall into the broad category of rock musical, though in a range of subsets of this style. We'll list them in that way:

Hard rock (including those that mix influences with hard rock) – *Hair, Tommy, Jesus Christ Superstar, Hedwig and the Angry Inch, Rent, Evita, Spring Awakening*

Revues and Jukebox musicals (those that use songs or performances by a specific group or performer as their musical score) – *Mamma Mia!, Movin' Out, Leader of the Pack, Smokey Joe's Café, Jersey Boys, Beehive, Buddy: The Buddy Holly Story, Ring of Fire, All Shook Up*

Pastiche musicals (those that try to sound like an earlier rock style, though they are written more recently) – *Little Shop of Horrors, Grease*

Motown/R&B – *Dreamgirls, The Wiz, The Color Purple*

Soft rock/pop music – *Pippin* (strong Motown influence), *Godspell* (strong folk influence), *Jekyll and Hyde, The Scarlet Pimpernel, Les Misérables, Miss Saigon, Aida, Wicked, The Last Five Years, Songs for a New World*

Research resources (film/audio/visual)

Soundtrack and cast albums for all of the shows listed above.
Films and video recordings of the following:
Dreamgirls (2006) Dreamworks – Knowles, Murphy, Hudson, et al.
Godspell (1973) Columbia Pictures – Garber, Thigpen, et al.
Hair (1979) MGM – Williams, Savage, Golden, et al.
Jekyll and Hyde (2001) Good Times Video – Hasselhoff and Broadway cast
Jesus Christ Superstar (1973) Universal – Neeley, Weathers, et al.
Pippin (1982) VCI Video – Vereen, Katt, Rivera, et al.
Rent (2006) Sony Pictures – nearly the complete original Broadway cast
Smokey Joe's Café (2007) Image Entertainment – Broadway cast
American Idol television series

Essential singers

Rock

The Beatles	The Rolling Stones
Foreigner	Janis Joplin
Robert Plant	Ann Wilson (Heart)
Bad Company	Pat Benatar
Blood, Sweat and Tears	Alannis Morrisette

Rhythm and Blues/Pop

Ray Charles	Mariah Carey
George Michael	Whitney Houston
Billy Joel	Celine Dion
Elton John	Luther Vandross
John Secada	Patti Labelle
James Brown	Aretha Franklin

Folk

Bob Dylan	Peter, Paul and Mary
Joni Mitchell	Joan Baez
Simon and Garfunkel	

Soft Rock

James Taylor	Carly Simon
Michael Jackson	Linda Ronstadt
The Carpenters	ABBA

Country music

Gary Morris	Bonnie Raitt
Larry Gatlin	Shania Twain
Johnny Cash	Faith Hill
Willie Nelson	Martina McBride
Dolly Parton	Trisha Yearwood

This series of exercises can be applied to any of the styles we have outlined in Chapter 16. Use them to contrast styles or to help you prepare for a role.

EXERCISE 16A   IN THE MANNER OF . . .

In the manner of the style you're entering, use the language, body movements, song and dance, fashion, etc. to do the following:

- Court or seduce a lover.
- Argue with a friend, a lover, a boss, a servant, a mother-in-law, or a central character from a show from this style (see resources for that style).

EXERCISE 16B   HAVE YOU HEARD THE ONE ABOUT . . .

Tell the same joke in each of the styles that we've outlined. So you'll step into the world of European operetta, Gilbert and Sullivan, musical comedy, Golden Age musical drama and the rock musical to tell this joke. You will need to rethink and rewrite the joke for each style. The way you use your body, voice, audience and partner will change, also.

Do the same exercise with a toast at a wedding for the central characters in a musical from each style.

EXERCISE 16C   I AM THE VERY MODEL

Dress as the social ideal for your gender in one of the styles we've studied. This may require some cooperation from your theatre's costume and prop departments. But it is also possible to approximate the silhouette using thrift store items that you've creatively reworked. Remember, it isn't just the clothing that makes the style. It's how you wear it!

Have a party for your group where everyone dresses from either the same style or different styles. Set up some party games for everyone to play that force interaction. Stay in character and see what happens with the culture clash.

EXERCISE 16D   SING WITH A PROP

Learn a song from the period you're entering. Perform that song using a prop from that period: a fan, a cape, a top hat, a cane, a martini glass, a lariat, a bouquet, a microphone, etc. How can you use that prop element to live in the style?

EXERCISE 16E   LOOK AT MY . . .

Identify the body part(s) that are most valued in the style you're entering. Sing a love song or song of seduction from that style to win a lover. Use a partner.

EXERCISE 16F   PERFORMANCE TRADITION

Pick a popular song from the style you're studying. It should be one that doesn't come from the theatre, or is not strongly associated with the theatre. Perform it as if in a concert, vaudeville, recital setting – not in the theatre as a character in a musical. Be a rock star, a big band singer, a vaudeville chanteuse or comedian, a British music hall comic or a Viennese recital artist. Focus on the performance tradition that influences the style. Have different members of your group each select a different style to present, then do all the songs back to back. See how you can embody those diverse traditions.

EXERCISE 16G   I'VE GOT A LITTLE PROBLEM

In the manner and behavior or the style you're studying, solve the following physical problems:

- Help someone on with a shoe.
- Help someone put on a piece of jewelry.
- Hide your drunkenness.
- You have to pee.

- A couple is preparing to go out for the evening. You're late.
- Try to steal something (from a lover, from a foe, from a boss).
- Get a stranger to give you some money. Pick a reason.

Include the physical and vocal tags for each style. Choose key clothing and silhouette elements to help you step into the style.

EXERCISE 16H CELEBRITY ROAST

Each member of your group is from a different style, and you're all at a celebrity roast for your teacher or director. You each present a story, joke, song, etc. to roast them. Have one member of your group serve as Master of Ceremonies for the event.

EXERCISE 16I YO, BABY! I LOVE YA!

Write a love note and read/perform it to your would-be lover in one of the styles. Choose the ideal setting. You can musicalize this if you like.

EXERCISE 16J ANYTHING YOU CAN DO, I CAN DO BETTER

Set up a debate where you champion the style you represent. What's great about your worldview, your performance conventions, the music and theatre of your style. Come as a character from that style and win converts.

EXERCISE 16K ARCHETYPES IN THE STYLE OF . . .

Play an archetype in one of the styles we've studied. Select one of the archetypes that we outlined in Section II. Choose a neutral song from the style as your text. You can also use an open scene that doesn't carry too many strong given circumstances. You can also try this by playing the same archetype in different styles. Or have different members of your group play the same archetype in different styles.

EXERCISE 16L I'M THE GREATEST STAR

Assign each member of your group a style and have them present a song as the quintessential performer. Assign the performer or allow each actor to pick. Have the actor pick a signature song to present. Don't just give a museum re-creation. Amplify important style tags for that performer. Pinpoint and parody Ethel Merman's warble, John Raitt's macho baritone, Joel Grey's impish charm, Ben Vereen's manic energy or Carol Channing's zaniness. Dress the part! Make this your own version of *Forbidden Broadway*.

EXERCISE 16M STYLE DAY

This is really a series of exercises to help you achieve a three-dimensional understanding of a style.

Divide your group into five smaller groups, each of which will pick one of the styles we've outlined. Each group will have about a week to prepare a full class or rehearsal period where everyone else will be immersed in and enter that style.

It's important that all members of the teaching group come in character and stay in character the whole time. Create a persona with a name. So, Joe Deer's musical comedy name might be Joey Katz. Rocco Dal Vera's Gilbert and Sullivan name could be Reginald Stanley. See if Janet Grey, Mitzi Minton or Madeline von Grossekleine show up.

This experience should involve all five senses. Include food from the period/style, music, visual art and images, clothing and behavior, popular culture. Have everyone learn a dance step. Have fun and be creative in how you do this.

The immersion should include a short performance (ten minutes or so) in the style. So, try:

- A Viennese parlor recital. Include a short poem of welcome, some delightful songs, perhaps some hors d'oeuvres. This is a very posh affair.
- A British music hall performance. Rewrite the lyrics to a Gilbert and Sullivan patter song to lampoon your theatre company, your class or national politics. Try the list song from *The Mikado* or *'I Am the Very Model of a Modern Major General'* from *The Pirates of Penzance*.
- A vaudeville show with different acts. Include some songs from the musical comedy stage. Try rewriting a Cole Porter, Ira Gershwin or Lorenz Hart lyric to poke fun at the values of your own culture.
- A U.S.O. show, or live radio broadcast from World War II. Include a comedy sketch, a song and dance routine, a love song, messages from home, inspirational anthems for the boys over there. You might also try a television variety show from the 1950s.
- A rock concert, a 1960s "happening," ten minutes from Woodstock or an MTV video (which you can actually shoot on video).

SECTION VI: THE PROFESSION

CHAPTER 17: DO YOU HAVE THE STUFF?

The Profession

Most actors aren't content to stay in the studio and sing and dance for the mirror. They want to share their work and to hear the applause. Many love theatre enough to want to do it as a profession. How do you take the step from the studio to the professional stage? First, you have to ask a very hard question:

CHAPTER 17   **DO YOU HAVE THE STUFF?**

Reaching the top of any field requires tenacity, talent and luck. But in show business the odds against you are even steeper than usual. There are often hundreds or even thousands of people auditioning for the same position. And as the cost of producing all types of theatre has gone up, the number of productions has gone down. So, for even the most talented performers, the chances of getting work at a given audition are slimmer than ever. Actors Equity Association, the union of professional actors, has lost a lot of ground in its effort to ensure work conditions and salaries for many theatres and tours. So, even if you are hired, your assurance of living wages and a safe, healthy work environment is uncertain.

These are some tough facts to face. In short, if you can do anything else with your life and be happy, you should.

Still with us?

Okay, if you're still committed to give it a go, you are doubtless wondering if you have "the stuff" to make it happen. The keys to success lie in your talent (which is your natural gift), your skill (which we've addressed significantly already), luck (which you can't control), and your professionalism and work habits (which *only* you can control). Here's a more detailed list of what you will need:

- Talent
- Charisma
- Castability and type
- Skills and know-how
- Connections and an understanding of the market
- A winning attitude
- Luck

Talent

UNIT 17.1

There's no getting around it. There's also no way to teach it. You can improve your craft and technique, but you must be personally endowed with exceptional talent in order to compete. How can you tell if you've got talent? Pay attention to the critical feedback you receive:

EXERCISE 17A HOW DO YOU MEASURE UP?

Usually, successful performers are recognized as having talent from a young age. It is rare for someone to explode from complete obscurity into fame. Even if they have poor technique and are untrained, they still get attention early on. Start with a little inventory:

1. What do your teachers tell you? Ask your dance, singing and acting teachers for their most critical assessment of your chances. Listen carefully to their answers.
2. What do theatre professionals tell you? Put the same question to directors and producers you know.
3. Are you getting cast? Are you currently competing successfully against your peers? Are you getting major roles (or at least the role you want, no matter what size)? Regardless of the kind things people will say about your talent, the defining test of whether you should pursue a career is whether directors are willing to put you in roles.

Although refusal to take no for an answer is one of the marks of an all-important will to succeed, self-deception on the talent question will only lead you into years of fruitless effort. One only has to watch the preliminary auditions for *American Idol* to see multiple examples of people who refuse to accept that they have no business in show business. Talent isn't something you can measure, and you certainly can't trust your mother to give you an unbiased evaluation. So, look carefully at the professional feedback you get. That's the best way to know if you should continue with acting as a professional career or as an avocation at the community theatre level.

UNIT 17.2   ## Charisma

Like talent, this can be hard to define, but everyone knows it when they see it. Call it stage presence, vitality, magnetism, charm, appeal, allure, confidence, virility, sexiness, danger, etc., this is the quality that makes people watch an actor. And the real issue is whether this attribute is expressed on stage. Plenty of actors are quite shy in their private lives, but when on the boards, their personalities leap all the way across the footlights and hit the back of the house. Don't, however, confuse this with energy. Charisma projects through moments of stillness just as powerfully as in times of high action. Charisma, like talent, is partly innate, but it can be developed and cultivated.

UNIT 17.3   ## Castability and type

What you look like and the nature of your personality are undeniably an important part of the product you're selling. Those factors, in combination with your talents and abilities, *are* what you're selling. Looks and personality are how we immediately assess someone; the subtleties come later. So, the first impression you make on casting people is the most important one. And casting for musical theatre (and most other performing arts) is often directly connected to what type of person you appear to be. The word "type" gets used a lot in casting and can often carry negative connotations for performers because actors like to feel that they are completely transformable. So, they tend to think they are perfect for every role. Though transformative skill is one of the goals of training, it isn't all that much of an actuality in the professional world. In truth, if you can't be typed, you can't be cast.

When you read a script or listen to a score for a show you immediately make decisions about the characters in it. Those immediate impressions need to be matched by the actors who play the roles. For instance, if you listen to and read Andrew Lloyd-Webber's *Phantom of the Opera*, you'll probably spot the following things straightaway. The Phantom is a mysterious, powerful man who sings in the baritone range, with strong falsetto capabilities. Christine is a lovely, innocent young woman who sings with a clear legitimate soprano voice. Those immediate impressions of the characters should guide you in your decisions about how to audition and how to present yourself at an audition. First, you can tell right off the bat if you should even bother to audition for those roles. If you are a man and aren't a baritone, then stay home or audition for a different role. If you are a baritone, but don't have strong falsetto capabilities, the same thing applies. If you can sing in a baritone range and have a strong falsetto, the next question is, "Am I right for this role?" Being "right" for a role means different things to different people. In this case you might decide whether you have the stature and physical bearing to play a tragic romantic figure like the Phantom. If you are 5'6" and weigh 225 pounds, you probably won't be taken seriously for that role, even if you can sing the pants off it. You simply don't look right. But if you were to audition for *The Most Happy Fella*, you'd be ideal for the lead role of Tony. In *Phantom*, though, you are visually a poor fit for the role. Similarly, if you have all the ideal attributes, including skills and physical appearance but are simply too young for the role, you probably won't be cast (though you might end up as the understudy).

When considering your type, you must face certain realities about what we can change in ourselves and what we can't. We can't change much about our vocal range. This may develop as we get older, but the essential nature of the voice is physiological and won't simply change because we work at it. However, you can sometimes enhance your range and develop what you've got. We also can't change our height, short of wearing lifts in our shoes or wearing low heels. But, if you're a woman who is almost six feet tall, you will be cast accordingly. If you have a stocky build, even when you're in prime health, then you will be seen that way.

But typing goes beyond what you look like alone. It also has to do with the kind of material that we are naturally drawn to. You may love to sing songs by Jerry Herman and feel totally at sea singing something by Michael John LaChiusa. You might feel that rock music is your natural style and that older, Golden Age show tunes are completely foreign to your experience. Flexibility is important, but so is an understanding of your likes and dislikes. If you can find unbounded passion and energy when approaching one type of material but feel lifeless when singing something else, this is important to understand.

The fourth aspect of type (after appearance, voice type and stylistic taste) is personality. This is probably the hardest to look at objectively. But it has a great deal to do with your casting potential. Your personality is the essential nature of who you are. Whether you are generally hopeful or pessimistic, anxious or carefree, silly or serious, you present personality traits wherever you go and to everyone you meet. Of course, we all have a huge variety in our personalities, and are not simply one thing or another. Everyone is a complex blend of qualities. But we do present an overall impression that probably does have a lot to do with our general nature. Some honest assessment of yourself and discussion with those whom you trust may help clarify the way others perceive you. Knowing that you appear to be an optimistic young woman might help guide you to certain choices if you're auditioning for a role that is unlike that, such as Fosca in Stephen Sondheim's *Passion*. You might decide to audition for Clara in the same show, instead. Or you might understand that you are also ideal for certain roles in classic musicals, while you might be less right for some other, more contemporary roles.

Here are some ways to get help answering the type question:

EXERCISE 17B YOUR BASIC PROFILE

Start by listing the basic type information you would supply on a resume:

- Weight (be honest, not optimistic!)
- Height
- Hair color
- Eye color
- Age (or as it is more commonly euphemized in the theatre: "age range")

Now look around and find several people who also fit those parameters. You will notice that very few of them really look like you. So, "type" surely isn't established by those characteristics alone. We need to look deeper.

EXERCISE 17C KNOW YOUR MUSICAL THEATRE TYPE

There are type imperatives in musicals. The material itself demands it. What is your musical theatre type?

Vocal fach:

1. Note your **singing range**. This should be the range where you have all your best notes; not those you can force out, but where you are at your functional excellence.
2. Make a list of **characters** in musicals whose range matches yours. (This should be an on-going project and may need to be constantly expanded and updated.)
3. Ask your voice teacher for an assessment of the **type of voice** you have: soprano, mezzo, belt, mix, etc. You may fall into more than one category. Don't list any that you can't sing with mastery.
4. From your earlier list of roles whose range you can sing, now narrow the list to those whose vocal type matches yours. For example, you may have the right range to sing a belt song, but if your sound is too "legit" you won't be cast.

Physical type.

Here is a list of standard physical character types. There are many sub-categories, but this is a place to start. Ask directors you know where they would place you:

- Children (20 and under)
- Preteen (13 to 15)
- Ingénue female and young leading men. These characters are the ones who discover first love. They are typically 16 to 21 and have qual-ities of romance, innocence, freshness and blossoming sexuality.
- Leading men and women. Usually 25 to 45, these characters are glamorous, sexually experienced, worldly and urbane.
- Character men and women. These characters are usually older (30 and up). They may be beautiful, but in an offbeat or quirky way. Their appearance is not likely to reflect a physical ideal, but rather represent an archetype like tall and thin, or short and fat, or birdlike, nerdy, muscular, etc.

Matching it up:

- Narrow your list of roles to those where you fit the character type, the singing range and the vocal type. When you're finished, share this list with directors, teachers and friends to see if you have placed yourself accurately into the roles that suit you best.

Now we need to go beyond the basics and into something deeper and more ephemeral: What is your projected essence? This is tricky, because we are almost beyond the capacity of language to express these ideas. But never fear. There are still ways to get at the answer. Don't try to gather this next kind of information from people who know you well. Essence is best determined by first impressions. The better we know the rich complexity of your personality, the less we are able to see your immediate impression, which is the way casting directors and audiences will experience you.

EXERCISE 17D YOU REMIND ME OF . . .

1. It may not be unusual for people to comment that you remind them of another person or a famous actor. Note what people say, and look for patterns. Write this down.
2. Go with a friend to a party where you don't know many people. Split up. Ask your friend to strike up conversations with people who don't know you and casually say. "See that guy (you) over there? He reminds me of someone, but I can't think of who." Now, with a little prompting, you have everyone trying to help you. When they toss off suggestions, have your friend remember and share them later.
3. When you begin to develop a list of people you are reputed to be like, do some research. If it is a person in your social sphere, study as much as you can about how they dress, their attitudes, their style. Try to understand what important type information you can glean from them. If you are frequently compared to an actor, study that person's career. Learn their roles. Read their reviews.

EXERCISE 17E THE SOCIOLOGY EXPERIMENT

Go with a friend to a local shopping mall. Dress in one of your typical outfits. Your job is to window shop, or read or sip coffee while your friend approaches strangers with the following pitch: "Hi, I'm doing a sociology survey for a class. Would you be able to take a couple of minutes to answer some questions for me? See that girl over there in the green jacket? I would like you to make a guess about some things about her. Don't think too deeply. Just say the first impression that comes into your head. What is her:

1. Age
2. Education
3. Income
4. Favorite TV show
5. Reading interest
6. Hobbies
7. Pets
8. Name
9. Nickname
10. Kind of car she owns
11. Profession
12. Marital status
13. Sexual preference (and the kind of person you would expect the subject to be paired with)
14. Sense of humor (does she like practical jokes, bawdy jokes, never get a joke)
15. If you were to set her in a particular time period, what would that be?
16. Does she remind you of any well-known person?
17. If you were casting her in a film, play, television show, etc., what role would you choose for her?

Sociology studies in the past have shown that people are not at all reluctant to project qualities or attributes onto another person, even in the complete absence of facts about them. This is also exactly what audiences unconsciously do when presented with a character. After you get several responses look for patterns.

EXERCISE 17F FILM/TELEVISION TYPING

In the casting breakdowns supplied to agents working in film and television, there are a number of phrases that are used to describe the character type being cast. These are some of the most common. Using the responses you are getting in the exercises above, see if any of these descriptors are being applied to you (Table 17-1).

Table 17-1

Young men

bad boy	boy-next-door	nerdy kid
bully	quirky/trendy	smart-ass
jock	brain	young dad

Adult men

leading man	the nice guy	that creepy weird guy
jock	blue-collar worker	cop/career military
executive	lawyer/politician	teacher/professor
dad	computer genius	salesman
slacker	doctor/nurse	jokester
player	slimy con man	criminal/thug/heavy
artist/poet/musician	redneck	pimp
effeminate gay	biker gay	

Young women

princess	girl-next-door	trendsetter
bully	jock	brain
awkward/gawky	ingénue	psycho-ex-girlfriend
sassy-smart ass	young mom	southern belle
valley girl	little sister	moody outcast

Adult women

leading lady	her best friend	bimbo/airhead
jock	sex goddess	cop
executive/lawyer/politician	social climber/bitch	teacher/professor
mom	frustrated housewife	saleswoman
doctor/nurse	wacky neighbor	criminal
artist/poet/musician	late-start careerist	vixen
cosmo-girl	hooker	nun
lipstick lesbian	dyke	earth mother/hippy
strict librarian	trailer trash	biker babe

Older actors

empty-nester	grandparent	judge
religious leader	codger/crone/senile	old salt

You may not like what you hear in these exercises. You may be surprised at what people say. But you can only begin to attune yourself to an employable theatrical type if you acknowledge and own how you appear to others. Remember that one of the fundamental axioms of communication theory is that the audience is never wrong. It doesn't matter what you think of yourself or how you mean to come across; if you get a distinct pattern of responses, then that is what you are projecting. Own it and learn to use it.

How do you process all this information and make it useful to you? It is time to bring it all into focus. Almost no one presents a completely unblurred picture, so focusing your presentation is essential.

EXERCISE 17G BRING IT INTO FOCUS

Work with a partner. (We are notoriously unable to do this kind of work for ourselves because we lack any objectivity.) Compile this information about each other.

1. Make lists of the different types of information you received in the previous exercise and look for patterns. Which actors are you regularly compared to? What roles or types of characters are most frequently suggested, etc.
2. Look for contradictions. This can be where some people say you look honest and simple where others say you look crafty and nervous, for example. Contradictions are the most frustrating but most helpful part of this investigation.
3. Evaluate the intensity of any contradictions. How often, how forcefully and in what specific areas does it show up? Try to narrow the issues to some specific areas. Get to the center of it.
4. Decide on the strongest image you seem to be projecting and look critically at the contradictions in light of that image. See if you can deduce the source of the opposing messages. "I seem to be coming off as . . . except for. . . . Can you see things that you can modify to remove those incongruities? Look at cosmetic issues of hair (cut and color), clothing, weight, muscularity, make-up, etc. to see what is keeping the picture from being crystal clear.
5. When you think you have refined your projected essence and unblurred the picture, repeat the sociology experiment exercise above,

> and see if the results are clearer. It may take several tries before you have sharpened the image enough to make the answers truly consistent. When you do present a clear image, however, you are ready to be cast.

Now comes the toughest part. You may not have seen yourself the way others are seeing you. You may now realize that you have to either lose 30 pounds or gain 20 in order to fit a castable type. You may have to get contact lenses, dye your hair and even start saving for that nose job. If your presentation is out of focus, it is up to you to bring it into clarity. If you can't, then you will be tough to cast. When you know what you want to adjust, make a common-sense plan for setting in these changes.

Perhaps a word about moderation here is necessary. Take the time to do this process thoroughly and correctly. You might need to go through the process several times as you make some modifications. Don't rush into permanent changes like cosmetic surgery without being sure you have really thought through your options. Also, be wary of extreme responses to issues such as weight and body shape. One of your goals is to stay radiantly healthy. Avoid compulsive behavior, extreme diets or immoderate fixes. They don't work and come with a host of other complications. They are acts of desperation and not an affirmative approach to the problem. Be steady and disciplined and take the long view, not the quick fix.

Many student actors spend their full college careers working through these issues, so don't try to do it in a couple of weeks. Realize, however, that you aren't ready to bring your product to market until you know exactly what you are selling and the package matches the contents. Don't slack on this important job.

UNIT 17.4   **Skills and know-how**

You not only need to have the stuff, you need to know your stuff. You need to be a triple threat. If you have a gap in your skills, it will keep you from being cast. Also, once you have a high level of skill, you have to work hard to maintain a professional level.

EXERCISE 17H SKILLS INVENTORY

Remember that this is about skills, not talent. The issues here should be measurable and provable. You might be wonderfully talented but either you can do a clean triple pirouette or you can't. That's a skill. Remember that these are abilities that you can confidently and consistently perform without undue strain.

Make a chart and rate yourself (using the highest professional standards) in the areas of precision, flexibility, strength and grace for:

Movement

1. Pirouettes
2. Tours en l'air
3. Jumps (ballon)
4. Partnering work
5. Pointe work
6. Handstands
7. Handsprings
8. Back flips
9. Time steps
10. Pullbacks
11. Wings

Give yourself extra points for fancy specialty steps like a coffee grinder or styles like hip-hop, tap improvisation, ethnic dance forms or swing dance. Note any other saleable skills like clowning, juggling, pantomime, acrobatics, unicycling, etc.

Singing

12. Belt
13. Pop
14. Legit
15. Mix
16. Range
17. Break/passagio
18. Sight singing
19. Skills at harmonizing

20. Theory
21. Keyboard skills

Give yourself extra points for skills like yodeling, trilling, or musical genres like jazz or scat. Also note any other instruments you play.

Bonus skills

22. Improvisational or stand-up comedy
23. Television or radio experience
24. Ability with ear prompter
25. Fluency in other languages
26. Impressions or impersonations of famous people (these must be spot on)

Make a plan to address any areas where your skills don't meet a competitive professional standard and for adding skills you know you need.

Very few people can do everything well. But the most useful person to hire is the one who can do the most! Get real about just how competitive you are and remember that although we are all given certain innate abilities, good old-fashioned sweat can overcome a lot. So get to work.

Finally, how's your acting? Acting is a less provable craft. Though it may be the most important skill of all, it is more challenging to objectively measure. We can all see whether you can do a triple pirouette. Acting isn't the same kind of game. But it can be key to your success. Your singing and dancing skills won't carry you very far in musical theatre unless you can believably embody and communicate an inner life through them. So, it is time to turn to trusted professionals for an honest check-in.

EXERCISE 171   CAN YOU ACT?

1. What do your teachers tell you? Ask your dance, singing and acting teachers for their most critical assessment of your acting ability (both your current skill and your potential). Listen carefully to their answers.
2. What do theatre professionals tell you? Put the same question to directors and producers you know.

Connections and an understanding of the market

So far we've discussed how you can develop an excellent product, how you can tune that product so that it will be useful and something people will pay for. Now it is time to talk about putting that product on the market – selling yourself.

"Oh, how cold," you might be saying. "I'm not a product." Alas, romantic notions aside, you are just that. And the sooner you look at show *business* in business terms, the sooner you can begin making a living at it. Let's assume you are a wonderful performer. Your job now is to get lots of people to agree with that fact. If only you know how good you are then you can continue singing for yourself in the shower. Let's get the word out.

Planning and setting goals

A business plan is an essential first step. Build your career through a thoughtful and clear strategy about the kinds of jobs you audition for, the kind of roles you take and the sort of training you spend your time and money on. Although the myth of being discovered at the soda counter or in the chorus and elevated to instant stardom used to permeate show business, most successful actors built their careers the old-fashioned way: they worked at it for many years. If you understand that successful careers on Broadway don't happen overnight, you'll be much happier as you begin your own career with jobs that are on the right tier of the business for your skill and experience level. Take a look at *Backstage* (the weekly New York show business newspaper – a publication that you should read regularly well before moving to New York) and see the many different auditions listed each week. Yes, some of them are for Broadway shows or Equity national tours. But far more of them are for summer theatres, showcases, regional theatre productions, concerts, children's theatre tours, etc. In the early stages of your career you will probably find many more opportunities to work in these types of theatre. It is there that you'll build career connections, learn about professionalism, gain the stamina and consistency to perform in long runs of varied circumstances, and so much more. You can and should audition for the big-time shows, but understand that you may not be ready for those jobs yet. So, get the experience of that kind of audition, learn all you can from the seasoned performers you're auditioning with, pay close attention to what the director, choreographer, music director and casting people ask of you, and treat the whole thing as a free class in how to audition. But take the pressure off yourself by expecting that you will be cut at some point. When you're ready for them, you'll get callbacks.

In the meantime, doing good work as an actor in summer stock, dinner theatre, even good community theatre, is perfectly acceptable as you tackle satisfying and challenging roles that will give you confidence, experience and the skills you wouldn't have gotten a chance for in higher levels of show business. Once you've mastered one level of show business, you're ready to move on to the next.

Develop a plan for how you want to build your career by examining the various tiers of work available and by identifying and targeting the best of those theatres to get work at. Talk to successful friends whom you respect, about theatres and directors they like and who they've learned from. Season by season, year by year, you'll see that you're rising up the ladder by doing good work and growing into your career.

UNIT 17.6 ## Market research

You can't sell your product if you don't know the territory – who is hiring and for what. There are numerous ways to learn about the market. As we mentioned earlier, *Backstage* is a fundamental tool, as is *The New York Times*. The main appeal of *Backstage* is the listing of the following week's auditions. The auditions are broken into a range of categories, such as: Equity Stage, Non-Union Stage, Dance, Film/Television, Student Films, Showcases, Staff, and so forth. These auditions are not solely in New York City, by the way. Many regional theatres post their auditions in *Backstage* because they know that everyone, including out of town actors, reads the newspaper. The majority of you reading this book don't live in or around New York City, but getting acquainted with *Backstage* is still important because of all the information and articles in it on a weekly basis. *The New York Times*, *Playbill* and other major newspapers, websites and culture publications form an important part of your ongoing professional study because they reflect and report on the important artistic developments in your field and offer a good idea of who is doing what where.

Other publications come and go, but look for titles like *Theatre Directory*, *Regional Theatre Directory*, *The Summer Theatre Directory*, *Straw Hat Guide to Summer Theatres* and *American Theatre*, to keep you abreast of who's doing what. Look for directories like the *Ross Reports* to help you connect with who's who in casting and agents. Most of these publications have an on-line component to accommodate rapidly changing information. You should spend a dedicated time every day studying the industry news.

Theatre bookstores are also good resources, as are phone-in hotlines (like the Actors' Equity hotlines for union members).

Aside from the fundamental information of what auditions are coming up, you are also learning who the players are. You need to know who is directing, who is casting, what theatres are coming to town to cast and what their seasons are. When you meet a director you should be able to speak knowledgeably about his past work and have an understanding of his aesthetic. It can be enormously helpful to know that the same casting director you are seeing for this particular call also casts for several other theatres and which roles you should be in consideration for with them.

Through doing your research, you'll get a sense of the scope of opportunities available to a musical theatre performer. It may be more diverse than you originally thought. Here are some of the places you might get hired.

Where the work is

UNIT 17.7

Nearly everyone who begins a career in musical theatre dreams of success on Broadway. Those lavish productions, with their enormous budgets (and equally enormous ticket prices), are probably the most visible jobs, but they make up a minute portion of the total marketplace for talent. There are literally hundreds of different productions in all variety of media and venue for every one mega-musical on Broadway. It is in these other job niches that most actors spend their time. As you build your career, you'll want to see which of these employment opportunities offers you work. Among these different job markets are:

Children's theatre

UNIT 17.7.1

A significant, though less visible sub-culture of show business is the children's theatre industry. These shows are usually geared toward children aged 4–13 and often involve adaptations of popular and classic literature. You might find yourself touring in a van with four other actors and a stage manager doing a sixty-minute musicalized *Nicholas Nickelby*, in which you play a dozen different characters that are identified by their own signature hat and funny voice. This sort of work can offer you rich opportunities for creativity and personal development as an actor. You will also learn to deal with as wide a range of performing circumstances and audience challenges as in any part of the business. There are a number of longstanding and reputable companies that send out numerous tours each year, including Theatreworks USA, American Family Theatre and others. The actors you work with in these shows often come straight from college and are enthusiastic and willing to deal with the grueling touring conditions. Some of the larger companies will give you your Equity card as part of the job. This is a big step that we'll discuss later on in this section.

UNIT 17.7.2   *Outdoor drama*

In virtually every part of the United States you'll find at least one large-scale epic drama that was written to extol the virtues of a local hero. Whether it's *Tecumseh* and *Blue Jacket* (celebrating Ohio Native Americans), *The Sword in the Land* (commemorating Spanish settlers), *Young Abe Lincoln* or any of the many shows being performed in amphitheatres by casts of fifty or more on horseback, with flaming arrows, these shows offer opportunities for young performers to learn about long runs, playing to large theatres, incorporating spectacle elements and so much more. Plus, they can just be fun. The Institute of Outdoor Drama holds collective auditions for many of these shows annually. Check out their website for more information.

UNIT 17.7.3   *Theme parks*

Similar in performing style to cruise ships, theme park shows offer the same career-building benefits, but allow you to have a full personal life. You may find that there is seasonal work available at theme parks that will allow you to continue training or to do other theatre work in the off-season. Though some theme parks, like Walt Disney World, fall under the jurisdiction of Actors' Equity Association, the majority are not union affiliated but still offer acceptable salaries for younger performers. The work can be demanding, as much of it is outdoors and can involve heavy costumes in high summer temperatures. But the opportunity to perform several hundred shows in the span of just a few months will give you a kind of seasoning that only years of traditional theatre could provide.

UNIT 17.7.4   *Arena shows*

Similar to Children's Theatre in many ways, arena shows like *Sesame Street Live*, *Blue's Clues Live*, *Disney on Parade* and others employ a large number of performers, many of whom spend a good deal of their stage time parading in large character costumes, dancing to canned music and lip synching to prerecorded music and dialogue tracks. These shows are very popular and can sometimes go on for years and years. The salary can be good and it's a great way to see the country. From the description above, you can see that the room for creativity and individual expression is less than in some other types of theatre, but there is still a lot to be said for learning to do a show like this well and with the full commitment and professionalism any long-running show requires.

Cruise ships

There are dozens of vacation cruise lines that feature Broadway and Top 40 styled revues and even full-scale book musicals as part of their entertainment package for customers. These shows require every bit of the skill and talent that so-called legitimate productions do. Performers often learn as many as three shows at a time and may be offered a chance to sing in cabaret settings as the star of their own mini-show. These cruise ships can help you build stamina and consistency as a performer that will be invaluable when you begin doing other jobs. The salary for these cruise ship jobs can be very good and, because you're living onboard, you can usually save a much higher portion of the weekly salary than in a typical theatre job. Most ships stop for one day a week in a home port, allowing you to do banking and take care of personal business. Probably the only disadvantage to cruise ship work is that you are stuck on a relatively small floating city for days and weeks at a time. And most ships ask for a minimum of six months commitment. So, you are unavailable for other auditions and training during this time. But the benefits of this kind of work, especially in the early part of your career, can be enormous.

Summer stock

The old tradition of spending the summer in the mountains as part of a repertory company doing plays and musicals for one or two weeks at a time is still thriving in many parts of the country and offers some of the best training and resume-building opportunities around. It is very possible for you to play Ellard in *The Foreigner*, the Nephew in *A Flea in Her Ear*, Tommy Djilas in *The Music Man*, a butler in *Rough Crossings*, Geoffrey in *The Lion in Winter* and finish up as part of the ensemble in *Godspell* all in one summer season. These summer theatres rehearse one show during the day and perform another at night. In a number of theatres you will also build scenery after rehearsal, rush to serve drinks in the canteen before the show, serve drinks again at intermission and then perform a cabaret show after the regular theatre event. Then, you go to bed and begin all over in the morning. As grueling as this sounds, the training can be irreplaceable and you can get a huge leap in your experience in just a few months. Summer stock is also a place where you may get to play roles you would not ordinarily be cast in, stretching you as an actor and forcing you to be resourceful and creative. As with most types of theatre, these summer stock experiences vary from place to place, ranging from bare-bones struggling artists to full-blown star tours. Housing at many of these theatres can be rustic and you will probably not make a good deal of money in the long run. But the real benefits of summer work are worth more than any big paycheck.

UNIT 17.7.7   *Dinner theatre*

Once upon a time every big city had at least one dinner theatre where patrons could enjoy a meal of rare roast beef, a rich dessert and a few drinks before turning their chairs toward the end of the banquet hall where a fading television star would perform the lead in a classic musical or the latest naughty sex farce involving infidelity and a near miss at being caught by her husband. All of this was punctuated by two intermissions where patrons had a chance to drink still more before driving home late at night. Those days are nearly behind us, but there are still a few diehard survivors who produce an ongoing season of plays and musicals that may or may not feature stars anymore. More often, these theatres simply employ hard-working local and regional actors who put out a respectable theatre product and offer customers entertaining live theatre. Dinner theatres offer steady, relatively long-running shows (up to ten weeks in many cases) and a chance to build your resume and skills. Occasionally you'll even get a regular dinner in the bargain. The salaries are sometimes meager but it can be a valuable experience.

UNIT 17.7.8   *Industrial shows*

Many large corporations hire production companies to create entertainment for their annual shareholder or sales meeting. These shows celebrate the virtues of the insurance product, cola, computer software or whatever else the client business makes their fortune at. These shows can be lucrative for a very short but intense work period. You may learn a forty-five minute show in a matter of days and perform it in a beautiful hotel or convention center. The best of these shows involve large budgets and offer you a chance to work with some of the highest production values in show business. It is not unusual to have a top star as a headliner. The creative talents for these productions often work in very good theatres, as well. The performers who do this kind of work well are adept at learning and performing complicated music and staging with ease and often have strong stage presence, an important commodity to sell as a performer.

Regional theatre

The term "regional theatre" has been used to describe a wide range of theatres. Some theatres that might otherwise be called summer stock have adopted the title because it has more prestige value and implies high art rather than pure entertainment. In other cases, regional theatres are genuinely excellent producers of year-round theatre seasons that usually include a healthy mixture of classics, new plays and musicals, workshops, staged readings, educational tours and a wide range of other theatre activities. Most large cities in America have at least one regional theatre. Increasingly, casting for these theatres is done in New York, with only small roles cast locally. In that case, the regional theatre is really a farm team of sorts for the big theatrical industry of New York, Chicago or Los Angeles. But the work at these theatres can be very rewarding and offers a chance to do plays and musicals that might not otherwise be seen or vital revivals of well-loved classics. It is very possible to develop an ongoing relationship with these theatres and to return again and again. Salary scales range widely, depending on the size of audience and the theatre's potential earnings. Actors' Equity Association is extremely accommodating of these theatres and works to create useful and fair contracts for this very important part of the theatrical economy. Increasingly, these regional theatres produce shows that later transfer to New York. This has become the new "try-out" mechanism for the theatrical industry.

Non-union tours (America and Europe)

Every year, more and more tours bearing the name "Broadway Tour" take off from New York City populated by actors who have chosen not to join Actors' Equity Association or who have not yet had the opportunity. These tours play major cities and large theatrical venues, much as their fully professional counter-parts do. In fact, it has become increasingly difficult to tell the difference between the union and non-union shows if you simply look at the advertising, sets and costumes. But the cast of a non-union tour is almost always much less experi-enced or fresh out of college. Some students even leave college for the chance to join a tour like this. We do not advocate that choice. Get your training first. This opportunity will be there when you graduate. The tours can run for several years and offer decent wages (usually with minimal or non-existent health and pension benefits). The schedule can be anything from one-week stops in mid-sized cities to one-night stands and split weeks in the high school auditorium of a very small town. The bus rides can be long and there is no guarantee of days off or rest. This kind of touring can build professional skills, but the absence of genuinely experienced upper-level performers in these tours often makes them more like a touring all-star college production. Apprenticeship under more experienced actors is unthinkable in these cases. Audiences are often never told that what they've just paid Broadway rates for is a wholly non-professional production only loosely based on its Broadway counterpart. There's a great deal of ongoing controversy over this, with producers and Actors' Equity Association negotiating more affordable contracts for the producers and getting lifelong professional actors back on the road with these shows. While some beginning performers may suffer at this change, it is ultimately better for the theatrical economy and will result in a higher-quality performance for regional audiences. Stay tuned for future developments on this category of work.

A number of European producers also mount multi-year tours of classic American musicals and cast them with American performers. Since Europe is not under the jurisdiction of any performing unions, these casts may include everyone from the newest conservatory graduate to Broadway veterans. Rehearsal and performance conditions are inconsistent with these tours and you have no legal recourse if you do encounter an unscrupulous producer. Nonetheless, this can be a great way to see the world and perform a wonderful show. It can also be a great way to get stranded in Antwerp without a return plane ticket. But the pros definitely outweigh the cons on these European tours.

UNIT 17.7.11 *Off-Broadway*

Though this term can be broadly defined (and on many resumes stretched to include almost anything) it usually describes productions occurring in New York City, but not directly within the Broadway Theatre district. You'll also hear the term "off-off-Broadway" for even more remote theatres that are still within the Boroughs of New York City. These theatres can range from tiny holes-in-the-wall hosting odd experimental work, to large houses mounting elaborate productions as big or bigger than the Broadway theatres. The salaries and quality of the work will also range widely.

Equity national tours

These productions are first-class replicas of the original Broadway shows, featuring top-ranked stars and highly experienced casts. They stand right up there with the Broadway productions in terms of salary and status. Many times they will take up residence, or "sit down" in a city like Los Angeles or Chicago for several months.

Broadway

The big time. The Great White Way. It is comprised of a group of about thirty-three theatres in and around Times Square in Manhattan. The vast majority of shows playing in Broadway theatres are musicals. There have even been times in the last few years when those were the *only* shows playing on Broadway.

Those are the primary places where you'll be looking for work. In addition, there are plenty of performance opportunities that will help you get your face in front of casting directors, build your performing experience and sharpen your skills.

Showcases

A fairly recent type of theatrical production is the showcase. It has become a way to give a production a short run in a small New York theatre while minimizing the salary costs to the fledgling producers. These showcases are most often intended as a way of featuring performing, directing and design talent rather than a new playwright, though that does happen as well. The showcase rarely pays anything – perhaps subway fare. But the hope of being seen by agents and casting directors is the brass ring that starving artists keep reaching for. And, occasionally, someone does get an agent out of the deal. But don't hold your breath. Think of it more as a way of getting a New York credit on your resume. Younger performers are fond of labeling these productions "Off-Broadway" shows. Don't do that. It is analogous to saying you had a role in a film if you were actually only an extra. Another variety of showcase is one in which you pay a fee to be part of a production or revue of talent. The idea is that you'll show your best material and that agents will come to see you. Be wary of this kind of showcase. Often, the only person getting anything out of it is the producer, who takes your fee and doesn't produce many industry representatives. It can be disappointing and costly for young performers.

UNIT 17.7.15   *Workshops*

Many mainstream producers employ this contract as a way to give their creative team a rehearsal process and bare-bones presentation of a new work. In exchange for participating in the development process for a new musical or play, the performer is given a minimal salary and small share in the future profits of the show, if it ever has any. This concept was pioneered in the 1970s and was most successful with *A Chorus Line*. Although the term "workshop" implies that a lot of developmental work is being done in rehearsal, this is often a way of simply rehearsing in advance and more cheaply than a full production contract would allow. But these are great opportunities to develop new material and create a role in a work that may have a future life.

UNIT 17.7.16   *Cabarets*

Guaranteed to pay virtually nothing and to cost you a fair amount in self-promotion, the cabaret scene in New York has a small but devoted following. Cabarets offer performers a chance to develop distinctive performing identities and establish direct audience rapport in ways that traditional theatre doesn't allow. Usually, a solo performer creates a 45–60 minute show that involves only herself and a pianist–music director. Many performers who work in traditional theatrical settings also do cabaret work. Most clubs require that patrons pay an admission charge and buy two drinks while they watch the featured performer. That performer usually gets a small percentage of the box office receipts. We don't know of many cabaret performers who make a living at it. But, the performance experience is unlike anything else and these shows can sometimes end up on cruise ships and in concert settings elsewhere. So, the potential for other work does exist.

This is just a sampling of the various performance possibilities that wait for you as you begin and build your career in the musical theatre. No one works in just one of these niches. A career is built out of many different theatrical experiences.

UNIT 17.8   **Finding the auditions**

There are a number of very useful groups that exist solely for the purpose of providing organized audition opportunities for young actors to be seen by literally hundreds of summer and year-round theatres. Chief among these are South Eastern Theatre Conference (SETC), New England Theatre Conference (NETC) and Unified Professional Theatre Auditions (UPTA). There are also the Straw Hat Auditions (usually held in New York). Many of these auditions are set up to coincide with as many college Spring Break schedules as possible. You will need to visit their websites to get registration information. These conferences are hugely popular and often require that you register months in advance. There is typically a non-refundable registration fee, as well. In most cases, you will need to provide a photograph of yourself, a resume (often on their application form, and sometimes you must send a whole stack of headshots and resumes), and one or two academic references.

Make no mistake, these auditions are the mother of all cattle calls. There will be hundreds of people being seen along with you. The time limits on your two selections are very specific and you will be cut off if you go one second over the posted limit. Know this in advance and cut your material to the appropriate length with a little time to spare. Practicing this kind of audition is important and could lead to your getting many callbacks. After you present your audition you will wait until the end of the day, when theatres from all over the region post callback lists. You will then go from room to room seeing potential employers, possibly doing callbacks and working to get the best summer employment possible.

Assessing the job

So you get some offers. Which should you take? Is this a good job? If you have a business plan, you can keep uppermost in mind whether this job will improve your connections, help you meet the next tier of producers, bring you to the attention of an important director or choreographer and in general take you to the next level. In addition to all that, there are some immediate practicalities you should watch for.

Take a folder or notebook with you and make notes about each of the theatres you talk to. Most places have flyers or brochures with their season dates and some basic information available to you. If you are eventually offered a job, you'll want to find out more than just what the salary is, though that's important. Be sure you find out the following:

- What is the weekly salary? Some theatres pay a lump sum for your services. Find out when you get that. Your best option is to be paid along the way.
- How often are you paid? Weekly? Bi-weekly? Monthly?
- Can you cash your paycheck nearby?

- What kind of housing will you be provided? (Private room, semi-private, shared bath, etc.)
- Is there any charge for housing? This is sometimes negotiable.
- Is there a kitchen and refrigerator available to you? (This can save you hundreds of dollars.) If not, can you bring a microwave with you?
- Does the theatre provide transportation to and from the theatre from your point of hiring?
- Is there a transportation stipend provided? You may be able to ask for the cash equivalent of their travel costs and apply it to gasoline for your own car.
- Do you need your own car to get around? Does the theatre provide a car or transportation for grocery store and laundry trips?
- What roles will you be playing? (Be sure you find out in advance.)
- Will you have any extra duties? (Scenery crew, bartending, waiting tables, children's theatre, cabarets, striking the set.)
- What are the rehearsal hours, typically?
- How many performances of each show will you do?
- Do you need to provide your own shoes, hairpieces or other costume elements? If you do, is there any reimbursement for use and cleaning?

None of these questions is unreasonable and any theatre that's been around for more than one season will have answered them all many times. So, don't worry about seeming too pushy. These should all be spelled out in your contract. Yes, there's that word. You must get a written contract from any employer that addresses these questions. Never go to a theatre without a contract that both you and the theatre owner have signed. (And never go on tour without a round-trip ticket.) There is no reason a producer can't provide you with a legal contract. If they resist, then you need to politely refuse the job.

UNIT 17.10 ## More than musicals

A full career as an actor will involve auditioning for and working in every aspect of the profession. You'll be looking for work in everything from straight plays to films, sitcoms, daytime drama, commercials, print and voiceovers. You should be prepared to audition for everything from Shakespeare to pouring blue liquid on a paper towel.

Training for musical theatre is an excellent preparation for much of this work. However, because you may have been concentrating on hitting that high C, you may not have had the time for classes on Restoration movement styles and may not have a voiceover demo. While it is beyond the scope of this book to offer detailed information about these other fields, it will be up to you to make sure you attend to all the dimensions of a full career as an actor. In many ways, you have an advantage over non-musical actors because there are more opportunities for you. It will be up to you to make sure you exploit those opportunities to their fullest.

Unions

Actors' Equity Association (AEA) is the primary union for actors performing in live theatre. You may also find yourself working under the aegis of The American Guild of Variety Artists (AGVA), The American Guild of Musical Artists (AGMA), The American Federation of Television and Radio Artists (AFTRA) and The Screen Actors Guild (SAG). These unions all establish safe working conditions and minimum salaries for the type of work being performed, supervise and franchise agents, and provide health and retirement benefits. If you are a professional actor, your career will certainly involve being a member of one or more of these unions at some point.

Union membership comes with some responsibilities. By joining, you agree to forego any non-union work. Because of this, you will want to think carefully about when it is best for you to join. AEA has a membership candidacy program that lets you work in union productions as you gather experience without having to join at the outset. This apprenticeship approach is useful to both young performers and producers. The producer can pay a much smaller salary and the performer gets experience working next to full-fledged professionals. In time, you will either gather enough points as a membership candidate to merit full membership, or a producer will offer you a full union contract. At that time you will join the union. You will have the right to attend union auditions and will be competing with experienced, professional actors.

Actors who are just starting their careers are occasionally cautioned against joining the union too soon. The reasoning here is that one should only focus exclusively in the union arena when you are confident you can compete with seasoned professionals. You must ask yourself if you're ready to compete against those performers you see onstage in the Equity national tours that may come through your town. Until you are, it's best to build your skills and experience toward that goal. Usually it is best to get out there, audition for everything, work hard and let the union card come to you in its own time. When a producer is ready to offer you a union contract, then you are probably ready to make that step.

Remember that union membership is a one-way street. Once you join, you cannot simply choose to work in non-union theatres if the going gets tough.

In the meantime, visit the websites for all these unions. Learn their regulations, and their membership programs. Start saving money for your initiation fees. Recognize that your future lies with these unions and that the more you know about how they work, the easier it will be for you to use the unions to your best advantage.

UNIT 17.12 ## Agents and personal managers

First, some definitions: an "agent" is an artist's representative. This person works for you and is empowered to negotiate contracts on your behalf. A reputable agent is one who is franchised by one or more of the actors' unions, agrees to abide by their regulations and earns a living exclusively by taking a commission from your earnings. That commission is regulated by their union agreement. Do not ever sign with an agent who isn't franchised by one of the actors' unions.

"Casting agents" work for the producer and help find actors to fill roles. They do exactly what a real estate agent does: learn what properties are for sale and try to fit the buyer to the property. They try to save the director time by not showing him beachfront property when he's looking for a townhouse. Many directors and artistic directors do their own casting, but increasingly the trend is to hire a casting agent to solicit submissions from agents, cull the most likely actors and collaborate throughout the casting process. As you can see, it is essential that you know these people and equally important for them to know who you are and the specifics of your type and talents. That's the primary goal of most showcases. Many actors have found it enormously beneficial to intern with casting agents and to volunteer as a reader for auditions. These experiences can offer you priceless insights into the casting process.

A "personal manager" is an individual hired by you to help develop your career. This profession is completely unregulated and unaffiliated with any union. As a result, although there are many reputable managers, the field is rife with unethical and unscrupulous charlatans. In the past, the best advice was to only take on a manager when your career became so busy that it was no longer manageable. That seems to be changing. Increasingly, managers are former agents who use their industry contacts to help new performers connect with agents, casting people, directors and others. They look for talents who are unknown but show a rich potential for future earnings and invest a lot of time and energy in developing their careers. This may be a good way to jump-start a career, but it isn't without troublesome aspects. Managers can charge whatever they can persuade you to pay – sometimes monthly fees and/or high-percentage commissions. They can pin you down to long-term contracts with no escape clauses. They can demand that you see their photographer or take a particular acting class (with the possibility that they'll be receiving kickbacks). The potential for coercion and thievery is quite high. You will still need a union franchised agent to negotiate any contracts (and remember that a franchised agent is forbidden to require you to see their photographer, can't sell you classes, and is strictly limited in the commissions they can charge). You could easily end up paying a 25 percent commission to your manager and another 10 percent to an agent. That's a lot to give up right off the top of your paycheck. Still, this may be one of the directions the business is taking, especially in representation for film and television. Just be careful. Before signing with anyone, do everything you can to check out that person's reputation and have a lawyer go over the contract with you.

Do you need an agent at all? For film, television and other media performance opportunities, the answer is yes. Those auditions aren't posted except through agents, so you'll never even hear about the jobs unless you have one. For live theatre, it is a bit less absolute. Many agents have good relationships with casting directors and can get you in on a call where you might otherwise be overlooked. Because of the economics of the live theatre, actors are usually paid the Equity minimum, so it is only in the advanced stages of your career that an agent is in a position to negotiate your salary. Some theatres only cast through open calls and never go through agents. Probably the best relationship to have with an agent for live theatre is one that is flexible: they help you when they can, but stay out of the way and don't charge you a commission when they haven't earned one. The most reputable and professional agencies adopt just this approach.

Personal networking and contacts

Every job you get will get you your next couple of jobs – provided that you are great to work with, completely professional and excellent in the role, contribute to the overall success of the production, and stay in touch after it is all over. It is the staying in touch part that is key.

You never know who will be the next person to help you, and the theatrical world is very small. There are rarely more than two degrees of separation between you and anyone else. So, you'll need to be unfailingly polite and professional – to everyone. That creepy guy lurking in the back of the box office might be the producer by next summer. That annoyingly whiny ingénue could be standing in rehearsal for a Broadway show when her partner (who reminds her of you) turns an ankle. It might be nice if all these folks remembered you fondly and had your contact information in their PDAs.

Professional salespeople know that networking and contacts are the life-blood of their careers. This is true for actors, too. Start developing great contact management habits today.

EXERCISE 17J   MANAGING YOUR CONTACTS

Look for a contact management system that works for you, is easy to use and is adaptable. We suggest one that is synchronized with your computer database, phone and/or PDA, but if you prefer to use a paper version, that's up to you.

1. Think of all the ways you might need to access someone and set up fields to enter that information. Be sure to include all the standard address and contact information as well as personal information like birthdays, anniversaries, and their kids' and spouse's names, information on how you know them, and the last time you spoke to or contacted them.
2. Start making entries. Look around you. If you are in school, start with the faculty and fellow students. Look back through the programs of every show you have ever done and put in everyone from the stage right flyman to the stars. Put in even incomplete information – just get in all the data you can. Yes, you can include your family and non-business related friends.
3. Get in the habit of updating your contacts on a regular basis. Salespeople do it a couple of times a day. Wherever you go, ask for business cards and file that information. Whenever you audition, make a note of as many people you contacted as possible – not just the director, but the stage manager and the reader, too.
4. Make up postcards with your headshot. Send a mailing of these whenever you can think up an excuse: you're about to open in a show, you have a commercial running, you're just back in town from a tour, thank you for the audition, thank you for the great master class, happy birthday, happy spring . . . Make sure your postcard includes your complete up-to-date contact information and the contacts for your

agents, too. If you put "address service requested" on the return address (yes, you'll pay for this service) the post office will let you know if any of your addresses are not good and if they have an address change. Make it a point to contact everyone at least twice a year, and make it your goal to have the world's best entertainment database!

Advertising tools – your resume, headshot, demo, website

In 1945, actor Conrad Cantzen bequeathed his estate to The Actors' Fund with the stipulation that it should be used to help actors purchase shoes so they did not appear "down at the heels" when auditioning. Mr. Cantzen believed that a good pair of shoes made a great first impression, and back in those days actors wore out a lot of shoes by "making the rounds" – walking to producers' offices looking for auditions. (Yes, any qualifying member of Actors' Equity can still receive $40 annually for a pair of shoes from this fund.)

Today, this seems sweetly quaint. Actors now need more than shoe leather to find work. They need to have a full range of promotional materials. They send out emails directing people to their websites where one can flip through their modeling portfolio, listen to their voiceover demo and see video clips of their film work. They give out business cards, headshots, resumes, voiceover demos, demo film reels on DVDs, headshot postcards, print tearsheets, comp and zed cards (folded postcards with several photos on them), etc. None of that is wasted energy. Get a pile of those and hand them out like candy. Yes, a lot of it will get tossed or forgotten, but some seeds are sure to fall on fertile soil.

Theatrical resumes

Every professional, regardless of his field, needs a resume that clearly and concisely advertises the skills and experience he has to offer. Professional theatre is no different. Unlike engineers, teachers, lawyers or other so-called professionals, the theatrical resume must be no longer than one page and must be readable in just a few moments. Those other resumes generally receive more time and deliberate attention. But the theatrical resume is intended to be read quickly while the actor is preparing to audition. Anything more elaborate than that is inappropriate for your purposes.

We will outline some of the basic guidelines for constructing your own theatrical resume in a way that reflects a serious young professional.

UNIT 17.15.1 *Functions*

Along with your headshot, the theatrical resume is your professional calling card. It serves a number of important functions.

- It offers contact information for you if/when a job comes up.
- It provides a clear and concise list of representative roles from your career.
- It gives potential employers a sense of what kinds of material you've done in the past and are likely to be doing for them.
- It can convey the range of skills that you've mastered.
- It tells the employer what kind of professional image you wish to project.

UNIT 17.15.2 *Formatting*

While there is a good deal of individuality allowed in a theatrical resume, it is also a fairly standardized document with a set of unwritten rules and conventions that are best to follow. Remember that your goal is to make the important information clear and easy to find. Here are some guidelines:

- Name at the top in clear, large print. Your name must be easily readable at a glance. Too small or too frilly and they won't even know who you are.
- Contact information at the top (either right or left), clearly separated from other information.
- Vital statistics (as you choose to give them) on the other side of the page – height, hair color, eye color, weight (if you choose), vocal range (top and bottom notes that you can reliably hit in the morning after a late night waiting tables).
- Roles that you've played are organized by larger category (usually type of theatre work or entertainment work). For instance, you might choose the following categories: University Theatre, Summer Stock, Community Theatre, Festivals and Fairs, Dinner Theatre, Regional Theatre, New York Theatre, Broadway and National Tours, Circus and Arena, Concert or any other areas that you've worked in. The purpose of this organization is so your experience can be easily available to the reader. If you have an extensive secondary career in commercials, voiceovers, industrial spokesperson work,

etc. be sure to note that a separate resume of this work is available. That is enough to pique the curiosity of anyone who might need that information.

- Your credits should be listed with the information for each production in three columns: the play, the role you played, the theatre where you performed. You may also include the name of a star associated with the production or a well-known director, choreographer or music director. Just be careful not to clutter up the page so the information is hard to access.

- Training and education, and special skills, go at the bottom of the resume. List only teachers that you've really studied with for long enough to have made an impact on your skills. One class with Patti LuPone is not enough to list her as a major teacher. But a summer workshop or ongoing lessons with someone of note absolutely entitles you to include them. If you know that these people will remember you, then include it. If you are in a college or conservatory program and expect to graduate at a specific time, you can list that, as well.

- Special skills include juggling, fencing, dialects, gymnastics, playing musical instruments or special musical abilities (sight reading or perfect pitch), odd things that are truly unique (can put entire fist in mouth!), special aspects of your abilities (licensed chauffer, certified child care specialist, trained welder, etc.) Do not lie – you'll be asked to do what you say you can do.

- Some actors leave room at the bottom of the page to highlight current projects. Keep your resume up-to-date and maintain the professional look.

Style

Style is important in creating the resume. But easy readability is the most important feature. Sacrifice the catchy font for easy access to your information at all costs. The information should be clearly organized and available at a glance. The following rules generally apply (though you can always find a way to do something original and still be clearly readable)

- Only two font families per page. A font is the term used for a particular design of typeface. You will usually use one display font for your name and the category headings. A display font is a typeface that is so ornate, bold or elaborate that it's difficult to read large sections of text printed in it. But it is fine for a headline, such as your name. A second font "family" will be used in listing the shows you've done, the roles you've played and where you did them. Most font families include plain (or roman), italic, bold, bold italic, etc. The second font that you use should be simpler and easier to read. Fonts like Times, Garamond, Helvetica, Bodoni and Stone are easy to read and can be used for large chunks of text.

- Avoid overly fancy or hard to read fonts, even for your name.
- In theatrical auditions, the standard size for pictures and resumes has always been 8 inches wide by 10 inches high (an "8 by 10"). And this is still generally true in New York City. But, as West Coast film and TV industry standards permeate the East Coast, the size of resumes and headshots has become more flexible and now includes the standard business page size of 8½ inches by 11 inches. In some cases the picture and resume are even three-hole punched for easy filing in notebooks of casting people. This is much more the exception than the rule in most theatrical auditions. But keep your eye open for changes in this standard. As with everything, theatrical audition standards evolve.
- The resume page must be solidly attached to the back of your picture – direct printing on the photo is the cleanest option.
- The resume should be printed on light-colored paper (white, off-white, very light creams, pale blue, etc.) Avoid brightly colored or dark paper. They are hard to read.
- It should be printed with black, very dark blue or dark brown ink. Avoid multiple colors. This can add to visual confusion.
- Maximize the amount of "white space" on the page. A densely written, edge-to-edge document is overwhelming to the eye. You may think you're going to impress the reader with the breadth of your range and experience. What you're really doing is making them put the page down out of frustration.
- Font sizes of 10–20 points are normal for listing credits. Section headings can be larger.

Here are some examples of various formatting styles for resumes. As you can see, there is room to personalize your layout and still make the information clear and easily accessible.

UNIT 17.15.4   *Keep it current*

As your career changes, you'll need to revise your resume to reflect the actor that you are today. There's nothing worse than seeing a grown young woman presenting a resume with the title role of *Annie* as the lead credit. This advertises one of two things. Either you haven't worked in ten years or you are unaware that you are now a grown up. In both cases, the actress is not well served by keeping it on her resume. Only include roles that you can still believably play.

Resume 1

Actor Name

Svc: (212) 555-5555

Height: 5'6"   Weight: 125 lbs.   Eyes: Brown   Hair: Brown

Professional Theatre

STEEL MAGNOLIAS	Enelle	Red Barn Theatre
BABES IN ARMS	Maggie	Red Barn Theatre
UP AND AWAY	Ensemble	Alphabet Repertory Theatre

University Theatre – Wright State University

STATES OF INDEPENDENCE (WKSHP)	Connie	Directed by Tina Landau Composer: Ricky Ian Gordon
BRIGADOON	Fiona	Festival Theatre
THE SEAGULL	Mdm. Arkadina	Festival Theatre
TOUCH	Annie	Jubilee Theatre
ARTSGALA 2001	Ensemble	Festival Theatre

Community Theatre

JOSEPH...DREAMCOAT	Narrator	Beavercreek Community Theatre
ALL MY SONS	Daughter	Muhlemberg Playhouse

Film, Television, Industrials & Print Work

WORKING GIRLS (STUDENT FILM)	Tanya (Lead)	New Dreams Film Festival
KOHL'S CHRISTMAS SPOT	Principal	Ohio Regional Spot
SNAP-ON-TOOLS	Spokesperson	Trade shows

Training

BFA in Acting with an Emphasis in Musical Theatre
Wright State University, Spring 2003
- Acting: Bruce Cromer, Joe Deer, Mary Donahoe, Greg Hellems
- Singing: Joseph Bates
- Dance: Greg Hellems, Terresa Wylie McWilliams, Joe Deer
- Special Skills: Unicycle, Banjo, Dialects, Fluent in Spanish, Sight Reading

---

Resume 2

Actor Name

Height: 5'6"
Weight: 125 lbs.
Hair: Blue
Eyes: Blue
Soprano: vocal range

Non-Equity	Svc (212) 555-5555	Agent (212) 555-555

Professional Theatre

STEEL MAGNOLIAS	Enelle	Red Barn Theatre
BABES IN ARMS	Maggie	Red Barn Theatre
UP AND AWAY	Ensemble	Alphabet Repertory Theatre

University Theatre – Wright State University

STATES OF INDEPENDENCE (WKSHP)	Connie	Directed by Tina Landau Composer: Ricky Ian Gordon
BRIGADOON	Fiona	Festival Theatre
THE SEAGULL	Mdm. Arkadina	Festival Theatre
TOUCH	Annie	Jubilee Theatre
ARTSGALA 2001	Ensemble	Festival Theatre

University Theatre – Wright State University

JOSEPH...DREAMCOAT	Narrator	Beavercreek Community Theatre
ALL MY SONS	Daughter	Muhlemberg Playhouse

Film, Television, Industrials & Print Work

WORKING GIRLS (STUDENT FILM)	Tanya (lead)	New Dreams Film Festival
KOHL'S CHRISTMAS SPOT	Principal	Ohio Regional Spot
SNAP-ON-TOOLS	Spokesperson	Trade shows

Training

BFA in Acting with an Emphasis in Musical Theatre
Wright State University, Spring 2003
- Acting: Bruce Cromer, Joe Deer, Mary Donahoe, Greg Hellems
- Singing: Joseph Bates
- Dance: Greg Hellems, Terresa Wylie McWilliams, Joe Deer
- Special Skills: Unicycle, Banjo, Dialects, Fluent in Spanish, Sight Reading

---

Resume 3

Actor Name

Svc: (212) 555-1212

Height: 5'6"
Weight: 120 lbs.
Range: —

Professional Theatre

STEEL MAGNOLIAS	Enelle	Red Barn Theatre
BABES IN ARMS	Maggie	Red Barn Theatre
UP AND AWAY	Ensemble	Alphabet Repertory Theatre

University Theatre

STATES OF INDEPENDENCE (WKSHP)	Connie	Directed by Tina Landau Composer: Ricky Ian Gordon
BRIGADOON	Fiona	Festival Theatre
THE SEAGULL	Mdm. Arkadina	Festival Theatre
TOUCH	Annie	Jubilee Theatre
ARTSGALA 2001	Ensemble	Festival Theatre

Community Theatre

JOSEPH...DREAMCOAT	Narrator	Beavercreek Community Theatre
ALL MY SONS	Daughter	Muhlemberg Playhouse

Film, Television and Industrials

WORKING GIRLS (STUDENT FILM)	Tanya (Lead)	New Dreams Film Festival
KOHL'S CHRISTMAS SPOT	Principal	Ohio Regional Spot
SNAP-ON-TOOLS	Spokesperson	Trade shows

Training

BFA in Acting with an Emphasis in Musical Theatre
Wright State University, Spring 2003
- Acting: Bruce Cromer, Joe Deer, Mary Donahoe, Greg Hellems
- Singing: Joseph Bates
- Dance: Greg Hellems, Terresa Wylie McWilliams, Joe Deer
- Special Skills: Unicycle, Banjo, Dialects, Fluent in Spanish, Sight Reading

---

Resume 4

Actor Name

Svc: (212) 555-1212

Height: 5'6"
Weight: 120 lbs.
Vocal Range: —

PROFESSIONAL	STEEL MAGNOLIAS	Enelle	Red Barn Theatre
	BABES IN ARMS	Maggie	Red Barn Theatre
	UP AND AWAY	Ensemble	Alphabet Repertory Theatre
UNIVERSITY	STATES OF INDEPENDENCE (WKSHP)	Connie	Directed by Tina Landau Composer: Ricky Ian Gordon
	BRIGADOON	Fiona	Festival Theatre
	THE SEAGULL	Mdm. Arkadina	Festival Theatre
	TOUCH	Annie	Jubilee Theatre
	ARTSGALA 2001	Ensemble	Festival Theatre
COMMUNITY	JOSEPH...DREAMCOAT	Narrator	Beavercreek Community Theatre
	ALL MY SONS	Daughter	Muhlemberg Playhouse
FILM, TELEVISION AND INDUSTRIAL	WORKING GIRLS (STUDENT FILM)	Tanya (Lead)	New Dreams Film Festival
	KOHL'S CHRISTMAS SPOT	Principal	Ohio Regional Spot
	SNAP-ON-TOOLS	Spokesperson	Trade shows
TRAINING	BFA in Acting with an Emphasis in Musical Theatre Wright State University, Spring 2003 Acting: Bruce Cromer, Joe Deer, Mary Donahoe, Greg Hellems Singing: Joseph Bates Dance: Greg Hellems, Terresa Wylie McWilliams, Joe Deer Special Skills: Unicycle, Banjo, Dialects, Fluent in Spanish, Sight Reading		

EXERCISE 17K   THE BUSINESS PLAN

Current position

Assess where you are now. We all start somewhere. Look at your resume. Evaluate your current level of skill, and professional contacts, knowledge of the market and general experience. Look at each element below and decide where you are in your present level of development.

Market research

- Get the tools to learn the market – trade papers, books, colleagues
- Learn who's who, who's doing what, etc. – study
- Decide where you want to base yourself – plan to enter a specific market
- Study and include plans for a full range of performance activities, not just musical theatre

Product development

- Study the competition

    Who's getting hired and why

- Fit the product to the market

    Define and clarify your type
    Develop and tune your skills

Taking the product to market – selling

- Advertising, headshots, postcards, resumes, website, demos, portfolio
- Allies – agents, managers
- Making and managing contacts
- Auditioning

Doing the job

- Performing well
- Getting rehired and recommended

Financing

- Paying for it all

    Budgeting and planning – know what you're getting into

    List expenses, be sure to include everything from headshots to pointe shoes: phone, clothing, make-up, hair, transportation, classes, food, apartment, utilities, computer equipment – get it all

    Survival job

    Skills
    Organizing the job so that it doesn't interfere with your real goals

Be prepared for change

- What if you are successful? How will this change your plan? Plan for success.
- How will you change over time? Can you see how your type, for example, will evolve over the next five or ten years? What other areas of your plan are likely to shift over time?

Step-by-step

After all this you have a good idea of where you are now. Use this outline to help you plan where you want to be. Develop a step-by-step plan to move yourself forward in each category.

- Develop a set of five-year objectives.
- Back that out to what you want to have achieved in the next year.
- Establish a month-by-month plan for getting to your goals.

Be as realistic and flexible as possible, but don't let yourself off the hook. Don't say that you want a lead on Broadway by Christmas unless you have solid reasons for knowing that is a real possibility. But also don't undersell yourself. And, since this is a fickle business, be adaptable to changing circumstances.

Money jobs

By now, it is probably abundantly clear that you'll need to have other skills besides acting, singing and dancing in order to get by while you build your career. Every actor in a major market has other job skills that they use to make a living in between show business gigs. These can range from waiting tables, temporary help in an office, to catering or cleaning apartments. Many people have other interests and specialized skills that allow them to make good money for short periods of work. Developing skills like legal proofreading, using technical software or medical billing can bring in better than average pay.

Aside from putting money in your pocket, these jobs must function within your real career in a few important ways. First, the job must allow you sufficient time to go to auditions, classes, lessons and interviews. Many employers in major cities are used to actors requesting flexibility to pursue these important professional interests. But there is a limit to any employer's understanding. So, choosing a job where you can get a coworker to fill in for you is important. Second, the work hours can't consistently overlap with normal 9 a.m. to 5 p.m. business hours. This is when auditions, lessons and classes take place. So, taking on a full-time office job or a teaching position might ultimately undermine your primary interest. Many actors have been permanently sidetracked by this kind of, sometimes lucrative, job. Soon, you're a secretary, not an actor. A third pitfall is the job that keeps you up until 4 a.m. every night. No matter how hard you try, you will not be able to make those morning auditions and classes. The occasional late night is reasonable for many restaurant or catering jobs. But taking the graveyard shift every night is going to seriously impact your career.

Our strongest advice is that you get some experience in one or several of these secondary professions before you leave school and head for the big city. These extra skills will hold you in very good stead as you begin your career. One young actor we know moved to New York City with several years of experience during college waiting tables at a high-end restaurant in a small Midwestern town. Because of this background, he immediately found a waiting job at a very nice restaurant in Mid-Town Manhattan, and soon he was making well over $600 a week in tips and salary. When his first big break came, performing the lead in a non-union national tour, he had to take a $250 a week pay cut to live his dream. He did take that tour and it has led to a number of subsequent jobs. But there is a lesson in his experience. First, he prepared himself with a second job skill. Then, he kept his eye on what was best for his acting career when opportunity knocked for him. Remember, you can wait tables, work in an office or clean apartments in far friendlier and cheaper cities than New York, Los Angeles or Chicago.

If you're going to endure the hardships of working and living in those cities, make it count.

So, now you have a good idea of your type and your abilities. You have studied the market and have found several opportunities to audition. You have your promotional material together and you have a way to feed yourself. Now it is time to get out there and get hired. Let's look at how we can make your audition a successful and positive experience.

SECTION VI: THE PROFESSION

CHAPTER 18

AUDITIONING

Audition guidelines

The audition is the most common gatekeeper for getting a job in theatre, film and television. Before you get a chance to do what you've trained for, you must be hired out of a pool of potential applicants. In other professions you fill out an application and go in for a job interview. You might have a second interview with someone else and take a job skills test before you are ultimately hired or not. The process for getting jobs in the theatre is the same, though the application and interview are slightly different. In almost every audition circumstance, you will face competition for the role you want. So, presenting yourself as the best-suited candidate for the role is essential.

Admittedly, auditions are an imperfect method of assessing a person's talent. Based on just a few minutes of contact with a performer, casting people (producers, directors, choreographers, casting directors) make decisions that can affect their production and your life. That brief encounter may not show all there is to know about a person. You've probably experienced auditions where you know you didn't do your best, or where the casting people didn't really understand all you had to offer. You may even have seen productions you'd auditioned for and weren't cast in where the person who ultimately got the job couldn't do what you could. It is an imperfect and highly subjective process built around the gut reactions and personal taste of those who are casting. But it's the best method anyone has come up with for finding unknown talent or for assessing a person's suitability for a role. Your job is to learn how to work comfortably and to show what you really can do in these situations.

Auditioning can be a stressful experience because it involves a great deal of scrutiny. You are being appraised for talent, personality, looks, specific kinds of skills and whatever else a casting person might need. But the experience doesn't have to be torture. In fact, it can be very positive. Preparation and under-standing of the process are essential to steer clear of some potential pitfalls and to make the most of a great opportunity for you.

UNIT 18.2 **A few words of encouragement**

Let us start by saying that you must have talent and competitive skill to get jobs in any theatrical setting; from community theatre to Broadway. It isn't enough to be good looking, be charming at parties or earnestly love the theatre. You have to work at becoming a good actor, singer and dancer. You must also take your health, work habits and attitude seriously. If you have begun doing these things, an audition is an opportunity to show what you have to offer a production.

Training for the musical theatre is often a process where all your deficiencies are constantly mirrored. But auditions are the time to trust what you do know, not to focus on what you *don't*.

An actor we know remembers being given some advice about auditioning early in his career. The well-meaning adult told him, "You just need to convince them you have confidence, then you'll get the job." What he later came to understand is he didn't need to convince anyone he had confidence. He needed to gain true confidence. And the way he discovered to do that was to work hard at developing his skills, get experience auditioning over and over again, prepare for each audition seriously and, finally, set aside doubts about his abilities so he could do his best work. Confidence is acquired in these ways and by allowing yourself to own how much you *can* do, as well as working on the things that you can't yet. The acting, singing or dance studio is the time to focus on improvement. The audition room is the time to trust what you can do today and to work with full confidence in yourself and your abilities. After the whole process is over, then you can decide what to improve for next time.

They're on your side

Although casting people can seem intimidating, rude or bored as they sit on the other side of the table, it will help you to remember that auditions are held because those casting people really do need to find talent. They all want you to be good and do well at your audition. No one holds an audition because they hate actors or want to scorn people for eight hours a day. The truth is, casting people pray for you to do well and offer them something wonderful, because they can't put on their shows without you. If you think you're not getting the attention or respect you deserve at an audition, put yourself in the shoes of a person who's already sat in a studio for seven hours listening to young women belting as high and as loud as possible. It is hard work to sort talent and consider all the casting requirements for a single show or a season of shows while they look at your resume and watch you. Talk about multi-tasking. Generally, if you think you're being treated poorly, you're probably just being sensitive.

Also remember that they have to hire someone. You do have a good chance of being considered for a role in the show you're auditioning for. And even if you don't get this show, you may give them something to remember for another show. There is no such thing as a wasted audition. So, stay positive about the whole experience.

Your best self

When we go to auditions, we are offering ourselves to casting people with the understanding that what we have to offer is good and worth hiring. You are presenting yourself – you – but not merely you on an average day. You are presenting the best possible you, regardless of the harsh realities of your life, work, romance, etc. We all have bad days where our car won't start, the weather is uncooperative, the dog eats our homework, or we have a fight with our parents or boyfriend. But even on those bad days we still need to audition well if we want to get cast. So, learning to avoid those problems in the first place and shake them off when they do happen is an important set of life skills to develop. Learning to laugh at the little things and set the bigger problems aside will enable you to audition from a place of control rather than powerlessness.

Appearance

How you dress and present yourself is the packaging for the product you sell: you. It often says as much about you as what you present in your audition. The packaging that you select to represent you can change from audition to audition, just as your costume changes from role to role, because you are capable of presenting many facets of yourself. If you don't know what the casting people are looking for, consider selecting the clothing for yourself that most flatters you and presents you in your best light, featuring your best attributes. It would be hard to overstate how important the visual appearance you make is. Consider the following questions:

What features do I like best about myself? Eyes, face, figure, legs, general physique. Select clothing, make-up and hairstyling that emphasize your best features. Purchasing clothing that is especially selected and saved for auditioning is important. That well-tailored suit or dress might be the perfect Christmas present. And it will serve you to keep it in good shape, clean and pressed.

Does my hair and makeup represent me well for the roles I'm auditioning for or that I'm most right for? If you look like a young leading man, boy-next-door type, are you serving yourself by wearing a nose ring, uncombed and untrimmed hair and a "Screw Authority" t-shirt? That is an extreme example. But in more subtle ways, you can convey the same message. Theatre producers and theatre audiences are generally more conservative than theatre artists. Yet, they are the people you must convince to hire you. So, striking the balance between rebellion and conformity is essential. Auditions are not the place to change society. Do that after you get the job through your passionate performances.

What is my "type"? We went over this question earlier. Here is where it all matters. If you have done your homework, you know what roles to go up for, how to dress and present yourself in order to look perfect for the part, and what material will best place you in line for the role.

You may have several possible niches. But you must identify and develop each type with your selection of audition material, clothing and persona in the audition circumstance. The role you play at the audition when you're not doing your material is the "you" that you select to represent. It *is* you. But, it is the best you possible – full of clarity, attention, positive energy and genuine connection to the auditors.

Audition material

The material you select is the second, immensely powerful tool you use to represent yourself. It tells the casting people about your taste, your personality, your image of yourself, and your understanding of what you are right for and which roles being cast best suit you. It behooves you, even if you only have two pieces in your repertoire, to choose songs that express something appropriate for your type and show two distinct qualities of your infinitely varied personality. Two songs that express longing and loneliness become depressing next to each other and tell the viewer you are glum by nature. Whereas one song of loneliness partnered with a song of joy show two opposite sides of you. This is a better choice.

Avoid overdone material or those songs associated with a famous performer or performance. *'Defying Gravity'* is Idina Menzel's song. Unless you redefine the song through technical or emotional means (or you intend to evoke her memory) you should avoid it. You'll be better served by finding a different, less known or less strongly identified song.

You must also select material that is appropriate to you. *'September Song'* by Kurt Weill is about an old man reflecting on his lost youth. It would be silly for a high school student, at the age of 17, to choose it. If you are strikingly handsome or beautiful and sing *'Nobody Makes a Pass at Me'*, you will seem oddly modest or simply unaware (though you might be able to do something very witty with that).

You can reframe a song that normally wouldn't suit you by placing it in a surprisingly comic or ironic context. This takes skill and polish as a performer. But it can be a way to show something unique about you and earn you a callback if done extremely well. This is a dicey call. The line between daring wit and bad taste might be hard to identify. While one person may think singing *'Thank Heaven for Little Girls'* as a dirty old man in the park is hysterical, another person may find it distasteful. Get some outside opinions before making a risky choice in an important audition.

The best choices of material are those that matter to you. Songs that speak to your soul, affect you strongly, and evoke a strong emotional response in you when you hear them or sing them are always the best choices. Just be sure to pick varied material and that you are not so caught up in the song that you become internalized. The audition/performance must affect the audience first – you come second in order of importance.

Passionate moments are the best selections. Whether you are in a fit of rage, of joy, of despair or of confusion, you will be at your most active. The brief time the casting people get to spend with you should not be wasted on mundane, pedestrian experiences. Go for the emotional gold. The mild stuff can be explored at callbacks or in rehearsal. No audition is long enough to waste on average experiences. We want to see people who are capable of grabbing our attention and commanding it. A word of caution, though. Being deeply engaged doesn't mean simply screaming, raging, jumping from chairs, etc. It has much more to do with your deep personal connection to what you're singing about. Caring whether you achieve your objective will result in an engaged performance.

UNIT 18.7

Audition portfolio of songs

As you scan the professional newspapers, websites and theatre listings for possible auditions, you'll discover an amazing array of potential jobs, each one requiring different styles of singing and acting. For each audition, you'll need songs that are just right for that particular show or theatre, sometimes with very little advance notice. But having to locate, learn and fully prepare a new song for every audition can be exhausting, expensive and an ineffective way of getting work. A far better answer is to have a portfolio of good audition songs already prepared in a wide range of styles and genres. So, as each audition comes up, you simply select from your menu of options, refresh yourself and make the minor adjustments necessary to present yourself in a polished and prepared manner. All the songs in your portfolio, regardless of style or genre, should be age and type appropriate for you. Here is a list of slightly more than twenty song types that a musical actor should have, at a minimum, to be prepared for the most common audition circumstances.

EXERCISE 18A   YOUR AUDITION SONG PORTFOLIO

Study each of the musical style divisions below. Make a checklist of those where you have a solid set of audition songs in full-length, 16 and 32 bar versions, in keys that suit your voice and for roles that are right for you. Make a plan to fill in the gaps in your portfolio.

- *Operatic aria or classical art song*. Have at least one piece of classical literature in your portfolio for those few occasions when you'll need to demonstrate some legitimate technique and a basic understanding of that repertoire. You must have perfect pronunciation and know what the lyric means in English. This can include popular arias, Neapolitan folk songs or any part of the classical repertoire you can sing with mastery.

- *Viennese operetta song* (in English). Shows like *The Merry Widow*, *The Desert Song*, *The Student Prince* and others from this genre are still produced frequently and no other musical style will demonstrate the blend of legit vocal technique and earnest acting approach that this repertoire does.

- *Gilbert and Sullivan song*. Different from the Viennese operetta, G&S operettas require diction and a sense of humor. For women, a song that sits in your vocal range and color. For men, a patter song *and* a ballad are appropriate. For both operetta styles, showing your best vocal technique is useful.

- *Early musical comedy/Tin Pan Alley song*. These simple early twentieth-century songs show an ability to simply put over a straightforward catchy tune. Songs like, 'Under the Bamboo Tree', 'Meet Me in St. Louis', anything by George M. Cohan or songs that became popular in the vaudeville era are appropriate here.

- *Optional: novelty comedy song from early twentieth century*. Vaudeville produced a seemingly endless array of silly comic songs that can fill a useful niche in your portfolio. A little research in the archives of many music libraries can yield unknown gems that might get the attention of auditors and provide the perfect piece to show your comic timing and personality. This is a must for character men and women.

- *Musical comedy ballad and up-tempo*: Early Irving Berlin, George Gershwin, Rodgers and Hart or early Cole Porter (a range of these selections are recommended). Still among the most popular in the repertoire, shows like *Anything Goes*, *The Boys from Syracuse*, *Girl Crazy* (and *Crazy for You*) require a specific repertoire and stylistic approach. The wit and sexiness of these lyrics and the pleasure of the melodies make both a ballad and an up-tempo from this period essential in your portfolio. Try to choose two songs by different composers to add variety to your selections. Having more than just two in this category is ultimately a good idea.

- *Golden Age ballad and up-tempo*: Rodgers and Hammerstein, Lerner and Loewe, Frank Loesser, late Cole Porter, late Irving Berlin. Different from the earlier period, these musical dramas that began with *Oklahoma!* and continue all the way through *Camelot* and even after are a world of their own. This repertoire is probably the most produced in the entire canon of musicals. Having a good understanding of the styles and popular repertoire from the period is essential if you want to work. There is hardly a summer stock season that doesn't include one show from this period.

- *Top 40 tunes*: Musical theatre is increasingly a world of "juke box" reviews featuring the top hits from a number of eras. So, having at least one song from each of these periods, and knowing how to sing it in the style it was written in, is a fundamental audition skill. We have listed shows that would require these songs after the category heading.

  1940s/World War II era: *Swingin' on a Star, My Way, Over Here*

  1950s pre-rock era: *Forever Plaid, The Taffetas*

  Early rock and roll: *Grease, Leader of the Pack, Hairspray*

  1960s/70s pop rock (Joni Mitchell, Carol King, Simon and Garfunkel, Billy Joel, Stevie Wonder, ABBA, etc.): *Mamma Mia, The Full Monty*

  Country western song: Can be from a wide range of periods. Just sing it faithfully, not as an unintentional lampoon of the song or genre. *Big River.*

If you sing particularly well in one of these styles, build up your repertoire in that area. You may have a valuable career niche as a crooner, folk singer or rockabilly.

- *Sondheim song*: Have at least one song by our greatest living composer. His work often demonstrates intelligence, maturity and musical dexterity in ways that most other composers' work will not. But the important stipulation here is that the song must be playable by an accompanist who hasn't rehearsed the piece. So, *'Another Hundred People'* from *Company* would be a bad choice. The simpler *'Joanna'*, from *Sweeney Todd*, is a good one, because the accompaniment is less complex.

- *Rock musical selection*: Shows like *Jesus Christ Superstar, Pippin, Godspell, Hair and Dreamgirls* require the singer to know how to blend pop singing styles from the 1960s and 70s with acting skills. This is one of the most useful areas of your portfolio. Develop it.

- *1960s show tunes* (ballad and up-tempo): Kander and Ebb, Cy Coleman, Jule Styne, Jerry Herman, etc. produced a rich and popular repertoire that many people call "show tunes." Shows like *Hello, Dolly!, Mame, Chicago, Cabaret, Gypsy* and the like are popular and require musical skills and styling unlike any other shows.

- *Contemporary musical theatre selection* (ballad and up-tempo): Frank Wildhorn, Jason Robert Brown and Michael John LaChiusa. Increasingly, the musical theatre is embracing a newer generation of composers who write using the popular musical styles of the last twenty-five years as the basis for their work. Knowing this repertoire will become more and more important as the next decade proceeds.

- *Disney or film tunes*: Menken and Ashman, Stephen Schwartz, Sherman Brothers, etc. If you do any revues, theme park shows, cruise ships or family-oriented entertainment, you will sing these songs. They are often catchy and are particularly well suited to young voices. Broadway has already become at least part theme park. Make sure you're prepared for this very important niche in the market.

- *Contemporary art songs*: Ricky Ian Gordon, Adam Guettel, John Bucchino and others write in a musical style that is something of a hybrid between contemporary opera and musical theatre. Their songs often fall into the category of art song, rather than show tune. The musical and acting requirements of these songs differ from other contemporary and more mainstream repertoire. These pieces should be used only when appropriate, but they are excellent acting and singing showpieces.

And last, but not least,

- *The "money" cutting*: Regardless of style or period, this short cutting shows off your voice, personality and various strengths ideally. It is the song you can always count on and know you feel great singing it. It is the callback getter that you'll probably sing more often than any other piece in your portfolio. You should be able to do a 32, 16 or 8 bar cutting of this song.

There are certainly many smaller categories of song that you could include in your repertoire. And you'll discover that you lean more naturally toward one or several of these song styles. But having this array of choices will prepare you for most eventualities. You will need to stay current with your changing type and review this repertoire regularly to stay on top of it.

UNIT 18.8   ## Preparation of sheet music

Every musical audition you do is a duet. While you may be the person who is trying out for the role, you are singing with an accompanist. So, optimizing that relationship is vital to your success in the audition. Your accompanist may or may not know the song you're singing. But they almost certainly don't know how you like to sing it, the tempo you're choosing or the length and specifics of your cutting for that particular song. So, before you begin singing, you must prepare your sheet music to communicate all of these things to the person at the keyboard.

Cuttings. Every selection of music that you have in your portfolio should be usable in three configurations: full song, 32 bar cutting, 16 bar cutting. Many large commercial auditions even require simply an 8 bar cutting. Each of these cuttings should be marked so that an unfamiliar accompanist could follow the music easily. Each cutting must have an easy introduction which leads you into the cutting easily. There should be a definite finish to each piece (don't leave us hanging mid-phrase with one bar to go just because you are at the end of 16 bars; you can sing the last bar). Most songs are written to allow for this kind of cutting. (It is true that many contemporary pieces don't fall exactly into these divisions. In those cases, make short cuttings that are as close as possible to the requested allotment.)

Music preparation. Your music should be photocopied or mounted onto card stock, a heavy paper that does not fold or bend easily. This is available at all office supply stores and print shops. That music should be taped on the back side with cloth tape or book binding tape. Scotch tape or masking tape is not substantial enough. Duct tape often gets too gummy and can cause music pages to stick to each other. The music should be able to fold accordion-style so that it can spread out easily on the music stand on the piano or be book folded for easy page turning.

Transposition, markings and internal cuts. It is never acceptable to ask an accompanist to make a transposition on the spot. If you need your music in another key, pay someone to transpose it and copy it clearly. If you are making internal cuts in a song, they should be photocopied, cut and pasted, then re-photocopied so that the unsung portion is deleted. Tell your accompanist that you've made the cut, in case they know the song without the cut. Alternately, if you are making a very short excision, you can simply cross through those bars so that the cut is very obvious. Any markings you make on your music should be clear and simple. Avoid written notes of explanation, zigzagging arrows or rewritten notes over existing ones. This will all conspire to give you a bad experience. You can include dynamic markings as needed, but be sure that these markings are in standard musical terminology and that you can explain them simply when you present your music. If you plan to take pauses, fermatas or rush ahead, you must tell the accompanist where it will happen. The less of this you do, the better, in auditions where you'll be working with an unfamiliar accompanist.

The Golden Rule of music preparation is that an accompanist should know everything they need to know about your audition piece except the tempo without any explanation from you.

Anatomy of the audition

Every audition has a distinct sequence of events. Understanding each and being prepared for them will give you confidence and minimize the fear that all of us feel at auditions. Typically, a private audition involves your presenting two contrasting selections. What follows is a blow-by-blow outline of that kind of audition. Even if this isn't the exact format of the audition you'll be going to, it still offers you a number of important reminders that will apply to almost every audition you go to.

Arrival. Getting to an audition 10 to 20 minutes early is essential. If you need to change your clothes (and know that you have facilities to do so) you must arrive earlier. Give yourself enough time to shake off the outside world and get acquainted with your surroundings. If it is a dance audition, there may be room for you to warm up physically. But this is not always true. If it is for a play or if you know you'll be doing a cold reading, you may be able to see copy for the sides being read or find out some important information that will help you adjust your audition material. The circumstances may have changed since you last had information – shorter or longer cuttings, different requirements, etc. While these changes are hard to anticipate, having a little extra time will allow you to adjust without being thrown off your game. Note that for some Chorus Calls in New York City, you may need to arrive several hours early to get your name on a list. Many performers show up early in the morning for that, then return home to dress and prepare for the audition appointment.

Entrance. Your entrance into the audition space is your first encounter with the casting people and their first look at you. First impressions carry huge weight. Let yourself become your best self before you enter. No complaining in the lobby, no negativity, no self-defeating comments. Stay positive and help set a good tone outside the room that you can bring in with you. An energetic, positive entrance is always best. A simple greeting before you go to the accompanist is a good way to make first contact with the auditors. Easy eye contact with those behind the table is important. At this point, you may need to give your resume to the auditors behind the table if it wasn't collected for them earlier. Again, an easy connection to those people as you do this with a simple "hello" is sufficient. Then, go to your accompanist.

Connection with the accompanist. You are dependent on the accompanist to help you. Greet her politely, succinctly convey the information needed about the cutting, a simple short phrase softly sung to convey tempo, then you're done. Practice saying what you need to tell the accompanist in advance. It should take a matter of 10–15 seconds, at most, to say what you need.

Your introduction. The cross from the piano to the performance place in the center of the room is your entrance onto the stage. You are playing the role of yourself. Arrive first, *then* speak – not on the way to the spot, but once you've gotten there. A simple self-introduction such as, "Hi, I'm . . . and I'll be singing . . . and . . ." will do. You don't need to tell the author of the piece or what show it's from. If they're curious, they'll ask and you'll have a chance to converse. Otherwise, keep it simple.

Brief preparation. You have no more than a few seconds to get into the mood and relationship for your first piece. This state should be very available to you through practice so that it happens almost immediately. You can do this without turning your back, staring at the floor, shaking away nerves, etc. Just let yourself step into the first moment of your one-act play.

Signal the accompanist. In the mood of the song and in character, simply nod to the accompanist to signal her to begin playing. Don't fall out of character or be overly solicitous. Accompanists are used to this procedure and are there to serve you.

The first piece. As soon as you look up to your imaginary partner or point of focus, you are engaged in the passionate pursuit of your objective. You remain so throughout the performance. When it is finished you complete the one-act play of the song. Your performance ends simultaneously with the music, not before or after the accompanist is done playing.

Transition and second piece. You have another brief moment to change moods. Then you repeat the signal to the accompanist and the performance of the second piece. Be sure that the pianist is settled before you signal her or you may be inviting a rocky start to the song.

Wrapping up. As you finish the last piece, stay intent all the way through the last note of the ride-out, then return to the positive persona that you entered with and thank the auditors. "Thank you very much" or "Have a good day." Don't be cute or charming – just yourself with positive energy. In some audition circumstances it's appropriate to repeat your name, as well.

Exit. If the casting people want to stop you and ask questions they will do so. Don't expect it or put them on the spot. Simply turn, get your music and anything else you brought in with you and leave with confidence.

In the wings. Nothing is more telling of an amateur or volatile actor than a shriek of self-disgust from the hallway or wings after the performer is out of sight. Even doing so quietly in the hallway is inappropriate. You don't know which stage manager, assistant or producer is in the wings or lobby when you leave the audition room. You must maintain professional decorum until you are out of the building, then you can cry, jump for joy, etc.

Audition "don'ts"

UNIT 18.10

Here are a few nearly absolute rules of auditioning:

- Props are almost always a no-no. They inevitably appear as a gimmick and distract from your performance. Unless you're auditioning for *Avenue Q* and need to demonstrate your skill as a puppeteer, stay away from props. (But bring juggling balls with you if you say you can do that.)
- Changing into specialized costume pieces is almost always unacceptable. You may remove a jacket or loosen your tie, but that's about it.
- Chairs should only be used if absolutely needed. You are seeking to command the space. If you have strong reasons of character, you may use a chair. But realize that you're potentially deflating your performance.
- Don't sit on the floor.
- Don't look directly at the people behind the table as you sing. They are not your acting partners and they need to be free to watch you, take notes, read your resume, etc. Pick a spot over their heads or off to one side slightly. This is standard.
- Don't act to a chair. They'll hire the chair and let you go.

- Don't attack or harass the auditors with your material. Anti-producer songs and monologues may seem cute to you and your friends. But they will never get you a job. In general, avoid material that is itself about auditioning. It is often insulting to the auditors, is based on how unfair and brutal the process is, and is guaranteed to drive everyone nuts no matter how accurate, insightful or funny it is. It is too close to home.

- Don't threaten those you're auditioning for. Grabbing someone's shirt or charging the table with a chair will only demonstrate that you're emotionally unstable.

- Profanity is almost never a good idea. Accept this and move on.

- Don't flirt with the auditors. This will probably not get you a job, but it might get you unwelcome phone calls.

- Unless you are an opera singer or the casting notice specifically asks for legit selections, stick to material in English and from popular music and musical theatre repertoire. In every case, you must act the song and know what all the words mean. Studying classical material and classical technique can be enormously useful to your development as an artist. Those songs are just not usually appropriate for a musical theatre audition unless the audition notice asks for it.

- Avoid songs that are difficult to play. If a song has numerous modulations in it, is written in a difficult key to read or play, or can't be played easily without practice, find another song or bring your own accompanist.

- Don't disobey the instructions. If they ask for a one-minute monologue and 8 bars of an up-tempo song, then give them exactly that. Actors are famous for thinking that the rules don't apply to them. They do. Break the rules and annoy everyone. Remember that one of the questions auditors are asking is whether they want to spend an intense rehearsal time with you. If they think you won't be easy or fun to work with or will disrupt the ensemble, they will pass on you. Most directors develop a radar for troublesome actors. Don't offer clues that you are anything less than a delight to work with.

UNIT 18.11   **Nerves**

One of the most common challenges of auditioning is getting nervous; some-times very nervous. This is natural because, as we've said over and over, you are being scrutinized on how you look, how you sound, what kind of personality you have, how charming and talented you are, and so forth. So why wouldn't you be nervous? An important audition can feel like a first date with the girl of your dreams *times ten*. But that doesn't mean that we have to be ruled by our nervousness and let it get in our way or ruin the audition. After a few experiences at auditioning you will probably discover what happens to you as a result of your nerves. It's different with everyone. Some people can't get a full, deep breath, while others may get jittery legs or a nervous twitch in their face. Some people sweat profusely while others get chills. These are all physical manifestations of your nerves.

It's interesting to note that the people who get uncontrollably nervous at auditions rarely have the same reaction when in performance. Instead they are calm, in control and very free onstage. But why is there such a difference? In both cases, you're performing material that you've rehearsed for an audience. You're probably doing material that you care about and are the right type for. You're singing in the perfect key and know the song backwards and forwards. Those are all the similarities. But the major difference is that you are acutely aware that you're being judged at the audition and you want to be liked enough to get a callback. So, all you can think about is whether you sound good, look sexy, have a pimple, seem too tall or short, are too fat or skinny or . . . you get the idea. You are essentially looking at yourself in a mirror the whole time. No wonder you're worried and self-conscious. And you probably already know most of what we've just said and still can't avoid the nerves. But there is a way out.

For our purposes, the most wonderful feature of the human mind is that you can't think of two things at the same time. You can only think of one thing at a time. You may be able to alternate between two different concerns, but can't think about them simultaneously. Try it and see. Think of the most perfectly faceted pear-shaped diamond in the world, resting on midnight blue velvet with a crisp, bright spotlight shining on it. Now try to think of your grocery list for dinner tonight. Get every ingredient for your favorite recipe clearly in your mind in alphabetical order. Now, try to think of both of them at the same time. No matter how hard you try, you'll concentrate on either the diamond or the chili con carne, but not both. This little parlor game can be your salvation at an audition because every time you try to think about how you sound or how ugly you are, you can switch your focus to what's really important. In this case, that will always be the essentials of good acting. So, asking yourself, "Who am I talking to and what is my critical relationship with him? What do I want from him? What am I doing to get it? Am I getting what I want from him?" is far more important than any other agenda.

As to the causes of your self-consciousness, if you feel that you're overweight, go on a diet *after the audition*. If you think your complexion is a mess, see a dermatologist *tomorrow*. If you wish you could hit that high C, call your singing teacher *tonight*. But, for right now, focus on what's really important and on what you can actually do to get the job. And that is to stay concentrated on the questions that will get you and keep you in your imaginary world. Chances are, those fears and self-doubts are probably irrational and unfounded. We all worry about silly things. Later on, when you're in a rational state of mind, if you really think you need to lose weight or get a nose job (or whatever else you worry about), seek good professional advice from people in the industry who can offer unbiased opinions. (That list doesn't include your mother or boyfriend.) After that, you can make whatever choice you like. But an audition is the last place in the world you should be worrying about these issues. And remember, if you are nervous, stop thinking about yourself, and start focusing on your acting partner – whether real or imagined.

When things go wrong

Sometimes you blow an audition. Sometimes the stage manager cuts you off before you're done with your selection. Sometimes the accompanist mangles your audition. In every case, you must act professionally and with dignity, regardless of how things went. Don't scream, blame or accuse anyone. If needed, politely go back to the accompanist and show her where she needs to start, what key you should be in, etc. But you must demonstrate professionalism, even if you are the only professional in the room.

We all have bad days. But, there will always be another audition. Don't let your bad behavior be the lasting impression. A truism of show business is "Good auditions and lousy people stick in a casting person's memory. Bad auditions fade away." If you bomb out, escape with your dignity and reputation intact.

Practice

Practicing these guidelines, feeling comfortable with the parts and sequence of an audition, and getting comfortable in your clothes are important and essential steps to learning how to audition with ease and confidence. None of this has to do with talent. You bring that to the table automatically. This all has to do with making that talent evident and available to potential employers.

Take advantage of every opportunity to practice these audition skills so you can get used to the inevitable nerves everyone feels when we're under pressure. Going to auditions for shows that don't matter so much to you will help you get accustomed to the mechanics of auditioning. Set up mock auditions with teachers and friends to help you have more practice. Consider going to "open mic" nights at local bars and clubs so you can try out new songs in front of people where there isn't a job at stake. After a while, the anxiety of putting yourself in front of those who are judging you will become less difficult and you can see the audition as a chance to perform material you love.

It's all about acting and singing well

UNIT 18.14

After having discussed all the minute technical aspects of auditioning, let's remind ourselves that it is finally about showing your ability as a singing actor. So, the same steps you go through in preparing and presenting any song or musical scene apply here. You still need to decide what the relationship with your imaginary partner is. You still need to decide on a beat breakdown, identify objectives and obstacles, choose tactics to use in achieving the objective, and live freely and truthfully within the imaginary circumstances of the song. None of the good acting work you've done in other exercises should be abandoned for an audition. It is not a different kind of acting. Auditioning is simply showing, in a very short time, what you can do as an actor. If you prepare thoroughly, do your technical and imaginative homework, warm up for the audition and go through the acting process as you present your audition you *will* do your best work for that day.

SECTION VI: THE PROFESSION

A WINNING ATTITUDE

Everyone builds a career in different ways and finds his own methods for sustaining long-running shows, getting past difficult work environments, surviving dry spells when the work just won't come, handling sudden success and so many other aspects of a life in professional show business. Most successful actors have either consciously or unconsciously followed a set of principles that helped them over the years in almost every phase of their career.

Focus on what you *can* control, not what you *can't*

In many ways it can seem as if your career isn't under your control. You are subject to the whims of casting, the economics of theatre production, the season selections of artistic directors, and on and on. Even a successful career can be an emotional rollercoaster. You may be employed for only brief stints at a time (15 minutes for a voiceover or up to a few weeks for most theatre gigs). Long-running Broadway shows still must close at some point. If you are lucky, you'll be looking for work all the time (the unlucky ones don't get called in to audition at all). You'll be doing really well to get 10 percent of what you audition for, so a really top-notch actor can still get turned down 90 percent of the time. A lot of the work is out of town, in short stints, or on tour. All these practical issues can make even a successful career (and remember how rare that is) so dislocating and jumbled that it is difficult to have any kind of normal life.

A winning attitude is one in which you don't focus on those things you can't control, and instead put your attention on those you can – the most important of which is yourself.

UNIT 19.2 ## Attitude and belief in yourself

In a field with so much uncertainty and change you need to have something that is unchangeable – a set of core values and self-knowledge that can't be shaken by circumstance or the opinions of critics, directors or casting agents. The meaning and purpose in your life needs to come from something deep and personal, not from the external approval of others or the applause of the crowd. This statement can come as a shock, because people who are attracted to the performing arts have a high need for public recognition. They are often drawn to performance precisely because of this need. It is almost paradoxical, but operating from that need, instead of from something deeper, will leave you vulnerable to the highs and lows of the business and will undercut your success. If the director or audience sees you as needy they will find that unappealing, and you won't get hired. It is a little like a bank that's only willing to lend money to those who don't require it. If you don't actually need applause, you'll get lots of it.

One of the reasons a career goes through apprentice and journeyman stages before hitting the big time is that through this process you will find a core belief in yourself and in your talents and abilities. You will have proven your worth to yourself over and over in difficult rehearsals and in front of many audiences. Convincing yourself can be the toughest part, and sometimes it is a long road to this knowledge.

If you look around you at the actors you know, you will see a wide spectrum of wisdom and self-awareness. High-level performers are said to radiate confidence, and they do, but that alone isn't it. You can also see their winning attitude expressed in certain behaviors:

- Respect
- Embracing criticism
- An on-going commitment to training and tuning
- Commitment to the success of the project
- Winners hang with winners
- Seeing the long term

Respect

For many years, Jerry Zaks, the highly successful director of plays, musicals, television and film, began each rehearsal process with a speech to his cast about respect. His guiding principle was that everyone works from a respectful point of view toward each other, the production, the script itself, their audience and everyone involved in making the show a success. This is one of the greatest habits of the successful actor. For the true professional actor, this sense of respect manifests itself in so many ways. An actor can show respect for his peers by being friendly and cordial, regardless of petty grievances. He can show respect for the production by mastering the script and score quickly and with accuracy. He can show respect for the director and choreographer by arriving at rehearsal early, warming up and attentively participating in the rehearsal with all possible diligence toward performing as he's been directed. When interpretive disagreements invariably occur, he can respectfully offer his views and know when to let go of a difference of opinion. An actor can show respect for the rest of his theatrical family by treating dressers, stagehands and ushers as the colleagues they are. No star is so big that they can put on a successful show without the support of an enormous network of talented, though less known, theatre artists. Working with this respectful attitude will help you gain the respect of your colleagues and will make you very desirable for the next job.

Embracing criticism

One of the hardest things for any actor to learn is to take criticism gracefully – even eagerly. If you think back to Chapter 1, you'll remember that we discussed this point there, as well. It's that important. If you are in the hands of a gifted creative team or teacher you will have opportunities for growth and deepening of your role at every rehearsal and performance. Your response to a note from the director can be, "Yes, *thank you*," or "Yes, *and* . . ." as opposed to "Yes, *but* . . ." – a secret resentment that they didn't love everything you did without exception. The best actors, regardless of their stature, all seek improvement and want notes to develop their performance.

Another key aspect of this is what some term the inner critic. Many people conceptualize this inner voice as the one that tells you, "you're fat" and "that note was flat" and "it's you they're laughing at."

A person with a winning attitude has the same inner voice, but she conceptualizes it differently. Instead of an inner critic, she has a co-pilot. This is a friend who looks out for you and reminds you to avoid scooping those high notes, to pull up and spot on those turns, and not to walk off the edge of the stage in the blackout. It can also remind you that your hair looks terrific today, and that last night they all applauded after you sang.

This inner voice is an essential part of our psyche. If you try to silence the critic, it will shout louder. If, instead, you bring it onto the team and give it a useful job, this co-pilot can be your best friend.

Winners have an inner co-pilot, not an inner critic.

UNIT 19.5   ## Training and tuning

Some of you who read this book will have been through nearly sixteen years of schooling, not including early childhood education or special summer programs that you've taken part in over the years. You're probably ready to be done with formal education and get out there to begin your career. Well, get ready, because you've chosen a career that requires a lifetime of continued training for new skills and maintenance of existing skills.

Remember that you're going into auditions and rehearsals that require you to be at the peak of your abilities at all times. Unlike the marathon runner or athlete who gears up for a specific competition, but can be in a less fit state at other times, you must be ready for top performance every day of your career. That means ongoing dance classes several times each week, continued vocal study with singing teachers and vocal coaches (not to mention your own solo practice), and acting classes to develop your skills and help you stay in emotional shape, as well. This ongoing regimen is time consuming and expensive. Especially in the early stages of your career, you will need to prioritize how you use your money and time. Even if you want to, you may not be able to do all the different types of training that you did in school. But there are ways to stay in shape without being supervised the whole time. Vocalizing and practicing with your tape recorded lessons, joining a church or community choir to get regular vocal practice, trading work for study with your singing or dance teacher, and applying for work/study scholarships at dance studios are all options for budget-conscious training. Successful career performers in musical theatre embrace ongoing training as an essential part of their life's work. Ignoring this important habit can be far more costly than the price of lessons; it can cost you your career. You probably have friends who were in great shape in college, but went to New York to begin their careers and were unable or unwilling to stay in competitive condition and subsequently lost the momentum they'd built early on. Their careers faltered and they now need to regain the skill levels they used to have in order to become competitive again. This is difficult and demoralizing.

Training and tuning applies to your physical condition and appearance, as well. As we've discussed already, the successful actor is one who is and appears to be physically fit and healthy. This requires an ongoing plan of exercise and nutrition. However, this doesn't really need to cost any more than living an unhealthy lifestyle. In fact, it can be cheaper. It is necessary, however, to constantly monitor your state and measure it against the demands of your type and career path.

For instance, if you are not at your ideal healthy weight because of poor eating or exercise habits, you can choose to change that in a healthy way. If you sound like a leading man, but look underfed or exhausted, there are ways to address that through lifestyle. If you come off as scruffy and rumpled, you can always take personal grooming more seriously. The same goes for complexion, hair color, muscularity and a variety of other external factors. The more competitive the market is, the more these external features become a determining issue in casting.

There are also other factors that weigh into the first impression you make. If you have a habit of appearing angry when you are nervous, you will need to address this if you want to be hired. If you habitually avoid eye contact in stressful situations, you are also limiting your possibilities. An important reality of casting is that most roles require you to appear healthy, fit and emotionally positive. Given all of this, what you are selling is still yourself. It is just you on your best day: full of energy, health, fitness, talent and skill.

Commitment to the success of the project

UNIT 19.6

Each of us has private ambitions, dreams of stardom and an appropriate level of self-interest. We want what is best for us, personally. This attitude is healthy and necessary to survive the slings and arrows of a life in show business. When we join a production, though, no matter the size of our role or importance of our position, we need to become part of a group that works together for the shared success of the overall production. Your big moment in a show may be cut during rehearsal, or the staging that had you in the front row of a big dance number may get revised to put you in the back instead. These can be difficult blows to take. But a faith in the creative leaders will help you see that these changes may be for the benefit of the total production. You will see that, as you prioritize the success of the show itself, your own star rises along with it. Instead of being a solo athlete, you are an individual member of a winning relay team. Even big stars, with their names above the title, are working for the success of the total production. Watch as that star helps her understudy with some new blocking, or as the stagehands and orchestra struggle to make a difficult transition more seamless. All of these professionals recognize that their small efforts add up to a complex tapestry of excellence that audiences will be moved by. The result is success for everyone – including you.

UNIT 19.7 **Winners hang with winners**

It is an axiom of psychotherapy that you can tell a person's mental health by what he attracts in his life. A healthy person has healthy friends and has a surprising knack for drawing good things to him. You can tell a lot about a person by the kind of people and circumstances he attracts.

Look around you. Do your friends push you to excel, or do they lounge about and complain? Are they putting themselves out there every day, working their career, staying in shape, making contacts, taking class, reading the trades, going to rehearsal? Or are they smoking pot and complaining about how unfair theatre is?

Real winners don't have the time to complain. They don't have the interest in complaining. Their entire focus is on getting out there and doing it.

EXERCISE 19A   THE WORKOUT BUDDY

- *Take stock.* We know this sounds brutal, but take a good look at the people in your life. Assess them on all the qualities listed in this section on attitudes. No one is perfect, but the question is whether they are moving forward, stagnating or regressing. Accept that if you are spending time with these people, they are a reflection of you!
- *Assess yourself.* What specific areas in your life (professionally and personally) could be better? Write them down and pick one to start.
- *Look around you.* Who do you know that seems to be excelling in that particular area?
- *Pick a workout buddy.* It is quite common for people to deliberately choose a "workout buddy." This is a person who will push you and not let you off the hook. That friend takes you to a level you couldn't achieve on your own. And you return the favor. Don't pick someone

you have competitive feelings about or who will be going up for the same roles as you.

- *Set goals.* Think of where you would like to be in five years, then back that out to three years, one year, six months and one month. Set specific, realistic and achievable goals for each interval. Don't set yourself up for failure by making the goals too idealistic or impossible.

- *Make a plan.* Now that you have goals, develop a specific plan for achieving them. Each buddy should review and assess the other's plan.

- *Hold each other accountable.* Decide how you will help each other stick to the plan. How are your activities and results measurable and provable to each other?

- *Establish rewards and punishments.* This needn't be draconian, but make it count. For example, if you are late for a meeting or don't keep a promise, put five bucks in the kitty, or donate it to a charity you both have chosen. Be creative about it. If you achieve a goal, give yourself a present. Pick it beforehand so you'll know what to anticipate and don't make it a reward that undoes all the good work you have done (like a gallon of ice cream). Don't focus on the guilt aspect as a motivation. The purpose of some sort of reckoning if you miss a goal isn't to make you feel bad, but to help you let go of the bad feelings associated with letting yourself and your buddy down. You can say, "Alright, I stood you up and didn't meet you at the gym. Okay, just as we agreed, I'll scrub your kitchen floor and then we'll be even." You do it, and then you can both move on.

- *Review your goals and plans.* Evaluate your progress regularly in terms of the person you are becoming, not the person you were back when you first set the goal. If you need to make adjustments based on newly acquired perspectives, feel free to do so.

- *Do it again.* When you're ready to take on a new project, consider adding another workout buddy. Tune the person to the project. In a short while, you will find your life filled with people who empower you and who help take you to the next level – all winners and no whiners!

UNIT 19.8 ## Seeing the long term

As a young actor beginning your profession it may be hard to imagine that you will, if you're lucky, build a career that lasts for the rest of your life. It will involve many of the same people you're beginning with right now, it will involve people who are already firmly established in their part of the business, and, later on, it will involve people who are much younger than you. All of these people can have a positive impact on your life and might be part of your career for many years and involved with you in many exciting projects. The person who is in the chorus with you today may be directing you in a show a few years from now or running a prestigious theatre at some point. She may go from being the assistant stage manager of one show to become the producer of another. So, building good relationships and making sure that you can work well with your colleagues is more important than you might think. Remember that any given show is only one production that will last as little as a few weeks or as long as a year or two. But the people you work with may have careers in show business for the rest of their, and your, lives. Letting your bad moods intrude into the workplace can give you a reputation that is difficult to change. Being professional means being able to work as part of a team for a long time.

Can you choose your attitude toward your career? Yes, certainly. And it will have a huge impact on your success and happiness along the way.

UNIT 19.9 ## Luck

Aside from truisms about making your own luck (which is something we passionately believe), the reason it is mentioned here is because fortune really does play a role in career success. It is important to come to terms with the arbitrary, unfair, irrational side of this business, or it will break your heart. You will see astonishingly talented people get passed over and venal, shallow, one-trick fools become stars. Since you can't do anything about that, place your focus on the areas of your life where you do have control. Over time, you'll also see that it is the performers with a solid basis of technique, self-discipline, a collegial spirit and a genuine love of performing that have the longest and most rewarding careers. Stardom may be a fickle thing, but a solid career is something else entirely. That's something you can earn.

And of course, we wish you great good luck!